Palgrave Studies in Cultural and Intellectual History

Series Editors

Anthony LaVopa
Department of History
North Carolina State University
Raleigh, North Carolina, USA

Javed Majeed
Department of English Language & Literature
King's College London
London, UK

Suzanne Marchand
Department of History
Louisiana State University
Baton Rouge, USA

The Palgrave Studies in Cultural and Intellectual History series has three primary aims: to close divides between intellectual and cultural approaches, thus bringing them into mutually enriching interactions; to encourage interdisciplinarity in intellectual and cultural history; and to globalize the field, both in geographical scope and in subjects and methods. This series is open to work on a range of modes of intellectual inquiry, including social theory and the social sciences; the natural sciences; economic thought; literature; religion; gender and sexuality; philosophy; political and legal thought; psychology; and music and the arts. It encompasses not just North America but also Africa, Asia, Eurasia, Europe, Latin America, and the Middle East. It includes both nationally focused studies and studies of intellectual and cultural exchanges between different nations and regions of the world, and encompasses research monographs, synthetic studies, edited collections, and broad works of reinterpretation. Regardless of methodology or geography, all books in the series are historical in the fundamental sense of undertaking rigorous contextual analysis.

More information about this series at
http://www.springer.com/series/14639

Julie L. Mell

The Myth of the Medieval Jewish Moneylender

Volume II

Julie L. Mell
North Carolina State University
Raleigh, USA

Palgrave Studies in Cultural and Intellectual History
ISBN 978-3-319-34185-9   ISBN 978-3-319-34186-6   (eBook)
DOI 10.1007/978-3-319-34186-6

Library of Congress Control Number: 2017947209

© The Editor(s) (if applicable) and The Author(s) 2018
This work is subject to copyright. All rights are solely and exclusively licensed by the
Publisher, whether the whole or part of the material is concerned, specifically the rights of
translation, reprinting, reuse of illustrations, recitation, broadcasting, reproduction on
microfilms or in any other physical way, and transmission or information storage and retrieval,
electronic adaptation, computer software, or by similar or dissimilar methodology now
known or hereafter developed.
The use of general descriptive names, registered names, trademarks, service marks, etc. in this
publication does not imply, even in the absence of a specific statement, that such names are
exempt from the relevant protective laws and regulations and therefore free for general use.
The publisher, the authors and the editors are safe to assume that the advice and information
in this book are believed to be true and accurate at the date of publication. Neither the publisher nor the authors or the editors give a warranty, express or implied, with respect to the
material contained herein or for any errors or omissions that may have been made. The
publisher remains neutral with regard to jurisdictional claims in published maps and institutional affiliations.

Cover image © Nadezhda Bolotina / Alamy Stock Photo

Printed on acid-free paper

This Palgrave Macmillan imprint is published by Springer Nature
The registered company is Springer International Publishing AG
The registered company address is: Gewerbestrasse 11, 6330 Cham, Switzerland

For Malachi

PREFACE TO VOLUME II

This book is a study of the so-called Jewish economic function in the middle ages, a deeply flawed historical narrative which has become part of common historical memory. In this narrative, Jews have been depicted as medieval Europe's principal moneylenders drawn, pushed, or pulled into moneylending by the Church's prohibition of Christian usury and by their exclusion from crafts, guilds, and landownership. As lenders, Jews purportedly provided much-needed credit for medieval Europe's expanding economy, yet suffered an antisemitic backlash for doing so. "The economic function of the Jews" has become a meta-narrative, a framework within which historians investigate the past, but which remains unquestioned itself. In the post-Holocaust period, when antisemitism has largely been delegitimized and transformed from a political platform to a subject of study, it is possible to break out of this framework. And it is imperative that we do so. For it limits and distorts our historical understanding of European and Jewish histories, and it perpetuates a dangerous discourse on Jews, Judaism, and money, despite its philosemitic politics.

Volume I established the fallacy of "the Jewish economic function" from both theoretical and empirical angles using the approaches of modern intellectual history (Part One) and medieval economic history (Part Two). Chapter 2 traced the historical narrative on Jewish moneylending from its roots in the Wissenschaft des Judentums to its emergence in the German academic mainstream with Wilhelm Roscher, Werner Sombart, and Max Weber. Roscher first formed the theory of "the Jewish economic function" by fusing it with a theory of economic stages (natural economy—barter—money—credit) and an organic *Volk* model. Organic *Volk* models presented

vii

the historical development of all "nations" as passing through the stages of the human life cycle from infancy to youth, from youth to adulthood, from adulthood to death. For Roscher, the ancient Jewish people were a mature nation, who served as "tutors" for the young Germanic tribes in Europe who were not yet ready for commercial trade. When the Germanic peoples matured in the high middle ages, they pushed Jews out of trade and imposed legal restrictions on them out of economic competition. Roscher articulated the Jewish economic function as a philosemitic response to the development of political antisemitism in the 1870s. Sombart and Weber inherited and adapted his model in significant ways. But all three shared a view of medieval European economy as a static, agrarian economy, bereft of capitalist profit motive. Only alien outsiders the Jews, or in Weber's more nuanced treatment, a Jewish influence via the Hebrew prophets, could jumpstart a credit economy.

In the first half of the twentieth century, this model came under attack from several directions. The Jewish economic function was broken off from the theory of a static, agrarian, precapitalist Europe. Chapter 3 traced the three intellectual trajectories that critiqued and refashioned this nineteenth-century model: (1) Jewish historians heavily critiqued Sombart's depiction of the Jewish capitalist, while Roscher received ambivalent treatment. During World War II, Toni Oelsner sharply criticized Roscher as contributing to rabid antisemitism, while Guido Kisch resuscitated Roscher's economic function of the Jew as a defense against antisemitism and sheared it of its organic *Volk* model to better fit twentieth-century historical conventions. (2) Medieval economic historians attacked the German Historical School's vision of Europe as a static, agrarian, anticapitalist economy, recovering a high medieval commercial revolution or high medieval expansion. Some of the main proponents were themselves Jewish émigrés to the Anglo-American world. (3) Sociologists and anthropologists, like Marcel Mauss and Karl Polanyi, critiqued the German Historical School's definition of economy around modern market economy, and posited gift exchange as an alternative contractual form that challenged the Historical School's progressive model of historical economic development in stages leading to modern capitalism. Building on these thinkers, Annales School historians developed a new narrative for European economic development that described the early medieval economy as a gift economy, which underwent a radical shift to a profit economy during the high middle ages, bringing with it a spiritual and social crisis. These three trajectories have provided the basis for post-war paradigms in medieval economic history.

A number of significant contradictions exist between these paradigms. Yet they remain unrecognized by scholars. One of principal importance to this study is that between "the commercial revolution of the high middle ages" and the "Jewish economic function." The medieval commercial revolution undercuts the theoretical basis for the Jewish economic function, yet the Jewish economic function has not been overturned, because it has served as the foremost counterresponse to the antisemitic discourses on Jews and money. Chapter 3 explains the obfuscation of these contradictions as a consequence of the lived experience of the émigrés who created these paradigms while suffering dislocation owing to their Jewish identities. The chapter argues that recognition of these contradictions will lead to significant innovations in both European history and Jewish history. It is the aim of this volume to realize that claim.

Part Two of Volume I presented the empirical evidence against the assumption that many or most Jews were concentrated solely in moneylending and provided an important economic function in being so concentrated. Part Two focused on the Jewish community of medieval England as the best case supporting the traditional narrative. Through the rich taxation and lending records preserved by the royal administration, Chapter 4 demonstrated that the distribution of wealth among the Jewish population was such that few individuals could have been moneylenders. The majority of the Jewish population was at or below the poverty line. And the distribution of wealth in the urban Jewish population roughly paralleled that in the urban Christian population. An analysis of the frequency, rate, and level of Jewish lending demonstrated that only a small group of families could have been professional moneylenders. Examining Jewish taxation within the context of English taxation more generally, Chapter 5 challenged the traditional picture of Anglo-Jewry as a "royal milk cow," which was privileged, protected, and extorted by the king. Rather, it was shown that Anglo-Jews had the legal status of free burgesses until shortly before the expulsion of 1290. Medieval Anglo-Jews participated collectively in the institutions of self-representation, long regarded as the seeds of representative government. Jews were different only in respect to their administrative segregation. The distinctive treatment of Jews was a consequence not of a Jewish economic difference, but of a growing anti-Judaism pushed by the Church, but taken up willingly by strong monarchs.

Volume II takes up the three postwar paradigms mapped out in Chapter 3 and explores the ramifications of dissolving the narrative of Jewish economic function for European history, as well as for Jewish history. It is essential to do so for two reasons. First, the intellectual critique of "the Jewish economic function" made in Volume I rejects the assumption that Jews were alien outsiders to Europe. Therefore a guiding principle of this work has been to configure Jewish history as fully European. Second, the narrative of the "Jewish economic function" is inextricably linked with the German Historical School's model of medieval European economy. To fully work out the implications of dissolving the "Jewish economic function" requires that we consider the implications for each of the postwar paradigms that emerged in response to this nineteenth-century model. In exploring the significance of dissolving the "Jewish economic function," this volume also extends the scope of the study beyond England to northern France, the Mediterranean, and central Europe.

Chapter 6 reconsiders the medieval usury campaign and historians' narration of it as a struggle between religious morals and market economy, in which the Church, whose morals were formed during the static, agrarian economy of the early middle ages, resisted economic development, but ultimately succumbed to market pressure. This chapter argues that the usury campaign was principally a campaign against Christian usury, not Jewish usury, yet from it emerged a rhetoric on Jewish usury that modern historians have misinterpreted as evidence for "the Jewish economic function." This chapter offers a new interpretation of the usury campaign and of the rhetoric on Jewish usury. It argues that the campaign itself, not market pressures, led to the simultaneous definition of legitimate and illegitimate forms of credit, from which emerged the binary of the good Christian merchant and the dangerous Jewish usurer. The usury campaign was part of a broad religious reform associated closely with the poverty movement and crusading. As crusading became endemic in the thirteenth century, the Church simultaneously launched an anti-Judaism campaign and extended protections originally meant for the Church to Christian society as a whole. When strong secular monarchs took up the Church's program, they went beyond papal precedent and expelled Jews, justifying an illegal measure with claims of Jewish usury. The rhetoric on Jewish usury is not a simple reflection of economic reality, but a theological polemic that must be understood within the context of the Christian usury campaign, on the one hand, and the anti-Judaism campaign, on the other.

Chapter 7 takes up the concept of the commercial revolution and explores the significance of Jewish merchants and their investments in Marseille for our understanding of Mediterranean trade in general and Jewish economic history in particular. It argues that the Jewish merchants of Marseille were participating in the commercial revolution alongside Christians. These Jewish traders were not capitalist precursors pushed out into moneylending. In fact in Marseille, moneychangers and bankers were municipally regulated, and Jews did not appear among those approved by the town. Jewish merchants used the Latin contract of *commenda* for their long-distance sea trade, even with their religious brethren. They chose this instrument to secure their commercial investments with municipal Marseille law. Marseille offers a counterpoint to case studies like that of Perpignan in which Jews were heavily involved in lending, suggesting that if historians look anew at the documentary evidence, a diversity of economic activities among the Jewish population in Europe will be uncovered. The difference read back into the medieval evidence by modern theoretical presumption of Jews as alien, non-European moneylenders dissolves. Marseille's Jewish merchants also contribute to our understanding of the European commercial revolution more broadly through the comparison they offer with Jewish merchants from the Islamic world. Despite the fact that Jewish merchants of Marseille and Cairo shared a religious law, each group of merchants made use of contracts rooted in the legal, political, and cultural institutions of the European Mediterranean or the Islamic Mediterranean.

Chapter 8 takes up the postwar model describing European economic development as a shift from gift economy to profit economy, a radical change that brought with it a spiritual and social crisis. Through an examination of the concepts of money, value, and consumption in moral texts known as *exempla*, this chapter argues that neither money nor the profit economy was the locus of anxiety. Rather, religious authors, Christian and Jewish, were concerned with the multiple layers of value created in acts of economic exchange. The moral and economic values created when a commodity or currency was exchanged operated in the mindset of these medieval thinkers according to the rules of both gift exchange and profit exchange. Medieval Europeans' sophisticated religious ideology of value implodes the very binary categories of gift economy and profit economy. Rather than describing European economic development as provoking a spiritual crisis, this chapter proposes that Christian and Jewish religious leaders constructed a more sophisticated, multivalent model of value that cut across the binaries gift/profit, money/nonmoney, economy/religion. Recognizing the complexity of the medieval categories and their shared existence across rabbinic Judaism and Western Christianity should also lead modern historians to reject the binary opposition often posited in scholarship between a medieval Christianity linked to the spirit of the gift and modernizing Judaism linked to the spirit of capitalism.

Contents

Part Three   Some Explorations: Ashkenaz and Beyond   1

6   The Discourse of Usury and the Emergence of the
    Stereotype of the Jewish Usurer in Medieval France   3

7   Commercialization among the Jewish Merchants
    of Marseille   113

8   From Gift Exchange to Profit Economy Reconsidered:
    Toward a Cultural History of Money   147

9   Which Is the Merchant Here? And Which the Jew?   175

Bibliography   199

Index   249

LIST OF FIGURES

Fig. 6.1 Conciliar legislation on Christian lay usury and Jewish usury
from Lateran III (1179) to Vienne (1311)   21

Fig. 6.2 Langmuir's model for the nature of Jewish legislation
pre-1223 and post-1223   45

LIST OF TABLES

Table 6.1	Frequency and placement of canons on Jewish usury in relation to canons on other Jewish issues	25
Table 6.2	Conciliar legislation on Jewish issues from 1179 to 1311	26
Table 7.1	Proportion of documents with Jewish agents in Amalric's register	121
Table 7.2	Proportion of Jewish commendators and tractators in Amalric's register	121
Table 7.3	Number of commendae per Jewish agent	123
Table 7.4	Types of investments made in Jewish commendae	126
Table 7.5	Comparison of types of investments expressed as a ratio of common investments	127
Table 7.6	Ships carrying Jewish tractators from Marseille in 1248	128
Table 7.7	Destination of commendae exported from Marseilles, spring 1248	129
Table 7.8	Values of commendae recorded in mixed money	131
Table 7.9	Destination of Jewish commendae by agent	131

ABBREVIATIONS

AJS	Association of Jewish Studies
CCR	*Calendar of the Close Rolls Preserved in the Public Record Office* (London, 1892–)
CPR	*Calendar of the Patent Rolls Preserved in the Public Record Office* (London, 1901–40)
Friedberg	Emil Friedberg, ed., *Corpus iuris canonici*, 2 vols. (Leipzig, 1879; repr. Graz, 1959)
GHS	German Historical School of Political Economy
Grayzel	Solomon Grayzel, *The Church and the Jews in the XIII Century*, vol. 1 (New York, 1966) and vol. 2, ed. Kenneth Stow (Detroit, 1989)
JHSET	*Jewish Historical Society of England—Transactions*
Mansi	G.D. Mansi, ed., *Sacrorum Conciliorum Nova et Amplissima Collectio*, 54 vols. (Paris, 1901–27)
MGH	*Monumenta Germaniae Historica* (Hannover, 1826–1934)
NA—UK	National Archives—UK, Kew
PL	*Patrologia Latina*, ed. Jacques-Paul Migne (Paris, 1844–55)
PREJ	*Calendar of the Plea Rolls of the Exchequer of the Jews* (London, 1905–2005)
SHB	Sefer Ḥasidim Bologna (*Sefer Ḥasidim*, ed. Reuven Margoliot (Jerusalem, 1944))
SHP	Sefer Ḥasidim Parma (*Sefer Ḥasidim*, ed. Judah Wistinetzki (Frankfurt am Main, 1924))
Tanner	Norman Tanner, ed., *Decrees of the Ecumenical Councils* (London, 1990)
WDJ	Wissenschaft des Judentums

xx ABBREVIATIONS

Units of Money and Their Abbreviations

England

12 denarii	= 1 shilling
20 shillings	= 1 pound
1 mark	= 13s 4d = 2/3 £
d	*denarius* (penny)
m	mark
s	shilling
£	pound

Marseille

mm   *monete miscui* (mixed money)

PART THREE

Some Explorations: Ashkenaz and Beyond

CHAPTER 6

The Discourse of Usury and the Emergence of the Stereotype of the Jewish Usurer in Medieval France

> What injustice do you find in usury greater than the prohibition on eating pork, forbidden animals, and fish without fins and scales? Since you transform everything into an allegory, called *figura*, why do you not interpret the commandment on usury likewise allegorically and permit even your own people to lend to each other on usury, as you do with the other prohibitions?...
>
> Also you are commanded to protect us and not to force us to receive the commandments (*mitzvot*) according to your interpretation—Meir ben Simeon of Narbonne (ha-Meili), *Milḥemet Mitzvah*[1]

A discourse on Jewish usury emerged in the mid-twelfth century, developed "legal teeth" in the thirteenth century, and was used to justify expulsions of Jews from western Europe by the early fourteenth century. Well-known texts mark this development: In a letter of 1146 preaching the Second Crusade, Bernard of Clairvaux wrote that "where there are no Jews, there Christian men Judaize even worse than they in extorting usury—if, indeed, we may call them Christians and not rather baptized Jews."[2] Around 1200, the Parisian theologians Thomas of Chobham and Robert of Courson asserted in their *summae* that "Jews have nothing except what they have gained through usury."[3] By 1215, legislation prohibiting Jews from extorting "heavy and immoderate usury from a Christian" was decreed at the Fourth Lateran Council and justified by the claim that "the perfidy of the Jews" in exacting usury was increasing so much that "in a short time they exhaust the wealth of Christians."[4] By

© The Author(s) 2018
J.L. Mell, *The Myth of the Medieval Jewish Moneylender,*
DOI 10.1007/978-3-319-34186-6_1

3

1290, Edward I King of England, justified the expulsion of Jews by claiming that "the Jews did...wickedly conspire and contrive a new species of usury more pernicious than the old...to the abasement of our...people... for which cause We, in requital of their crimes and for the honour of the Crucified, have banished them from our realm as traitors."[5]

These texts traditionally have not been read as markers of a new discourse, but as straightforward evidence of a social and economic fact—that European Jews concentrated in moneylending by the later twelfth century and served an important role as moneylenders by the thirteenth century. This chapter offers a new reading of these texts by placing them within the larger context of an anti-usury campaign directed primarily toward Christians and a new anti-Judaism campaign. The central question this chapter examines is why a discourse on Jewish usury arose in the later twelfth and thirteenth centuries. The answer involves a complex range of historical causes: a Church campaign against usury among lay Christians, an intensifying crusading ethos, a new virulent Christian anti-Judaism, and the emergence of increasingly powerful and centralized monarchies, among them a papal monarchy, which were constructing their power through the expansion of legal jurisdiction, in part. But it is the legislation on usury that gives real force to these changes. Hence it is the legislation that will be the focus of my analysis. The usury legislation originates in Church councils, but becomes the blueprint for royal legislation. Alongside canon law and royal legislation, there exists a third legal tradition which is actively regulating usury in thirteenth-century Europe, rabbinic law. The competition between the legal judgments and legal jurisdictions of Church, Crown, and rabbinic authorities stands at the heart of the emergence of a medieval stereotype of Jews as usurers.

In the current historical model, the elaboration of canon law and theological tracts on usury is regarded as a reactionary response to the economic takeoff of the high middle ages:[6] the Church's position is considered to have been inherited from and reflect the "dark ages," when Europe was an agrarian society. A rigid opposition to usury was codified in Gratian's *Decretum* in the mid-twelfth century, where usury was defined as "any gain stemming from a loan, no matter how small."[7] But "even when it was pronounced, some time about the year 1140," it "was not compatible with reality."[8] The history of the development of canon law and theology on usury is the story of the Church forced to come to terms with the reality of the market.

The need to come to terms with the realities of the market drove Parisian theologians like Robert de Curzon (d. 1219) and his master Peter Cantor (d. 1197) to consider, though not necessarily approve, the possibility of indemnifying a lender for forfeit he was losing (*lucrum cessans*) and for damages he would suffer (*damnum emergens*) when lending money. Even Thomas Aquinas, half a century later, was bound to accept such compensations as legitimate, considering that "human laws leave certain sins unpunished because of the imperfection of man." He was driven to admit the existence of usury.[9]

In this historical narrative, more and more "loopholes" were defined by canon law. But this narrative overlooks the fact that at the same time the rhetoric against usury reached a new pitch and spread beyond ecclesiastics to secular rulers. When historians pay attention to the references to Jews, they present Jews as caught in the crossfire: "Jews' involvement in moneylending made them subject to restrictive legislation and to hostile political actions, not to mention social opprobrium and physical violence."[10]

Three elements in this traditional narrative are problematic and will be challenged in this chapter. First, encoded in the historical paradigm is the presumption of a radical split between "economy" and "religion," represented by "the needs of the market" on the one hand and the anti-usury law of "the Church" on the other. This interpretation fails to give proper attention to chronology. The same medieval churchmen who railed against usury also created the concept of *interesse* (interest) and defined legitimate forms of credit and moneylending. At the very same time as the canonists defined 13 exceptions to the usury prohibition, they increased the severity of the penalties on usurers and extended these penalties to ever-wider circles of individuals. Both the campaign against usury *and* the widening definitions of licit forms of credit are aspects of the same developments in Christian economic thought. What we have then is not the opposition of economy and religion, but the invention of economic concepts within religious thought.[11] By means of these concepts, the boundaries were drawn between permissible and impermissible economic forms. To understand the campaign against usury, we must refrain from translating usury as "interest," "moneylending," or "credit," and we must seek to understand what was encompassed in the illicit and dangerous category of *usura*.

Second, the attack on Jewish usury is elided in the literature with the campaign against usury among Christians. This may be a consequence

6 J.L. MELL

of Benjamin Nelson's work in the 1940s, *The Idea of Usury: From Tribal Brotherhood to Universal Otherhood*. Nelson read all of Christian intellectual thought on usury as a contest between Jewish tribalism and Christian universalism.[12] He flattened out the dynamic history of the high medieval usury campaign by adhering to an old-style intellectual history of ideas and projected back to the early Church a consistent usury campaign and a static definition of usury. Consequently, he misconstrued what was primarily an internal Christian fight, presenting it as a contest between Jewish and Christian interpretation. Only in the mid-thirteenth century when the Talmud came under attack would a contest between Jewish and Christian interpretation surface in the polemical literature. Even then, this contest would remain on the sidelines of the Jewish-Christian polemical debate and the Christian anti-usury campaign. The result of Nelson's influence is an odd split in the historiography. Jewish historians[13] write as if the usury campaign is directed entirely at Jews, while scholars of canon law[14] rarely refer to Jews at all. This chapter will avoid conflating the two by discussing first the conciliar legislation on Christian usury, and only then the conciliar legislation on Jewish usury. This theoretical approach is supported by two facts which will become apparent below: the campaign against Christian usury preceded the campaign against Jewish usury by 70 years, and the canons themselves textually separate the legislation on Jewish usury from that on Christian usury.

Third, the campaign against Jewish usury is treated as a rational, economic response to Jews cornering the market, while the antisemitic fantasies of ritual murder, blood libel, and host desecration are treated as irrational, religious responses to Christian doubt.[15] Framing the attack on Jewish usury as rational naturalizes it as economic and disguises its religious aspects. The historical literature fails to consider "Jewish usury" as part of a developing anti-Judaic discourse. This is due not only to the presumption that the texts reflect an economic and social reality, but also to the reification of the royal legislation as political history unconnected with ecclesiastical legislation and ecclesiastical issues. The charges of both ritual murder and usury should be understood as intertwined parts of a developing anti-Judaic discourse. Dissolving the binaries irrational/rational and religious/economic will provide a more satisfactory answer to the old question raised by Stobbe on the decline of Jewish status than Roscher's answer—"the economic function of the Jews."

Several historians have pointed the way toward a discursive approach to Jewish usury. In the 1940s, Joshua Trachtenberg approached the

Jewish usurer as an overblown myth linked to a constellation of stereotypes clustered around the Devil and heresy, even as he tipped his hat to the historical narrative on Jewish concentration in moneylending.[16] R. Po-Chia Hsia's work on the fantasy of ritual murder in early modern Germany led him to approach Jewish usury as an antisemitic discourse disjoined from the reality of Jewish economic activities.[17] The art historian Sara Lipton has analyzed the association between Jews and usury within the imagery of the earliest *Bible moralisée* manuscripts produced for the royal court of France between 1220 and 1229. She shows how the association between Jews and usury works as a complex strategy "in which a negative polemic against an economic activity—moneylending— is displaced through the use of increasingly more sophisticated figurations (borrowed from the disciplines of logic, rhetoric, and the natural sciences) onto the Jew, who appears as a sign for usury, avarice, and the destructive effects of money capital as a whole." Lipton's deep understanding of these representative strategies leads her to suggest the need for a reconsideration of the traditional narrative on Jewish concentration in moneylending.[18]

Giacomo Todeschini has produced path-breaking work on the discourse of the usurious Jew over a long and productive scholarly career. But his work has not yet received the recognition that it should in the Anglo-American world for several reasons.[19] Focusing on Franciscan economic thought and the Christian stereotypes on Jewish economic activity, he has made sharp and incisive critiques of the standard narrative on Jewish moneylending. For example, in a recent article on the emergence of the "manifest usurer" in canon law, he notes that medieval references to Christian usurers as "Judaei nostri" (our Jews) did not signify that usury was considered a typical Jewish profession, as generations of historians have presumed. Rather it signals that "from the twelfth to the thirteenth century the infamy of Judas and the Jews became a clear representation of manifold types of civic irregularity."[20] In "Franciscan Economics and the Jews," Todeschini defines three ways in which Jews were stereotyped in Franciscan economic writings between 1260 and 1380: as enemies of Franciscan poverty, as supporters of a usury economy in connection with the interpretation of Deuteronomy 23, and as usurers, dangerous for the Christian moral and economic order.[21] The end point of his analysis is a breathtakingly revisionist insight: Franciscans granted a positive religious and civic role to Christian merchants, because they defined them as making use of money not to accumulate it, but to utilize it as a means of exchange.

This civic role was set in opposition to that of the infidel businessman. Consequently, the sterility of the money and wealth of the Jewish usurer derived not from the nature of money, but from its economic immobility. Its wrong and depraved use flowed from the infidelity of the unconverted Jew.[22] Franciscan economics, Todeschini suggests, constructed a binary economics in which the permissible profit was linked intrinsically with the morally good Christian and the non-Christian with impermissible profit. The "Jew" was ensnared as the quintessential *infidel* whose profit was harmful to the Christian community.

Recently Todeschini has critiqued the "long surviving stereotype of the Jewish usurer" in contemporary historiography, seeing it as a problem of the long duration of Christian economic language in the West.[23] His monograph *Franciscan Wealth* provides us with insight into how and why the stereotype of the Jewish usurer formed by the Christian culture of the middle ages has been sustained through to the present day: the Franciscan conception of voluntary poverty, that is, their interpretation of Christian perfection, was intrinsically an economic language. And it ultimately shaped some of the most basic categories in the economic thought of Western civilization:[24]

> the Christian world was never extraneous from the market, as fantasized between the 1800s and 1900s, nor was there a clear separation between morality and business. Franciscanism, in the very heart of Roman catholicity, identified in deprivation and renunciation the decisive elements for understanding the value of trade....As a consequence, Franciscans were not the "first economists," but rather those who made the appearance of economists in the Christian West of the following centuries possible.[25]

Todeschini's work has been of tremendous value and shaped my analysis here significantly. This chapter builds on his work. Where Todeschini focuses on the intellectual history of Franciscan thought particularly in the thirteenth through fifteenth centuries, I focus on the ecclesiastical law prior to the emergence of Franciscan intellectuals as key players. And I trace how this ecclesiastical law was both appropriated and contested by secular authorities in medieval France. I hope thereby to recover the prehistory for the later spiritual Franciscans in the late-twelfth-century and early-thirteenth-century Church.

Although this chapter tracks canonical legislation across western Europe, it comes to focus on France. For the majority of the rulings on usury came from provincial and local councils in France, and the secular rulers who took the lead in repressing Jewish usury in secular legislation were the Capetian kings of France. Typically, historians have assumed that Jews in medieval France were second only to Anglo-Jewry in concentrating heavily in moneylending in the twelfth and thirteenth centuries.[26] This judgment is based on the legislation examined below and occasional references to Jewish usury made in theological texts and chronicles. Both, I shall argue, are evidence for the birth of a new discourse on Jews, not for Jewish economic activity. For the actual documentary evidence on medieval Jewish moneylending in France is extremely sparse.[27] It consists of a set of rolls from 1227 to 1228 listing Jewish debts, a set of inquests on Jewish usury from 1247 to 1248, and a series of notarial registers from the town of Perpignan (1261–87). In 1959, Richard Emery produced a fine study of the notarial registers from Perpignan.[28] Although the 1063 Jewish loans provide a statistically significant sample, the Perpignan case cannot represent Jewish moneylending in medieval France. For Perpignan was part of the Aragonese realm, and Jewish lending in France had been outlawed well before 1261. Perpignan seems to have been an unusual local case, which may have been the result of Franco-Jewish lenders immigrating when Jewish lending was outlawed in France. Perpignan will be discussed in the following chapter, together with other Mediterranean port towns and Jewish mercantile trade. In 1969, Gérard Nahon studied 124 cases concerning Jewish usury in the inquests ordered by Louis IX to reform abuses in the realm prior to his departure on crusade.[29] In 1979, William Jordan added to these another 50 cases from a newly discovered manuscript fragment.[30] These cases mostly involved pawns, reflecting the success of the Crown in quelling Jewish lending by the 1240s. Nor are these inquests bias-free records of economic activity; they must be understood within the context of crusading and the campaign against usury and Judaism, as this chapter will demonstrate. The only significant sources for Franco-Jewish lending are three rolls from 1227 to 1228, so poorly reproduced in the *Layettes du Trésor des Chartes* that they have been largely inaccessible to scholars.[31] William Jordan, working from the originals, redated them to the *captio* (tallage) of June 1227 levied on royal Jews and counted 700 debts owed to 60 Jewish creditors, half of whom had fewer than five clients.[32] Significant Jewish lending in France, as we will see, would cease shortly thereafter.

Conciliar Legislation against Christian Usury

Historians writing on usury have typically focused primarily on the compilations of canon law and their commentaries and secondarily on theological *summae*, which followed the principles laid out by canon lawyers.[33] I have neglected neither in my research, but will focus principally on conciliar legislation. For the Church councils were the front line of the campaign against usury. The prohibitions and the penalties levied on sinners therefore provide the best gauge of the intensity and direction of the campaign. The compilations of canon law, as textbooks for the legal schools, were one step removed from the campaign of the parish clergy to reform the lay population. After discussion of the legislation itself, the jurisdictional reach and representative nature of these councils will be analyzed.

Conciliar legislation against usury emerged around 1140, escalated between the late twelfth and mid-thirteenth centuries, and deepened in the late thirteenth and early fourteenth centuries. This campaign targeted Christian lay usury. For over 150 years, conciliar legislation spearheaded the campaign through the imposition of new penalties on the Christian faithful. These penalties, intended to correct the sinner, were levied on ever-wider circles of individuals in contact with usurers. None of this legislation was applicable to Jews, as is evident from the fact that the penalties had no relevance for non-Christians.

The high medieval usury campaign burst onto the European scene with the general council of Lateran II (1139).[34] Canon 13 denounced the "insatiable rapacity of moneylenders," severed usurers from "all ecclesiastical consolations," and warned clergy against receiving usurers "unless with the greatest caution." Usurers were declared "infamous" and unfit to receive Christian burial unless they repented.[35] Early church councils had prohibited clerics, but never laity, from practicing usury.[36] Other than a few Carolingian capitularies in the ninth century, the early medieval Church never referred to usury by clerics or lay persons.[37] We have virtually no information on discussions or debates that resulted in the new conciliar legislation.

But a sea change in ecclesiastical concern with usury around 1140 can be discerned in Gratian's *Decretum*, the famous textbook of canon law completed around this time.[38] Gratian included eight canons on usury among the roughly 1000 canons listed in Part One. But all referred to clerical usury, and all derived from the early Church.[39] The meaning of usury in these canons was ambiguous and open to semantic fluctuation. The canons on usury were grouped within two Distinctions addressing vices which disqualify individuals from clerical office: quarrelsomeness, arrogance, jealousy, sedition, usury, and cupidity. Usury was not specified as a type of monetary contract (selling of money) by a particular type of individual (*infidelis* or *carnalis*). This dramatic change in meaning would come only in the later twelfth century.[40] In part II, where Gratian expounded cases and questions arising from them, the new clerical concern with usury came to the fore. Gratian queried what usury might be exacted, whether clergy or laity might demand usury, whether alms from usury might be received, and whether penance for usury might be undertaken without first making restitution.[41] Yet again the only proof texts Gratian could bring were from the fourth, fifth, and sixth centuries. Gratian's "extremely brief" commentary established these points: "To demand or receive or even to lend expecting to receive something above the capital is to be guilty of usury; usury may exist on money or anything else; one who receives usury is guilty of rapine and is just as culpable as a thief; the prohibition against usury holds for laymen as well as clerics but, when guilty, the latter will be more severely punished."[42] As Gratian's *Decretum* became the standard law text, these points were accepted as the basic principles upon which an analysis of usury was founded. Circa 1140, their very articulation reflected the newness of the ecclesiastical concern with usury, and their content established a ground zero from which canon law on usury would develop.

Forty years later at Lateran III, new legislation against usurers was justified with this logic: "in almost every place the crime of usuries so grows, that many, overlooking other business, practice, as if licit, usuries, and do not attend [to the fact that] the pages of both the old and new Testament condemn it."[43] Lateran III (1179) renewed the substance of Lateran II by denying usurers admission to communion at the altar,[44] Christian burial, and acceptance of oblations. But it also introduced two significantly new elements. It narrowed the application of the legislation by targeting "manifest usurers" (*usurarii manifesti*). And it automatically suspended from office clergy who received alms from a usurer or buried a usurer:

> we decree that manifest usurers neither shall be admitted to the communion of the altar nor receive Christian burial, if they die in this sin, nor shall anyone receive from them oblations. Whoever will have received them and their oblations, in order to give them Christian burial, shall be compelled to return those oblations and until he has received judgment by his bishop, he will remain suspended from the execution of his office.[45]

12   J.L. MELL

It is this canon, rather than Lateran II, that became the cornerstone of high medieval legislation against usurers.[46] Here too for the first time emerged the strategy of strengthening the campaign by imposing penalties on those in contact with usurers, a strategy that would be deployed more and more in later legislation.

Over the course of the thirteenth century, conciliar legislation would intensify the campaign against usurers by stiffening the requirements for restitution,[47] by making excommunication public,[48] and by denying the validity of their wills.[49] But it primarily ramped up the pressure on usurers by extending the sphere of penalties in concentric rings out from usurers to other members of society with whom they came into contact. The clergy were the first group to whom penalties were extended. But later legislation would penalize merchants, clerics, and notaries who assisted in writing contracts or wills for usurers, as well as attorneys who defended a usurer in court,[50] landlords who rented houses to outsiders who were usurers,[51] and judges or secular authorities who wrote statutes legitimating usury.[52] The most radical legislation penalized the servants, wives, and heirs of usurers.[53] By the early fourteenth century, anyone who stated that usury was not a sin, whether or not they practiced usury, was prosecuted as a heretic.[54]

The jurisdictional reach of councils varied widely depending on whether they were local, provincial, or general. Local councils were called by a bishop and attended by the clergy in his diocese, and the rulings reflect the sole decision of the bishop. Provincial councils had a wider jurisdictional range and reflect a wider clerical viewpoint, as they were held under an archbishop with the participation of bishops and clergy from several dioceses. The broadest of all were the ecumenical councils. Held under the auspices of the pope, the councils reflect the consensus of hundreds of clergy attending the council.[55] At times, secular rulers also participated in a provincial or general council. More councils enacting usury legislation were provincial than local, reflecting a relatively broad base of clerical opinion and application. The most radical legislation, such as that of Paris (1212) and Vienna (1267), came out of councils called by a papal legate, whose role suggests at least nominal papacy approval. The most significant and far-reaching canons on usury came from the high medieval ecumenical councils called by the papacy: Lateran II (1139), Lateran III (1179), Lateran IV (1215), Lyon I (1245), Lyon II (1274), and Vienne (1311–2). All but Lyon I (1245) enacted significant legislation against usury and usurers.

THE DISCOURSE OF USURY AND THE EMERGENCE OF THE STEREOTYPE... 13

The two ecumenical councils of the late thirteenth and early fourteenth centuries illustrate well the increasing severity of the usury campaign 100 years after Lateran III. Lyon II (1274) was called by Pope Gregory X and attended by the Patriarchs of Antioch and Constantinople, 15 cardinals, 500 bishops, and more than 1000 other dignitaries.[56] The council "wishing to close up the abyss of usury, which devours souls and swallows up property," ordered "under the threat of divine malediction" that canon 25 of Lateran III be "inviolably observed."[57] Lyon II not only transformed Lateran III's minor excommunication into anathema, it decreed new legislation against secular authorities, corporations, and lay persons with clear penalties. Guilds (*collegium*), corporations (*universitas*), and lay individuals were prohibited from renting lodgings to any foreigner who practiced or intended to lend money on usury publicly: they were ordered to expel manifest usurers from their territories within three months and never allow them to return. High-ranking ecclesiastics who did not do so incurred automatic suspension from their office; guilds and corporations who did not do so, interdict; and lay persons, ecclesiastical censure.[58] Canon 27 at Lyon II stiffened the requirements for repentance necessary to receive Christian burial:[59] a will made by a notorious usurer which included orders for restitution of usuries was to be refused until full restitution had been made, as far as means allowed, or until a pledge of fitting restitution had been given. The canon also stipulated precisely how such a pledge should be made, and it closed loopholes by declaring that nobody was to assist at the wills of manifest usurers, hear their confessions, or absolve them, unless the usurers had made restitution or given a fitting pledge as stipulated in the canon. Wills made in any other way were declared null and void.

The general council of Vienne (1311–3) called by Clement V and attended by the Patriarchs of Antioch and Alexandria, 300 bishops, and three kings—Philip IV of France, Edward II of England, and James II of Aragon—also enacted new legislation that extended ecclesiastical jurisdiction over secular law.[60] Canon 29 invalidated statutes that not only granted the demand and payment of usury, but required debtors to pay it.[61] It penalized with excommunication all secular authorities (*potestates, capitanei, rectores, consules, iudices, consiliarii aut alii quivis officiales*) who made or upheld statutes or customs permitting usury, or who did not delete them from their books within three months. Suspicious that moneylenders "enter into usurious contracts so frequently with secrecy and guile that they can be convicted only with difficulty," canon 29 decreed that moneylenders be required under ecclesiastical censure to open their books to investigation when there was a question of usury. And it further decreed that anyone who maintained that the practice of usury was not sinful be investigated and punished as a heretic, whether the person practiced usury or not. It strictly enjoined local ordinaries and inquisitors to proceed against those suspected of such error.

While the campaign against lay usury was escalating over the course of the thirteenth century, canon lawyers were at the same time defining and refining what constituted usury. By the mid-thirteenth century, well before the stringent legislation of Lyon II and Vienne (1311–3), 13 cases were accepted in which "something may be received in excess of the principal," in other words, cases which flatly contradicted Gratian's definition of usury. The historical development then does not move from a rigid prohibition established by an early medieval Church rooted in an agricultural society to a high medieval Church yielding to market necessity. Rather, there was a double movement. At one and the same time, the Church escalated its campaign against *lay* usury through canon law and rendered increasingly permissible forms of credit through canon law. This duality is reflected in the dual terminology of "interest" and "usury" born in this period, but which itself reflects a more ancient semantic duality encased in usury, the one spiritual, the other carnal, represented in the New Testament parable of the talents.[62]

Conciliar Legislation against Jewish Usury

The ecclesiastical campaign against usury was extended to Jews in the early thirteenth century some 70 years after Lateran II, during the reign of Pope Innocent. The canons on Jewish usury were decreed separately from those on Christian usury.[63] For none of the Christian legislation could in practice or in theory apply to Jews. In practice, the penalties of minor and major excommunication that cut off a believer from the consolations of the Church had no force for non-Christians. In theory, the jurisdiction of canon law extended only to Christians.

The first canons on Jewish usury appeared at the provincial council of Avignon (1209) and the ecumenical council of Lateran IV (1215).[64] Both councils instituted legislation aimed at restraining Jewish usury and compelling restitution for usury already exacted from Christians. Jews were threatened with what one might quippingly call "material excommunication," that is, isolation from Christians particularly in commerce. Both can be read as extensions of Lateran III. Later conciliar legislation, primarily from France, stiffened Lateran IV's canon against Jewish usury by using the same techniques used to restrain Christian usury—enacting new legislation on those supporting usurers. In the 1250s, judges and bailiffs were ordered not to compel debtors to pay usury to Jews. In the 1280s and 1290s, legislation penalized clerics and notaries for writing contracts on behalf of Jewish usurers, just as did the canons against writing contracts and wills for Christian usurers.[65] These canons are an extension of the Christian usury campaign to a new frontier, Jews, in accord with the escalation of the general campaign by means of extending penalties to new social groups. Most surprising, the canons on Jewish usury, when compared to the canons on Christian usury, are relatively light and late.

The councils of Avignon (1209) and Lateran IV (1215) both extended Lateran III's canon on manifest (Christian) usurers to (manifest) Jewish usurers. Avignon's canon on Jewish usurers immediately follows a decree renewing Lateran III's canon on Christian usurers:

3. That usurers should be excommunicated

Although both the Old and New testaments agree on rooting out usury, and likewise many canons, but because nevertheless…many practice usuries, as if lawful, we command: that on solemn feast days, and especially when synods are held, that all those practicing usury, whether by his own agency or by another shall be tied in the chains of excommunication. If they are public usurers, and have been convicted of that crime: if after three admonitions they are unwilling to make satisfaction, by their name they shall be struck with censure & in addition they will be inflicted with the penalties against usurers decreed in the [Third] Lateran council: namely, that no one shall receive oblations from them, nor if they depart life in that sin, shall they have ecclesiastical burial.

4. That Jews should make restitution for usury, should not publicly work on the Sundays or feast days, or eat meat on fast days

Concerning Jewish usurers, this council decrees that through the sentence of excommunication on Christians, who are in commerce with them, or in any other way engage with them, they shall be restrained from exacting usury; and following the constitutions of the lord pope Innocent III, they shall be compelled to remit these [usuries]. We also prohibit them, and order that it be prohibited them by the bishops on pain of similar punishment, to presume to work in public on Sundays or feast days. Nor shall they eat meat on days of abstinence.[66]

The heading and the opening link canon 4 to canon 3, revealing the ecclesiastic authors' understanding of this radical new legislation as an extension of the law on Christian usurers to Jewish usurers. However, the substance of the ruling the text declaims comes from an application and expansion of "the constitutions of Innocent III" on the Jews. These constitutions are not the "Constitutio pro Judeis" given by Innocent III to the Jews in 1199, but the papal bull of 1198 "Post miserabile" addressed to the Archbishop of Narbonne and circulated throughout the kingdoms of France, England, Hungary, and Sicily.[67]

"Post miserabile" preached the Fourth Crusade, took the property of crusaders under the protection of the Church, and required Christian creditors to absolve crusaders from oaths to pay usury and to desist from further exactions of usury. Should any of the Christian creditors compel crusaders to pay usury, the clergy were to force the creditor to return it under threat of minor excommunication. The bull then added an additional clause extending the requirement of remittance to Jewish creditors: "We order that Jews shall be compelled by you, my sons the princes, and by the secular powers, to remit usury to them; and until they remit it, we order that all intercourse with faithful Christians, whether through commerce or other ways, shall be denied Jews by means of a sentence of excommunication."[68] Christian lenders alone were pressured to release debtors from their oaths to pay usury, and only when this failed were lenders pressured to remit usury already paid.[69] This policy would be ratified at Lateran IV (1215) in a canon separate from that on Jewish usury and again at the following ecumenical council, Lyon I (1245).[70]

The council of Avignon (1209) adopted the regulation of restitution by Jewish usurers and the penalty of indirect excommunication from "Post miserabile," but made two bold new moves. Where "Post miserabile" was restricted to crusaders only, the Avignon canon amplified its application to all Christians. And it went beyond "Post miserabile" in aiming to *restrain* Jews from exacting interest before it has been paid (*ab usurarum exactionibus compescantur*) and demanding restitution only when restraint has failed.

The Avignon canon on Jewish usury seems to accord with Innocent III's own policy. The council was an important one convened by papal legates appointed under Innocent III to address the Albigensian heresy in Provence. Innocent III remained in communication with his legates, the Bishop of Riez, Milon, and later Theodosio, as several letters in Innocent III's Register attest.[71] It is clear that Innocent III was highly

THE DISCOURSE OF USURY AND THE EMERGENCE OF THE STEREOTYPE... 17

concerned about Jewish usury in the years preceding the Avignon council of 1209. For in his letters from 1205 to 1208, Innocent III rebukes King Philip Augustus of France and the Count of Nevers for allowing Jews to extort "usury upon usury," thereby appropriating ecclesiastical goods and Christian possessions.[72] In 1208, however, Innocent III was still calling on secular princes to reform Jewish usury. Direct canonical legislation on Jewish usury to any Christian came only with the radicalization prompted by crusading against heresy. In 1210, following the Avignon decree, the amplification of "Post miserabile" to *all Christians* was incorporated in *Compilatio III*, the collection of canons approved by Innocent III and edited by the papal notary and sub deacon, Peter of Benevento.[73] In this version, it would later enter the Decretals of Gregory IX in 1239.[74]

The substance of the Avignon canon was ratified at the Lateran IV Council of 1215, the most important ecumenical council of the medieval period and the pinnacle of Innocent III's reign. Canon 67 of Lateran IV titled "On the Usury of the Jews" in its entirety reads:

> The more the Christian religion is restrained from usurious practices, so much more does the perfidy of the Jews become used to this practice, so that in a short time the Jews exhaust the financial strength of the Christians. Therefore, in our desire to protect the Christians in this matter, that they should not be excessively oppressed by the Jews, we order by a decree of this Synod, that when in the future a Jew, under any pretext, extort heavy and immoderate usury from a Christian, all relationship with Christians shall therefore be denied him until he shall have made sufficient amends for his exorbitant exactions. The Christians moreover, if need be, shall be compelled by ecclesiastical punishment without appeal, to abstain from such commerce. We also impose this upon the princes, not to be aroused against the Christians because of this, but rather to try to keep the Jews from this practice. We decree that by means of the same punishment the Jews shall be compelled to offer satisfaction to the churches for the tithes and offerings due them and which these churches were wont to receive from the houses and possessions of Christians before these properties had under some title or other passed into Jewish hands. Thus shall this property be conserved to the Church without any loss.[75]

The opening obliquely refers to the success of Lateran III, when it claims that "the more the Christian religion is restrained from usurious practices, so much more does the perfidy of the Jews become used to this practice." In this way this new Jewish legislation is positioned as an extension of or complement to that on Christian usurers made at Lateran III, just as was Avignon (1209). The heart of Lateran IV is in complete accord with Avignon (1209): it focuses first on restraining Jews from extorting usury from all Christians and second on compelling Jews to make restitution of usury taken from Christians, and it applies the penalty of "material excommunication" to do so.

The qualification "heavy and immoderate usury" (*graves immoderatasve usuras*) has troubled both modern historians and medieval canonists, who have wondered whether the phrasing implies that moderate usury was permissible for Jews.[76] Both a prominent Jewish historian, Kenneth Stow, and a prominent church historian, John Moore, have suggested that Innocent III took a soft line on Jewish usury.[77] Indeed, it seems possible that "immoderate and heavy usury" might apply to something more than the rate of "two pennies per pound per week" set in France by Philip Augustus and in use in England, particularly as the terminology seems to have been taken from Roman law, which did have a legally set rate.[78] Although the meaning of these adjectives may elude us, they seem to have been clear enough to late twelfth- and early-thirteenth-century clerics. For Pope Alexander III (1159–81), under whom the canon on "manifest usurers" was made at Lateran III, used the adjective "immoderate" to object to a creditor who was forcing a debtor to pay "immoderate usury" (*ad immoderatum foenus solvendum*).[79] Innocent III himself used the adjective "heavy" in a bull of 1208 to the Count of Nevers when he objected to Jews who compel debtors to make "heavy payment of usuries" (*ad solutionem gravissimam usurarum*) even after they have received the principal and "more besides."[80]

Perhaps immoderate attention has been given to the qualifiers "heavy and immoderate." For within a longer historical perspective, Innocent III's reign clearly marks the onset of canonical legislation on Jewish usury. And it is this that is the important fact. Lateran IV is the first and only ecumenical council that legislates on Jewish usury, and its legislation with the distinctive language of "immoderate usury" would be renewed several times in mid-thirteenth-century provincial councils. Lateran IV accords with the unqualified canon of Avignon (1209) both in amplifying "Post miserabile" to all Christians and in attempting to *restrain*, not merely remit, Jewish usury. One may even detect a subtle escalation in the rhetoric between Avignon 1209 and Lateran IV. Where the Avignon canon refers to "Jewish usurers" designating a subset of Jews who are usurers, Lateran IV refers flatly to "the usuries of the Jews," to the "Jews" and the "perfidy of the Jews," implying a stereotyping of all Jews as usurers. Given the accord between Avignon (1209) and Lateran IV emphasized in the analysis here, I would propose that Lateran IV's qualifier "heavy and immoderate" may function in the text as a directive to clergy to penalize the egregious cases, just as the qualifier "manifest" does in Lateran III and later papal bulls.[81] This reading accords with that of later decretalists from the thirteenth century who also puzzled over the implications of these qualifiers.[82]

Canon 67 from Lateran IV became the cornerstone of canonical legislation against Jewish usury. It was renewed at the provincial council of Narbonne (1227) with language that reiterated the justification of Lateran IV via Jewish oppression of Christians, the prohibition of "immoderate usury," and the penalty of material excommunication:

> Because usurious Jews oppress Christians greatly by exactions [of usury], when by God generally usuries have been prohibited: we are led to make the provision by the synodal council, that no Jew at all shall receive from a Christian at all immoderate usuries. But if they do, they will be compelled to restore them by the church: namely through the excommunication of Christians, who have a partnership (*participationem*) with them in commerce or other things.[83]

The Narbonne canon was repeated almost verbatim 20 years later at the provincial council of Béziers (1246), also held under the Archbishop of Narbonne.[84] The canon from Lateran IV would be repeated verbatim, but without its introductory justification, at the council of Vienna (1267) held under a papal legate.[85]

In the 1250s, three French councils decreed new legislation against Jewish usury that went radically beyond Lateran IV and previous canon law. The council of Albi (1254) ordered ecclesiastical and secular judges not to compel debtors to pay usury to Jews *or to others*, to compel Jews to tell the truth about whether a loan included usury by swearing on the Torah, and to apply this ruling even to loans *between Jews*.

> Furthermore, no ecclesiastical or secular judge may compel the Christians to pay any usury whatsoever to Jews or to any other persons. Moreover, we order that in cases where there is a doubt whether any usury forms part of those debts which now and then the Jews demand that the Christians shall pay them, the said Jews shall first be bound to tell the truth by taking an oath over the Law of Moses. This does not mean that any other methods

20   J.L. MELL

which have been found for the discovery of usurious practices shall be given up. This is also to be observed in case of loans contracted among the Jews themselves. We decree and order that in the case of such loans, and in the case of loans hereafter to be made to Christians by the Jews, a simple oath by the said Christians shall be sufficient to establish whether there is any taint of usury about them; and in cases where they state that there is usury, those who have so sworn shall be absolved from payment.[86]

This decree breaks several precedents. It abjures all Jewish usury, not only immoderate usury. It commands secular as well as ecclesiastical judges. It says nothing about cases where debtors had sworn to pay usury, suggesting that even in these cases, usury should not be paid, thus reversing earlier canon law. Finally, it orders judges to apply the same rule of no usury to loans *between Jews*. The language here makes clear that Jews are singled out as the final frontier for the usury campaign, not as the prototypical moneylenders. They are dangerous, because in theory they do not fall under ecclesiastical jurisdiction. But theory is changing.

In the following year, the mixed council of Béziers (1255), held under Louis IX on his return from the Seventh Crusade, decreed:

Jews shall desist from usury, blasphemy, and magic. The Talmud as well as other books in which blasphemies are found, shall be burned. The Jews who refuse to obey this shall be expelled, and transgressors shall suffer punishment according to the law. All Jews shall live from the labor of their hands, or from commerce (*negotiationibus*) without terms (*terminis*) and usuries.[87]

The flat denunciation of all usury and its equivalence with blasphemy and magic stand out. The decrees of Béziers, as a mixed council held under the king, must be considered as reflecting both ecclesiastical and secular legislation. The role of the king in the council is an important indicator that the secular legislation on Jewish usury is closely linked to the ecclesiastical legislation, as will be discussed later in the chapter.

At the council of Montpellier (1258), all Jewish usury is again forbidden and legal measures are decreed similar to those of Albi.

5. That Jews shall not extort usuries; but only principle.

Moreover to restrain the deadly avarice of the Jews, as far as we are able with justice, we establish that no one in the future shall hear a Jewish case against a Christian over the exaction of debts, nor offer him any occasion for audacity: unless first by the sacred law of Moses placed before him, the Jew himself, who claims justice be exhibited to him, by means of his advocate declares, what and how much of the debt he extorts, was usury or principal.[88]

These three councils reflect a radicalization in France during the 1250s. In the 1280s and 1290s, in the territory of modern France of today, three local councils instituted legislation preventing clerics and notaries from writing or sealing documents which contained usury exacted by Jews from Christians.[89]

To summarize, the conciliar legislation on Jewish usury appeared during the reign of Pope Innocent III, in the context of the radicalization prompted by the crusade against the Albigensians in southern France. When compared with the legislation against Christian lay usury, that on Jewish usury was not a primary ecclesiastical concern (see Fig. 6.1). To be

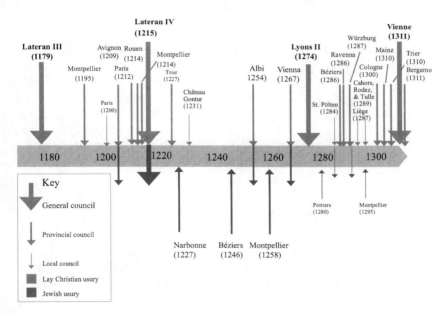

Fig. 6.1 Conciliar legislation on Christian lay usury and Jewish usury from Lateran III (1179) to Vienne (1311).
Note: only legislation directed at lay usurers or Jewish usurers has been included. Legislation directed at clerical usury or clerical indebtedness, as at Melun (1216) and Rouen (1231), and crusader indebtedness, as in Lyon I (1245), has been excluded. Mixed councils with secular monarchs at their head, such as Béziers (1255), have been excluded from this list.

sure, the ecclesiastical authorities were concerned with it, but no more so than with Christian lay usury, and until the thirteenth century their hands were tied completely. The discrete canons decreed on Jews and usury were necessary in order to apply the same laws already in effect for Christians to the non-Christian population. Consequently, the Jewish legislation was both later and lighter than that on Christian lay usury. The legislation on Jewish usury, often misread as a transparent reflection of an economic fact (the dominance of Jews in moneylending), was in fact the extension of a long ecclesiastical campaign against usury to a new frontier, wholly in keeping with its *modus operandi*.

The legislation is not good evidence for the prominence or pervasiveness of Jewish lending, even according to the outdated methodology in which legislation reflects economic and social facts. For the far more extensive legislation on Christian usury would mean that Christians were far more prominent than Jews in lending on usury. Yet, how much weight should be given to the fact that the legislation on Jewish usury trails that on Christian usury? Two facts complicate our assessment. First, the papacy only began to legislate on Jews in the late twelfth century, as the popes began pushing the boundaries of their legislative jurisdiction. And second, French royal legislation is weighted almost exclusively against Jewish usury and only lightly touches on Christian usury, reflecting an obverse pattern to that of the ecclesiastical legislation. The remainder of this chapter will deal with these two issues. Lurking under all these questions is a more fundamental one: why do the Jews get marked out as usurers? The answer shall emerge from an investigation of the others.

Conciliar Legislation on Jews

The emergence of the legislation on Jewish usury is entangled with the extension of the Church's claim to have jurisdictional power over the Jewish community, a group properly outside the legal jurisdiction of the community of the Christian faithful. The ecclesiastical authorities themselves seem to have been aware of this fact, as the famous statement at the beginning of Lateran IV's canon—"the Jews exhaust the financial strength of the Christians"—functions to justify an unprecedented and unwarranted legal move by asserting the need to protect Christians.[90] Does this undermine the proposed interpretation of these canons as reflecting the extension of a general usury campaign rather than reflecting the economic fact of Jewish concentration in moneylending? I think not. When the legislation on Jewish usury is contextualized within the ecclesiastical legislation on Jews more generally, we find that Jewish usury comes later and receives less attention than other issues. That is to say, Jewish usury was of secondary importance to ecclesiastical authorities whether one looks at it in relation to Jewish issues in general or in relation to usury in general. Most significantly, placing Jewish usury within the context of conciliar legislation on Jews illuminates why Jews began to be marked out as usurers.

Prior to the late twelfth century, conciliar legislation relating to Jews was restricted almost exclusively to Jewish converts to Christianity, with the exception of a few canons restricting Jews from holding public office.[91] In the late twelfth century, Italian canonists and popes began proposing that the Church could punish Jews for temporal offenses. The break with the long medieval tradition of respecting rabbinic jurisdiction began with two rulings by Pope Alexander III (1159–81). One concerned Jews refusing to pay tithes on lands acquired from Christians, and the other concerned Jews leaving their doors and windows open on Easter. The Italian canonist Huguccino of Pisa was the first to assert ecclesiastical jurisdiction over Jews, claiming that when "they sinned or did wrong ('cum enim peccant vel forisfaciunt'), a bishop or his court could fine them, mutilate them or hang them."[92]

During the pontificates of Celestine III (1191–98) and his nephew Innocent III (1198–1216), "indirect excommunication" was developed as a remedy against recalcitrant Jews applicable in many circumstances, including usury. This penalty, known as the "Judgment of the Jews," was what I have called "material excommunication," as it cut Jews off from business relations with Christians. It was enforced by threatening Christians with excommunication should they violate the ban. Celestine III first used material excommunication in Rouen in 1193 to compel Jews to pay tithes on what had formerly been Christian land. Innocent III then used this penalty in 1198 to compel Jewish creditors to make restitution of usury owed and paid by crusaders, as discussed above. When "Post miserabile" was included in the official collection of Innocent III's bulls *Compilatio III* (1210), ecclesiastical jurisdiction over Jews was confirmed.[93]

Thereafter cases developed rapidly, even though northern canonists still doubted whether the Church could judge Jews at all. By 1229, Jews were appearing in canonical courts "on at least three grounds: failure to pay tithes, usury, and assaults on clerics."[94] And "by 1239, the papacy asserted its right to punish Jews communally for a purely religious offense—the study of the Talmud—without even alleging that Christians were being injured."[95] The expansion of jurisdiction over Jews paralleled the concurrent papal expansion into secular affairs.[96] As Walter Pakter has commented, "it would have been an anomaly for the papacy to exercise authority over Christian kings and emperors while granting immunity to the weakest of western minorities."[97]

The extension of jurisdiction over Jews was accomplished via anti-Judaic legislation. Usury was not among the first or foremost subjects of canonical legislation on Jews in the high middle ages. From Lateran III (1179) to Vienne (1311–2), over 70 councils decreed legislation on Jews. Among these fewer than 15 (<20 percent) directly legislated against Jewish usury or Jewish usurers.[98] Table 6.1 depicts the frequency of canons on Jewish usury and the order in which the canon was placed in relation to other Jewish issues. Much more significant was the legislation on Christian wet nurses nursing Jewish babies, Christian servants working and living in Jewish homes, the imposition of distinctive dress on Jews, the repression of public office holding by Jews, and the regulation of Jewish presence in public spaces on Sundays and Christian feast days. As frequent as canons on usury were canons concerning food issues, handling of conversions and converts' property, and sex across religious lines (see Table 6.2). Among the ecumenical councils, only Lateran IV ruled on Jewish usury, while Lateran III and IV contained new Jewish legislation and Lyon II (1274) and Vienne (1311–2) contained new legislation on Christian usury.[99]

The legislation on Jewish usury appears clustered with other pieces of anti-Jewish legislation, with one exception.[100] Often one canon contains legislation on several issues. For example, canon 4 of Avignon (1209) coupled the legislation on Jewish usurers with prohibitions on Jews publicly working on Christian holy days and eating meat on Christian fast days.[101] Lateran IV tacked onto the usury legislation the requirement that Jews pay tithes on land formerly owned by Christians, and the two canons following the usury decree ordered that Jews (and Muslims) should wear distinctive dress, should not appear in public on the days of lamentation and Passion Sunday, should not blaspheme, and should not hold public office.[102] The council of Narbonne (1227) when renewing Lateran IV's decree on Jewish usury incorporated prohibitions on Jews hiring Christian servants, eating or selling meat on fast days, and holding public office, and in two following canons prescribed the Jewish badge, prohibited Jews working on Christian holy days and appearing in public during Holy Week, and required an offering by Jews to parish churches on Easter.[103] The later councils legislating on Jewish usury include some or all of these

THE DISCOURSE OF USURY AND THE EMERGENCE OF THE STEREOTYPE... 25

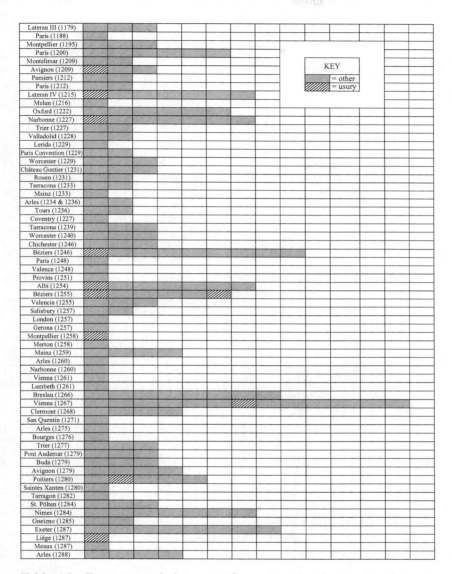

Table 6.1 Frequency and placement of canons on Jewish usury in relation to canons on other Jewish issues

Table 6.2 Conciliar legislation on Jewish issues from 1179 to 1311

On Jews and...	No. of canons
Christian servants	29
Clothing	28
Sundays, feast days, processions, or viewing holy objects	21
Public office	19
Jewish usury	14
Sex or cohabitation	13
Food	11
Tithes and obligations to the Church	11
On clerics pledging Church articles or borrowing from Jews	10
Jewish testimony in court	9
Jewish doctors and medicine	9
Jewish converts to Christianity	8
On Jews and Christians dining, celebrating, or gaming together	8
Converts' property	6
On clerics acting as sureties for Jews or using churches as depositories for Jews	6
Other	6
Synagogues	5
On lay Christians and uneducated clergy disputing with Jews	4
On Jews and Christians mixing in public places (baths, taverns)	4
Ghettos	2
Magic	2
Blasphemy	1

Note: Canons are arranged in order of frequency. The data is based on my reading of the canons collected in Grayzel.

issues, as well as prohibitions on Christians interacting with Jews in regard to medical care, sexual intercourse or cohabitation, gaming, drinking, celebrating, and disputing religious doctrine.

The coupling of Jewish usury with other anti-Judaic legislation suggests a conceptual link among the disparate topics of food, office holding, servants, clothing, and usury. The clergy who passed this legislation were making a concerted, even fierce, effort to separate Jews from Christians, subordinate Jews to Christians, and repress Jewish religious difference, regarded more and more as deviant and dangerous. The canons on dress were made so that "in all Christian lands, at all times," Jews "shall easily be distinguishable from the rest of the populations by the quality of their clothes."[104] Their stated aim was to prevent sexual intercourse. Social separation was reinforced through canons prohibiting Christians and Jews from drinking, celebrating, gaming, and cohabiting together.[105] But the most extensive legislation was aimed at subordinating Jews to Christians by preventing Jews from hiring Christian servants or holding public office. The holding of public office was offensive because "it is quite absurd that any who blaspheme against Christ should have power over Christians."[106] For the canon assumes that public office offers Jews "the pretext to vent their wrath against Christians."[107] The legislation on food similarly was motivated by a sense that it was denigrating to Christians to purchase what was deemed ritually unfit for Jews.

When Jewish religious practice conflicted with Christian practice, Jews were made to conform to Christian customs. Jews could not work publicly on Christian holy days or eat meat on fast days. Jews should not dress ornately on Christian days of lamentation. These were seen as acts of insolence. Canons restricted Jewish presence in public on Christian holy days, because the clergy feared that Jews would mock "Christians who are presenting a memorial of the most sacred passion and are displaying signs of grief" and would "deride the Redeemer."[108]

In making these laws the clergy overstepped ecclesiastical jurisdiction and infringed on rabbinic legal authority. The Church could not do so with impunity, even over a weak minority, much less over Christian kings. Legal and theological justifications had to be given, and they were. In papal bull after papal bull, and canon after canon, we find Jews decried as blasphemers, as despisers, and as murderers of the Redeemer, who oppress Christians though they should be in servitude to them.[109] Underlying this development is a conceptual shift in the understanding of Jews and Judaism as deviant Christians, akin to heretics.

Canon law on Jewish usury was likewise motivated by the desire to subordinate Jews to Christians, repress Jewish religious difference, and even separate Jews from Christians. In Lateran IV's ground-breaking canon, the entire issue of Jewish usury was cast as a struggle between "the Christian religion" and the "Jewish perfidy," not as a matter of restraining individual usurers: "The more the Christian religion is restrained from usurious practices, so much more does the perfidy of the Jews become used to this practice, that in a short time Jews exhaust the financial strength of Christians."[110] Jewish usury was not regarded primarily as a matter of economic justice, but of the injustice of Jewish dominance over Christians, the subversion of the right superiority of the *fideles* over the infidel and blasphemer. The anxiety over Jewish usury was prompted not by the economic activity of Jews, but by the rab-

28   J.L. MELL

binic interpretation of Deuteronomy 23:21, which permitted usury on loans to Christians, in dissonance with the development of canon law on Christian usury.

Rabbinic Legislation against Jewish Usury

The Jewish community had its own religious law, which regulated its community just as canon law regulated the Christian community. Rabbinic law had developed legislation against Jewish usury long before the high medieval Christian campaign against lay Christian usury, and rabbinic authorities continued to refine it throughout the medieval period.[111]

The prohibition against usury is biblical. It is found in three passages in the Torah: Exodus 22:24–5, Leviticus 25:35–8, and Deuteronomy 23:20–1.[112] Both the Exodus and Leviticus passages limit the injunction specifically to the poor, and ground the injunction in Israel's experience as sojourners in Egypt:[113]

> You shall not wrong a resident alien (*ger*) or oppress him, for you were strangers in the land of Egypt....If you lend money to my people, to the poor among you, do not act as a creditor towards them; exact no usury (*neshekh*) from them. (Ex. 22:20, 24)
> And if your brother, being impoverished, sinks among you, and you hold him [as] a resident alien (*ger*) or sojourner, let him live among you. Do not take from him usury (*neshek ve-tarbit*), but fear your Lord. Let him live among you as a brother (*aḥ*). Your money you shall not lend him on usury, nor for usurious increase (*marbit*) shall you give him your food. I the Lord am your God, who brought you out of the land of Egypt, to give you the land of Canaan, to be your God. (Lev. 25:35–8)

The third biblical passage expands the prohibition from the poor to any "brother." But like the Leviticus prohibition, that of Deuteronomy ties it to God's gift of land:

> You shall not take from your brother (*aḥ*) interest (*neshek*) on money, interest on food, or interest on anything else on which one can take interest. From a foreigner (*nokhri*) you may exact interest, but from your brother you may not exact interest, so that the Lord your God may bless you in all your undertakings in the land that you are about to enter and possess. (Deut. 23:20–1)

While expanding the scope of the prohibition to all Israelites, the Deuteronomic injunction simultaneously explicitly permits usury to be exacted from foreigners. The determination of who is a foreigner (*nokhri*) and who a brother (*ah*) would lie at the heart of the high medieval dispute.

The Mishnah (c. 70–200 CE) adopted Deuteronomy's absolute prohibition on usury between Jews, whether poor or not. What generated discussion among the rabbis of the Mishnah, known as the Tannaim, were the gray zones, the economic exchanges that could be defined either as loan or sale: loans of produce paid in produce when the market value of produce fluctuates, advance payment for the purchase of goods, a sale in which the buyer delays payment, mortgages where the lender receives the property of the borrower as security for the loan, investments where the money given to the recipient is used to engage in a business enterprise.[114] These contracts are often parallel to those that would be considered a thousand years later by high medieval canon lawyers, such as loans on security, buying and selling on credit, rent charges, rentals of houses, loans of produce, and investments.[115] The solutions reached by the early and later rabbis (the Tannaim, Amoraim, and Rishonim) are often similar to those of the canonists. For example, both legal traditions defined a similar type of investment contract as non-usurious—the *iska* in rabbinic law and the *commenda* in canon law. Although the protocol of these contracts differs slightly, both are based on the principle that profit is permissible when the investor shares the risk of the enterprise.[116] In short, rabbinic law, like canon law, prohibited usury among its own and developed a sophisticated legal discourse on contracts, prices, and torts that distinguished licit and illicit forms of advance payment, buying on credit, mortgages, and investments. As Giacomo Todeschini has recently argued, medieval scholars' ignorance about the existence of the rich tradition of Jewish economic law and thought on usury has skewed our understanding of Jewish history.[117] And as Toni Oelsner argued decades ago, a double standard has been applied to Jews and Christians, owing in large part to the prominence of Weber and his concept of the double morality of in-group/out-group ethics.[118] What complicates matters is how these parallel legal traditions on usury played out within the historical dynamics of majority/minority relations.

In the thirteenth century, there existed a difference in the interpretation of a shared scriptural text: Jewish law interpreted Deuteronomy 23:20–1 as permitting lending on usury to the "stranger," understood as any non-Jew, and prohibiting it to the brother, "any Jew."[119] Although a similar line of interpretation existed in Western Christianity, stemming from no less an authority than the Church Father Ambrose, it was largely discarded by the mid-thirteenth century.[120] Christian theologians and polemicists in consequence often attacked Jewish interpretation, arguing that Christians were brothers too.[121] If so, then Christian interpretation should hold sway over Jews too, and the infringement of rabbinic jurisdiction by the papacy was justified by more than defense of Christians. This friction between theological interpretations and legal jurisdictions underlies the ecclesiastical and secular legislation on Jewish usury in the thirteenth century. The following discussion of polemic will demonstrate that Christian legislation on Jewish usury pressed forward laws directly in contradiction to rabbinic law and in contestation with the jurisdiction of rabbinic law. Although in theory each religious law should dictate the rules for lenders in their religious communities alone, the Church increasingly found obnoxious the dissonance between Jewish and Christian law on lenders. Canon law was increasingly imposed on Jewish lenders in the gray zone of loans by Jews to Christians.[122] Evidence of this shift can be seen most clearly in the Hebrew polemical literature recording disputations between Jews and Christians in the late twelfth and thirteenth centuries.

JEWISH-CHRISTIAN POLEMICS AND THE ANTI-JUDAISM CAMPAIGN

The Christian construction of the Jew as the quintessential usurer is in part a consequence of the difference between Christian and Jewish interpretation of the biblical prohibitions on usury, particularly Deuteronomy 23:20–21. Through the Hebrew disputation literature, one can see clearly that Jews maintained interpretations of the biblical prohibitions on usury at odds with Christian theology, that Jews resisted Christian pressure to conform to Christian theological interpretation, and that Jews struggled to maintain the independent jurisdiction of rabbinic law against the encroachments of canon law and royal legislation. It is the Jewish refusal to accept the dictates of the Christian usury campaign which generates the medieval stereotype of the usurious Jew. In short the caricature of the usurious Jew reflects a theological dispute, not an economic fact.

Among Jews, anti-Christian polemics were nonexistent prior to the twelfth century, with the exception of the ancient *Toledot Yeshu*.[123] With the works by Joseph Kimḥi and Jacob ben Reuben, the writing of Jewish polemic began. The Hebrew treatises reached a peak in the thirteenth century with nine works written by, among others, the anonymous author of the *Vikkuaḥ lehaRadak*, Yehiel mi-Paris, Meir b. Simeon of Narbonne, and Yosef ha-Mekanne.[124] The small number of Jewish texts is vastly outweighed by the hundreds of Christian polemics.

Latin Christian writings on Jews and Judaism stretch back to the early Church. This vast *adversus Judaeos* literature has been classified into six types of genre: (1) collections of scriptures (*testimonia*), (2) treatises in epistolary form, (3) homilies, (4) poetical works, (5) sermons, and (6) dialogs.[125] The dialog was a classical form, but it resurfaced and came to predominate in the high middle ages. The prominence of the dialog form corresponded to a dramatic upsurge in Christian polemic that began in the late eleventh century and reached a crescendo in the twelfth century with works by Peter Damian, Gilbert Crispin, Petrus Alfonsi, Rupert of Deutz, Peter the Venerable, William of Champeaux, Peter of Blois, Walter of Châtillon, Alan of Lille, and others.

In the twelfth century, the dialogs addressing Judaism were literary constructions, sometimes loosely based on actual discussions between a learned Jew and the learned Christian author. By the thirteenth century, the fictitious literary dialog was supplanted by staged disputations, whose participants circulated a written account such as those in Paris (1240) and Barcelona (1263). The disputation was a common debating form in medieval university culture, as it conformed to the primary mode of medieval reasoning, dialectic, and served to hone skills in reasoning and rhetoric. When staged between Jews and Christians, the dispute was compulsory for Jews and had potentially dangerous consequences. Disputes were held in the presence of the king and his court, and the participants were carefully chosen leaders selected from preeminent rabbinic and ecclesiastical authorities.[126]

From the fifth to the early twelfth century, none of the approximately 150 Christian authors who wrote on Jews and Judaism discussed any biblical passages on usury.[127] The polemics from the twelfth and thirteenth centuries too focused on theological themes, such as Jesus as the Messiah, the Trinity, the abolition of the ritual law of Moses, the immaculate conception, the salvation effected by Jesus Christ, and God's abandonment of the Jewish people.[128] Usury entered high medieval polemics only as the ecclesiastical campaign against usury gained ground in the later twelfth century. Contrary to the statements of some scholars, usury was not a major issue in disputations or polemic literature.[129] Usury was not

32 J.L. MELL

discussed at all in the two most important and well-documented Jewish-Christian disputations of the thirteenth century, those at Paris (1240) and Barcelona (1263). But usury did make a minor appearance in a handful of Hebrew polemics and commentaries on the Bible or the Talmud in the late twelfth and thirteenth centuries, most notably in the writings of Rabbenu Tam, Joseph Kimhi, Joseph b. Nathan ha-Mekanne, Bahya ben Asher, Gersonides, and Meir ben Simon of Narbonne.[130] I will bring three examples of Hebrew polemic to demonstrate Jewish knowledge of the Christian campaign against usury and to illustrate how the Jewish response maintained the validity of an independent Jewish interpretation: the earliest medieval Hebrew polemic, Joseph Kimhi's *Sefer ha-Brit* (Book of the Covenant) composed in Narbonne;[131] a late-thirteenth-century or early-fourteenth-century compilation, *Sefer Nizzahon Yashan*; and the lengthy thirteenth-century compilation of disputations and *testimonia*, *Milhemet Mitzvah*, by Meir ben Simeon of Narbonne, also known by the acronym ha-Meili.[132]

Joseph Kimhi (1105?–70?, Provence) explicitly states that he wrote *Sefer ha-Brit* at the request of one of his students. The text is constructed as a literary dialog between a Jew and a Christian, the *ma'amin* (believer) and the *min* (unbeliever).[133] And it conforms to the Latin literary genre of *testimonia* and fictionalized dialogs, though it may also reflect a composite version of discussions Kimhi held with Christian theologians.[134]

The text opens with the Jewish interlocutor refuting the doctrines of the Trinity and original sin. The Christian in response challenges the Jew: "You have neither faith nor deeds, dominion nor sovereignty, for you have lost all."[135] The Jewish believer responds by illustrating Jews' adherence to the Ten Commandments and their moral superiority over Christians. The good deeds of Jews are elaborated at great length and contrasted to the evil deeds of Christians: "There are no murderers or adulterers among [the Jews]. Oppression and theft are not as widespread among Jews as among Christians who rob people on the highways and hang them and sometimes gouge out their eyes. You cannot establish any of these things with respect to the Jews."[136] Jews offer free hospitality to Jewish travelers, ransom Jewish captives, clothe and feed the poor, and keep the Shabbat, unlike Christians. Only then, in response, is the charge of usury raised by the Christian: "You are right in part....[But] I will show you other deeds that you do that are contrary to religious law. You lend on usury, although David said *Who will dwell in your tabernacle? He who has not lent his money with usury* (Ps. 15:1, 5)."[137]

THE DISCOURSE OF USURY AND THE EMERGENCE OF THE STEREOTYPE... 33

Kimḥi answers him by interpreting the Psalm as referring to the more limited case of taking usury from your brethren, forbidden in Deuteronomy 23:21:

> Usury, to which you refer is mentioned in the Torah of Moses: *You may take usury on loans to foreigners but not on loans to your countrymen* (Deut. 23:21). Thus when David said *he who has not lent his money with usury* (Ps. 15:5), he reiterated what had been forbidden them. Do you not see that although Scripture said *You shall not kill* (Exod. 20:13), David killed thousands from among the nations? This is because *you shall not kill* means that you shall not kill one who is innocent. Similarly, *He who has not lent his money with usury* is to be interpreted with reference to what the Torah forbade. There was no need for David to refer to this since Moses had already stated it.[138]

He concludes by contrasting the scrupulousness of Jews in not lending on usury to their brethren with the flagrant lending on usury by Christians to their brethren:

> A Jew will not lend his brother wheat, wine, or any commodity on a term basis in order to increase his profit, while you, who have disdained usury, sell all commodities to your brethren on a term basis at twice the price. You should be ashamed to say that you do not lend with usury for this is enormous usury. Furthermore, many gentiles clearly lend on interest to [both] Jews and gentiles, although Jews do not lend to their fellow Jews.[139]

That this theological dispute had a long life is evident from its appearance in the *Sefer Nizzahon Yashan*, a text dating to the late thirteenth or early fourteenth century with a German provenance. *Sefer Nizzahon Yashan* incorporates earlier polemical material, particularly from *Sefer Yosef HaMekanne* and an anonymous anthology of Ashkenazic polemical literature found in the Vittorio Emanuele library in Rome.[140] Its inclusion of the Deuteronomy debate largely follows Kimḥi's formula, but also reflects developments in Christian counterarguments. The passage in *Sefer Nizzahon Yashan* likewise begins with a challenge raised from Psalm 15:5. Again the Jewish response is to delimit Psalm 15 within the parameters set by Deuteronomy 23:21. But one can detect the development of Christian counterarguments in the claim that Jews ought to consider Christians as "brethren," since they are Edomites according to Jewish lore:[141]

> On the basis of this psalm, the heretics curse us and ask why we take interest from Gentiles....If you then say that the descendants of Esau are also called

34   J.L. MELL

brethren, as it is written, "You shall not abhor an Edomite, for he is your brother" [Deut. 23:8], the answer is: It is true that they were once brethren and it was forbidden to take interest from them; now however, they have disqualified themselves and are considered strangers.[142]

Sefer Nizzahon Yashan also counters the Christian theological principle popularized by the school of Peter the Chanter that usury is equivalent to theft.[143]

Moreover, one can respond concerning interest that it represents legitimate gain, for Solomon said, "He who increases his wealth through usury and unjust gain will gather it for one who pities the poor" [Prov. 28:8], i.e., his sin can be expiated through charity. Now if this were regarded as robbery, how could charity help?[144]

Our third example is Meir b. Simeon's *Milhemet Mitzvah*, the longest Hebrew work of the thirteenth century, running to over 250 folios. Meir b. Simeon was a prominent rabbinic authority, living in Narbonne in the mid-thirteenth century. His manuscript is a complex composite of his numerous disputations with priests and archbishops, sermons, *testimonia*, a letter to Louis IX, commentary on liturgy, and an attack on the Kabbalistic work *Sefer ha-Bahir*. *Milhemet Mitzvah* contains the lengthiest medieval Hebrew discussion of usury, contained in two separate disputations and the letter to Louis IX. Meir b. Simeon had close knowledge of the Christian usury campaign and recent conciliar and royal legislation. This is not surprising, given that Narbonne was the seat of the 1227 provincial council, the first council to re-enforce Lateran IV's decrees prohibiting Jewish usury (as well as Jews hiring Christian nurses, holding public office, and eating meat in public on fast days or selling meat).[145] The neighboring town of Béziers was the seat of the provincial council of 1246 and the mixed council of 1255, both of which ruled on Jewish usury.

Milhemet Mitzvah provides extensive evidence for the contest between Jewish and Christian interpretation of the biblical prohibitions on usury. And it provides evidence of the legal encroachment on rabbinic jurisdiction by both the Church and the Crown. Folios 3b–7a record an extensive debate on usury with a clergyman.[146] Because the opening folio of the manuscript is damaged, we do not know the identity of the disputant or the context giving rise to the dispute, or even if Meir b. Simeon included them. Where the manuscript becomes readable, it is clear that the first

THE DISCOURSE OF USURY AND THE EMERGENCE OF THE STEREOTYPE...   35

subject is Christology and the conversion of the Jews. But the Christian interlocutor also raises the issue of usury, to which Meir b. Simeon quickly responds with four separate arguments.

First, Meir b. Simeon argues that Christians should not object to usury at all by pointing out an inconsistency in the Christian application of allegorical interpretation to the *mitzvot* in the Hebrew Bible: According to your opinion, he says, the laws on kashrut, Passover, circumcision are interpreted allegorically; therefore so too should the laws on usury.

> What injustice do you find in usury greater than the prohibition on eating pork, forbidden animals, and fish without fins and scales? Since you transform everything into an allegory, called *figura*, why do you not interpret the commandment on usury likewise allegorically and permit even your own people to lend to each other on usury, as you do with the other prohibitions?[147]

The Christian answers by drawing a distinction between commandments which human intellect teaches, such as not committing theft, adultery, and murder, and commandments of righteousness and loving kindness, into which category usury falls: "because it is righteousness and loving kindness not to take interest for the lending of money."[148] Again, Meir b. Simeon replies by raising an inconsistency in Christian interpretation of scripture: "If that is so you should observe all the commandments of loving kindness and righteousness according to their literal meaning, such as the *shemitah* year...(Exodus 23:11), and the jubilee year..., and the returning of a pledge at night to a poor person, and [leaving in the field] the gleanings, the [forgotten] sheaf, the corners, and the poor tithe." Meir b. Simeon seals his argument with a proof text from the New Testament book of Matthew in which Jesus commanded his followers to observe the commandments on loving kindness and not to abrogate one *yod* from the law:

> "Whoever therefore shall break one of the minor commandments and shall teach men so, he shall be small in the kingdom of heaven." And there are many similar sayings....You turn them all into their opposites by your deeds and interpret them figuratively or mystically. I am therefore very surprised at you. Why do you gather yourselves together against us in connexion with the taking of interest? According to your opinion about the interpretation of the laws—namely to explain them figuratively and to abolish their plain sense, as e.g. in the case of pork, leavened bread on Passover, and circumcision,—you should also allow to lend on interest.[149]

Meir b. Simeon's second line of attack is to defend the Jewish interpretation of Deuteronomy 23:21, which differentiates between the brother and the stranger regarding the taking of interest: According to Jewish interpretation, the Torah distinguishes between the foreigner and the brother in regard to usury, but not in regard to theft or murder. Only toward a brother must one show loving kindness.[150] In an aside, Meir b. Simeon deploys high medieval poverty critiques to charge that the Church does not even show loving kindness to other Christians: "But you and your church dignitaries close your eyes, collect tithes and other gifts and taxes running into thousands and thousands, and do not lend to the poor who go a-begging at the doors. You do not see to it that the poor young maiden[s] get married. Thus they turn to licentiousness and harlotry because of their want."[151]

The Christian objects to the Jewish distinction between brother and stranger on the basis of Psalm 15: "he who puts out his money on usury" shall not dwell in the tabernacle of the Lord. This appears to be the standard Christian objection. Meir b. Simeon answers as previous rabbinic authorities have: King David did not introduce a new commandment in the Torah received from Moses; rather he spoke only in reference to a more limited case of "the brother." For,

> Do you not see that the Torah makes a general statement in many places and relies on a more specific wording given elsewhere? It says, e.g., in an unqualified manner: Thou shalt not kill. Yet there is no doubt that it is a commandment to kill the murder, the adulterer, and him that desecrates the Sabbath or worships an idol...Therefore, "thou shalt not kill" refers certainly to him only, who should not be killed. In the same way, the general statement in *Psalm xv* can be referred to the brother only, to whom no loans on interest should be made.[152]

Meir b. Simeon then concludes with an additional rejoinder from Isaiah, which ties back into his first argument on allegorical interpretation.

But the Christian objects: if the distinction between brother and stranger is followed in Deuteronomy 23:21, then it also should be followed in the cases where the language of "neighbor" or "friend" is used, leading to the absurd position that one should permit false testimony, fraud, and coveting of another's wife and house in all cases where the injured is not a "neighbor" or a "friend."

THE DISCOURSE OF USURY AND THE EMERGENCE OF THE STEREOTYPE... 37

Meir b. Simeon responds with linguistic distinctions between "brother" and "neighbor" or "friend." The latter are used consistently in the Hebrew Bible to refer to all individuals with whom one has business dealings. But "brother" is never used in these passages, and conversely "neighbor" and "friend" are never used in the usury passages. Moreover, if one should argue that all three are the same, one can answer that in the case of usury, there is an explicit permission to take usury from the foreigner, but in the case of fraud, covetousness, and false testimony, there is no explicit permission to take it from anyone.

> No distinction is there made between the neighbour and the foreigner; but regarding a loan on interest you will never find that Scripture forbids it, except in the case of a brother.[153]

Meir b. Simeon's third line of attack is to argue that the Torah in fact only prohibits taking usury from the poor among one's people, on the basis of Exodus 22:24 and Leviticus 25:35: "if thou lend money to any of my people, to the poor with thee, thou shalt not be to him as a creditor" (Ex. 22:24) and "if thy brother be waxen poor, take no interest of him" (Lev. 25:35). Essentially, Meir b. Simeon treats Deuteronomy 23:21 under the more limited case of the usury prohibitions in Exodus 22:24 and Leviticus 25:35—that the Torah only forbids lending on usury to one who is poor among one's people. He introduces several aspects of rabbinic law on usury to support his case: We do not even collect the capital from the poor, though from a strict legal point of view, one is permitted to collect a debt even from the cloak of the poor man. The rabbis permitted collecting usufruct of houses, fields, and vineyards (defined as usury in both rabbinic and canon law) "except for the nominal penny that is deducted, because they realized that the prohibition of the Torah (of taking interest) refers to the poor only."[154]

The Christian accepts these arguments and then introduces a final objection again on the point of whether a Christian is a "brother":

> I will show you from Scripture that even he who does not belong to your people and faith is called "thy brother" as it says: "thou shalt not abhor an Edomite for he is thy brother" (Deut. xxiii:8) or: "thus saith thy brother Israel" (Numb. xx:14).[155]

Meir b. Simeon makes four responses:[156] (1) The scripture does not call the Egyptian, Ammonite, or Moabite "brothers," but only the Edomites. If you claim to be Edomites, that is, descendants of Esau, and therefore Jews should not lend on usury to Christians, you would be applying a bad and hard testimony to yourselves. For it is prophesied that none of the house of Edom will remain and there are other evil prophesies about Edom. (2) If you say you are not sure whether you are Esau, then we must go with the majority rule. Since most nations are not Edomites, then you are not Edomites. (3) If you really are Edomites, according to the prophet Obadiah, Edomites are no longer considered brothers.[157] And (4) scripture uses "brother" with two meanings: with the meaning of a family relationship and with the meaning of members of the same faith, as when all Israel are called brothers through their faith and their Torah. When it says, "Do not abhor an Edomite, for he is thy brother" (Deut. 23:8), the term is used in the sense of a family relationship, as it is written: "Was not Esau Jacob's brother?" (Mal. 1:2). Meir b. Simeon concludes by noting that he takes up again the question of Christian brotherhood in the notes on his later disputation with the Archbishop of Narbonne.[158] There Meir b. Simeon would actually modify his answer, conceding that Christians are brothers, while still maintaining that it is permissible for Jews to lend on interest to Christians.

The second lengthy passage on usury (f. 32a–37b)[159] records a disputation with the Archbishop of Narbonne,[160] which included a discussion of usury three times. It opens with an account of the archbishop preaching to the Jewish community, urging them to cease taking usury and receive back only the principal on loans already given, seemingly on the occasion of an order from the King of France for the cancellation of all usury on debts owed to Jews.[161] Meir b. Simeon argues fiercely that it is a great sin for a borrower to break an oath taken for repayment of a debt and conversely no sin for a borrower to pay usury. Furthermore, according to Jewish law and faith, the Jewish lender does not transgress a prohibition in accepting usury from a "stranger" (*nokhri*). "Also you are commanded to protect us and not to force us to receive the commandments (*mitzvot*) according to your interpretation."[162] Meir b. Simeon brings proof of this from one of "the strictest commandments in the Torah, according to both your opinion and our opinion." That commandment concerns divorce and remarriage, which is impermissible in canon law and permissible in rabbinic law.

THE DISCOURSE OF USURY AND THE EMERGENCE OF THE STEREOTYPE... 39

You do not force the divorcee to be separated from her second husband. Not only this, but you overstep your religious law (*dat*), if you compel her to leave her second husband, since this is our religious law (*dat*). Therefore, in the matter of usury (*ribit*) you should not compel us to never take it from a non-Jew, since it is permitted to us according to our religious law and our tradition.[163]

Meir b. Simeon argues therefore that Christian authorities, both ecclesiastical and royal, have overstepped the legitimate bounds of their legal jurisdiction in the matter of usury. Just as Jews are permitted to maintain their religious law on marriage even when it stands in contradiction to canon law, so too should they be able to maintain rabbinic law on usury when it stands in contradiction to canon law. This passage is fundamental for clarifying what is obscured from view when we read only legislation emanating from Church councils and royal courts.

The first round of the disputation concludes with Meir b. Simeon arguing that the king is not learned like the archbishop, the pope, and other ecclesiastical authorities, and should be instructed by the churchmen on the necessity of fulfilling oaths and permissibility of Jews following rabbinic law on usury. The archbishop agrees with the necessity of fulfilling oaths. But he challenges the application of Deuteronomy 23:21 to Christians, arguing that Christians are not "strangers" (*nokhrim*), but brothers, because "we protect you and your property from the violence of lords....Therefore you ought to interpret 'to a stranger you may lend on usury, but to your brother you may not lend on usury' (Deut. 23:21) as referring to those whom you do not live among and who are not at peace with you....If you listen to this word, it will be held as righteousness to you, and you will merit a blessing from the Lord and justice."[164]

Meir b. Simeon then concedes that Christians are brothers: "for you are like a faithful father to us, and all the non-Jews [i.e., Christians] are like brothers and friends." But Meir b. Simeon corrects the archbishop's understanding of rabbinic law:

The permission to take usury from Christians is not justified solely in the way that you said. Know then what is correct, that in the whole Torah of Moses, in the Scriptures spoken by the mouth of God, you will not find a prohibition on usury except when it is taken from the poor, as it is written in *Mishpatim* "If you lend money to any of my people that is poor among you, you shall not be to him like a creditor and you shall not lay on him usury." (Ex. 22:24) And it is written in the portion *be-Har Sinai*, "If your brother become poor, and fallen in decay with you; then you shall relieve him, though he be a stranger, or a sojourner; that he may live with thee. Take no usury from him, or increase, but fear your God; that your brother may live with you. You shall not give him your money on usury, nor lend him victuals for increase." (Lev. 25:35–37). Therefore taking usury is only prohibited in reference to the poor, and this is an act of loving kindness, like the commandment to return the cloak at night to the poor person out of mercy. But it is not fitting to say that he must likewise return [the cloak] to a wealthy person. Therefore, the Torah contains no prohibition on taking usury from a wealthy person at all.[165]

The course of the disputation then runs along familiar lines: The archbishop argues that Psalm 15 makes no distinction, but condemns all usury. Meir b. Simeon asserts that Psalm 15 is governed by the limited case already defined in the Torah, just as the commandment "You shall not murder" is governed by the more limited case of those who are innocent.

The archbishop challenges the rabbinic interpretation of the usury prohibition, as presented by Meir b. Simeon,[166] on the basis of logic and custom: (1) Where in the scriptures do you find an explicit permission to lend to the wealthy? And (2) do Jews in fact lend on usury to wealthy Jews? The first question Meir b. Simeon dispenses with by arguing that actions permissible before the Torah was given do not require an explicit permission after the Torah was given. In regard to the second question, Meir b. Simeon answers, yes, and gives examples permitted within rabbinic law, namely the permission for the lender to consume the fruits of immovable property on the basis of which a loan was made, and the permission for Torah scholars to give and receive usury.[167] The archbishop offers no more rejoinders.

Meir b. Simeon concludes with one new and striking argument from common sense—that it is not possible to do without loans. For if even the kings and lords need to borrow, then how much more so the common people? In conclusion, he repeats the earlier arguments from this section on fulfilling oaths and from the earlier section on the use of the biblical terms "brother," "friend," and "stranger" in support of his contention that Deuteronomy 23:21 is a commandment of loving kindness which obligates one only in regard to one's brother, unlike the laws on robbing, stealing, and cheating which apply to all men.[168]

The Hebrew polemics reveal what is obscured by the Latin documents—the stereotype of the Jewish usurer emerges from a theological and legal difference over the interpretation of shared scripture. According

THE DISCOURSE OF USURY AND THE EMERGENCE OF THE STEREOTYPE... 41

to medieval rabbinic law, lending in which one received back something more than was given was permissible between Jews and Christians, either on the grounds that Christians were "strangers" and therefore the Torah explicitly gave permission in Deuteronomy 23:21, or because the Torah only forbade usury on loans to the poor, that is, that Deuteronomy 23:21 was governed by Exodus 22:24 and Leviticus 25:35–7. Church councils overstepped the customary autonomy of Jewish law when they decreed on Jewish lending practice. One can hear the outcry of the rabbinic leadership in Meir b. Simeon's polemic. And one can sense the ecclesiastical authorities' response in the justifications which frame the new canons on Jewish usury, as at Lateran IV, where the harm to Christians is explicitly invoked as a rationale. But the jurisdictional tussle between the Church and the rabbis was not the only contest. The French Crown too was engaged in a struggle over Jewish jurisdiction. Though often working in concert with the aims of the Church, the Crown was simultaneously in competition with the church authorities over Jewish jurisdiction. Louis IX's biographer reports him as saying:

> The matter of Christian usurers and their usury seems to pertain to the prelates of the Church. The matter of the Jews, who are subjected to me by the yoke of servitude, pertains to me, lest they oppress Christians by their usury and lest, under shelter of my protection, they be permitted to do this and to infect my land with their poison. Let those prelates do what devolves upon them concerning their subject Christians. I wish to do what pertains to me concerning the Jews.[169]

In fact, Louis IX took up the Church's usury campaign and, by applying it with force to the Jewish population, made himself into "the most-Christian king." Viewing either the royal or the conciliar legislation in isolation produces a myopic perspective, which has only reinforced the modern myth of the Jewish moneylender. The following section will offer a rereading of the royal legislation in the context of the conciliar legislation.

ROYAL LEGISLATION AGAINST JEWISH USURY

As the Christian usury campaign was gaining ground in the late twelfth and early thirteenth centuries, royal regulation on Jewish loans was developing in France and, to a lesser degree, in England. Within 35 years, the

Capetian kings of France outlawed Jewish usury, a step that their vassals, the Anglo-Norman kings, would take 50 years later. By the early fourteenth century, both monarchies would justify major expulsions of the Jews with the claim that Jews continued to practice usury despite its prohibition.

The ordinances of the French kings from the early thirteenth century have received significant scholarly attention. Three separate historical analyses have appeared by foremost historians: Gavin Langmuir's 1960 article "'Judei Nostri' and the Beginning of Capetian Legislation,"[170] Robert Chazan's 1973 monograph *Medieval Jewry in Northern France*, and William Jordan's 1989 monograph *The French Monarchy and the Jews*. All three take as a foundational assumption the narrative of the "economic function of the Jews" and assume that the legislation reflects economic facts: Jewish predominance in moneylending and Jewish moneylending as financially significant to the Crown.

But these studies of French royal legislation have failed to take fully into consideration the ecclesiastical legislation on usury, whether by Christians or by Jews. Seen within the Church campaign against usury, the royal ordinances on Jewish usury complement the canonical legislation on Christian usury and reflect the jurisdictional division between Church and Crown. Capetian kings were first solicited by popes to restrain Jewish usury, because Jews lay outside ecclesiastical jurisdiction. By the mid-thirteenth century, the Capetians took up the role of "most-Christian kings" by adopting the ecclesiastical campaign against usury in the environment of a radical crusading ethos and its attendant dark discourse on Jews and Judaism. This move can be seen at one and the same time as driven by their personal piety and by their jostling with the papal monarchy for power. For the first royal claims that Jews were "the king's serfs" correspond to the development of the ecclesiastical jurisdictional claims over Jews. Ultimately the most powerful and centralized western European monarchies in England, France, and Spain would go beyond ecclesiastical dictates, expelling the Jews *en masse*. The monarchies would justify the expulsions by claiming the persistence of Jewish usury against their decrees. But the expulsions are not explained by this rhetoric. Rather the rhetoric of the Jewish usurer is part of a new anti-Judaism, which gained ground during the thirteenth century.

The story of the French regulation of Jewish usury begins after Philip Augustus (r. 1180–1223) retracted an early and unusual expulsion of the Jews from the royal domain in 1198. With the Jewish community back in his domain, Philip Augustus made three ordinances on Jewish lending between 1206 and 1219.[171] At the heart of his regulation of Jewish loans was a system of seals and scribes attesting the loans, whose rate of interest was set at two pennies per pound per week. Shortly after Philip Augustus' death, his son Louis VIII (r. 1223–6) made an ordinance in 1223 with the "archbishops, bishops, counts, barons, and knights of the kingdom of France" which effectively attempted to end Jewish usury and constrict non-usurious loans by Jews. It declared that, henceforth, Jewish loans would not accumulate usury; it established a repayment schedule for three years; and it revoked the system of seals for contracting new loans.[172] These provisions were extended in 1227 in a now lost ordinance that decreed "prolongation by nine payments through three years of outstanding debts" between 1223 and 1227.[173] In 1228, Louis VIII "laid down a procedure for dealing with contracts that might conceal usury, provided for the recording of debts by chirography, and prohibited the enforcement of usury from 1 June 1228."[174] This ordinance applied only to the royal domain. In 1230, Louis IX (r. 1226–70) in an assembly of barons reaffirmed his father's legislation, decreeing that henceforth no newly contracted debts be repaid to Jews, and that debts owed up to this point should be paid off within three years.[175] By 1235, Louis IX had made a series of new laws on the Jews, which began, "that they live by their own labor or by trade, but without usury."[176] Agreements that no magnate retain the Jews of another were coupled with this Capetian legislation.

The ordinances of 1223 and 1230 have long been regarded by French historians as "the beginning of effective general legislation by the Capetian kings of France."[177] Yet generations of French historians who debated the meaning and significance of these decrees paid little attention to the Jewish "problem," which occupied the magnates who drew up the texts. Gavin Langmuir intervened in the historical debates over the 1223 and 1230 decrees by recovering the dense history of the baronial and royal negotiation of possessory rights over Jews that went back to 1198. Langmuir's article, though a model of historical scholarship, drew on the standard narrative of the economic function of the Jews, imputing a central economic role where there was little evidence:

> After the First Crusade, economic motives led secular rulers increasingly to protect and control Jews. Jews had been profiting from the economic revival...but the hostility unleashed by the crusades...and the development of Christian commerce apparently made many occupations uncertain

44   J.L. MELL

for them. Increasingly they turned to moneylending in competition with Christian merchants and monasteries.[178]

He interpreted the regulation of Jewish lending as therefore stemming from economic motives: in short, the French Jews like the English were a royal (or baronial) "milch cow." The king and barons were protecting their economic interests in the early legislation, but this fiscal motivation gave way to a religious motivation under the "influence of the church" and a changing attitude toward the Jews.[179] Therefore, "by 1223, Louis VIII, Blanche of Castile, and their advisers were more concerned with the dangers and disadvantages of supporting the Jews than with possible profits from them."[180]

Essentially the model Langmuir set up was this: there was a leap between "conventions between individuals" over retaining Jews to "general legislation on economically important problems, which involved not only innovation in the law but innovation in the form of law."[181] The conventions before 1223 are individually based and economically motivated. The ordinances of 1223 and 1230 are general in nature and religiously motivated (see Fig. 6.2). The problem as Langmuir saw it was to explain the "leap" from the individual to the general. For "neither royal power nor the interest of several magnates are sufficient to explain" it.[182]

Langmuir argued that "the influence of the church was necessary" for this leap to have been made. The influence of the Church was shaped by changing "attitudes toward the Jews."

> The Jews had been protected by secular authorities for economic reasons and tolerated by the church for religious reasons, and their status depended on an uneasy equilibrium between those conflicting interests and authorities. The balance was disturbed as royal-baronial demands drained Jewish wealth and as the church, increasingly concerned with both the economic and religious activities of the Jews, defined their status more precisely by canonical regulation....And when the Jews as a religious issue were becoming more important than the Jews as an economic asset, Capetian legislation was first able to move from covenant and individual consent to effective general legislation on the question of the right to control the Jews, with explicit reference to a theological concept.[183]

Even though Langmuir assumed a radical antithesis between economy and religion, between secular and ecclesiastical legislation, he saw in the legislation from Louis VIII on the influence of the Church and a radical-

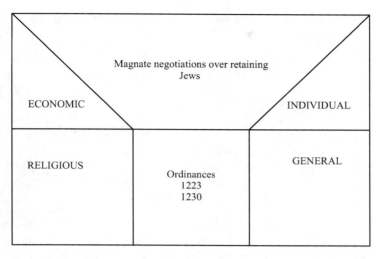

Fig. 6.2 Langmuir's model for the nature of Jewish legislation pre-1223 and post-1223

ization of an anti-Judaic policy in the secular sphere that would go beyond the ecclesiastical program.

There is no doubt that the legislation on Jews under Louis VIII and IX was religiously motivated. But contra Langmuir, I will argue that the legislation under Philip Augustus was also religiously motivated. The early ordinances do not reflect the economic interests of the Crown, or protection of Jewish business interests. The purpose of Philip Augustus' legislation was to contain Jewish usury. There was no about-face in royal policy from Philip Augustus to Louis IX, but a step-by-step development leading from containment to elimination of Jewish usury, to elimination of Jews. Decisive for interpreting these documents properly is the context of the long chronology of ecclesiastical legislation on Christian usury and its association with crusading. For as we shall see, it is the isolation of the Jewish legislation and its location in royal decrees that has given rise to the most persistent myths about Jewish moneylending.

46   J.L. MELL

The Crusading Origins of Royal Legislation on Jewish Usury

The legislation on Jewish loans and usury, like that on Christian usury, grew out of crusading privileges. The first legislation referring to Jewish loans came from Capetian kings in the twelfth century in preparation for the Second and Third Crusades. Both crusades were launched with papal appeals that promised economic privileges to crusaders.[184] In 1145, when Pope Eugenius III called for a Second Crusade, he renewed the remission of sins for crusaders granted by Urban II. He also issued a new privilege that placed crusaders' wives, sons, goods, and possessions under the protection of the Church; placed a moratorium on lawsuits involving their property until their return or their death was confirmed; and absolved indebted crusaders from the obligation of paying usury: "Those who are pressed by debt and truly with a pure heart begin the journey shall not pay usuries with regard to the past, and if they themselves or others for them are bound by pledge or oath in regard to usuries, we absolve them by apostolic authority."[185] Eugenius III in effect took crusaders' families and property under the jurisdictional wing of the Church for the duration of the crusade. The exemption from usury specifically reflected the new legislation on Christian usury made at Lateran II (1139).[186] But the privilege would have applied only to debts from Christian lenders.[187] For the 1140s are too early for the papacy to have claimed jurisdiction over Jewish debts, even in regard to crusader privileges.

Two letters written in 1146, in connection with the Second Crusade, mark the emergence of the discursive construct of the Jewish usurer. Written by Bernard of Clairvaux and Peter the Venerable, the heads of the Cistercian and Cluniac orders, respectively, the letters reflect the views of the most powerful and educated monastics in western Europe during the summer and fall following Eugenius III's bull "Quantum praedecessores" issued on 1 December 1145.[188] Both letters were addressed to secular rulers, and both argued against killing European Jews out of crusade enthusiasm. Yet both letters expressed a new notion of Jewish hostility against Christians and saw economic practices as one arena in which this Jewish hostility could manifest itself against Christians.

Bernard of Clairvaux's letter was an encyclical, which circulated widely in western Europe, exhorting princes and nobles, secular clergy, and the people of the land to join the crusade.[189] Following an impassioned plea for the enlistment of knights, Bernard of Clairvaux warned against excessive enthusiasm: crusaders should not persecute or kill Jews or set out on crusade before their leaders. Both strictures had been violated by the People's Crusade of 1096, in which Rhineland Jewish communities were massacred en route to the Holy Land. And, in the summer of 1146, a Cistercian monk, Rudolph, had been inciting murder of Jews in the Rhineland with enthusiastic preaching. Violence against Jews during both the First and Second Crusades was governed by the logic of avenging Christ's crucifixion.[190] Peter the Venerable expressed the logic of contemporary crusaders in this way: "Why should we pursue the enemies of the Christian faith in a far and distant land while vile blasphemers far worse than any Saracens, namely the Jews, who are not far away from us, but who live in our midst, blaspheme, abuse, and trample on Christ and the Christian Sacraments so freely and insolently and with impunity?"[191] Robert Chazan has forcefully and perceptively argued that the notion of Jews as enemies developed spontaneously during both the First and Second Crusades across all levels of society. But while in 1096 the notion of Jewish hostility was located in the "historic" claim of culpability for crucifying Christ, "a new perception of contemporary Jewish hostility" emerged in 1146. This shift in the notion of Jewish hostility, from historic to contemporary, can be seen in Peter the Venerable's quote above: rather than pointing to the crucifixion of Christ as the Jews' crime, he evokes an image of Jews trampling and abusing Christ and his sacraments in the present day. As Chazan has suggested, "the most accurate gauge for the development of these new stereotypes is the rapid emergence and spread of the accusation of gratuitous Jewish murder" in the charges of ritual murder, which coincide precisely with the Second Crusade.[192]

Events of 1146 suggested a repetition of the People's Crusade, and Bernard of Clairvaux attempted to restrain the inflammatory preaching of Rudolph by writing to the Archbishop of Mainz.[193] But "Bernard of Clairvaux by no means rejected the conviction expressed by the 1096 anti-Jewish crusaders of historic Jewish enmity. By basing his argument [against slaying the Jews] on Psalm 59, Bernard in fact reinforced the sense of age-old Jewish hostility."[194] And in the midst of arguing against killing Jews, Bernard of Clairvaux makes what has become a famous reference to Jewish usury: "I will not mention that where there are no Jews, Christian usurers, if they can be called Christian, rather than baptized Jews, judaize worse, we are sorry to say."[195] The oblique reference to Jewish usury vis-à-vis Christian usury suggests that Bernard of Clairvaux saw Jewish usury as a rallying cry for the crusader violence he wished to avert.

48   J.L. MELL

The emergence of a discourse on Jewish usury here is not the result of Jewish control over the credit market—there is simply no evidence for the predominance of Jews in moneylending in the mid-twelfth century. Rather, it is explained by the confluence of the imagined enmity of Jews toward Christians and the new campaign against usury among Christians. In short, Christians imagined usury as a mode for Jews to wreak vengeance on contemporary Christians, a vengeance imagined to be persistent, perennial, and all consuming. The ecclesiastical campaign against usury had been launched six years before the Second Crusade at Lateran II (1139). With the crusading privilege, which granted crusaders absolution from the oath to pay usury, Eugenius III went a step beyond the canon of Lateran II. He made the contract to pay usury null and void. This bold legislative move was possible only because he made crusaders and their property legally part of the Church. But canon law had no reach (yet) over the Jewish community: the crusading privilege did not apply to loans from Jews, precisely those seen as the enemies of Christ within Christendom. Bernard of Clairvaux's letter itself bears witness to the limited reach of the jurisdiction of canon law in the 1140s. For the letter concludes that Jews should be spared, but secular rulers should require them to release crusaders from usury:

> It is moreover [an act of] Christian piety…"to spare the conquered" (Aeneid, 6, 853), especially "[the people of Israel] to whom belong […] the giving of the law […] and the promises, theirs are the patriarchs, and from them is Christ according to the flesh, who is over all things, God be blessed forever."(Rom. 9:4–5) Nevertheless, it ought be demanded from them in keeping with the tenor of the apostolic order ["Quantum praedecessores" that]: all who take the sign of the cross, shall be entirely free and released from all exactions of usury.[196]

Jewish usury then was doubly obnoxious in the 1140s. Usury of any sort harmed the crusading venture. But when usury was taken from crusaders by the very enemies of Christ, it became identified with an attack on Christ's body, historically enacted at the crucifixion on Christ's physical body and presently re-enacted on Christ's metaphysical body, the Church. Usury injures the Church and her crusaders as they war for "the land which," in Bernard of Clairvaux's words, "is his: his, I say, in which the word of the Father was taught, and where he dwelt for more than thirty years, a man among men; his, for he enlightened it with miracles, he consecrated

THE DISCOURSE OF USURY AND THE EMERGENCE OF THE STEREOTYPE... 49

it with his own blood; in it appeared the first fruits of his resurrection." It is a short leap from the *external* "enemies of the cross" who "raise blaspheming heads, ravaging with the edge of the sword the land of promise...and polluting the holy places" to the *internal* enemies who injure the mystical body of Christ by injuring the crusading enterprise with usurious exactions.[197]

It is essential to read Bernard of Clairvaux's references to Jewish usury within the theological constellation that he and other twelfth-century Christians constructed around it:[198] Underlying the theology was a widespread certainty of Jewish enmity toward Christ and by extension Christians. The first and foremost theological issue consequently became whether to slay European Jews as the internal enemies of Christendom. The theological answer that both Bernard of Clairvaux and Peter the Venerable gave was—no. God commanded, "Slay them not...for they are living signs to us [Christians] representing the Lord's passion...[and] they shall be converted."[199] If they die now, they "will remain in death." The second theological issue was this: with Jews remaining alive within Christendom, Christians were faced with the fact that the "enemies of Christ" could and did injure the crusading effort by economic means. Bernard of Clairvaux deflected the issue by focusing instead on Christian usury: "I will not mention that...worse Judaizing, I am sorry to say, is done by Christian usurers (*feneratores*)." In effect, he said, "Jewish usury really is not what we should be focusing on—forget it! If we take up the speck in our brother's eye, we should take care first of the log in our own!" Peter the Venerable gave a different answer: Jewish wealth should be seized and made to finance the crusade:

> I do not admonish that they should be murdered, rather I exhort that they should be punished in a way congruent with their iniquity. What is a more congruous way for those impious ones to be punished than that by which both iniquity is condemned and charity is sustained? What is more just than that those who fraudulently have made a profit, shall be left destitute, those who wickedly have stolen, like thieves and what is worse, up to this time with audacity and impunity, shall be stolen from?[200]

The "iniquity" for which they should be punished is not usury, but rather, as the sentence preceding this passage makes clear, the Jews' killing of Christ: "Because they poured out Christ's blood certainly akin to their brother's flesh, Jews are servile, miserable, fearful, lamenting and exiled over the earth, until the time prophesied, when a miserable remnant of that people, having been called into the fullness of the peoples, shall be converted to God, and thus according to the apostle, *all Israel shall be saved.* But I do not admonish that they should be murdered."

Peter the Venerable's letter was not an encyclical like Bernard of Clairvaux's, but addressed solely to Louis VII, King of France. Its main objective was to apologize for not participating in the crusade and to offer "counsel and aid" (*devotione tamen, oratione, consilio, et auxilio*).[201] The last two terms are a set phrase used to evoke feudal dues owed by a vassal to a lord, which typically included military support and military council, but *auxilium* might take a monetary form, used to hire mercenaries or supply troops. An early tallage on the Jewish community, as we saw in Chapter 5, was called an *auxilium.* To the feudal terms *consilio et auxilio*, Peter the Venerable added two additional items, *devotione* and *oratione*, which evoked the special role of the Cluniac order in offering aid through prayer. But the letter swiftly turned *consilio et auxilio* into advice to despoil the Jews, modeled on the Israelites' despoiling of the Egyptians. The heart of Peter the Venerable's letter can be boiled down to three points:

> B—A comparison between the Crusaders and the Children of Israel. Both fought at the command of the Lord, but the Crusaders' aims are pure, while those of ancient Israelites were materialistic.
> C—Nevertheless, Jews are not to be killed, because the Bible forbids this.
> D—The Jews should be made to finance the Crusade, whereas Christians should be exempted from payment, since Jews obtained their money illegally.[202]

At no point does Peter the Venerable charge Jews with usury.[203] Rather, he portrays all Jewish economic activity with Christians as "fraudulent profit," "like stealing," "profit craftily acquired," and "misappropriated from the worshippers of Christ." The central charge, however, is blasphemy—blasphemy of Christ and shaming of Christians—through the acquisition of sacred vessels. Peter the Venerable develops this charge through a hypothetical scenario of a thief, nominally a Christian, who breaks into a church and carries away "candelabrums, pitchers, censers, even those sacred crosses and consecrated chalices," and then takes refuge with the Jews. From the "condemned ones," the thief receives not only refuge, but a buyer for his stolen goods: "that which he has stolen from holy churches, he sells to the synagogues of Satan." The vessels which hold Christ's body and blood in the mass are identified by Peter the Venerable

THE DISCOURSE OF USURY AND THE EMERGENCE OF THE STEREOTYPE... 51

with Christ's body and blood. Just as the mass re-enacts the salvific sacrifice of Christ, so too does the Jewish misuse of the holy vessels re-enact the crime of killing Christ.

> The thief sells the vessels for Christ's body and blood to those who killed His body and to those who poured out the blood of Christ, [those vessels] by which means now He [Christ] dwells among mortals, and with as much abuse and injury as they are able to afflict, on He who now sits in the majesty of divine eternity, they dare with blasphemous words to assail [Him] without desisting....Christ clearly feels in these [vessels], which are not in themselves sentient as sacred vessels, the Jewish abuses of Christ, because, as I have heard from truthful men, to the shame of Christ and ourselves, these wicked ones [Jews] apply these celestial vessels to uses, which are horrible to contemplate and detestable to speak of.[204]

Peter the Venerable concludes his hypothetical scenario with a shockingly modern antisemitic image: the Jew "grows fat and wallows in luxuries" while "the Christian is hung from the noose."[205] The very word "thief," linked to a Christian at the beginning of the passage, is elided in this sentence to heighten the sentiment of outrage against Jews. Peter the Venerable has cultivated an image of the Jew "as a rich parasite...in order to justify the proposal to take money from them."[206] Jewish riches "wickedly acquired for the sake of growing fat" shall be carried away, "for the sake of the Christian army assaulting the Saracens," just as the Israelites took the Egyptian riches upon their journey to the Holy Land. This is the *consilio et auxilio* of Peter the Venerable.[207]

The fact that Peter the Venerable never mentions usury is strong evidence for the claim here that Jewish usury in the mid-twelfth century must be understood within the theological constellation of enmity toward Jews emerging from Christian crusading ethos. The letters of both Peter the Venerable and Bernard of Clairvaux reveal that Jewish economic activity of any sort became fused in the crusading ethos with imagined Jewish intent to injure Christians presently, as they had, presumably, historically injured Christ. There was no sharp split between religion and economics in the twelfth-century Christian mind. Rather the soil in which the image of the Jew as an economic parasite took root is that of imagined Jewish hostility and enmity toward Christ and Christians.[208] In an environment where Christian usury was being repressed and the imagination of Jewish hostility encouraged, Jewish usury easily became an imagined manifestation of Jewish injury of Christ's body, the Church, closely linked with the contemporaneous, fantastical ritual murder accusations. In assessing the textual evidence, we should not lose sight of the fact that the overarching framework for the discourse on Jews as usurers was a theological debate on whether European Jews ought to be killed, despoiled, or preserved for conversion, when Christian crusaders were traveling great distances to kill the Saracen enemy, who, unlike Jews, acknowledged Christ and the Virgin.[209]

There is some indication that Louis VII took Bernard of Clairvaux's advice and imposed on Jewish lenders the obligation to forgive usury on crusaders' debts. The sole reference comes from Rabbi Ephraim of Bonn's Hebrew account of the Second Crusade, of which Ephraim of Bonn was an eyewitness as a child. His account of the Second Crusade accords with that of the Christian chroniclers and is generally treated as a solid authority. However, the passage referring to Louis VII's decree is often judged to be inaccurate.[210] Ephraim of Bonn reports, after relating the beating and near death of the famous Tosephist Rabbenu Tam:

> As for the other French communities, we have not heard of any person being slain or forcibly converted at that time, but they did lose much of their wealth, for the king of France had proclaimed: "Whosoever volunteers to go to Jerusalem will receive remission of any debt he owes to the Jews." Most of the loans of the Jews in France were on trust, and so they lost their money.[211]

Given the meager documentary evidence for Louis VII's far more important act of levying monetary aid from the prelates of France for the crusade, it is not surprising that we have no documentary evidence for what would have been a minor extension of a papal privilege to debts owed Jews. But Ephraim of Bonn's understanding of "remission" as a cancellation of the loan is inconsistent with the general development of French legislation on Jewish laws. The best resolution of the puzzle seems to me to assume that Rabbi Ephraim's reference reflects an actual decree, but muddles the details at a distance of 30 or more years by replacing "remission of usury" with "remission of debts." If this interpretation is correct, this would be the first piece of royal legislation on Jewish lending.

When calling for a Third Crusade to respond to Saladin's capture of Jerusalem in 1187, Gregory VIII made a privilege similar to Eugenius III's.

THE DISCOURSE OF USURY AND THE EMERGENCE OF THE STEREOTYPE... 53

> The property also of such persons, from the time that they shall have assumed the cross, together with their families, are to be under the protection of the Holy Church of Rome, and of the archbishops, bishops, and other prelates of the Church of God, and no person is to make any claim against the property of which, on assuming the cross, they were in quiet possession, until it is known for certain as to their return or death, but their property is to remain in the meantime untouched, and in their quiet possession; they are also not to pay interest to any person, if they have so bound themselves.[212]

Gregory VIII's privilege would be included in the canon law compendia *Compilatio II* and later the *Decretals of Gregory IX*.[213] Gregory VIII died shortly after making this call for crusade, and was succeeded by Celestine III, who repeated his appeal. The appeal placed "three imperatives at the forefront of Christian preoccupations: penitence, peace and the taking of the cross."[214] In accord with these aims, papal envoys were instructed to make peace between princes, kings, and cities. Accordingly, in January of 1188 under the eye of Archbishop Josias, the king of France and the Count of Flanders not only made peace, but took the cross, together with the future English king Richard I.[215]

Consequently, in March 1188 Philip Augustus as a crusader king made a statute to aid the crusades with the counsel of the archbishops, bishops, and barons of France.[216] The statute opens by giving respite on the repayment of debts of "bishops, prelates, and clerics of the conventual churches, and knights who have taken the cross." The document explicitly includes Jews along with Christians: Whether the debts were owed "to Jews or Christians," the debtors were to repay their debts in three equal installments over a period of two years following the king's departure for the crusade. "Also, for each one, from the day on which he takes the cross, interest on debts previously contracted shall cease." The following 11 articles spell out the limitations and details of this privilege: whether fathers and mothers of crusader knights receive the privilege; the assignment of lands, revenues, sureties, or bail to the creditors for repayment; the time limit for the respite; conditions under which the respite does not apply; punishment for uncooperative lords; and how to handle the respite when both the creditor and borrower have taken the cross. The following article grants respite from new lawsuits on a crusader's lands from the day he took the cross until the day he returns.

The second part of the statute lays down the provision for the Saladin Tithe—a tenth of the movables and revenues of non-crusaders taken in support of the crusade, with the exception of ordained Cistercians, Carthusians, Fontevraultians, and lepers. Lords who took the cross directly received the tenth of their vassals who did not take the cross, and knights who took the cross received the tenth of their parents who did not take the cross. Henry II of England, following Philip Augustus' lead, also decreed a Saladin Tithe, though not the respite on loans.[217] Both tithes are regarded by historians as the first instance of general taxation.[218]

Several things are noteworthy about Philip Augustus' decree: The council is equally a church council and a constitutional assembly with Philip at its head.[219] The most important element of the statute is the Saladin Tithe, signaled by its opening words, "his imprimis constitutum est de decimis" (above all, a tenth is decreed).[220] The main substance of the relief for indebted crusaders is a delayed repayment for their loans. This technique would be used again in the later decrees of the Capetian kings. But the rights of the creditors too are not overlooked; for the respite only applies when proper securities are given for repayment of the loan. Loans from Jews are not singled out or given undue weight. The specification "whether from Jews or Christians" seems to have been made because the papal privileges could only apply to loans from Christians. Finally, the respite on debts was given among the laity only to crusader knights—not to foot soldiers, women, or others who took the cross. But it seems to have been given generally to the secular clergy whether or not they participated in the crusade, while the Saladin Tithe was not levied on the principal monastic orders of the twelfth century.

Philip Augustus' decree seems to have influenced Innocent III, when he was elected to the papal seat ten years later, both in regard to a tithe and in regard to the inclusion of loans taken from Jews as well as Christians. Innocent levied on ecclesiastics a fortieth of their revenue in support of the Fourth Crusade in "Graves orientalis terrae" (1199) and in "Ad liberandam" (1215) a twentieth of their ecclesiastical revenue, while donating a tenth part of papal revenue for each crusade.[221] In "Post miserabile" (1198), Innocent III was the first pope to include a provision for crusaders that remitted interest from Jewish loans.[222] Jewish creditors were to be compelled by the secular powers, under threat of the "Judgment of the Jews," that is, material excommunication. This stipulation was repeated in the calls for the Fifth Crusade made in "Quia maior" (1213) and "Ad liberandam" (1215).[223] Moreover, in "Ad liberandam" (1215) Innocent

III called for secular princes "to provide a suitable delay to those who cannot at present pay their debts to Jews, so that after hasty departures they do not incur the disadvantages of usurious debts." Even more, he ordered that "Jews must be made to keep accounts of the yields of the securities they have received in the meantime, after the deduction of necessary expenses according to the capital lent," evoking the regulations first established by Philip II in 1188.[224]

Underlying the royal and papal privileges was a close identification of lay crusaders with the Church jurisdictionally and financially, and the protection of both in the interests of furthering the crusade. It seems no accident that the first canons against lay Christian usury passed at Lateran II and III shortly preceded the crusade privileges for the Second and Third Crusades. Remission of interest and delayed repayment of loans for knights became part of galvanizing "Christendom." As Innocent III would write in 1214, "the pest of usury has grown to unusual proportions, consuming and devouring the potentialities of the churches, the knights, and of many others to such an extent that, unless an effective medicine be found for so great a disease, there would not be enough for a subsidy to the Holy Land."[225]

I have dwelt at length on this legislation to show that the usury campaign over the twelfth and thirteenth centuries was closely related to crusading. The crusade privileges illuminate how the roots of the usury campaign lay hidden in the humus of the twelfth century and point to its roots in the eleventh-century reform program which sought to "free" the Church from lay influence by protecting the Church's financial base. This was the ground in which the usury campaign first sprouted, as crusaders were identified with the Church. The usury campaign was propelled forward by the radicalization of European society in the crusades. The First and Second Crusades were limited engagements, but from the Third Crusade on, crusading became endemic. A crucial period in this radicalization was that during which Philip August and Innocent III reigned, and a center for this radicalization was Paris and its university theologians associated with Peter the Chanter and deployed by Innocent III as preachers, judges, and legates to prepare the ground for Lateran IV and the Fifth Crusade.[226] Under Philip Augustus the first decrees on Jewish loans would be made in the interests of protecting the Christian population from the infidel Jew, who held a dangerous position inside Christendom itself. In effect, "Christendom"—that utopian community of faithful Christians and Christian property—as a whole became equivalent to the crusaders taken under the jurisdictional wing of the Church.

From Crusader to All Christendom

When in January 1204 the Fourth Crusade came to a close, Innocent III turned his attention to the problem of Jews and heretics within Europe.[227] The concern with heresy would blaze into the Albigensian Crusade when the papal legate Peter of Castelnau was murdered in 1208, but European Jews were as much a concern for Innocent III. He sent a series of letters complaining of "Jewish insolence" and "perfidy" to secular lords throughout Europe and the powerful ecclesiastics in their realms.[228] The letters addressed the range of issues which were or would be the subject of conciliar legislation—Jewish employment of Christian wet nurses and servants, tithes on lands acquired by Jews, employment of Jews in public office, loud prayer, high synagogues, blasphemy against Christ, and retailing stolen goods. Jewish usury occasionally received mention, and when it did, it took pride of place. From the crusading privileges with their balanced language of loans "whether by Christians or Jews," a radical step was taken by Philip Augustus at the prompting of Innocent III to render what had been privileges awarded only to crusader knights *to all Christians indebted to Jews.* But this developed only in several steps over the course of Philip Augustus' reign. The following discussion will trace its development through the decrees of 1206, c. 1210, and 1219, and then turn to consider why this Jewish legislation was separate from that on Christian usurers.

The earliest of these papal letters was sent to Philip Augustus in January 1205 and promised him remission of his sins should he "restrain the presumption" of Jews. This is quite an extraordinary move that makes Philip's action on Jewish "presumption" *the equivalent of a crusade.* Usury took pride of place. Innocent III began by complaining to Philip Augustus that "in the French Kingdom the Jews have become so insolent that by means of their vicious usury…they appropriate ecclesiastical goods and Christian possessions. Thus seems to be fulfilled among the Christians that which the prophet bewailed in the case of Jews, saying, 'Our heritage has been turned over to strangers, our houses to outsiders.'"[229] But as with the ecclesiastical legislation, Jewish usury is not disassociated from other Jewish outrages: Innocent III complains that contrary to the legislation of Lateran III, Jews have Christian servants and nurses. In court,

Jewish testimony and documents in the hands of Jews have been given preference over Christian witnesses. Jews have built a new synagogue at Sens that towers over the Church. They pray "with great shouting," disturbing the services in the Church. They blaspheme God's name, publicly insult Christians saying that Christians "believe in a peasant who had been hung by the Jewish people," and gad about on Good Friday. Going beyond the canons of Lateran III, Innocent III claimed: "the doors of the Jews are also open to thieves half the night," and Jews "kill their Christian hosts" as in the recent report of "a certain poor scholar...found murdered in their latrine." Innocent III pulls out all the stops, exhorting Philip Augustus: "Lest through them the name of God be blasphemed, and Christian liberty become less than Jewish servitude, we admonish the Royal Serenity and exhort [you] in the Lord, and grant [you] the remission of sins, that you restrain the Jews from their presumptions in these and similar matters, that you try to remove from the French Kingdom abuses of this sort."[230] The promise of remission of sins strikingly equates action against Jews with a crusade, a supposition strengthened by the fact that the concluding lines tack on a charge "to remove heretics from the French Kingdom."

In 1208, Innocent III again wrote on a series of Jewish issues in French territory—this time in the territory under the control of the Count of Nevers:

> It has been brought to our notice that certain princes...while they themselves are ashamed to exact usury, they receive Jews into their villages and towns and appoint them their agents for the collection of usury; and they are not afraid to afflict the churches of God and oppress the poor of Christ. Moreover, when the Christians, who had taken a loan from the Jews, have paid them back the principal and more besides, it often happens that these appointees (of the princes) and the servants of their power, after seizing the pledges, and after casting these Christians into prison, compel them to pay most exorbitant usury. Thus are widows and orphans robbed of their inheritance, and churches defrauded of their tithes and other regular sources of income.[231]

Joined to the issue of Jewish usury are again the issues of tithes, food, and court testimony. And Innocent III justifies his exhortation by the perceived harm to the "poor of Christ" and church property and tithes.

58   J.L. MELL

The letter concludes with a threat of papal intervention and punishment should the Count of Nevers not correct the abuses.

Philip Augustus' Decrees on Jewish Lending

A year and a half after Innocent III's letter of 1205, Philip Augustus made the first ordinance on Jewish loans.[232] There is no paper trail that allows us to say with certainty that Philip intended it to address Innocent's bull. The question of papal-Crown relations during these years was sticky, to say the least, with the ongoing tussle over Philip's repudiation of Ingeborg of Denmark and the papacy's refusal to validate the divorce.[233] Nonetheless, the decree addressed thoroughly Innocent III's complaints over Jewish economic issues and shows at the very least that the Crown and the papacy were moving in similar directions. It established a rate of interest, limited compound interest, and set up a new system of seals on Jewish loans. Several examples of such royal seals on Jewish charters have survived.[234] The royal supervision of Jewish debts must therefore have been established between 1198, when Jews were readmitted to the lands of the French royal domain, and 1204, when the order for new seals was issued. Made with the assent of the Countess of Troyes and Guy of Dampierre, the order was not a piece of general legislation but pertained only to their lands.

> No Jew shall lend at a rate higher than two pennies per pound per week nor can a Jew reckon with his debtor before a year is out, unless the debtor wishes to reckon and repay before the year is out. Whenever the debtor wishes to reckon and repay, the Jew may not refuse this to him, after the day which will be set by our bailiffs. The Jews shall have all their debts sealed with new seals, and if after the date set, these debts will not have been sealed, from then on nothing will be repaid which the Jews exact on the basis of the old seals.[235]

The next two clauses attempt to deal with situations that may fall outside the purview of the system of new seals. The debts of anyone who is a fugitive[236] or detained on pilgrimage shall be halted and not accumulate usury beyond that of two pennies in the pound. Jews shall not lend on pawns of ecclesiastical vessels and ornaments, or bloody and stained garments, nor may they receive in pledge ecclesiastical lands without the consent of the king, the countess, or the other barons under whose jurisdiction they

THE DISCOURSE OF USURY AND THE EMERGENCE OF THE STEREOTYPE... 59

fall. Finally, the ordinance limits the possibility of fraud by Jewish lenders and collusion by the royal officials: evasion of the ordinance with a verbal agreement beyond the contract or without a sealed contract will result in loss of the debt. The keepers of the seal must swear that they have good information on the oath, and the appointed scribe must give security that "he will write and fulfill that office properly."

The ordinance responds effectively to Innocent III's complaint about Jewish usury and addresses other touchy points related to Jewish loans which arise in later conciliar legislation. In evaluating Philip Augustus' response, it is important to keep in mind that in 1206 there was not *yet* any legislation on Jewish loans. So the regulation of Jewish loans and rates of profit did not flout canon law, but rather was the first step in its containment. The rate of two out of 240 pennies per week set by Philip Augustus was less than that legally permitted by the *Corpus Juris Civilis*, as Philip Augustus must surely have known had he consulted with masters of law or theology at Paris. For Robert of Courson, in his *Summa* composed in Paris between 1204 and 1208, raised the question of the legitimacy of the Justinian *centesimas usuras* (one out of 100 pennies) in discussing whether there were certain cases in which usury was legally permitted.[237] Moreover, the ordinance effectively put an end to compound interest by deferring the "reckoning" (*computare*) of the debt to the end of one full year, for medieval loans were usually taken for shorter periods. It is significant that the term *usura* never appears in the ordinance; only *lucrum* is used in reference to the old debts of pilgrims and political fugitives, when it states that these loans shall not accrue *lucrum* except for two pennies per pound per week. Philip Augustus, one could argue, has put an end to Jewish usury, as understood in the first decade of the thirteenth century. Philip Augustus also addressed Innocent III's charge that Jews often procured stolen goods and escaped justice by prohibiting Jews from lending on pawned garments that were bloody or stained. And similarly, he addressed Innocent III's charge that *sub specie usurarie pravitatis...ecclesiarum bona et possessiones Christianorum usurpent* (by means of their vicious usury... they appropriate ecclesiastical goods and Christian possessions) by prohibiting Jews lending on church vessels or ornaments as pawns or church lands as gages. These would subsequently become the subject of conciliar legislation directed to the clergy,[238] the earliest of which was the roughly contemporaneous council called by Odo, the Bishop of Paris, between 1198 and 1208.[239]

60   J.L. MELL

Overall, the ordinance appears to have been made to limit Jewish usury and fraud, in keeping with papal concerns.[240] There are no economic incentives for the Crown here; rather it is religiously motivated regulation of Jewish lending. The establishment of the Capetian system of seals was roughly contemporaneous with the establishment of the *archae* under Richard I in England in 1194.[241] As Robert Stacey has recently argued for the archae in England, the seals would have offered little or no economic advantage to the king, only protection to the borrower.[242] Neither the English loan chests nor the French seals were effective tools for a king to exploit Jewish loans.[243] Only later when the debts were enrolled could the rolls have been used as a basis for taxation or as a means for seizing unpaid taxes. Even then, Stacey regards the loan chests as an ineffective system for exploitation.

Philip Augustus further refined the system regulating Jewish loans in a letter addressed to all bailiffs in the royal domain and in Normandy.[244] Dating the document is difficult, but if, as some historians with good reason suggest, it dates to around 1212–1213, it would be contemporaneous with Robert of Courson's attack on usury in northern France undertaken in conjunction with preaching the Fifth Crusade.[245] The document orders Philip Augustus' bailiffs to appoint two lawful men as keepers of the seal, who would seal all debts between Christians and Jews worth 60s or more, and retain a record for the king's use. Most importantly, the document stipulates the formula to be used in each document:

> This is moreover the form of the agreement, namely that if at the first term which is set in the document, the Christian has not repaid his debt to the Jew, from then on, [that is] after the first term has elapsed, the Christian will be legally held to pay to the Jew per week for each pound two pennies, up to one year only: if the Christian wishes to retain the debt all this time, & the Jew wishes him to discharge (*dimittere*) it; and for more than that year the Jew shall not be able to exact usury (*usuras*) from the Christian on the pretext of that debt, inasmuch as more than a year that debt itself may not accrue usury (*currere ad usuram*).[246]

The new regulation requires that the set rate of two pennies per pound per week cannot be collected *until after the Christian defaults on the first term for repayment*, and then only for one year.[247]

In fact, the decree transforms the limited Jewish usury permitted in the 1206 ordinance into a *penalty for late payment*, a payment that the

THE DISCOURSE OF USURY AND THE EMERGENCE OF THE STEREOTYPE... 61

canonists will later call *interesse* (interest) to distinguish it from illegitimate usury.[248] And the decree absolutely cancels the possibility of compound interest by limiting interest to one year. According to the decretist Bernard of Pavia (d. 1213), penal clauses are legitimate in monetary loans unless they have been attached with the fraudulent intent to exact usury. One can see the idea of *interesse* emerging in the *Summa* of his teacher Huguccio (d. 1210), where he says that it may be lawful or unlawful depending on whether the creditor *intends to exact usury*.[249] Half a century later, Raymund of Penafort (d. 1275) would define the intent as usurious in regard to penalty clauses for late payment if the creditor was a habitual usurer or if the penalty was stipulated at so much a month or a year.[250] But Raymund of Penafort's time stipulation was yet in the future.

Moreover, the royal decree attempts to safeguard against usurious intent by mandating that the charge of two pennies on the pound is limited to cases where *the Christian wishes to retain the debt and the Jew wishes the loan to be discharged*.[251] It is noteworthy that the language in the decree flatly refers to *usura,* a notable shift from the term *lucrum* in the 1206 ordinance. But if the definition of usury hangs on intention, then the designation of the penalty as *usura* hangs on the Christian assumption that Jews intend to exact usury from Christians. Jewish lending emerges here as always already usurious. By virtue of being a Jew, the lender is already designated a usurer. This accords with the increasingly strong notion of Jewish enmity that seeks to injure Christians through any means.

The rest of the provisions in the document are directed to making the system work well. Borrowers and lenders need only seal debts of 60s and above. The cost of the parchment, the scribe, and the seal would render it burdensome to require a seal for smaller debts.[252] Testimony for proving debts will be handled only in the old way. And when requested by the Jewish creditor, the bailiff should ensure that the debt be repaid without delay. But the document includes one other important innovation glossed over above. It requires the keepers to keep a record of the debts for the king's use.[253] Here for the first time may be found an economic incentive for the Crown. As in England, the records of Jewish loans could be used to assess tallages and to seize loans of Jewish lenders defaulting on taxes or fines to the Crown, though without a loan chest, seizure would be rather difficult. The system of registration must have been in place by 1212, when an inquest of Jewish debts in the royal domains and Normandy was made, which would have been impossible without a system of registration.[254] This inquest may have been used as the basis for a large tallage, as the most prominent lenders in the inquest were among the large group of Jews held in the Châtelet du Petit Pont in Paris.[255]

Four years after Lateran IV's canon prohibited Jews from taking "immoderate and heavy usury" from Christians, Philip Augustus issued legislation further restricting Jewish loans in the royal domain and Normandy.[256] The 1219 legislation forbids certain types of loans to Christians, reinforces ecclesiastical law, and most strikingly applies crusader privileges to common Christians. The ordinance distinguishes between loans to laborers, clergy, and propertied knights, burghers, and merchants. Henceforth, Jews are forbidden to lend to "any Christians who work with their hands, such as agricultural laborers, leatherworkers, and carpenters, who do not have inheritance or movable goods by which they can be sustained." When loans are made to propertied peasants and laborers, the earlier legislation applies: "the debts shall not run for more than a year...and the pound shall not make a profit weekly but for two pennies."[257]

Jews are forbidden for the first time to lend to monks, canon regulars, or other regular clergy without the assent of their superiors through a letter patent. And the prohibition from 1206 on taking church ornaments or bloody and stained garments as pledges is renewed and to it are added plowshares, plow teams, and unwinnowed grain.[258] Just as the prohibition of taking church ornaments as pledges was mirrored in the thirteenth-century conciliar legislation, so too was the prohibition on clergy taking loans. A brief aside will help clarify this important point. At a provincial council within the Ile-de-France, priors and conventuals were forbidden to take loans larger than 40s from Christians and loans of any amount from Jews:

3: That a prior shall not take a monetary loan greater than 40 shillings
We decreed that no prior, nor conventual, shall receive a monetary loan greater than 40 shillings, from anyone, without the permission of his abbot or of his bishop, if the abbot shall be far away: if it should happen that he does so, he shall be thrown out of the priory, nor shall he be allowed to gain a priory a second time, until he is restored by a provincial council.

4: That a prior may take no money from a Jew
A prior is subject to the same penalties for receiving any sum of money from a Jew.[259]

Both articles of this Melun ordinance would be repeated at the provincial councils of Rouen (1231) and Paris (1248).[260] All three councils notably fell within lands under the control of the French king.[261] These canons, which are directed first and foremost to loans from Christians, are a significant indicator of the kind of distortion produced by historians' focus on secular legislation alone. And yet, they tell us too about a more serious anxiety over loans from Jews, for the loans from Jews are prohibited *no matter how small*. The reason for the mirroring of the conciliar legislation is this: the king directly ordered the Jews in the royal lands not to violate these strictures, while the ecclesiastical legislation ordered the clergy not to do so. Each authority had no jurisdiction over the other, but they could and did cooperate. These articles are important clues to the interlocking nature of the secular and ecclesiastical legislation, showing that the general campaign against usury was a shared one.

Returning to the 1219 ordinance, it furthermore stipulates that Jews may make loans to knights, burghers, and merchants, but only on the assignment of land or revenues for repayment. Philip Augustus essentially applied the 1188 privilege granted to crusader knights on loans "whether made by Christians or Jews" to all loans made by Jews to all propertied Christians, but he did not require the set repayment schedule of two years: "if any Jew lends money to a knight or a burgher or a merchant, he shall accept for his debt from his debtor an assigned income of inherited property or of tenured property or of rights, with the assent of the lord from whom the debtor holds it."[262] Moreover, two pennies on the pound per week will accrue only if the debtor does "violence" to the assigned income. And it will accrue only after the Jewish lender has lodged the legal complaint and only so long as the violence continues.

What historians have failed to note previously is that this is in fact strictly speaking a usury-free loan, even when two pennies per pound were paid. For the payment is a penalty for damages, which according to canon law is a permissible case of *poena nec in fraudem* in which "something in excess of the principal may be received," like the penalty for late payment.[263] Where no violence is done to the assigned income, it is in effect the purchase of the usufruct of land for one year (*venditio fructus*).[264] And yet, the term *usura* is used in the ordinance, just as it was in the mandate to bailiffs in regard to the penalty for late payment. Again, it seems the position of Jews as Jews predetermines the intent of the creditor. After

64   J.L. MELL

the following two articles adjust the system of assignment to the Norman legal assize and permit pledges on horses, garments, and other movables, the ordinance concludes by addressing the debts contracted prior to this new legislation.

Here the ordinance once again uses the crusader privileges of 1188 as a template for handling debts owed by Christians to Jews. Propertied debtors, and their guarantors, are protected from being compelled to sell their property, arrested, or having their plow teams, bedding, or household utensils seized. Rather the system of assigned income will be used to pay off the debt: two-thirds of the inherited property or income of debtor and guarantor shall be assigned to the Jewish creditor, one-third to the debtor for his maintenance. Though it is not expressly stated, it can be assumed based on the mandate to the bailiffs that usury will not be paid over one year on these loans, making them in effect not much different from the loans of crusaders addressed in the 1188 privilege. For unpropertied debtors who labor by their hands, the crusader privilege of returning one-third each year on security kicks in: "All debtors…who lack inherited property or valuable goods by means of which they might sustain themselves, but who rather labor by their hands, shall have a moratorium of three years for paying their debts. They must make security for returning one-third each year." Christian laborers *when indebted to Jewish lenders* are given the privileges formerly granted only to crusading knights indebted to Christians or Jews.

To summarize: Over the course of 30 years (1188–1219), Philip Augustus' policy moved from issuing privileges *to crusaders alone* on loans *from Christian or Jew* to issuing privileges *to all Christians*—laborers, merchants, burghers, and knights alike—on loans *from Jews alone*. The crusader privilege of 1188 cancelled interest on loans to "bishops, prelates, and clerics of the conventual churches, and knights who have taken the cross" and granted a moratorium on repayment of debts backed with the assignment of securities of land, rent, or movables on loans whether from Christian or Jew. If Ephraim of Bonn's report on the privilege granted by Louis VII for the Second Crusade is accurate, then Philip Augustus' privilege of 1188 was nothing new. But what was new was that within 20 years, Philip Augustus set up a system for regulating Jewish loans and only Jewish loans. This was a profoundly innovative move which mirrored that of the Angevins across the channel. The 1206 ordinance moderated Jewish usury with a set rate and limited the possibility for compound interest. The mandate to the bailiffs (c. 1210–2?) abolished compound interest and transformed usury into a penalty for late payment on Jewish loans. The ordinance of 1219 retained this system only for peasants of means, abolishing Jewish loans to common laborers and clergy. The crusading privilege's system of assigned income was adapted for the future loans of propertied knights, merchants, and burghers, and the crusading moratorium was adapted for the repayment of all Christians' loans to Jews.

The legislation under Philip Augustus does not mirror a simple economic fact—that most loans were made by Jews—nor does it suggest a simple causality—that Jewish lending was profitable for the king. Rather it reflects an anxiety about *Jewish* loans and a radicalization of Christendom through the Third, Fourth, Fifth, and Albigensian Crusades, which increasingly opposed all Christians to all Jews. An escalating anti-usury campaign, itself generated by a crusading ethos, meshed with a growing anti-Judaism. The Jew metamorphosed into a dangerous internal enemy of Christendom, whose ability to injure Christians by wielding authority through public office or household service, by selling food rejected for Jewish consumption, and by wielding economic power as a lender had to be constrained.

The Church would come to rule on all these in the thirteenth century. But at the turn of the thirteenth century, when the Church was only beginning to extend its jurisdictional claims on Jews, church authorities first turned to Christian monarchs to legislate on Jewish loans. Consequently, an administrative segregation of Jews developed, which has skewed our historical vision. During the very same years in which Philip Augustus was establishing administrative oversight of Jewish loans, a usury campaign led by clerics was raging in the area around Paris. "From 1195 to 1215 [Peter] the Chanter's circle was responsible for two concerted drives against usury."[265] These campaigns were not directed at Jews, but at Christians and the moral reform of the West in connection with crusading.

Peter the Chanter's Paris School, Anti-usury, and Crusade Preaching

Innocent III transformed the very concept of crusade by making the moral reform of the West necessary for the success of the crusades in the East.

> Although this association had been made in the past, Innocent III...was able to achieve what Urban II and Gregory VII could not. By commissioning "Paris" men such as James of Vitry, Robert of Courson, Stephen

66 J.L. MELL

Langton, Fulk of Neuilly, and Eustace of Flay to preach the crusade and, in Robert and Stephen's case, to hold regional councils preparatory to the Fourth Lateran itself, he invested them with the authority to combine the crusade with an insistence upon a reformed church and a pastorally guided laity. For both Innocent and the Paris preachers, usury became one of the prime concerns associated with crusade preaching and the new extension of the vow to non-military classes, including the merchant class.[266]

Innocent III himself had studied at Paris under Peter the Chanter, as well as at Rome and Bologna.[267] Paris was his "second home." He probably arrived there at the age of 15 and stayed six to 10 years. His studies may have overlapped with those of three noteworthy companions—Stephen Langton, Robert of Courson, and Odo of Sully.[268] Innocent III would in time appoint Stephen Langton as archbishop of Canterbury, Odo as bishop of Paris, and Robert of Courson as cardinal and papal legate with a special mission to preach the crusade in France. It was the councils held under Robert and Odo that made new inroads against usury.[269]

The "Paris men" whom Innocent III commissioned to preach the crusades were all members of Peter the Chanter's circle. Master of theology at Paris from around 1173 to shortly before his death in 1197, Peter the Chanter founded what has been called "the biblical-moral school," which applied the intellectual heights that theology had reached at Paris to the moral reform of Christian life.[270] Many of the earliest theologians writing on usury were members of the Chanter's circle. In addition to the Chanter, Robert of Courson, Thomas of Chobham, and Jacques de Vitry discussed usury extensively in their *Summae*, popular manuals, and sermons.[271]

The connection between the theological discussions of usury in the Parisian schools and the moral campaign for the reform of Christendom is exemplified in one of the Chanter's disciples, Fulk of Neuilly.[272] While a parish priest of Neuilly, Fulk underwent a conversion, leading him to study in Paris under Peter the Chanter. With the encouragement of the Chanter, Fulk preached in the vicinity of Paris and Neuilly, denouncing usury, avarice, extravagance, prostitution, and clerical marriage. As a charismatic preacher, Fulk belongs to that group of innovative religious figures who created a medieval Reformation,[273] which changed the course of western European Christianity—among them Henry of Lausanne, Peter Waldo, Francis of Assisi, and Dominic of Osma. (It was part of the institutional brilliance of Innocent III and Honorius III to make these later charismatic preachers and their followers into the Franciscan and Dominican orders. These orders would in time come to dominate the universities and economic thought, lead campaigns preaching crusade, anti-heresy, and anti-usury, and attempt to convert Jews and Muslims.) When Innocent III launched the Fourth Crusade in 1198, Fulk was enlisted to preach the crusade in France. The moral reform he had been preaching easily could have been tailored to the taking of the cross. For what better way for the converted to demonstrate their repentance than in going on a crusade, already conceived for a hundred years as a form of pilgrimage and penance? This campaign, which traveled widely in Champagne, Burgundy, Normandy, and the urban areas of Picardy, Flanders, and Brabant, probably lasted until about 1200. Some chroniclers suggest that Robert of Courson assisted Fulk on this preaching campaign.[274]

Robert of Courson, while a master of theology in Paris, wrote about usury and, seemingly together with Stephen Langton, preached against usury in the urbanized regions of Arras, Saint-Omer, and Flanders during 1213.[275] As a cardinal legate from 1213 to 1215, Robert of Courson traveled widely throughout France and held provincial councils in preparation for Lateran IV, which addressed, among other issues, usury. The canons passed under his direction at Paris (1213), Rouen (1214), and Montpellier (1214), discussed earlier in this chapter, were some of the most severe ever passed on usury. But even Robert of Courson, the most radical of the Paris reformers, did not institute conciliar legislation on Jewish usury, because both ecclesiastics and secular lords recognized Jewish lending as properly under secular jurisdiction. The legislation of Lateran IV (1215) was exceptional. Hence it had to be justified by the claim that Jews were appropriating the goods of all Christians. Even then, it had to limit itself to "immoderate and heavy" Jewish usury.

The really innovative legislation on Jewish usury came from Philip Augustus, Louis VIII, and Louis IX. It is important to recognize that papal policy was not in tension with the Capetian royal decrees. Rather, the point of tension was the struggle between Crown and papacy over jurisdictional authority. Philip Augustus would complain to Innocent III about Robert of Courson's severity against Christian usurers and claim that he lacked papal authority. But the Capetian legislation on Jewish usury applied papal directives, and in doing so established the secular lords' jurisdiction over the Jewish population. It was when the Church began extending her jurisdiction over Jews in the first quarter of the thirteenth century that monarchs initiated claims of Jewish serfdom.[276] Secular lords

68   J.L. MELL

contested the growing ecclesiastical jurisdiction over Jews by adapting the theological idea of Jewish servitude to secular rule. But European leaders, whether secular or sacred, were not only moved by power politics, they deeply believed in the religious program that called for the repression of Judaism and the Jews. The radicalization of Christian society continued, and by the later thirteenth century, most-Christian kings went beyond papal directives in their legislation on Jews. This movement concluded in expulsion. The decisive shift appears to have been a consequence of the radicalization of Christendom through the crusading efforts directed against the Albigensians and in support of the Fourth and Fifth Crusades. Usury, together with prostitution, was already a target for moral reformers. It was not only dangerous to the financial well-being of the Church and her crusaders, but it was a spiritual threat to the West whose moral reform was necessary for her success in the East.

The Ordinances of Louis VIII and Louis IX

While Philip Augustus' legislation made the radical move of transforming all Christians into the equivalent of crusaders vis-à-vis Jewish loans, it is the ordinances of his successors which have been seen as decisive. The ordinances made by Louis VIII in 1223 and Louis IX in 1230 have been regarded as watersheds in French political history and in Jewish history. As discussed above, French institutional historians have considered them the first general ordinances by the French kings not related to religious issues. Jewish historians have considered them an about-face in the Capetians' policy toward Jewish moneylending.[277] But these ordinances were rather extensions and expansions of earlier Capetian legislation. What does make these ordinances watersheds is that they extend legislation which had formerly applied only to the French royal domain and Normandy to the French realm as a whole, and in order to make the legislation work, they make the first French claims for Jewish serfdom.

On the Octave of All Saints Day, Louis VIII (r. 1223–6) made a *stabilimentum* with the assent of "the archbishops, bishops, counts, barons, and knights of the kingdom of France." Though this is not considered by scholars a church council, the assemblage of ecclesiastical and secular lords makes it akin to a "mixed" or "national council," like that which enacted the Saladin Tithe in 1188 under Philip Augustus.[278] The ordinance was sworn to and sealed by 26 nobles. It first and foremost ordained that "No debt to Jews shall incur usury from this day, the Octave of All Saint's, henceforth. Neither we nor our barons shall from here on out cause usuries to be paid to Jews, which are incurred from this day, the Octave of All Saints, henceforth."[279] In regard to the legislation in place in the royal domain and Normandy, this prohibition only took a small step forward. Usury was already prohibited except on loans to propertied peasants for one year at two pennies per pound per week and as damages on loans to propertied knights, burghers, and merchants when the debtor did violence to immovable property assigned to a Jew for repayment of a loan. But in other French lands, this probably was the first legislation against Jewish usury.

The second clause disposes of all Christian loans to Jews through a three-year moratorium. What is really significant is that the two articles together apply the crusader privilege of 1188 to all Christians in French lands in regard to Jewish loans (and only Jewish loans).[280] As with the crusading privilege, the aim of this order is the relief of debtors. However, the moratorium of the 1223 ordinance contains a significant difference from that of the 1219 ordinance: all debts are to be repaid "to the lords under whom the Jews are subject" (*ad reddendum dominis quibus Judaei subsunt*), rather than directly to the Jewish lenders. Repayment via the lord was clearly intended to proactively enforce the new legislation by protecting the debtor against the Jewish creditor squeezing usury out of them behind the backs of the authorities. But in the absence of any additional information which might illuminate what was going on, one can only speculate on whether the Jewish lenders ever saw the principal of the loan. It is possible that the lords may have counted the debts in lieu of taxation owed by Jewish lenders, as was done in England when Jewish creditors defaulted on their tallage to the Crown. But it has also been suggested that the loans were simply seized by the lords.[281]

The third clause ordains that neither the king nor barons may receive or retain the Jew of another, a step necessary to enforce the other items of the decree. The fourth clause decrees that "Jews shall henceforth not have seals for sealing their debts." This has been understood as the withdrawal of the rulers' support for Jewish lending. However, it is unlikely that a system like that of the royal seals had been put in place by most French barons. The fifth clause, which mandates enrolling debts, suggests that what is taking place is a shift from Jews sealing their own debts to lords enrolling Jewish debts: "Jews ought to have enrolled, by the authority of the lords under whom they are, all of their debts by the next Feast of the

70 J.L. MELL

Purification of the Blessed Mary," that is, in three months' time. Finally, debts five years and older are decreed void.

In short, the *stabilimentum* of 1223 (1) ended Jewish usury, but not Jewish loans, (2) established a system of regulating Jewish loans vis-à-vis rolls, and (3) liquidated old loans to Jews through a three-year moratorium and invalidated loans more than five years old. To make this new legislation work across the lands of 26 barons and the king, an agreement was made not to receive or retain the Jews from other baronies. The institutional framework is equivalent to, if not actually, a national council. With Louis VIII's untimely demise within three years, the next piece of legislation was passed in his son's reign.

The ordinance of 1230, made when Louis IX was 16, capped 30 years of Capetian legislation on Jewish usury.[282] Where the first article of 1223 revoked a legal right for Jewish usury, the first article of 1230 revokes legal support for Jewish loans as a whole: "We order that neither we nor our barons shall cause Jews to have any debt which henceforth will be entered into." Articles two and three repeat in reverse order the second and third articles of 1223: Article two is a non-retention agreement on "lords' Jews" which gives lords the legal right to seize "their Jews" outside their domain. Article three enacts a three-year moratorium for all old debts to Jews. The fourth article revokes legal support for Christian lenders receiving usury. The fifth makes compulsory the decree on all barons, even those who did not sign. The final article repeats the requirement found in 1223 that Jews enroll all old loans with their lords.

The 1230 decree has been considered a watershed document for both French political history and Jewish history on three counts. For the first time, the monarchy with the agreement of a large number of barons imposes a decree on recalcitrant barons by force: "if any barons do not wish to observe these decrees, we shall compel them." Secondly, Jews are defined for the first time in France as serfs: "Wherever anyone shall find his Jew, he may legally seize him as his serf, whatever the custom which the Jew may enjoy under the rule of another or in another kingdom." Thirdly, the decree retracts legal support for all Jewish loans, whether usurious or not: "we and our barons shall henceforth cause no contracted debts to be repaid to the Jews."

Yet a fourth innovation should be noted, which clarifies the highly charged religious context of the Capetian legislation. This ordinance for the first time legislates broadly on Christian usury and attempts to quell its practice by retracting legal recourse for Christian lenders attempting to

THE DISCOURSE OF USURY AND THE EMERGENCE OF THE STEREOTYPE... 71

collect usury on loans owed by Christian debtors: "Concerning Christians we order that neither we nor our barons cause them to have usury from debts contracted. We understand usury to be anything above the principal." The language is adopted from the 1223 ordinance on Jewish usury: the retraction of legal support for collecting usury by Jewish lenders has been applied here to Christian lenders. The Capetian monarchy is assuming leadership and legal jurisdiction over the usury campaign initiated and heretofore legislated on by ecclesiastical courts.

Unlike the ordinance of 1223, this was not the work of a mixed council attended by archbishops and bishops, but a decree of secular lords alone. But Louis IX shaped the legislation as a religious act by making it a religious donation: "Let all know, present and future equally, that we for the salvation of our soul and that of King Louis our father of illustrious memory, and that of our ancestors, weighing the usefulness for our whole realm, with our whole will, and with the general council of our barons..." The barons too signed for the good of their and their ancestors' souls.[283] By legislating on usury, whether Christian or Jewish, Louis IX was taking the lead in the moral reform of Christendom. In doing so, he supported the ecclesiastical program, but also competed with the Church's jurisdiction. But Jewish loans were treated more severely. As an appendix to the 1230 decree, Louis IX released Christian debtors in royal lands from one-third of their loans to Jews, presumably on the assumption that a third part would have been usury.[284] No similar order was issued on Christian loans, perhaps because it was assumed that usury could be reclaimed in ecclesiastical court. At roughly this period, however, Jews begin to be sued for the first time for usury in ecclesiastical court.

In 1235, Louis IX issued decrees that took up the broader canonical anti-Judaism program. He paired prohibitions on social and sexual contact between Christians and Jews with an absolute prohibition of lending as an occupation and a dissolution of all debts to Jews owed by Crown, Church, or monastery. If the Melun ordinance of 1230 was made when Louis IX at the age of 16 was still under the influence of the queen mother, the 1235 ordinance was made when Louis IX at the age of 21 had reached majority.

The new constitution made by the Lord King concerning the Jews: That they shall live by their own labor or by trade (*mercatura*) without usury; From brothels and prostitutes, they shall be thrown out; That they shall not be received in taverns except as travellers; Concerning the Christian ser-

72 J.L. MELL

vants of Jews who have been excommunicated, the Jews shall dismiss them; Concerning the debts which are owed by the Lord King, churches, or local religious orders, that the Jews shall completely release them; Concerning the grain owed to the Lord King, that it shall be received at the set terms.[285]

It cannot be emphasized strongly enough that these decrees reiterate the conciliar legislation discussed earlier in this chapter. In effect, the Crown has assimilated to itself the position of the Church. But one significant difference marks the royal legislation: it claims direct jurisdictional authority over Jews, where the Church could only impose legislation on Jews indirectly by excommunicating Christians in contact with Jews. For example, Lateran III (1179) decreed that Christian servants in the homes of Jews or Saracens would be excommunicated, while the royal decree directly orders Jews to dismiss Christian servants who have been excommunicated.[286] Similarly, where canonical legislation forbade priors from taking loans from Jews, the royal legislation here dissolves the debts of Church or Crown in one blow.[287] The jurisdictional reach claimed by royal and canon law was different, but the moral program was the same. Louis IX, by legislating directly on the Jewish population, reinforced the Church's program on a population formally outside the jurisdiction of the Church. In doing so, he likened the French realm to the sacred Church.

Louis IX continued to support the Church's anti-Judaism program. In 1239, when Pope Gregory IX called on European monarchies to suppress the Talmud, only Louis IX responded.[288] The Talmud was seized in France on 3 March 1240. The trial of the Talmud, held in the presence of Queen Blanche, ended with 24 cartloads of Talmuds burned in Paris in 1242. In 1244 Louis IX took a crusader vow while on a sickbed and prepared morally for the crusade by correcting abuses in his kingdom from late 1244 until his departure in August 1248.[289] The preaching of the crusade by the papal legate was joined with a renewal of the condemnation of the Talmud. Franciscan and Dominican investigators were commissioned "to hear petitions from disgruntled subjects," including complaints on Jewish usury. Among these are found 174 complaints about usury involving around 109 Jews.[290] These inquests also include complaints against manifest Christian usurers.

When Louis IX returned from six years of crusading (1248–54), "he then engaged in a political and moral reform of the realm, aiming to make God's justice reign on earth."[291] On his return, he decreed in December 1254 that

THE DISCOURSE OF USURY AND THE EMERGENCE OF THE STEREOTYPE... 73

(32) Jews shall desist from usury, blasphemy, and magic. The Talmud as well as other books in which blasphemies are found, shall be burned. The Jews who refuse to obey this shall be expelled, and transgressors shall suffer punishment according to the law. All Jews shall live from the labor of their hands, or from commerce (*negotiationibus*) without terms (*terminis*) and usuries.

(33) Moreover, we command that the decrees issued by us with the advice of our nobles at Melun, shall be adhered to and observed.[292]

These decrees were issued again some months later at the mixed council of Béziers (1255) held under Louis IX. During the same period, the provincial council at Albi (1254) held under the jurisdiction of Zoën, who was both papal legate and bishop of Avignon, ordered ecclesiastical *and secular judges* not to compel Christians to pay usury to Jews.[293] The directive to secular judges suggests that the conciliar legislation was made in concert with, if not directed by, Louis IX. These decrees mark the extent to which Louis IX had assumed the papal anti-Judaism program and in the wake of crusading went beyond the papal dictates expressed in the provisions of 1235, by ordering the expulsion of Jewish usurers.[294] Though only Jewish usurers are mentioned in the 1254 ordinance, there is evidence from a 1257–1258 ordinance, which refers back to 1254, that Christian usurers in Normandy were expelled as well.[295] An expulsion could only have been ordered by Louis IX; for the Church did not have the jurisdictional authority to legislate directly on Jews or to expel Jews from French lands. The fact that Louis IX's program was the Church's program of moral reform deeply enmeshed with crusading is evident in the fact that he prosecuted both Christian usury and Jewish usury, and implemented the Church's policy of repressing the Talmud and enforcing Jewish segregation. In 1269 in preparation for his last crusade, Louis IX became the first French ruler to impose the Jewish badge mandated by Lateran IV (1215).[296] Significantly, he was influenced by the Dominican preacher and Jewish convert Paul Christiani, who after his famous disputation with Nahmanides in Barcelona (1263) had made his way to the French court by the late 1260s and acted as Louis IX's advisor during his preparations for the crusade on which he would die in 1270.[297]

The Capetian legislation on Jewish usury does not reflect an economic fact, that is, a preponderance of Jewish lenders and their predominance, but rather the secular rulers' assumption of the mantle of a religious program of moral regeneration of Christendom deeply enmeshed with crusading, which had as one of its corollaries the repression of (an imagined) Jewish hostility to Christians by attacking Jews and Judaism. By the late thirteenth century, western European monarchies took the lead over the Church in imposing legislation on Jews in their role as most-Christian kings. They expressed their new claim to a jurisdictional monopoly on the Jews in the conceptual language of Jewish serfdom and exercised it in expulsion.

EXPULSION

In the late 1280s and 1290s, large-scale expulsions of Jews in France and England began a cycle that would, with the Spanish and Portuguese expulsions of 1492 and 1497, make western Europe largely *Judenrein* by 1500.[298] In late 1287, King Edward I of England expelled the Jews from his French province of Gascony, held as a vassal of Philip IV, after recovering from an illness and taking the cross for a new crusade.[299] In 1289, Charles II, King of Naples, nephew of Louis IX, expelled the Jews from his French territories of Maine and Anjou, shortly after Edward I arranged Charles' release from imprisonment by Peter III of Aragon.[300] In 1290, Edward I expelled the Jews from England.[301] In 1294 the Count of Nevers expelled the Jews.[302] In 1306, Philip IV expelled the Jews from the French royal domain, though this expulsion would only become final in 1394 under Charles VI, and southeastern France would not be included until 1501.[303]

The official expulsion decrees for Gascony (1287), England (1290), and France (1306) have not survived. That for Anjou and Maine is therefore particularly valuable.[304] The expulsion from England is partially illuminated through a letter to the treasurer and barons of the exchequer issued at the time of the expulsion, as it is also through Edward I's Statute of Jewry (1275), to which it refers.[305] A close reading of these three documents shows the way in which the issue of Jewish usury is embedded in a cluster of religious issues and assumptions of Jewish hostility and intent to injure Christians, which derive straight from the ecclesiastical anti-Judaism program.

The expulsion order from Anjou and Maine opens by justifying the expulsion with reference to Jewish enmity and perfidy.

> We have ascertained the state of the aforesaid land and have found that it is subject to many enormities and crimes odious to God and abhorrent to the Christian faith. In many locales of that land, numerous Jews, enemies of

THE DISCOURSE OF USURY AND THE EMERGENCE OF THE STEREOTYPE... 75

the life-giving Cross and of all Christianity, dwelling randomly and publicly among Christians and deviating from the way of truth, subvert perfidiously many of both sexes who are considered adherents of the Christian faith. They seem to subvert all whom they can. They despoil these Christians of their movable and immovable goods by their devious deceits and by the endless abyss of usury, and thus they wickedly force these Christians to beg for alms. What is most horrible to consider, they evilly cohabit with many Christian maidens.[306]

Here is a composite picture of Jewish perfidy derived directly from ecclesiastical thought and legislation. Usury is not the primary issue. It is a subcategory of Jewish "deceit" and "fraud," themselves merely the material manifestation of the spiritual subversion of Christianity. Note the order of the concepts: Jewish hostility, dwelling among Christians, religious subversion, despoiling of Christians, cohabitating with Christian women. Jewish hostility to Christ and all Christians means that Jews dwelling "randomly and publicly" among Christians subvert the Christian faith. Spiritual subversion is paralleled in the material despoiling of Christians, economically and sexually. The rhetoric of Jewish enmity and despoiling is that articulated over a hundred years earlier by Peter the Venerable. Over the course of 140 years, these themes have become the subject of ecclesiastical legislation, then secular legislation. Now the Christian princes and kings deeply imbued with crusading ideology take responsibility for the spiritual state of their realms and purge them of Jews. Charles II sees it as his "responsibility to purge the territories" of evil men. His act is a religious one: "we, pierced by the arrow of compassion, have consulted... with the reverend father the bishop and with many clerics." He acts "with the assent of God," "exhibiting zeal for the life-giving Cross" and "for the honour of God":

> We have, for the honour of God and the peace of the aforesaid areas, expelled from our aforesaid counties of Anjou and Maine all Jews, male and female, adults and young people, children and infants, of whatever sex or condition they might have been born and raised.

Using the language of a religious donation, he makes this binding: "not only for the present but for all times, both for our time as well as that of our successors." That Charles II assumes on himself the ecclesiastical program emerges as well in the final act of the decree: the expelling

76   J.L. MELL

of all Lombards, Cahorsins, and other foreigners who engage in public usury and who are properly considered usurers as mandated by the general council of Lyon II (1274).[307]

In the aftermath of the English expulsion, Edward I wrote to the treasurer and barons of the exchequer with orders to recover only the principal on debts owed by Christians to Jews. Because of the business of collection with which the letter is concerned, usury is front and center. But a close reading of it together with the Statute of Jewry (1275) reveals a range of issues similar to those in the Anjou and Maine expulsion decree. The letter opens with a reference back to the 1275 decree:

> In the third year of our reign, We, moved by solicitude for the honour of God and the wellbeing of the people of our realm, did ordain and decree that no Jew should thenceforth lend to any Christian at usury upon security of lands, rents, or aught else, but that they should live by their own commerce and labour; and whereas the said Jews did thereafter wickedly conspire and contrive a new species of usury more pernicious than the old, which contrivance they have termed curialitas, and have made use of the specious device to the abasement of our said people on every side, thereby making their last offence twice as heinous as the first; for which cause We, in requital of their crimes and for the honour of the Crucified, have banished them [from] our realm as traitors.[308]

As in Anjou and Maine, the expulsion must be legalized with a claim of Jewish maleficence. Here the claim is that Jews have violated the proscription of usury made in 1275. For this, they are deemed traitors and banished. The claim is a specious one. For as Robin Mundill has shown decisively in *England's Jewish Solution*, Anglo-Jewish lenders effectively shifted their business from moneylending to commodity trade after 1275.[309] Edward I's perception of Jews "wickedly conspiring and contriving a new species of usury more pernicious than the old" therefore seems to be grounded in the assumption of Jewish enmity against Christians and Christ which we have seen previously. The last lines quoted above suggest as much in the coupling of Jewish "crimes" with "the honour of the Crucified."

The Statute of Jewry confirms this interpretation. The statute opens by depicting Jewish usury as "disheriting the good Men of his Land." Usury is prohibited "for the Honour of God and the common benefit of the People." That the crux of the issue is *Jewish* dominance over Christians is clear from the fact that no similar provisions were made to protect Christian debtors from Christian usurers. The statute goes on to impose a regulation derived directly from canon law: Jews are to wear a badge "in the Form of Two Tables joined, of yellow Felt, of the Length of Six Inches, and of the Breadth of Three Inches." Nor are Jews to hold advowsons of churches—a perennial problem addressed in canon law. But "as it is the will and sufferance of Holy Church, that they may live and be preserved, the King taketh them under his Protection." But the royal legislation goes beyond that of the Church, regarding residence, legal status, and ownership of real estate. Jews are restricted to dwelling in the king's cities and boroughs where archae are found. Jews are defined legally as the king's serfs and must, like serfs, now pay a head tax. Jews are denied henceforth the power to enfeoff another, whether Jew or Christian, or to alienate houses, rents, or tenements. Jews henceforth may only buy houses and curtilages in the towns where they dwell if held directly from the king. All of these moves effectively ensure that Jews will not hold positions of dominance over Christians. One can also point to the *Chapitles Tuchaunz la Gyuerie* (Articles Touching the Jewry) as further evidence that Edward I took up the anti-Jewish program first outlined by canon law: the articles address Jews holding church vessels as pawns, usury, sexual intercourse with Christian women, relapsed converts, Christian servants living in Jewish homes. Whether these articles and their statute on usury were only a draft never to be issued, and to what date in the 1270s and 1280s they belong, will likely never be resolved.[310]

The 1275 Statute of Jewry was part of an "Edwardian experiment,"[311] in which Jewish injury was to be quelled, pernicious Jewish influence contained, and Jewish conversion attained. At the same time as the statute "was issued, orders were given to enlarge the *Domus Conversorum* in London."[312] In 1279, "relapsed converts from Judaism were subject to the secular arm." In 1280, Edward backed the Dominicans' desire to force Jews to attend their sermons. In the mid-1280s, Edward I attempted to entice new converts to Christianity by allowing them to retain half the value of their possessions. Edward I not only attempted to convert Jews, he cracked down on Jewish "blasphemy" and reputed ritual murder.[313] The Edwardian experiment itself was undertaken on Edward's return to England following his participation in the crusade and his attendance at the ecumenical council of Lyon II (1274), which, though it did not legislate on Jews, passed new and more stringent laws against Christian usury. But in 1287, Edward's policy underwent a sudden change.[314] By the late 1280s, he realized that his aim of converting the Jews had failed. And following his recovering from a sickbed and his oath to undertake a new crusade in Gascony, he ordered the expulsion of Gascon Jewry in late 1287.

Edward's reign, moreover, coincided with a decisive shift in papal attitudes to Jews that went hand in hand with close papal ties to the mendicant orders.[315] In 1272, as Edward took the throne, a former provincial prior of the Dominicans was appointed Archbishop of Canterbury, Robert Kilwardby. In 1279 John Peckham, formerly provincial Franciscan minister for England, replaced Kilwardby as Archbishop of Canterbury and began a "deliberate campaign against the Jews."[316] In 1286, Honorius IV complained to the Archbishops of Canterbury and York of "the accursed and perfidious Jews" who "have done unspeakable things and horrible acts, to the shame of our Creator and the detriment of the Catholic faith." He condemned Jews for study of the Talmud, accused them of seducing converts with gifts, inviting Christians to synagogues, lodging Christian servants in their homes, using Christian wet nurses, feasting with Christians, and abusing Christians. Peckham responded. A spate of ritual murder and host desecration charges in the 1270s–1290s probably contributed to the deterioration of Jewish security: In 1276, Edward turned over to parliament an accusation of ritual murder made by London Jews.[317] From 1286 to 1289, Jews in the Rhenish town Oberwesel suffered persecutions in connection with the alleged ritual murder of the boy Werner. Between the Gascon and the English expulsions, 13 Troyes Jews were put to death by an inquisition for an alleged ritual murder in 1288, and Parisian Jews suffered a host desecration charge in 1290. Jews were accused in 1294 in Bern of the death of the boy Rudolph. In 1298 the Rindfleish massacres were set off by a claim of host desecration.[318]

In light of Robin Mundill's superb analysis of the English expulsion,[319] it is now beyond dispute that neither the Jews' legal status nor their financial debility had anything to do with the expulsion, nor was the expulsion a political gambit for popular support, new taxes, or the appropriation of Jewish wealth.[320] Among the long-term causes was the need to find a solution to the "Jewish problem" itself defined out of the new anti-Judaism movement. But the long-term causes were mediated by Edward's own personal and religious attitude to the Jews, which unfolded during his reign in concert with more general shifts in the European landscape. "In the last resort the English Final Solution was Edward's own decision and

THE DISCOURSE OF USURY AND THE EMERGENCE OF THE STEREOTYPE... 79

not that of his people."[321] The details of the Angevin story illuminate roughly the other French expulsions.

In 1291, Philip the Fair expelled Jews newly arrived from England and renewed his father's order expelling Jews from villages and small towns. In 1300, he expelled the Jews from the town of Angy,[322] and in 1306, the Jews in all royal domains. Although we do not have Philip IV's expulsion order from 1306, a clue to the motives behind the expulsion may be found in his 1299 decree instituting an inquest by royal justices into Jewish blasphemy and maleficence.[323] He charged that Jews were inciting Christians to "heretical depravity" and by their "great cunning (*astuciis*) deceiving" them and "luring them with gifts and promises." Even more, with "their wicked hands" they dared to "handle the sacred body of Christ and blaspheme other sacraments of our faith." They receive and hide fugitive heretics,[324] they build new synagogues in which their loud voices disturb ecclesiastical offices, and they teach the "hateful book called Talmud, containing innumerable blasphemies about the glorious Virgin Mary," to the degradation of the Christian faith. The ecclesiastical anti-Judaic program has become the subject of royal justice administered by secular judges. The subsequent expulsion must have been in part effected by charges of blasphemy such as these.

The French princes—Charles II, Edward I of England (who as an Anglo-Norman properly is numbered as French), Louis I, Count of Nevers, and Philip IV—assumed the mantle of Christian king, took up the ecclesiastical anti-Judaic program, applied it to their subject Jews, and ultimately went beyond the strict bounds of ecclesiastical doctrine in expelling their Jewish populations. It is perhaps ironic that the papal states alone did not expel their Jews. But it is also an important indication of the shift in the anti-Judaism program that had taken place over the thirteenth century, from a program led by the papacy and ecclesiastical elite to one led by the princes and kings of western Europe.[325]

CONCLUSION

This chapter has argued that the usury campaign initiated in the mid-twelfth century by the Church was not, first and foremost, directed against Jews or Judaism. But by the end of the thirteenth century, Jews had become increasingly identified with usury and even become a potent

80   J.L. MELL

symbol of the usurer. Increasingly severe ecclesiastical legislation against Christian usury was haltingly extended to Jewish usury, as the Church began to claim greater jurisdiction over the Jewish community. This jurisdictional claim went hand in hand with a new anti-Judaism designed to protect Christians from the "nefarious influence" of Jews. The ecclesiastical authorities were painfully aware of the fact that they were overstepping traditional jurisdictional boundaries by legislating on the Jewish community. Therefore, ecclesiastical authorities first appealed to secular lords, particularly strong centralizing monarchies, to rein in Jewish usury. The Capetian and Angevin monarchs responded by regulating Jewish usury at the turn of the thirteenth century and by strengthening their claims to jurisdiction over the Jewish population. Their new claims that Jews were the king's serfs drew on the theological language of perpetual Jewish servitude *and* directly competed with the papal monarchy's growing claims for jurisdictional authority over Jewish communities. Both papal and royal claims on Jewish jurisdiction infringed on the authority and freedom of rabbinic law. Rare rabbinic authorities, such as Meir b. Simeon, may have protested the usurpation of rabbinic legal jurisdiction, but to little effect.

Ecclesiastical legislation on Christian usury and secular legislation on Jewish usury were complementary and interlocking parts of a single campaign. This campaign in the broadest sense was a campaign for the moral reform of Christendom intimately tied to crusading—in the Land of Israel against Muslims and in southern France against the Albigensians. Growing anti-Judaism expressed in the attacks on the Talmud, seen as a form of blasphemy and heresy, the public disputations aimed at the conversion of the Jews, the segregation of Jews through badges and other legislation—all heightened the sense of Jews as public enemy number one. By the second half of the thirteenth century, the secular monarchs in France and England, who had been personally radicalized in the crusades, went beyond the initial ecclesiastical campaign. To purify their Christian kingdoms, Jews were expelled *en masse* in France and England by the late thirteenth century. To justify what was patently an illegal action, monarchs claimed that Jews continued to practice usury even after it had been outlawed and even though most Jews were probably too poor to lend much money. The conceptual matrix in which this claim was made, however, was a religious one based on a fictitious notion of Jewish enmity and a perception of Jewish religious difference as blasphemy. A new discourse on Jews as usurers was born between the failures of the Third, Fourth, and Fifth Crusades and the expulsions of 1290 and 1306. It would have longev-

THE DISCOURSE OF USURY AND THE EMERGENCE OF THE STEREOTYPE... 81

ity far beyond the crusading context in which it emerged: the concept of Jewish enmity with the intent to injure by economic means remains a staple of antisemitism to this day.

NOTES

1. *Milḥemet Mitzvah* f. 3b, 33b. For full reference, see discussion below.
2. Bernhard von Clairvaux, *Sämtliche Werke: lateinisch/deutsch* (Innsbruck, 1990), 3:316; trans. J.H. Robinson, *Readings in European History* (Boston, 1904), 1:333.
3. Robert de Courson, *Le traité "De Usura" de Robert de Courson*, ed. George Lefèvre (Lille, 1902), 53; Thomas de Chobham, *Summa Confessorum*, ed. F. Broomfield (Louvain, 1968), 510.
4. Lateran IV (1215), can. 67 (Norman Tanner, ed., *Decrees of the Ecumenical Councils* (London, 1990), 265 (hereafter cited as Tanner); trans. by Jacob Marcus, *The Jew in the Medieval World*, rev. ed. (Cincinnati, 1999), 153.
5. J.M. Rigg, ed., *Select Pleas, Starrs, and Other Records from the Rolls of the Exchequer of the Jews, A.D. 1220–1284* (London, 1902), xli.
6. Patrick Cleary, *The Church and Usury* (Dublin, 1914); Benjamin Nelson, *The Idea of Usury: From Tribal Brotherhood to Universal Otherhood*, 2nd ed. (1949; reprt., Chicago, 1969); John Gilchrist, *The Church and Economic Activity in the Middle Ages* (London, 1969); Aryeh Grabois, "Du crédit juif a Paris au temps de saint Louis," *Revue des études Juives* 129 (1970): 5–22; William Jordan, *The French Monarchy and the Jews* (Philadelphia, 1989); Joseph Shatzmiller, *Shylock Reconsidered: Jews, Moneylending, and Medieval Society* (Berkeley, 1990); Jacques Le Goff, *Your Money or Your Life: Economy and Religion in the Middle Ages*, trans. Patricia Ranum (New York, 1988), and *Money and the Middle Ages: An Essay in Historical Anthropology*, trans. Jean Birrell (Cambridge, 2012); Diana Wood, *Medieval Economic Thought* (Cambridge, 2002); Steven Epstein, *An Economic and Social History of Later Medieval Europe, 1000–1500* (Cambridge, 2009), esp. 132–41.
7. Shatzmiller, *Shylock Reconsidered*, 45, summarizing Gratian. I use *Shylock Reconsidered* here as concisely presenting the accepted his-

torical paradigm, even though it is in other regards one of the most innovative monographs.

8. Ibid.

9. Ibid.

10. Ibid., 46.

11. On this point, see: the introduction to Giacomo Todeschini, *Franciscan Wealth: From Voluntary Poverty to Market Society*, trans. Donatella Melucci (Saint Bonaventure, NY, 2009).

12. Nelson, *The Idea of Usury*.

13. For example, Robert Chazan, *Medieval Jewry in Northern France: A Political and Social History* (Baltimore, 1973); Jordan, *French Monarchy and the Jews*; and Shatzmiller, *Shylock Reconsidered*.

14. For example, T.P. McLaughlin, "The Teaching of the Canonists on Usury," *Mediaeval Studies* 1 (1939): 81–147; 2 (1940): 1–22; John Noonan, *The Scholastic Analysis of Usury* (Cambridge, MA, 1957); John Baldwin, *Masters, Princes, and Merchants: The Social Views of Peter the Chanter and His Circle* (Princeton, 1970); Odd Langholm, *Economics in the Medieval Schools: Wealth, Exchange, Value, Money, and Usury According to the Paris Theological Tradition, 1200–1500* (Leiden, 1992), and *The Merchant in the Confessional: Trade and Price in the pre-Reformation Penitential Handbooks* (Leiden, 2003).

15. The central example is the path-breaking work of Gavin Langmuir, *Toward a Definition of Antisemitism* (Berkeley, 1990). Anna Abulafia has pushed back against this model, locating the emergence of medieval antisemitism in the Christian concept of reason. See: her *Christians and Jews in the Twelfth Century Renaissance* (London, 1995).

16. Joshua Trachtenberg, *The Devil and the Jews: The Medieval Conception of the Jew and Its Relation to Modern Antisemitism* (Philadelphia, 1983), 188–95. He says, "The Jew-heresy-usury equation became a medieval cliché" (ibid., 191).

17. R. Po-Chia Hsia, "The Usurious Jew: Economic Structure and Religious Representations in an Anti-Semitic Discourse," in *In and Out of the Ghetto: Jewish-Gentile Relations in Late Medieval and Early Modern Germany*, ed. R. Po-Chia Hsia and Hartmut Lehmann (Cambridge, 1995), 161–212. See also: R. Po-Chia Hsia, *The Myth of Ritual Murder: Jews and Magic in Reformation Germany* (New Haven, 1988), and *Trent 1475: Stories of a Ritual Murder Trial* (New Haven, 1992).

18. Sara Lipton, *Images of Intolerance: The Representation of Jews and Judaism in the Bible Moralisée* (Berkeley, 1999), 33, and "The Root of All Evil: Jews, Money and Metaphor in the *Bible Moralisée*," *Medieval Encounters* 1 no. 3 (1995): 301–22, citation on 31.

19. Foremost among them is the fact that his work was available only in Italian until recently, a language not typically mastered by Anglo-American medievalists or Jewish historians who do not work in Italian history. Among his more important monographs are *Un trattato di economia politica francescano: il "De emptionibus et venditionibus, De usuris, De restitutionibus" di Pietro di Giovanni Olivi* (Rome, 1980); *La ricchezza degli ebrei. Merci e denaro nella riflessione ebraica e nella definizione cristiana dell'usura alla fine del Medioevo* (Spoleto, 1989); *Franciscan Wealth*; and *Come Guida: le gente commune e i giochi dell'economia all'inizio dell'epoca moderna* (Bologna, 2011). Among his many articles are "Usura Ebraica e identità economica cristiana: la discussion medievale," in *Ebrei in Italia*, ed. C. Vivanti et al. (Turin, 1996), 291–318; "'*Judas mercator pessimus*,' Ebrei e simoniaci dall'XI al XIII secolo," *Zakhor* 1 (1997): 11–23; "Franciscan Economics and Jews in the Middle Ages: From a Theological to an Economic Lexicon," in *Friars and Jews in the Middle Ages and Renaissance*, ed. Steven McMichael and Susan Myers (Leiden, 2004), 99–117; "Christian Perceptions of Jewish Economic Activity in the Middle Ages," in *Wirtschaftsgeschichte der mittelalterlichen Juden: Fragen und Einschäzungen*, ed. Michael Toch (Munich, 2008), 1–16; "Theological Roots of the Medieval/Modern Merchants' Self-Representation," in *The Self-Perception of Early Modern Capitalists*, ed. Margaret Jacob and Catherine Secretan (New York, 2008), 17–48; "The Incivility of Judas: 'Manifest' Usury as a Metaphor for the 'Infamy of Fact' (*infamia facti*)," in *Money, Morality, and Culture in Late Medieval and Early Modern Europe*, ed. Juliann Vitullo and Diane Wolfthal (Farnham, 2010), 33–52.

20. Todeschini, "The Incivility of Judas," 43.

21. Todeschini, "Franciscan Economics and Jews," 102.

22. Ibid., 111.

23. Todeschini, "Christian Perceptions," 1, 6.

24. Todeschini, *Franciscan Wealth*, 7.

25. Ibid., 7–8.

26. For example, Chazan, *Medieval Jewry in Northern France*; Jordan, *French Monarchy and the Jews*; and Shatzmiller, *Shylock Reconsidered*.

27. This is accurate based on what has been studied by scholars to date. It is possible that other documents may come to light, as with that found by Jordan discussed below.

28. Richard Emery, *The Jews of Perpignan in the Thirteenth Century* (New York, 1959).

29. Gérard Nahon, "Le credit et les Juifs dans la France du XIIIe siècle," *Annales, Histoire, Sciences Sociales* 24 (1969): 1121–48. The inquests were published in Léopold Delisle, *Recueil Historiens des Gaules et de la France*, vol. 24, 2 parts (Paris, 1904).

30. William Jordan, "Jewish-Christian Relations in Mid-Thirteenth Century France: An Unpublished *Enquête* from Picardy," *Revue des études juives* 138 (1979): 47–55, and "An Aspect of Credit in Picardy in the 1240s: The Deterioration of Jewish-Christian Financial Relations," *Revue des études juives* 142 (1983): 141–52.

31. J. 1028/2, J. 943/17–18, Archives Nationales, Paris, published in extremely abbreviated form in *Layettes du Trésor des Chartes*, ed. H. François Delaborde, vol. 5 (Paris, 1909), 122–5, nos. 571–3. Unfortunately, I have not been able to consult the original rolls because of their fragile condition.

32. Jordan, *French Monarchy and the Jews*, 129–31, esp. note 13.

33. Noonan, *Scholastic Analysis of Usury*; Baldwin, *Peter the Chanter and His Circle*, and see esp. 270 for his comment on the subordination of theology to canon law in regard to usury; Langholm, *Economics in the Medieval Schools*.

34. The prohibition of clergy practicing usury was renewed in two local English councils of the twelfth century prior to Lateran II: London (1126), can. 14; Westminster (1138), can. 9 (David Wilkins, *Concilia Magnae Britanniae et Hiberniae*, 4 vols. (London, 1737), 1:408, 415). But I am aware of no legislation against *lay* usury before Lateran II.

35. II Lateran, can. 13 (Tanner 200). Translation is my own.

36. Councils of Elvira (305 or 306), can. 20 (G.D. Mansi, ed., *Sacrorum Conciliorum Nova et Amplissima Collectio*, 54 vols. (Paris, 1901–27), 2:20) (hereafter cited as Mansi); Arles (314), can. 12 (Mansi 2:472); Carthage I (348), can. 13 (Mansi 3:149). Nicaea I (325), can. 17 and Arabic Canons 15, 52 attributed to

Council of Nicaea; Laodicea (343–81), can. 4; African Code (419), can. 5; Apostolic Canon 44, respectively in *Nicene and Post-Nicene Fathers of the Christian Church*, Second Series (New York, 1900), 14:36, 46, 49, 126, 445, 597. Vermeersch regards the mention of laymen in a text of the Council of Elvira as of "extremely doubtful authenticity" (Arthur Vermeersch, s.v. "Usury," in *The Catholic Encyclopedia*, vol. 15 (New York, 1913), http://www.newadvent.org/cathen/15235c.htm (accessed 15 Feb. 2014)).

37. Noonan, *Scholastic Analysis of Usury*, 15–7. After surveying the conciliar and royal legislation, Noonan concludes: "Nonetheless, the period's thought on usury is primitive. Strong sanctions are laid only against clerical usurers. The papacy sponsors no general legislation on the subject."

38. On Gratian's *Decretum* and its place in the development of high medieval canon law, see: James Brundage, *Medieval Canon Law* (London, 1995), 44–69, 190–4.

39. *Decretum Gratiani*, D.46.c.8–10, D.47.c.1–5; Decretals, X.V.19.c.7, in *Corpus iuris canonici*, ed. Emil Friedberg, 2 vols. (Leipzig, 1879–81; repr. Graz, 1959), 169–71 (hereafter cited as Friedberg).

40. Todeschini, "Christian Perceptions," 10–11.

41. *Decretum Gratiani*, C.14q.3–6 (Friedberg 732–44).

42. McLaughlin, "Teaching of the Canonists on Usury," 1:82.

43. III Lateran, can. 25 (Tanner 223). My translation.

44. Early canonists interpret this as receiving the Eucharist. Later canonists interpret it as being present at Mass. See: McLaughlin, "Teaching of the Canonists on Usury," 2:4.

45. III Lateran, 25 (Tanner 223). My translation.

46. Montpellier (1195) (Mansi 22:670); Paris (1200), can. 6.11 (Mansi 22:679); Avignon (1209), can. 1.3 (Mansi 22:786); Paris (1212), can. 2.7 (Mansi 22:827); Trier (1227), can. 10 (Mansi 23:34); Lyon II (1275), can. 26 (Tanner 328–9).

47. Paris (1200), can. 6.11 (Mansi 22:679); Paris (1212), can. 5.4 (Mansi 22:843–54). The first canon is directed not only at usury, but at theft, robbery, and fraud.

48. Avignon (1209), can. 1.3 (Mansi 22:786); Paris (1212), can. 5.5 (Mansi 22:843–54); Château Gontur (1231), can. 30 (Mansi

23:239); Albi (1254), can. 62 (Mansi 23:850); Vienna (1267), can. 8 (Mansi 23:1172); Mainz (1310) (Mansi 25:340–1).

49. Rouen (1214), Add. 36 (Mansi 22:898–924).

50. Liège (1287) (Mansi 24:934; Solomon Grayzel, *The Church and the Jews in the XIII Century*, vol. 1 (New York, 1966) and vol. 2, ed. Kenneth Stow (Detroit, 1989) (hereafter cited as Grayzel), 2:281); Cologne (1280) (Mansi 24:359); Wurzburg (1287), can. 23 (Mansi 24:859–60); Mainz (1310) (Mansi 25:340–1); Bergamo (1311), can. 24–5 (Mansi 25:498–501).

51. Lyon II (1274), renewed at Tours (1282), Wurzburg (1287), Auch (1308), Lucca (1308), Bergamo (1311), can. 24–5 (Mansi 25:498–501).

52. Paris (1212), can. 5.9 (Mansi 22:843–54); Vienne (1313), can. [29] (Tanner 384–5).

53. Paris (1212), can. 5.1, 5.6, 5.10 (Mansi 22:843–54); Mainz (1310) (Mansi 25:340–1).

54. Vienne (1311), can. [29] (Tanner 384–5).

55. Karl Joseph von Hefele, *A History of the Christian Councils*, trans. William Clark (Edinburgh, 1894), 1:1–41; Joseph Wilhelm, "General Councils," in *The Catholic Encyclopedia*, vol. 4 (New York, 1908), http://www.newadvent.org/cathen/04423f.htm (accessed 30 Apr. 2014).

56. Wilhelm, "General Councils."

57. Lyon II, can. 26 (Tanner 328). On malediction, see: Lester Little, *Benedictine Maledictions* (Ithaca, 1993), 32.

58. Lyon II, can. 26 (Tanner 329).

59. Lyon II, can. 27 (Tanner 329–30).

60. Karl Joseph von Hefele, *Conciliengeschichte: nach den Quellen bearbeitet*, 9 vols. (Freiburg, 1869–90), 6:515–6.

61. Vienne, can. [29] (Tanner 384–5).

62. Todeschini, "Christian Perceptions," 7.

63. The one exception is the decrees on crusader loans.

64. A local council at Paris held under Bishop Odo mentions usury in prohibiting the Christian laity from all economic exchange with Jews: "Priests shall prohibit publicly to the laity under anathema to do commerce with Jews, to receive money by loan (*mutuo*) from them for the sake of usury [or] anything, to sell to them or to give them by loan, or from them to acquire; where there is a disparity of worship, there ought not to be a consensus of spirit."

THE DISCOURSE OF USURY AND THE EMERGENCE OF THE STEREOTYPE... 87

This radical canon was not be repeated by any later councils and should be distinguished from that targeting Jewish usury in two respects: it is legislation directed to lay Christians rather than Jews, and it bans all commercial exchange with all Jews whether usurious or not, whether a loan or a sale (Paris (1200), Add. 1 (Mansi 22:685); Grayzel 1:300–1. My translation).

65. See, for example, the reference above to Liège (1287), Cologne (1287), Wurzburg (1287), Mainz (1310), Bergamo (1311).

66. Avignon (1209), can. 1.4 (Mansi 22:786; Grayzel 1:304–5). My translation.

67. Grayzel 1:92–3 for the "Constitutio" and 1:86–7 for "Post miserabile."

68. Innocent III, "Post miserabile," in Grayzel 1:86–7.

69. The reason that it is necessary to compel remission of oaths is that according to canon law borrowers who have taken an oath to pay usury are obliged to pay usury, even though the creditor sins in taking it (McLaughlin, "Teaching of Canonists on Usury," 2:15). Why Jews would not have been compelled to release borrowers from oaths remains unclear.

70. Lateran IV, can. 71 (Tanner 269); Lyon I, can. II.5 (Tanner 297–301).

71. Hefele, *Conciliengeschichte*, 5:843–7.

72. Grayzel 1:104–9, and 126–31.

73. Kenneth Stow, "Papal and Royal Attitudes toward Jewish Lending in the Thirteenth Century," *AJS Review* 6 (1981): 167. Stow does not see this shift as reflecting Innocent III's own policy, but that of hardline canonists. Given that *Compilatio III* accords with can. 67 of Lateran IV as discussed below, I find it more reasonable to regard the amplification as condoned, if not directed, by Innocent III. For the texts, see: Emil Friedberg, ed., *Quinque Compilations Antiquae* (Leipzig, 1882; reprt., Graz, 1956), 131, and Friedberg, *Corpus Iuris Canonici*, X.5, 19, 12: Post miserabilem.

74. Decretals, Lib. V, titl. XIX, c. 12 (*Corpus Iuris Canonici*, Friedberg, 2: 814–15).

75. Lateran IV, can. 67 (Tanner 265; Grayzel 1:306–9). Translation follows Grayzel.

76. For modern historians, see the citations below; for medieval commentators, see: McLaughlin, "Teaching of the Canonists on Usury," 1:99.

77. Stow, "Attitudes toward Jewish Lending," 162–6; and John Moore, "Pope Innocent III and Usury," in *Pope, Church, and City: Essays in Honour of Brenda M. Bolton*, ed. Frances Andrews et al. (Leiden, 2004), 59–75.
78. For France, see Philip Augustus' legislation of 1206 in H.-François Delaborde, ed., *Recueil des Actes de Philippe Auguste* (Paris, 1916–79), 2:549–51 (no. 955), and of 1206–10? in Edmond Martène and Ursin Durand, eds., *Veterum scriptorum et monumentorum historicorum* (Paris, 1724), 1:1181–2. For 1219: Eusèbe de Laurière et al., ed., *Ordonnances des rois de France de la troisième race* (Paris, 1723–1849), 1:35–7. Translated by Robert Chazan, ed., *Church, State, and Jew in the Middle Ages* (West Orange, NJ, 1980), 206–10. For use in England, see: the Norwich Daybook transcribed in V.D. Lipman, *The Jews of Medieval Norwich* (London, 1967), 187 f.
79. McLaughlin, "Teaching of the canonists on Usury," 1:99.
80. Innocent III to Count of Nevers (1208); Grayzel 1:126–7.
81. Lateran III, can. 25 (Tanner 223); Innocent III to Bishop of Auxerre (1207) (Grayzel 1:124–5).
82. Particularly Hostiensis and Bernard of Parma: see: McLaughlin, "Teaching of the Canonists on Usury," 1:99.
83. Narbonne (1227), can. 2 (Mansi 23:21; Grayzel 316–9). But note that Narbonne uses the more limited language of Avignon when it specifies "usurious Jews."
84. Béziers (1246), can. 37 (Mansi 23:701; Grayzel 1:332).
85. Vienna (1267), can. 19 (Mansi 23:1175–6; Grazyel 2:248). One might also include in this list the councils at Arles in 1234 and 1236, which renewed "all the canons of Lateran IV" without directly mentioning usury, though the nature of the Jewish badge and tithes to the churches were specified (Mansi 23:340, 342 note; Grayzel 1:327).
86. Albi (1254), can. 63 (Mansi 23:850, Grayzel 1:334–5). Translation by Grayzel.
87. Béziers (1255), can. 23 (Mansi 23:882–3; Grayzel 1:336). Citation follows Grayzel's translation except for his translation of *terminis* as "contracts."
88. Montpellier (1258) (Mansi 23:992; Grayzel 2:277). The council of Béziers (1255) was a mixed council preceded over by Louis IX and thus represented both canon and secular law. It shall be discussed in connection with secular law more fully below.

THE DISCOURSE OF USURY AND THE EMERGENCE OF THE STEREOTYPE... 89

89. Poitiers (1280), can. 6 (Mansi 24:384; Grayzel 2:252–3); Synod of Saintes (Xanten), can. 13 (Mansi 24:378); and Montpellier (1295) (Grayzel 2:260–2).
90. Lateran IV, can. 67 (Tanner 265; Grayzel 1:306–9).
91. John Gilchrist, "The Canonistic Treatment of Jews in the Latin West in the Eleventh and Early Twelfth Centuries," *Zeitschrift der Savigny-Stiftung für Rechtsgeschichte Kanonistische Abteilung* 75 (1989): 70–103.
92. Walter Pakter, Medieval Canon Law and the Jews (Ebelsbach, 1988), 51–8.
93. Ibid., 60–2.
94. Ibid., 46, 63.
95. Ibid., 46.
96. Ibid., 64–5.
97. Ibid., 66.
98. I have not included in this number the legislation directed against clergy taking loans from Jews or Christians swapping money with Jews in order for Christians to lend it out on usuries. For the former refers generally to the danger of Jewish money, and the latter, to Christian usury.
99. I have excluded legislation relating to crusaders' debts and church debts.
100. The one exception is Montpellier (1258) (Mansi 23:992; Grayzel 2:277).
101. "Quibus etiam prohibemus, & jubemus, per episcopos poena simili prohiberi, ne diebus Dominicis & solemnibus publice laborare praesumant; nec carnibus, abstinentiae diebus, vescantur" (Avignon (1209), can. I.4 (Mansi 22:786)).
102. Lateran IV, can. 67–9 (1215) (Tanner 265–6; Grayzel 1:306–11).
103. Narbonne (1227), can. 2–4 (Mansi 23:21; Grayzel 1:316–9.)
104. Lateran IV, can. 68 (Grayzel 1:308–9). Lateran IV justifies the new legislation with the fact that it "is imposed upon them also by Moses," in other words, by rabbinic law. See also: Pamiers (1212) (Grayzel 1:320–1), which states that Jews "should be set apart and separated from the Christians by some definite sign."
105. Vienna (1261), Breslau (1266), Vienna (1267), Clermont (1268), and Bourges (1276) in Grayzel 2, nos. V–VIII, XLIX.
106. Lateran IV, can. 69 (Tanner 266; Grayzel 1:310–1). Translation by Grayzel.

107. Ibid.
108. Lateran IV, can. 68 (Tanner 266; Grayzel 1:309).
109. Grayzel 1:14, 24, 41, 71.
110. Lateran IV, can. 67 (Tanner 265). The justification of the oppression of Christians by Jews is repeated in the renewals of Lateran IV at Narbonne (1227) and Béziers (1246).
111. For a general historical summary, see: Hillel Gamoran, *Jewish Law in Transition: How Economic Forces Overcame the Prohibition against Lending on Interest* (Cincinnati, 2008). On the rabbinic period, see: Judah Rosenthal, "Ribit min-ha-Nokri," *Talpiyot* 5 (1952): 475–92 and 6 (1953): 130–52. On medieval developments, see: Haym Soloveitchik, *Halakhah, Kalkalah ve-Dimui 'Atsmi: ha-Mashkona'ut bi-Yemei ha-Beinayim* (Jerusalem, 1985), originally published in a shorter English version as "Pawnbroking: A Study in Ribbit and of the Halakhah in Exile," *Proceedings of the American Academy of Jewish Research* 38–9 (1972): 203–68, and republished in a revised English version in his *Collected Essays* (Oxford, 2013), I:57–166; Haym Soloveitchik, "The Jewish Attitude to Usury in the High and Late Middle Ages (1000–1500)," in *Credito e usura fra teologia, dirit to e amministrazione*, ed. Diego Quaglioni et al. (Rome, 2005), 115–27, and republished in *Collected Essays* 1: 44–56; Siegfried Stein, "The Development of Jewish Law on Interest from the biblical Period to the Expulsion of the Jews from England," *Historia Judaica* 1 (1955): 3–40.
112. The usury prohibition numbered 23:20–21 in the Hebrew Bible appears in the Vulgate and New Revised Standard as Deut. 23:19–20. Translations below are my own. Several verses from the prophets and the writings also contain injunctions against usury: Ez. 18:8, 16–17; 22:12; Ps. 15:5; and Prov. 28:8. Though cited in rabbinic discussions, they do not have the same legal weight as these verses from the Torah.
113. I am indebted to Luke Bretherton for the insight that it is grounded in Israel's experience as sojourners in Egypt and their covenantal relationship. He discusses these briefly in *Resurrecting Democracy: Faith, Citizenship, and the Politics of a Common Life* (New York, 2015), 246–9.
114. I follow here the categories defined by Hillel Gamoran in *Jewish Law in Transition*.
115. I follow the categories defined by McLaughlin in "Teaching of the Canonists," 1.

THE DISCOURSE OF USURY AND THE EMERGENCE OF THE STEREOTYPE... 91

116. The *iska* and *commenda* are discussed more extensively in Chap. 7.

117. Todeschini, "Christian Perceptions," 1–7.

118. Toni Oelsner, "The Place of the Jews in Economic History as Viewed by German Scholars: A Critical-Comparative Analysis," *Leo Baeck Institute Yearbook* 7 (1962): 183–212, citation on 197. Quoted above in Volume I, Chap. 3, 88.

119. In fact, the history of this line of interpretation is not so simple. Rabbinic literature proper generally permitted the taking of interest from gentiles, except around the time of pagan festivals, but a variety of rabbinic views can be found, as Siegfried Stein explains: "According to the Gemara in *Makhoth*, one should refrain from lending money at interest altogether. The Gemara in *Babha Metzia*, if properly analyzed, left the decision open, the first version restricting it to economic necessity, the second permitting it without restriction....Some of the Geonim reduce the permission to a minimum" (Stein, "Development of Jewish Law on Interest," 28). But by the high medieval period, European rabbinic authorities generally treated moneylending to gentiles as permissible, even on non-Jewish festivals.

120. As Aaron Kirschenbaum notes: "Ambrose defined 'brother' as 'your sharer in nature, co-heir in grace, every people which, first, is in the Faith, then under the Roman Law'; and 'foreigner' he defined as the Amalekite, the Amorite, the Canaanite, the notorious foes of God's people. [The early medieval commentator] Rabanus Maurus, like Ambrose, defines 'brother,' as any and every Catholic, and 'foreigner' as infidels and criminals. And in the same spirit [the decretalists] Rolandus Bandinelli, Rufinus, Bernard of Pavia, Huguccio, Johannes Teutonicus, and Henricus Bohic. This distinction, however was opposed by an equally long list of Catholic authorities" (Aaron Kirschenbaum, "Jewish and Christian Theories of Usury in the Middle Ages," *Jewish Quarterly Review* 75 (1985): 270–89, citation on 286).

121. Aaron Kirschenbaum suggests that there is an underlying theoretical difference between Jewish and Christian theories of usury which explains their different conclusions on Deuteronomy's distinction between "brother" and "stranger": "For the rabbis, theoretically there can be no objection to an agreement freely entered into by both sides according to the standards of natural justice (*sedek*). The prohibition against a creditor taking any interest at all runs counter to natural justice and is based on charity (*hesed*).

92 J.L. MELL

In contrast, for the scholastics, the taking of interest runs counter to natural justice, not simply charity" (ibid., 270–1). While this is an attractively clean and neat theory, underlying it is the old assumption that Jewish law forwarded economic progress and Christian law stifled economic progress. The historical process was much messier and more polemical, as I shall try to explain.

122. Stein reaches similar conclusions in his "Development of Jewish Law on Interest," 34, 38.

123. David Berger, *The Jewish-Christian Debate in the High Middle Ages: A Critical Edition of the Nizzahon Vetus with an Introduction, Translation, and Commentary* (Philadelphia, 1979), 3–37, esp. 7.

124. Ibid., 16.

125. Lee Fields, "An Anonymous Dialog with a Jew: An Introduction and Annotated Translation" (Ph.D. diss., Hebrew Union College, 2001), viii–xi.

126. Amos Funkenstein, "Changes in Christian Anti-Jewish Polemics in the Twelfth Century," in *Perceptions of Jewish History* (Berkeley, 1993), 172–201, originally published as "Changes in the Patterns of Christian Anti-Jewish Polemic in the Twelfth Century" [Hebrew], *Zion* 33 (1968): 125–44; Gilbert Dahan, *Les intellectuels chrétiens et les juifs au Moyen Âge* (Paris, 1990), and *The Christian Polemic against the Jews in the Middle Ages*, trans. Jody Gladding (Notre Dame, 1998).

127. Bernhard Blumenkranz, *Les auteurs chrétiens latins du Moyen Âge sur les juifs et le judaïsme* (Paris, 1963), 289–90.

128. Berger, *Jewish-Christian Debate*, 8–15; and Dahan, *Christian Polemic against the Jews*, 19–40.

129. Contra Frank Talmage in his translation of Joseph Kimhi, *The Book of the Covenant* (Toronto, 1972), 35, note 19.

130. Rosenthal, "Ribit min-ha-Nokri"; Stein, "Development of Jewish Law on Interest," 23–34.

131. Joseph Kimhi, *Sefer ha-Brit*, ed. Efraim Talmage (Jerusalem, 1974). Frank Talmage also published a translation, cited above: Kimhi, *Book of the Covenant*.

132. *Milhemet Mitzvah*, ms. 2749 (De Rossi 155), Biblioteca Palatina, Parma; Zeev Herskowitz, ed., "Milhemet Mitzvah shel R. Meir HaMeili," in William Herskowitz, "Judaeo-Christian Dialogue in Provence as Reflected in *Milhemet Mitzva* of R. Meir Hameili" (Ph.D. diss., Yeshiva University, 1974). Citations to the text

THE DISCOURSE OF USURY AND THE EMERGENCE OF THE STEREOTYPE... 93

include the folio page followed by the page numbers of Herskowitz' transcription. In addition to Herskowitz' dissertation, see: Siegfried Stein, *Jewish-Christian Disputations in Thirteenth Century Narbonne: An Inaugural Lecture Delivered at University College London 22 October 1964* (London, 1969), and "A Disputation on Moneylending between Jews and Gentiles in Me'ir b. Simeon's *Milḥemeth Miswah* (Narbonne, 13th Cent.)," *Journal of Jewish Studies* 10 (1959): 45–61.

133. In general, *min* is translated as "heretic." But "unbeliever" seems to me more in keeping with Kimḥi's meaning as indicated by the juxtaposition with *ma'amin* (believer). For heretic implies an erring member of the same religion. Jews did not recognize Christians as erring Jews, although Christians in this period were beginning to see Jews as akin to heretics.

134. Introduction to Kimḥi, *Book of the Covenant*, 11–26.

135. Kimḥi, *Sefer ha-Brit*, 25; *Book of the Covenant*, 32.

136. Ibid.

137. Kimḥi, *Sefer ha-Brit*, 27; *Book of the Covenant*, 33–4. My translation slightly alters Talmage's.

138. Kimḥi, *Sefer ha-Brit*, 27; *Book of the Covenant*, 34.

139. Kimḥi, *Sefer ha-Brit*, 27; *Book of the Covenant*, 34–5.

140. Berger, *Jewish-Christian Debate*, 3–40.

141. Malachi Hacohen, *Jacob and Esau between Nation and Empire: A Jewish-European History* (Cambridge, forthcoming 2018), Chap. 3, "From Empire to Church: Medieval Edom."

142. Berger, *Jewish-Christian Debate*, 133; Hebrew text, 81.

143. Baldwin, *Peter the Chanter and His Circle*, 301–7.

144. Berger, *Jewish-Christian Debate*, 134; Hebrew text, 81.

145. Narbonne (1227), can. 2 (Mansi 23:21; Grayzel 316–9).

146. *Milḥemet Mitzvah*, f. 3b–7a; Herskowitz, 4–10. Unless otherwise indicated, the translation of this section follows that of Stein, "Meir b. Simeon's *Milḥemeth Miswah*," 51–7.

147. *Milḥemet Mitzvah*, f. 3b; Herskowitz, 4–5. Translation my own.

148. *Milḥemet Mitzvah*, f. 3b; Herskowitz, 5; Stein, "Meir b. Simeon's *Milḥemeth Miswah*," 51.

149. *Milḥemet Mitzvah*, f. 4a; Herskowitz, 5; Stein, "Meir b. Simeon's *Milḥemeth Miswah*," 52.

150. This distinction is drawn also by David Kimḥi and R. Yehiel of Paris: Stein, "Meir b. Simeon's *Milḥemeth Miswah*," 52, note 32.

94   J.L. MELL

151. *Milḥemet Mitzvah*, f. 4b; Herskowitz, 6; Stein, "Meir b. Simeon's *Milḥemeth Miswah*," 53.
152. Ibid.
153. *Milḥemet Mitzvah*, f. 5b; Herskowitz, 7; Stein, "Meir b. Simeon's *Milḥemeth Miswah*," 54.
154. *Milḥemet Mitzvah*, f. 6a; Herskowitz, 8; Stein, "Meir b. Simeon's *Milḥemeth Miswah*," 55.
155. *Milḥemet Mitzvah*, f. 6a; Herskowitz, 9; Stein, "Meir b. Simeon's *Milḥemeth Miswah*," 56.
156. *Milḥemet Mitzvah*, f. 6b; Herskowitz, 9; Stein, "Meir b. Simeon's *Milḥemeth Miswah*," 56–7. I paraphrase the argument here.
157. Joseph b. Nathan ha-Mekanne gives this same explanation in the name of R. Moses of Paris. (Stein, "Meir b. Simeon's *Milḥemeth Miswah*," 56, note 43.)
158. *Milḥemet Mitzvah*, f. 7a; Herskowitz, 10; Stein, "Meir b. Simeon's *Milḥemeth Miswah*," 57.
159. *Milḥemet Mitzvah*, f. 32a–b; Herskowitz, 92–101. Robert Chazan gives a partial translation of this passage in his *Church, State, and Jew*, 201–4.
160. Scholars have identified him as Guillaume I de la Brue on the basis that he is mentioned elsewhere in the manuscript as the disputant of a later disputation. Guillaume I de la Brue was bishop from 1226 to 1245 and archbishop from 1245 to 1257. See: Herskowitz, 40, notes 75–6; Stein, *Jewish-Christian Disputations*, 10, 25, note 31.
161. Meir b. Simeon does not identify the king, the archbishop, or the year in this passage. It is possible that it refers to the 1223 decree by Louis VIII, to the 1230 Melun decree, or to a now lost decree. Stein assumed that it referred to Louis IX and his decree of Melun (1230), which forbade repayment of all debts to Jews. But only the repayment of interest seems to be at issue here. Hence, it seems equally possible that the reference is to Louis VIII's decree of 1223, which prohibited payment of interest on loans to Jews. (For a discussion and references to the primary sources on royal decrees, see below.)
162. *Milḥemet Mitzvah*, f. 33b.
163. *Milḥemet Mitzvah* f. 33b; Herskowitz, 95.
164. *Milḥemet Mitzvah*, f. 34a–b; Herskowitz, 95–6.

165. *Milḥemet Mitzvah*, f. 34b–35a; Herskowitz, 96.

166. It is not clear that all contemporary rabbinic authorities would agree with Meir b. Simeon's rendering of halachah. See the range of opinions on usury surveyed in Rosenthal, "Ribit min-ha-Nokri."

167. On these rabbinic permissions, see: Gamoran, *Jewish Law in Transition*, 32–6; Stein, "Development of Jewish Law on Interest," 14.

168. Meir b. Simeon glosses here one's brother as "one who is a child of our Torah." This seems to contradict his early admission that Christians who have protected the Jewish population are brothers and friends. He offers no resolution.

169. Guillelmo Carnotensi, "De Vita et Actibus inclytae recordationis Regis Francorum Ludovici et de Miraculis," in *Recueil des historiens des Gaules et de la France*, ed. Martin Bouquet et al. (Paris, 1840), 20:34; trans., Chazan, *Church, State, and Jew*, 217.

170. Gavin Langmuir, "'Judei Nostri' and the Beginning of Capetian Legislation," *Traditio* 16 (1960): 203–69; republ. Langmuir, *Toward a Definition of Antisemitism*, 137–66.

171. 1206: Delaborde, *Recueil actes de Philippe Auguste*, 2:549–51 (no. 955). 1206–10?: Martène and Durand, *Veterum scriptorum*, 1:1181–2; Laurière et al., *Ordonnances*, 11:315; Delaborde, *Recueil actes de Philippe Auguste*, 4:190–1, no. 1555. 1219: Laurière et al., *Ordonnances*, 1:35–7. English translations are available, but contain problematic readings: Chazan, *Church, State, and Jew*, 205–10.

172. Alexandre Teulet et al., eds., *Layettes du Trésor des Chartes*, 5 vols. (Paris, 1863–1909), 2:14, no. 1610.

173. Langmuir, "'Judei Nostri,'" 153.

174. Ibid.

175. Teulet et al., *Layettes*, 2:192–3, no. 2083; English trans. by Chazan, *Church, State, and Jew*, 213–5.

176. Léopold Delisle, ed., *Recueil de jugements de l'echiquier de Normandie au XIIIe siècle (1207–1270)* (Paris, 1864), 2:370, no. 581. One important ordinance was also passed in 1234: Laurière et al., *Ordonnances*, 1:54–55; Chazan, *Church, State, and Jew*, 283–4.

177. Langmuir, "'Judei Nostri,'" 137.

178. Ibid., 140.

96 J.L. MELL

179. "Secular regulation of the Jews in the early thirteenth century, despite the religious premises involved, did not fall into this category of religiously inspired ordinances for the simple reason that, at least until 1223, both king and magnates were well aware that they were inspired by fiscal, not religious motives. But attitudes toward the Jews were changing" (ibid., 165).

180. Ibid.

181. Ibid., 164.

182. Ibid.

183. Ibid.

184. On usury and crusading, see: Rebecca Rist, "The Power of the Purse: Usury, Jews, and Crusaders, 1198–1245," in *Aspects of Power and Authority in the Middle Ages*, ed. Brenda Bolton and Christine Meek (Turnhout, 2007), 197–213; Jessalynn Bird, "Reform or Crusade? Anti-Usury and Crusade Preaching during the Pontificate of Innocent III," in *Pope Innocent III and His World*, ed. John Moore (Brookfield, 1999), 165–85; James Brundage, *Medieval Canon Law and the Crusader* (Madison, 1969), 179–83; Giles Constable, "The Financing of the Crusades in the Twelfth Century," in *Outremer: Studies in the History of the Crusading Kingdom of Jerusalem*, ed. B.Z. Kedar et al. (Jerusalem, 1982), 64–88, republ. in altered form as "The Financing of the Crusaders" in his *Crusaders and Crusading in the Twelfth Century* (Farnham, 2008), 117–41.

185. Eugenius III, "Quantum praedecessores" (1 Dec. 1145), in *Ottonis et Rahewini Gesta Friderci I Imperatoris*, ed. Bernard von Simson, Scriptores Rerum Germanicarum in usum scholarum, 3rd ed (Hannover, 1978), 55–7; trans. Louise and Jonathan Riley-Smith, *The Crusades: Idea and Reality, 1095–1274* (London, 1981), 57–9.

186. Brundage, *Medieval Canon Law and the Crusader*, 180.

187. Kenneth Stow, one of the few experts on canon law and the Jews, likewise reads Eugenius III's privilege in "Quantum praedecessores" as applying only to Christian lenders: Stow, *Alienated Minority: The Jews of Medieval Latin Europe* (Cambridge, MA, 1992), 114, 223.

188. Bernhard von Clairvaux, Epistola 363, in *Sämtliche Werke*, 3:311–22; Peter the Venerable, Letter 130, in *The Letters of Peter the Venerable*, ed. Giles Constable, 2 vols. (Cambridge, MA,

1967), 1:327–30. Peter the Venerable wrote sometime after Easter 1146 (Peter the Venerable, *Letters*, 2:185), Bernard during late summer or autumn of 1146 (Yvonne Friedmann, "Anatomy of Anti-Semitism: Peter the Venerable's Letter to Louis VII, King of France (1146)," in *Bar-Ilan Studies in History* (Ramat-Gan, 1978), 89, note 11).

The scholarly literature on Bernard of Clairvaux and Peter the Venerable is extensive. I give here only the studies that deal directly with their thought on Jews and Judaism in the order of significance to my account: Jeremy Cohen, *Living Letters of the Law: Ideas of the Jew in Medieval Christianity* (Berkeley, 1999), 219–70; Friedmann, "Anatomy of Anti-Semitism"; Robert Chazan, "From the First Crusade to the Second: Evolving Perceptions of the Christian-Jewish Conflict," in *Jews and Christians in Twelfth-Century Europe*, ed. Michael Signer and John Van Engen (Notre Dame, 2001), 46–62; Robert Chazan, "Twelfth-Century Perceptions of the Jews: A Case Study of Bernard of Clairvaux and Peter the Venerable," in *From Witness to Witchcraft: Jews and Judaism in Medieval Christian Thought*, ed. Jeremy Cohen (Wiesbaden, 1996), 187–201; Robert Chazan, *Medieval Stereotypes and Modern Antisemitism* (Berkeley, 1997), 41–52; Manfred Kniewasser, "Die antijüdische Polemik des Petrus Alfonsi und des Abtes Petrus Venerabilis von Cluny," *Kairos: Zeitschrift für Religionswissenschaft und Theologie* 22 (1980): 34–76; Gilbert Dahan, "Bernard de Clairvaux et les Juifs," *Archives juives* 23 (1987): 59–64; Gavin Langmuir, "Peter the Venerable: Defense against Doubts," in *Toward a Definition of Antisemitism*, 197–208; David Berger, "The Attitude of St. Bernard of Clairvaux toward the Jews," *Proceedings of the American Academy for Jewish Research* 40 (1972): 89–108; Marianne Awerbuch, "Petrus Venerabilis: Ein Wendepunkt im Anti-judaismus des Mittelalters?" in *Christlich-jüdische Begegnung im Zeitalter der Frühscholastik* (Munich, 1980), 177–96; Jean-Pierre Torrell, "Les Juifs dans l'oeuvre de Pierre le Vénérable," *Cahiers de civilization médiévale* 30 (1987): 331–46; Funkenstein, "Changes in Christian Anti-Jewish Polemics."

189. In addition to Bernard of Clairvaux's encyclical, there is a second letter addressed to Duke Wladislaus, and the nobles and people of Bohemia, whose message is close to that of the encyclical, but

98 J.L. MELL

without the warnings in the encyclical discussed here: Bernhard von Clairvaux, "Epistola 365," in *Sämtliche Werke*, 3:320–2, trans. Bruno James, *The Letters of St. Bernard of Clairvaux* (Kalamazoo, 1998), no. 392, 463–4. On the manuscripts and transmission of both letters, see: Jean Leclerq, "L'Encyclique de Saint Bernard en faveur de la croisade," *Revue bénédictine* 81 (1971): 295–330.

190. Articulations of the crusaders' logic of violence against Jews during the First Crusade can be found widely in both the Jewish and Christian chroniclers. For references and discussion, see: Robert Chazan, *European Jewry and the First Crusade* (Berkeley, 1987), 59–60, and his articles "From First Crusade to Second," and "Twelfth-Century Perceptions of Jews," 189.

191. Peter the Venerable, *Letters*, 1:328; trans. follows Friedman, "Anatomy of Anti-Semitism," 93. Peter the Venerable goes on to explain that Muslims are to be hated even though they acknowledge along with Christians Christ born of a virgin, as opposed to Jews who believe nothing concerning Christ and the Christian faith, and reject and blaspheme the virgin birth and all the sacraments. (For a discussion of this passage, see: Chazan, "Twelfth-Century Perceptions of Jews," 197.)

192. Chazan, "From First Crusade to Second," esp. 50–1. The two earliest accusations of Jews ritually murdering Christians are those concerning William of Norwich, made only several years after his death in 1144, and a dismembered corpse in Wurzburg in 1147. For William of Norwich, see: Thomas of Monmouth, *The Life and Miracles of St. William of Norwich* (Cambridge, 1896); Gavin Langmuir, "Thomas of Monmouth: Detector of Ritual Murder," in *Toward a Definition of Antisemitism*, 209–36. For the Wurzburg accusation, see: *Annales Herbipolenses* in MGH, 16:3–4.

193. Bernhard von Clairvaux, "Epistola 365," 3:320–2.

194. Chazan, "From First Crusade to Second," 48.

195. "Taceo quod sicubi illi desunt, peius iudaizare dolemus christianos feneratores, si tamen christianos, et non magis baptizatos Iudaeos convenit appellari" (Bernhard von Clairvaux, "Epistola 363," 3:316. Translation is my own. Compare: James, *Letters of St. Bernard of Clairvaux*, 463; and Robinson, *Readings in European History*, 1:333. It is worth noting that the first Jewish

THE DISCOURSE OF USURY AND THE EMERGENCE OF THE STEREOTYPE... 99

historians to highlight Bernard of Clairvaux's use of *judaizare* in an economic sense were central Europeans working in the 1920–40s in the context of heightened antisemitism with its sharp economic stereotypes. They were Posener, Trachtenberg, and Baron (Berger, "Attitude of St. Bernard of Clairvaux," 104, note 65).

196. Bernhard von Clairvaux, "Epistola 363," 3:317. My translation. This passage is left out of the most accessible English translation, that by Robinson, *Readings in European History*, 1:330–3.

197. Bernhard von Clairvaux, "Epistola 363," 3:316. Trans. follows Robinson, *Readings in European History*, 1:333.

198. Similarly argue Jeremy Cohen, *Living Letters*, 239, 242, 245, 249, 266, 270, and Dahan, "Bernard de Clairvaux et les Juifs." Cohen in particular emphasizes the context of the crusading for both Bernard's and Peter's thought on Jews.

199. Bernhard von Clairvaux, "Epistola 363," 3:316. Trans. follows Robinson, *Readings in European History*, 1:333. Peter the Venerable, *Letters*, 1:328.

200. Peter the Venerable, *Letters*, 1:329.

201. Ibid., 1:327; Friedman, "Anatomy of Anti-Semitism," 91–2.

202. Friedman, "Anatomy of Anti-Semitism," 91.

203. Nor is Peter's animosity rooted in Cluny's indebtedness to Jewish lenders, as some earlier historians have speculated, such as Duby and following him Langmuir. On this, see: ibid., 95–7. On the development of Peter the Venerable's anti-Jewish economic polemic and its relationship to both anti-simony rhetoric and crusading, see: Kniewasser, "Die antijüdische Polemik," 49–55.

204. "Pinguescit inde et deliciis affluit Iudaeus, unde laqueo suspenditur Christianus" (Peter the Venerable, *Letters*, 1:329). We should not imagine the "horrible and detestable uses" to be some grotesque demonic rite of a warped imagination; it may rather be that Peter the Venerable is referring to a prosaic instance, such as a Jew using a pawned chalice at a Shabbat table for the benediction over wine.

205. Ibid., 1:330.

206. Friedman, "Anatomy of Anti-Semitism," 100.

100 J.L. MELL

207. One reads with dismay the recent address of Pope Benedict XVI (St. Peter's Square, Wednesday, 14 Oct. 2009, http://w2.vatican.va/content/benedict-xvi/en/audiences/2009/documents/hf_ben-xvi_aud_20091014.html (accessed 5 May 2015): "In addition, he [Peter the Venerable] also showed care and concern for people outside the Church, in particular Jews and Muslims: to increase knowledge of the latter he provided for the translation of the Qur'an. A historian recently remarked on this subject: 'In the midst of the intransigence of medieval people, even the greatest among them, we admire here a sublime example of the sensitivity to which Christian charity leads' (J. Leclercq, *Pietro il Venerabile,* Jaca Book, 1991, p. 189)."

208. As Robert Chazan puts it, "the underlying issue is surely not economic; the underlying issue is the alleged contemporary Jewish hatred and abuse of Christianity" (Chazan, *Medieval Stereotypes,* 51).

209. Peter the Venerable, *Letters,* 1:328.

210. Shlomo Eidelberg, trans. and ed., *The Jews and the Crusaders: The Hebrew Chronicles of the First and Second Crusades* (Madison, 1977), 117–9; Constable, "Financing of the Crusades," 46. (Constable however is unaware of the fact that the papal privilege would have applied only to loans from Christian lenders.)

211. Avraham Habermann, ed., *Sefer Gezirot Ashkenaz ve-Sarfat* (Jerusalem, 1945), 121; trans. Eidelberg, *Jews and the Crusaders,* 131.

212. "Audita tremendi" (29 Oct. 1187), in *Gesta regis Henrici Secundi Benedicti abbatis. The Chronicle of the Reigns of Henry II and Richard I,* ed. William Stubbs, 2 vols. (London, 1867), 2:15–9; Riley-Smith and Riley-Smith, *Crusades: Idea and Reality,* 63–7.

213. Brundage, *Medieval Canon Law and the Crusader,* 180.

214. Jean Richard, *The Crusades, c. 1071–c. 1291* (Cambridge, 1999), 217.

215. Ibid., 218.

216. H.F. Delaborde, ed., *Oeuvres de Rigord et de Guillaume le Breton, historiens de Philippe-Auguste* (Paris, 1882), 1:85–90; the first decree is also found in Mansi 22:577–80. These are sometimes treated as two separate statutes, but as they seem to have been passed together, there is reason to treat them as two parts of one statute.

THE DISCOURSE OF USURY AND THE EMERGENCE OF THE STEREOTYPE... 101

217. William Stubbs, ed., *Select Charters and Other Illustrations of English Constitutional History*, 9th ed. (Oxford, 1913), 189; trans. in Riley-Smith and Riley-Smith, *Crusades*, 143–4.
218. See the discussion of taxation in Chap. 5.
219. Rigord calls it a "general council" (Delaborde, *Oeuvres de Rigord*, 84). According to modern criteria, it would be considered a "mixed council," as discussed earlier in this chapter.
220. Ibid., 88.
221. For "Graves orientalis terrae," see: Jacques-Paul Migne, ed., *Patrologia Latina* (hereafter PL), 214:829–31; trans. Riley-Smith and Riley-Smith, *Crusades*, 144–8. For "Ad liberandam," see: Lateran IV, can. 71 (Tanner 267–71).
222. "Post miserabile," in *Chronica magistri Rogeri de Hovedene*, ed. William Stubbs, 4 vols. (London, 1868–71), 4:70–5; PL 216:817–21. Translation available in *Crusade and Christendom: Annotated Documents in Translation from Innocent III to the Fall of Acre, 1187–1191*, ed. Jessalynn Bird, Edward Peters, and James Powell (Philadelphia, 2013), 28–37.
223. For "Quia maior," see: PL 216:817–21; trans. Bird, Peters, and Powell, *Crusade and Christendom*, 107–12, 124–9.
224. Citations from trans. of Riley-Smith and Riley-Smith, *Crusades*, 127. For decree of 1188, see above.
225. Innocent III to Philip Augustus (14 May 1214), Grayzel 1:138–41. This letter clearly refers to Christian usury, not Jewish, as Jews are not mentioned here by Innocent III.
226. See discussion later in this chapter.
227. John Moore, *Pope Innocent III (1160/1–1216): To Root Up and to Plant* (Leiden, 2003), 136, 140–68.
228. Innocent III to the King of France (16 Jan. 1205), to Bishops, Abbots, and other clergy of Constantinople (21 Jan. 1205), to Alphonso, King of Castile (5 May 1205), to the Archbishop of Sens and the Bishop of Paris (15 July 1205), to Bishop of Auxerre (16 May 1207), to Raymund Count of Toulouse (29 May 1207), to the Count of Nevers (17 Jan. 1208): Grazyel 1:105–18.
229. Innocent III to King Philip Augustus (16 Jan. 1205): Grazyel 1:104–9, citation on 107.
230. Grayzel 1:108–9, translation my own.
231. Grayzel 1:126–31, citation on 127.

232. Delaborde, *Recueil des actes de Philippe Auguste*, 2:549–51, no. 955; trans. Chazan, *Church, State, and Jew*, 206, but see Jordan's corrections: *French Monarchy and the Jews*, 277, notes 32, 34. For discussion of the decree, see: Chazan, *Medieval Jewry in Northern France*, 84; Jordan, *French Monarchy and the Jews*, 61–3.

233. John Baldwin, *The Government of Philip Augustus* (Berkeley, 1986), 82–7.

234. Brigitte Bedos, "Les sceaux," in *Art et archeology des Juifs en France médiévale*, ed. Bernard Blumenkranz (Toulouse, 1980), 207–28, esp. 207, 218–9. Two of the charters were published by Adolf Neubauer, "Documents inédits," *Revue des études Juives* 9 (1884): 51–65, esp. 63–4.

235. My translation. There is an intriguing precursor to the limitation of Jewish usury to one year in the charter granted by the Count of Nevers to the burghers of Auxerre in 1194 which states: "If a Jew should extort usury from a Christian, he may only extort usuries for two years on the lawful testimony of a Christian and a Jew" (Maximilien Quantin, *Recueil de pièces pour faire suite au Cartulaire général de l'Yonne, XIIIe siècle* (Paris, 1873), 2:416).

236. "Fugitive" here applies to political dissidents (F.M. Powicke, *Loss of Normandy (1189–1204): Studies in the History of the Angevin Empire* (Manchester, 1960), 284–5).

237. Robert de Courson, *Le traité "De Usura,"* 5. Although Robert of Courson does not consider the *centesimas usuras* legitimate, it is quite possible that others did. As will be discussed below, Robert of Courson was one of the most radical voices against usury.

238. Contra pledging of church vessels and ornaments: Paris (1200), can. 8.15 (Mansi 22:681; Grayzel 1:300–1); Trier (1227), can. 10 (Mansi 23:34; Grayzel 1:318–9); Worcester (1229) (Mansi 23:176; Grayzel 320–1); Valencia (1255) (Mansi 23:893; Grayzel 2:276); Poland (1285) (Grayzel 2:280); Meaux (1287) (Grayzel 2:281); Würzburg (1298), can. 7 (Mansi 24:1191; Grayzel 2:282). For examples of church vessels pledged to Jews, see: Joseph Shatzmiller, *Cultural Exchange: Jews, Christians and Art in the Medieval Marketplace* (Princeton, 2013), 22–44. Clergy were forbidden to take loans without the authorization of their superiors from both Christians and Jews: Melun (1216), can. 4 (Mansi 22:1087–8; Grayzel 313); Rouen (1231), can. 1 (Mansi

THE DISCOURSE OF USURY AND THE EMERGENCE OF THE STEREOTYPE... 103

23:213; partial Grayzel 1:322–3); Lyon I (1245), can. II.1 (Tanner 293–5); Paris (1248), can. 9 (Mansi 23:765; Grayzel 1:332–3).

239. On the dating of the Paris council, see: Grayzel 1:300, note 2.

240. Chazan likewise sees the Church influence: "the major legislation of the reign of Philip Augustus definitely shows the growing impact of Church objection to Jewish usury, grounded in both theological and social concerns" (Chazan, *Medieval Jewry in Northern France*, 84). Where I disagree with him is on whether the legislation aided exploitation.

241. Roger de Hoveden, *Chronica magistri Rogri de Hovedene*, 3:266–7; trans. *Annals of Roger of Hoveden*, trans. Henry Riley, 2 vols. (London, 1853), 2:338–9.

242. Robert Stacey, "The Massacres of 1189–90 and the Origins of the Jewish Exchequer, 1186–1226," in *Christians and Jews in Angevin England: The York Massacre of 1190, Narratives and Contexts*, ed. Sarah Jones and Sethina Watson (Woodbridge, 2013), 106–24, esp. 117–8.

243. Jordan also concludes that "Philip himself had access to very little precise information on the extent of Jewish lending" circa 1206 and that whatever his motivations were, they were *not* driven by a fiscal crisis (Jordan, *French Monarchy*, 65).

244. This document is distinguished from the 1206 and 1219 ordinances, which were directed largely to Jews, in being a mandate to the royal bailiffs on Jewish loans. There are three printed editions: Martène and Durand, *Veterum scriptorum*, 1:1181–2, taken from Register E or F; Laurière et al., *Ordonnances*, 11:315, taken from Register E; and most recently Delaborde, *Recueil des actes de Philippe Auguste*, 4:190–1, no. 1555, taken from Register C. An English translation was made by Chazan (*Church, State, and Jew*, 207–8) from the Martène and Durand text, but "it does not make good sense," as Jordan notes (*French Monarchy*, 281, note 3). Some of the difficulties in the text will be dealt with below.

245. None of the Register texts contain an internal date. The most recent editors of the *Recueil des actes de Philippe Auguste* date it to 1219–20 because it follows the ordinance on Jewish loans of 1219 in Register C of Philip Augustus. But as Register C became encumbered near 1220, documents were inserted wherever room

104   J.L. MELL

could be found (Baldwin, *Government of Philip Augustus*, 413). Its inclusion in Register C (1212–20) and not in Register A (1204–11) suggests a date between 1212 and 1220. But Jewish historians have suggested an earlier dating. Chazan places it between the 1206 and 1219 ordinances. Jordan argues for a date shortly after a 1210 inquest, as he sees the inquest "pointing the way" to registration of debts (Jordan, *French Monarchy*, 74). In my opinion, the inquest could only have been made with the aid of a register like that mandated here. If this document is the first royal mandate to register Jewish loans, then it seems likely that it dates to 1206–10. But with more than half of the royal acts lost, it is impossible to say for certain.

246. I follow here the version in Martène and Durand, *Veterum scriptorum*, 1:1181–2. See the discussion below of a problematic clause.

247. Ibid. Because no records of loan documents have survived it is unclear what their structure was. It is possible that "the first term of payment" signals that the loans were to be repaid in several installments designated in the document, as we find in the Norwich Daybook of 1225–6. The payment of two pennies per pound, also common in the Norwich Daybook, is effective only when the Jew wishes the debt to be repaid at the first term. For a transcription of the Norwich Daybook, see: Lipman, *Jews of Medieval Norwich*, 187 f.

248. McLaughlin, "Teaching of the Canonists on Usury," 1:140–3.

249. *Summa* on C.14.q.3.c.3 cited in McLaughlin, "Teaching of the Canonists on Usury," 1:140, note 479.

250. McLaughlin, "Teaching of the Canonists on Usury," 1:141.

251. Each of the modern editions gives a different version of this clause. *Veterum scriptorum*, followed here, gives the text as "si tamen Christianus tamdiu *voluerit* debitum retinere, & Judaeus *voluerit* ei dimittere." *Ordonnances* gives the text as "si tamen Christianus tandiu *voluerit* debitum retinere & Judaeus *noluerit* ei dimittere." The modern editors of the *Recueil* give "si tamen Christianus tamdiu noluerit debitum retinere, & Judaeus noluerit ei dimittere." It is easy to imagine that either two of the modern editors or the medieval scribe of Register E misread "v" as an "n" or vice versa, letters often difficult to distinguish in manuscript. On the basis of logical meaning *voluerit...voluerit* seems to me to

be the best reading. For the Christian debtor could discharge his debt whenever he wished according to the 1206 ordinance, and hence *Christianus noluerit* (the Christian does not wish) does not make good sense. *Judaeus noluerit* (the Jew does not wish) does not make good sense, since the clause does not exclude anything. Interest runs after the first payment has been defaulted, and it is generally assumed that Jews wish debts to accrue interest.

252. Contra Jordan, who attributes it to the keepers being overburdened by the number of small loans and the king's interest in exploiting only major lending (Jordan, *French Monarchy*, 74). See: Robin Mundill, "The 'Archa' System and Its Legacy after 1194," in *Christians and Jews in Angevin England*, ed. Jones and Watson, 148–62.

253. Given the large number of missing acts of Philip Augustus it is possible that this mandate does not reflect the first order to keep a register.

254. John Baldwin et al., eds., *Les Registres de Philippe Auguste* (Paris, 1992), 1:240–1. Jordan dates the inquest to 1210 precisely on the basis of the names of the bailiffs (Jordan, *French Monarchy*, 279, note 64.)

255. Baldwin, *Registres de Philippe Auguste*, 570–1. The correlation of these two documents is, however, speculative. First suggested by Baldwin (*Government of Philip Augustus*, 232), it was used by Jordan to concoct a more questionable series of events (*French Monarchy*, 66–8).

256. Laurière et al., *Ordonnances*, 1:35–7; and Delaborde, *Recueil des actes de Philippe Auguste*, 4:188–90, no. 1554; trans. Chazan, *Church, State, and Jew*, 208–10. The text of the ordinance and the editorial note in the edition by Laurière gives February 1218, but the date is corrected in *Recueil* to February 1219. See also: Chazan, *Medieval Jewry in Northern France*, 85–6; and Jordan, *French Monarchy*, 81–8, 97.

257. It is not entirely clear whether this second article of the ordinance applies to the more restricted case of propertied peasants, as I read it, or to all Jewish loans. The assignment of properties in loans to knights, burghers, and merchants suggests that this second clause applies only to peasants. Also, it is curious that this text does not include the restriction found in the mandate to the bailiffs which stipulated that interest does not begin until the

106   J.L. MELL

debtor defaults on the first term of payment. There are three possible resolutions: one could assume that the orders to the bailiff are still in force though not mentioned here; one could assume that this ordinance supersedes entirely the previous orders, though it seems unlikely that the system of seals and registration would have been done away with, particularly as in a few years Louis VIII would do so overtly; or one could assume that the mandate to the bailiffs post-dates this ordinance, which then raises innumerable problems as this ordinance is more restrictive. It seems preferable to me to assume that the mandate to the bailiffs was in force with these additional restrictions added.

258. The prohibition in 1206 on lending on church lands without the permission of the secular lord is curiously dropped.

259. Melun (1216), can. 3–4 (Mansi 22:1088).

260. Rouen (1231), can. 1 (Mansi 23:213; partial Grayzel 1:322–3); Paris (1248) can. 9 (Mansi 23:765; Grayzel 332–3). Rouen moderates the Melun canon 3 by allowing loans up to 60s and allowing abbeys with rich revenues loans up to 100s, but it also imposes a penalty on abbots who without the permission of the bishop take a monetary loan from a Jew. The general council of Lyon I (1245) prohibited in a general way "troublesome debts," ones based on usury "if possible," and ones contracted at a fair or public market, but without any specific reference to Jews (Tanner 293–5).

261. Baldwin, *Government of Philip Augustus*, 39–40, 442–4.

262. There are some differences in the details. Here the terms for repayment are not set, nor are pledges of movables included, though these are permitted in article 8 of the current ordinance.

263. McLaughlin, "Teaching of the Canonists," 1:140–3.

264. Ibid., 1:136.

265. Baldwin, *Peter the Chanter and His Circle*, 1:206.

266. Bird, "Reform or Crusade?" 166.

267. On Innocent III, see: James Powell, trans., *The Deeds of Pope Innocent III by an Anonymous Author* (Washington, DC, 2004); Oliver Guyotjeannin, "Innocent III," in *The Papacy: An Encyclopedia* (New York, 2002), 2:785–90; Moore, *Pope Innocent III*; and Jane Sayers, *Innocent III: Leader of Europe, 1198–1216* (London, 1994).

268. Guyotjeannin, "Innocent III"; Sayers, *Innocent III*, 17–21.

THE DISCOURSE OF USURY AND THE EMERGENCE OF THE STEREOTYPE... 107

269. See the discussion of these councils earlier in this chapter.
270. Baldwin, *Peter the Chanter and His Circle*.
271. Ibid., 279–311; Le Goff, *Your Money or Your Life*; Langholm, *Economics in the Medieval Schools*, 37–62; and especially for unpublished sermons, Bird, "Reform or Crusade?"
272. Milton Gutsch, "A Twelfth Century Preacher—Fulk of Neuilly," in *The Crusades and Other Historical Essays Presented to Dana Munro*, ed. Louis Paetow (New York, 1928), 183–206.
273. The "medieval Reformation" is a term coined by Brenda Bolton in her *The Medieval Reformation* (New York, 1983).
274. Baldwin, *Peter the Chanter and His Circle*, 206.
275. On Robert of Courson, see: Ch. Dickson, "Vie de Robert de Courson," *Archives d'histoire Doctrinale et Littéraire du Moyen Age* 9 (1934): 53–142; Baldwin, *Peter the Chanter and His Circle*, 1:19–25; Langholm, *Economics in the Medieval Schools*, 37–62. *Le traité "De Usura" de Robert de Courson*, ed. Georges Lefèvre, is but a piece of his larger *Summa*, still available only in manuscript. On Robert of Courson and Stephen Langton's preaching tour, see: Baldwin, *Peter the Chanter and His Circle*, 2:12, note 40.
276. See: Chap. 5 for a discussion of Jewish serfdom and the relevant literature.
277. But Chazan sees them as a consistent extension of earlier Capetian legislation, as I do.
278. There are two extant versions: one is a draft dated 1 Nov. and one is sealed on 8 Nov.: Teulet et al., *Layettes*, 2:14 (no. 1610), and Martène and Durand, *Veterum scriptorum*, 1:1182–3, respectively; trans. Chazan, *Church, State, and Jew*, 211–2. Cf. Jordan, *French Monarchy and the Jews*, 93–104; Chazan, *Medieval Jewry in Northern France*, 104–8.
279. The double construction here seems at first sight puzzling. Why was it necessary both to prohibit Jewish loans with usury *and* to ordain that secular lords will not cause it to be repaid? The reason may lie in the nature of the strength of an oath. If a borrower swore to pay the usury, even if it was prohibited, the borrower would still be obligated. In general, courts would require an individual to uphold their oath. For even the ecclesiastical courts required the borrower to fulfill their oath by paying usury, if the

108   J.L. MELL

creditor demanded. By ordaining that secular lords will not cause it to be paid, perhaps they avert the problem of requiring the borrower to fulfill the oath.

280. This has gone virtually unnoticed, except in a short footnote: Chazan, *Medieval Jewry in Northern France*, 106, note 15.

281. As per Jordan, *French Monarchy and the Jews*, 95. However, this raises a problem. For why then would Jews be willing to comply with the fifth article of the ordinance, which required enrolling their debts with their respective lords within three months? Moreover, even a *captio* probably had to have a legal basis as a tax or fine.

282. Teulet et al., *Layettes*, 2:192–3, no. 2083, trans. Chazan, *Church, State, and Jew*, 213–5; Chazan, *Medieval Jewry in Northern France*, 109–10; Jordan, *French Monarchy and Jews*, 128–34. I have chosen not to discuss the *captiones* treated at length by Jordan in this discussion of royal legislation, because it seems the *captiones* should be treated in a larger discussion of taxation, Jewish and non-Jewish.

283. "We also have desired, resolved, and sworn to these things for the salvation of our souls and those of our ancestors" (Chazan, *Church, State, and Jew*, 215).

284. Laurière et al., *Ordonnances*, 1:54–5; trans. Chazan, *Church, State, and Jew*, 283–4. The last *captio* and enrollment mentioned in the document must almost certainly have been connected with the general legislation of 1230, since the decree made in December 1230 required debts to be enrolled and first payments to be made on 1 Nov. 1231. The three-year repayment schedule then would have concluded in 1234 when this decree was made (Chazan, *Medieval Jewry in Northern France*, 110–1; Jordan, *French Monarchy and Jews*, 133–4).

285. Delisle, *Recueil de jugements de l'echiquier de Normandie*, 133, no. 581. Translation my own. Cf. Chazan, *Church, State, and Jew*, 216.

286. Lateran III (1179), no. 26 (Tanner 223–4). See earlier discussion.

287. Melun (1216), can. 4 (Mansi 22:1087–8; Grayzel 1:313); Paris (1248), can. 9 (Mansi 23:765; Grayzel 1:332–3).

288. Grayzel 1:239–43; Salo Baron, *A Social and Religious History of the Jews*, 2nd ed. (New York, 1952–83), 9:64–71; Hyam Maccoby,

THE DISCOURSE OF USURY AND THE EMERGENCE OF THE STEREOTYPE... 109

Judaism on Trial (London, 1982); Chazan, *Medieval Jewry in Northern France*, 124–33; Jordan, *French Monarchy and Jews*, 137–40; Cohen, *Living Letters*, 317–63; Gilbert Dahan, ed., *Le Brûlement du Talmud à Paris, 1242–1244* (Paris, 1999).

289. On Louis IX and crusading, see the extensive study of William Jordan, *Louis IX and the Challenge of the Crusade* (Princeton, 1979).

290. Jordan, *French Monarchy and Jews*, 144–5; Nahon, "Le credit et les Juifs dans la France du XIIIe siècle"; Jordan, "Jewish-Christian Relations in Mid-Thirteenth Century France" and "An Aspect of Credit in Picardy in the 1240s."

291. s.v. "Louis IX (Saint Louis)," *The Encyclopedia of the Middle Ages* (2005), Oxford Reference Library (accessed 9 Mar. 2015).

292. Laurière et al., *Ordonnances*, 1:75a, nos. 32–3; and Béziers (1255), can. 23 (Mansi 23:882–3; Grayzel 1:336). Citation follows Grayzel's translation except for his translation of *terminis* as "contracts."

293. Grayzel 1:334–7.

294. Matthew Paris reports that Louis IX first ordered this expulsion in 1253 while on crusade via a letter (Jordan, *French Monarchy*, 148).

295. Laurière et al., *Ordonnances*, 1: 85; trans., Chazan, *Church, State, and Jew*, 287. Note too that the men executing these orders are clergy.

296. Laurière et al., *Ordonnances*, 1:294. Cf., Chazan, *Medieval Jewry in Northern France*, 150. On the badge generally and its delayed appearance in France, see: Grayzel 1:60–70; and Stow, *Alienated Minority*, 247–9.

297. Chazan, *Medieval Jewry in Northern France*, 149–50.

298. For comparative work on expulsions, see: Gerd Mentgen, "Die Vertreibungen der Juden aus England und Frankreich im Mittelalter," *Aschkenas* 7 (1997): 11–53; Stow, *Alienated Minority*, 281–308; Sophia Menache, "The King, the Church and the Jews: Some Considerations on the Expulsions from England and France," *Journal of Medieval History* 13 (1987): 223–36, and her "Faith, Myth, and Politics—The Stereotype of the Jews and Their Expulsion from England and France," *Jewish Quarterly Review* 75 (1985): 351–74; Maurice Kriegel,

"Mobilisation politique et modernisation organique: les expulsions de Juifs au bas moyen age," *Archives de sciences sociales des religions* 46 (1978): 5–20.

There are earlier expulsions from French and English lands and towns: French royal domain, 1182; readmitted, 1198 (Delaborde, *Oeuvres de Rigord*, 1:27–31; trans. Chazan, *Church, State, and Jew*, 310–2); Brittany, 1239 (Grayzel 1:344–5); Bury St. Edmond, 1190 (Jocelin de Brakelond, *Chronica Jocelini de Brakelond* (London, 1840), 33–4; trans. Jocelin de Brakelond, *Chronicle of Jocelin of Brakelond* (London, 1949), 45–6; reprt. in Chazan, *Church, State, and Jew*, 309–10); Leicester, 1231 (John Nichols, *History and Antiquities of the County of Leicester*, 4 vols. (London, 1795–1815), I, pt. 2, App. p. 38, no. 13; James Thompson, *History of Leicester from the Time of the Romans to the End of the Seventeenth Century* (Leicester, 1849), 72; *Roberti Grosseteste episcopi quondam lincolniensis. Epistolae*, ed. Henry Luard (London, 1861), 33–8; trans. *The Letters of Robert Grosseteste, Bishop of Lincoln*, trans. and ed. F.A.C. Mantello and Joseph Goering (Toronto, 2010), 65–70); Newcastle, 1234; Warwick, 1234; Wycombe, 1235; Southampton, 1236; Berkhamstead, 1242; Newbury and Speenhamland, 1243; Derby, 1261; Romsey, 1266; Winchelsea, 1273; Bridgnorth, 1274 (Robin Mundill, *England's Jewish Solution: Experiment and Expulsion 1262–1290* (Cambridge, 1998), 265, note 88); from all small towns and villages to royal towns with archae, 1275 (*Statutes of the Realm (1225–1713)*, (London, 1810–22), 1:220–1; trans. Mundill, *England's Jewish Solution*, 291–3).

299. Mundill, *England's Jewish Solution*, 276–7, and for the dating of the Gascon expulsion, see esp. his note 172; H.G. Richardson, *The English Jewry under Angevin Kings* (London, 1960), 213, 225–8.

300. Pierre Rangeard, *Histoire de l'université d'Angers* (Angers, 1877), 2:183–7; trans. Chazan, *Church, State, and Jew*, 313–7; reprt. in Mundill, *England's Jewish Solution*, 299–302.

301. On the expulsion from England, see: Mundill, *England's Jewish Solution*, 249–85; Robert Stacey, "Parliamentary Negotiation and the Expulsion of the Jews from England," *Thirteenth Century England: Proceedings of the New Castle upon Tyne Conference* 6

(1995): 77–101; Richard Huscroft, *Expulsion: England's Jewish Solution* (Stroud, 2006), 140–60; Richardson, *English Jewry*, 213–33; Lionel Abrahams, "The Expulsion of the Jews from England in 1290," *Jewish Quarterly Review* 7 (1894–5): 75–100, 236–58, 428–58; republ. as *The Expulsion of the Jews from England in 1290* (Oxford, 1895); Abrahams "Condition of the Jews of England at the Time of Their Expulsion in 1290," *JHSET* 2 (1894–5): 76–105; G.H. Leonard, "The Expulsion of the Jews by Edward 1st—An Essay in Explanation of the Exodus A.D. 1290," *Transactions of the Royal Historical Society* 5 (1891): 103–46; Paul Hyams, "The Jewish Minority in Medieval England 1066–1290," *Journal of Jewish Studies* 25 (1974): 270–93; and Cecil Roth, *A History of the Jews in England* (Oxford, 1964), 68–90. To be avoided is Peter Elman, "The Economic Causes of the Expulsion of the Jews in 1290," *Economic History Review* 7 (1937): 145–54.

302. René de Lespinasse, *Le Nivernais et les comtes de Nevers*, 3 vols. (Paris, 1909–14), 2:373.

303. The French expulsion was checkered. Not only were there local or partial expulsions in the thirteenth century, but over the fourteenth century, the French monarchs withdrew and renewed the Jewish expulsion from the royal domain several times. Louis X recalled the Jews in 1315. Philip VI expelled them in 1322. John II recalled them in 1359, and Charles VI evicted them in 1394. On the French royal expulsions, see: Chazan, *Medieval Jewry in Northern France*, 182–8, 191–205; Jordan, *French Monarchy*, 180–6, 246–51.

304. Rangeard, *Histoire de l'université d'Angers*, 2:183–7; trans. Chazan, *Church, State, and Jew*, 313–7; reprt. in Mundill, *England's Jewish Solution*, App. IV, 299–302.

305. Rigg, *Select Pleas, Starrs and Other Records*, xl–xlii, liv–lxi; Mundill, *England's Jewish Solution*, 291–8; Chazan, *Church, State, and Jew*, 317–9. An alternative translation of the statute appears in the *Calender of the close Rolls Preserved in the Public Record Office, Edward I: Volume 3, 1288-1296*, (London, 1892–), 109 (5 Nov. 1290).

306. This and all following quotations are from Chazan, *Church, State and Jew*, 314–7.

307. Lyon II (1274), can. 27 (Tanner 329).

112   J.L. MELL

308. Rigg, *Select Pleas, Starrs, and Other Records*, xli.
309. Mundill, *England's Jewish Solution*, esp. 108–45.
310. For the document, see: Rigg, *Select Pleas, Starrs, and Other Records*, liv–lxi; translation reprinted. in Mundill, *England's Jewish Solution*, 294–8.
311. Vivian Lipman first coined this term, later embraced by Robin Mundill: Lipman, *Jews of Medieval Norwich*, 162–85.
312. Mundill, *England's Jewish Solution*, 275.
313. Ibid., 274–6; F.D. Logan, "Thirteen London Jews and Conversion to Christianity: Problems of Apostasy in the 1280s," *Bulletin of the Institute of Historical Research* 45 (1972): 214–49; Robert Stacy, "The Conversion of Jews to Christianity in Thirteenth-Century England," *Speculum* 67 (1992): 263–83.
314. Mundill, *England's Jewish Solution*, 269–70.
315. Ibid., 270–3.
316. Ibid., 273; Logan, "Thirteen London Jews," 214–29; Mentgen, "Die Vertreibungen," 25–7.
317. Mundill, *England's Jewish Solution*, 275, 277–85.
318. Stow, *Alienated Minority*, 231–42; Robert Stacey, "From Ritual Crucifixion to Host Desecration: Jews and the Body of Christ," *Jewish History* 12 (1998): 11–28; Miri Rubin, *Gentile Tales: The Narrative Assault on Late Medieval Jews* (New Haven, 1999); Gerd Mentgen, "Die Ritualmordaffäre um den 'Guten Werner' von Oberwesel und ihre Folgen," *Jahrbuch für Westdeutsche Landesgeschichte* 21 (1995): 159–98.
319. Mundill, *England Jewish Solution*, 249–85.
320. Ibid., 260.
321. Ibid., 253.
322. Chazan, *Medieval Jewry in Northern France*, 183.
323. Gustave Saige, *Les Juifs du Languedoc antèrieurement au XIVe siècle* (Paris, 1881), 235; Chazan, *Medieval Jewry in Northern France*, 187–8.
324. Perhaps converts who returned to Judaism.
325. The examples limited here to France and England could easily be extended to the rulers in the Iberian Peninsula and in central Europe.

CHAPTER 7

Commercialization among the Jewish Merchants of Marseille

Tinker, Tailor, Soldier, Sailor, Rich Man, Poor Man, Beggar Man, Thief, Doctor, Lawyer, Merchant, Chief—*Jump Rope Rhyme*

Chapters 4 and 5 refuted the "economic function of the medieval Jew" with data from the economic, legal, and political histories of Anglo-Jewry. Chapter 6 traced the emergence of the stereotype of the Jewish usurer in the interstices of the ecclesiastical campaign against Christian usury, crusading, and an anti-Judaism program in northern France. It is time to return to the broader question of medieval economic history. For as Part 1 clarified, the "economic function of the Jew" was grounded in a view of medieval European economy as static and agrarian, developed by the German Historical School. Two scholarly currents in the interwar and postwar periods challenged this perspective. One recovered "medieval capitalism," or what later came to be called the commercial revolution of the high middle ages. The other recast early medieval economy as a gift economy, which transformed with the commercial revolution into a profit economy. Yet, the "Jewish economic function" did not wither away. Rather it became more deeply entrenched in response to twentieth-century antisemitism and its stereotypes of Jews and money. The masterminds of the postwar paradigms re-inscribed the Jewish economic function into the paradigms of commercial revolution and gift economy/profit economy. This latent contradiction hampers our historical understanding of both Jewish history and European history.

© The Author(s) 2018   113
J.L. Mell, *The Myth of the Medieval Jewish Moneylender*,
DOI 10.1007/978-3-319-34186-6_2

In this chapter and the following, I take up commercialization and gift/profit exchange in order to show how dissolving the myth of the Jewish moneylender may contribute to both Jewish history and European history. I begin with the working assumption that Jews in Europe were Europeans; therefore they participated in broad historical processes, even as Jewish difference may have morphed the result in a different direction. This chapter will bring an example of Jewish merchants who participated in the commercial revolution and actively used what was, according to Robert Lopez, its key institution, the investment contract known as a *commenda*. The contracts recorded in the notarial register of Giraud d'Amalric at the port of Marseille in 1248 document Jewish merchants sailing the Mediterranean Sea at the height of the commercial revolution who were entrusted with investments from Christians and Jews alike.

But the Marseille commendae do not merely provide evidence for Jewish merchants that contradicts Roscher's narrative of early medieval Jewish merchants pushed out of trade into the lucrative but despised profession of moneylending. The commendae demonstrate Jewish participation in the European process of commercialization vis-à-vis European civic institutions. For Jewish merchants and investors, *even when dealing only with other Jews,* chose to use a Latin contract, written by a Christian notary, to be upheld in Christian courts. Jews could have used the equivalent Hebrew contract, *iska*, or relied upon the older form of oral contract protected by the *lex mercatoria*.[1] The use of commendae by Jews demonstrates that Jews were embedded in the legal and civic institutions undergirding European commerce in the Mediterranean. This has significance for "general" economic history and for Jewish economic history. In regard to "general" economic history, Jewish merchants provide a fruitful point for comparing European and Islamic modes of commercialization in the Mediterranean. A comparison of the trade, institutions, and geographical networks of both groups of Jewish merchants brings into relief the European preference for partnerships constructed through the commenda versus the Islamic preference for reciprocal agency instituted in the *suḥba*. I will return to this at the end of the chapter.

In regard to Jewish economic history, this chapter aims to open our historical imagination to the variety of economic occupations engaged in by medieval European Jews, their local variations, and their connection with processes of commercialization. I offer the Jewish merchants of Marseille as a counterpoint to Richard Emery's study of the Jewish moneylending in Perpignan during the same period.[2] Using 15 notarial registers running from 1261 to 1287, Emery documented moneylending by recent Jewish immigrants, who supplied Perpignan with needed credit as it was developing commercially and industrially. Both the Perpignan and the Marseille stories are limited and local, and yet both are deeply connected with broader regional changes and commercialization in the Mediterranean. More significantly, inasmuch as both loans and investment partnerships were grounded in Latin contracts and an urban law inflected with legal concepts derived from Roman law, both were part and parcel of European commercialization. By setting merchants alongside moneylenders, and both alongside Jewish craftsmen working with coral, soap, silk, and gold, Jewish landowners and vintners, and Jewish doctors, we can begin to recover a more varied and, therefore, more accurate picture of Jewish economic activity.[3]

COMMENDA

The commenda has been called the "linch-pin of the Commercial Revolution" and widely credited by scholars with making the expansion of trade possible.[4] The commenda was a commercial loan or partnership, which allowed investors and agents to pool capital and labor for long-distance sea voyages. Profits were split 50/50 in the bilateral commenda, where the passive partner (commendator) contributed two-thirds of the capital and the active partner (tractator) one-third. Losses were borne according to one's share of capital. Profits were split 75/25 in the unilateral commenda, where the commendator contributed all the capital and the tractator only the labor. The tractator in this case bore no obligation for loss.

The bilateral commenda was the favored contract in the twelfth century; the unilateral commenda that of the thirteenth century.[5] In mid-thirteenth-century Marseille, the unilateral commenda had entirely supplanted the bilateral commenda, and the division of profits 75/25 was so customary it was no longer usually specified in the contracts. Eugene Byrne suggested some causes behind this shift in relation to Genoa.[6] In the twelfth century, the bilateral commenda was favored when risky foreign trade with Syria was monopolized by a few leading Genoese families. The capital required for such a lengthy sea voyage and the risks attendant on it necessitated several partners. In the thirteenth century, when trade had been regularized, risk reduced, and exports increased, individual merchants were able to operate alone. The unilateral commenda was more suitable to investments of merchandise than currency, and allowed the tractator more freedom

116 J.L. MELL

to take on multiple commendae. The Genoese case analyzed by Byrne probably illuminates the situation elsewhere. For the unilateral commenda became the prototypical contract for Mediterranean sea trade during the peak of the commercial revolution.

Precedents for the commenda have been found in the Roman sea loan, the Muslim *muqarada*, the rabbinic *iska*, the Byzantine *chreokoinonia*, and even the Babylonian *tapputum*. Disputes over the origin of the commenda have been fierce.[7] But judicious scholars emphasize that "the commenda as it appears in the Western Mediterranean from the tenth century on seems to [be]…the fruit of a slow development in customary law."[8] The question of origin is perhaps irrelevant, for when the commenda comes into full view in the twelfth-century notarial registers (the earliest extant is from 1155), it has a similarity of form throughout the western Mediterranean, even though called by different names—*societas, accommendatio, commenda, comanda, collegantia*.

Because we will be investigating Jewish commendae, it is important to point out that the *iska* continued to be used by European Jews throughout the middle ages. The *iska*, like the commenda, was a loan made for the purpose of a business venture. But the entire capital was contributed by the investor as in the unilateral commenda, not by two partners together as in the bilateral commenda or *societas maris*. As with the commenda, the fact that the risk was borne by the investor prevented the transaction from being usurious in the eyes of religious authorities. The *iska* was defined in the Talmud over the course of several hundred years, and continued to be refined in the middle ages. The Mishnah (Bava Metzia 5:4) states that one may loan capital for a business venture for a half share of the profits only if one also pays wages to the active business partner. The intent, as is clear from the context, is the avoidance of usury (*avak ribit*). Later Talmudic discussion clarifies the juridical logic underlying the arrangement: the contract is half loan and half deposit (B.T. Bava Metziah 104b). The active partner therefore is entitled to the profit on the half given as a loan, and the investor on the half given as a deposit. Similarly the active partner is liable for the loss of the half made as a loan, the investor for the half made as a deposit. But the investor must pay wages for management of his or her share in order to avoid "usury." Several legal points left unclear were resolved by medieval rabbinic authorities, including the amount of wages which ought to be paid and the active partner's liability for loss and theft or an unavoidable accident.[9] The whole question of the relationship between commercialization and the *iska* deserves careful study, both in regard to theoretical legal developments and in regard to its practical use with attention to regional variations. Such a study might make it possible to understand more deeply the evolution of the law on *iska* in relation to commercialization within local medieval customs and urban law.[10] For the purposes of this chapter, it is sufficient to know that a Hebrew contract parallel to the commenda was available to European Jews making investments with Jewish partners.

The most important source for the study of the commenda has been notarial records from western Mediterranean ports, stretching from Venice to Valencia. While the commenda was effected by entrusting merchandise or coins, the notarial record together with the verbal testimony of the witnesses who signed it provided a legal guarantee for the commercial venture. Notaries, licensed and regulated by the commune or feudal lord, recorded a draft (*notula*) for a legal document in their register, or cartulary, from which they might later draw up a formal charter (*instrumentum*) if the parties requested.[11] A *notula* in a notary's register or *instrumentum* provided a record of the transaction and the witnesses, but did not effect the transaction. Notarial registers were part of a complex set of legal, social, and institutional changes. In particular, the notary's register was recognized in courts as sufficient proof of obligation or contract. In general, the rise of the public notary in the twelfth and thirteenth centuries formed part of Europe's shift from an oral culture to a written culture, linked to changes in legal proof.[12]

The earliest extant medieval notarial register from modern-day France is that of Giraud d'Amalric of Marseille, which will provide the data for this chapter.[13] Written between March and July of 1248, the cartulary includes 1031 entries, one-half of which are commendae. Although other documents survive illuminating Marseille trade, notably the charters of the merchant de Manduel family from 1191 to 1263 and notarial cartularies from 1278 to 1300, several fortuitous circumstances make Amalric's register unrivaled for a study of mercantile trade:[14] Giraud d'Amalric worked near the docks of Marseille, next to the moneychangers (*iuxta tabulas campsorum*), unlike any of the other thirteenth-century notaries whose cartularies survive. His clientele included merchants, ship masters, bankers, shopkeepers, artisans, and others involved in the international network of commerce in Marseille. In addition, the months covered in his register were those of the spring sailing season when commercial business was at a peak, and the year 1248 was one in which Marseille was at the height of its commercial prominence.

The notarial registers from the Italian merchant cities of Genoa and Venice hold pride of place in the study of medieval commerce and the commenda.[15] Yet, when the volume of trade in Amalric's register is compared with that of the Genoese notarial registers, it gains in consequence. Amalric's register contains 466 commenda contracts during a four-month period. The famed Genoese cartulary of Giovanni Scriba contains 1400 commenda contracts for a 10-year period.[16] Amalric's register thus provides a significant sample, which allows for statistical analysis, even though limited temporally to a short cross section of Marseille trade.

Amalric's register contains a large number of commenda contracts with Jewish agents, but these have received little comment beyond an 1888 article by Isidore Loeb.[17] John Pryor has produced an excellent statistical study of all commendae in thirteenth-century Marseille documents, which I relied on here, but he no more than notes the presence of Jewish agents.[18] Writing shortly after Louis Blancard published his edition of the thirteenth-century documents on commerce in Marseille, Loeb emphasized the importance of the documents Blancard had collected for the study of Jewish history. The attention Loeb drew to these documents insured them a place in the histories of Jews in Marseille and in Baron's synthesis of Jewish economic history.[19] But no attempt has been made to study the Jewish commenda contracts in a serious statistical manner as has been done for the contracts in general. Even less has any scholar broached the questions of the significance of the Marseille documents for our understanding of Jews and commercialization.

The following discussion will analyze the Jewish commenda contracts statistically. Statistical analysis provides the clearest means for reading the repetitive documents of a notarial register. However, it is important to keep in mind that the clear and concise figures of statistical analysis are only rough and hazy approximations of Marseille's trade and the Jewish involvement. Anyone working with notarial registers from the thirteenth century is painfully aware of their fragmentary nature. Richard Emery estimated that the surviving registers from thirteenth-century Perpignan comprised only 17 out of 1000 contemporary registers.[20] Moreover, even the *notulae* in a register need to be read with attention to the marginalia and cancellations made by the notary signaling that the contract was fulfilled or closed.[21] Finally, it is possible that oral contracts continued to be used alongside notarial records, and in the case of intra-Jewish business, Hebrew contracts (*iska*) recorded by Hebrew scribes. Consequently, the following statistics, though given as hard numbers, cannot reflect the real

COMMERCIALIZATION AMONG THE JEWISH MERCHANTS OF MARSEILLE   119

proportion of Jewish mercantile trade. We can, however, safely assume that the absolute number of commenda contracts involving Jewish merchants and investors in Giraud d'Amalric's register reflects only a percentage of those undertaken in the mid-thirteenth century. In short, the real numbers would have been higher than the numbers I shall give below, while the relative proportion of Jewish agents may have been lower or higher, and would have varied over the course of the thirteenth century.

THE JEWISH COMMUNITY IN MARSEILLE

A Jewish community was established in Marseille as early as the Merovingian period and lasted until the late fifteenth century, when Charles VIII expelled the Provençal Jews in 1481 after Provence was unified with the royal French domain.[22] In the mid-thirteenth century, Jews were admitted as citizens of Marseille, treated as equals in regard to customs and privileges, and treated with respect in regard to their religious observance. They were granted the right to organize as a corporate body, the *universitas Judeorum*. Jews owned houses and property in and around Marseille. There were two Jewish quarters, one in the lower town that had two synagogues, a *mikveh*, a hospital, schools, and a market, and one in the upper town.[23] But Jews were not restricted to residence within their quarters. Jews were allowed to practice all trades and are known to have been doctors, middlemen in the internal land trade in wool and grain, merchants in seaborne trade, cloth merchants and tailors, and craftsmen involved in the working of coral and the production of soap. Loans on interest were tolerated and regulated at 15 percent in Marseille, but Jews were not distinguished as moneylenders or moneychangers. Giraud d'Amalric's cartulary mentions 26 to 28 Christian moneychangers, but no Jewish moneychangers, an office regulated by town officials; and Jews more often appear as debtors than as lenders.[24] In the course of the thirteenth and fourteenth centuries, some restrictions were placed on Marseille Jews. All stemmed from the ecclesiastical anti-Judaism program discussed in Chapter 6: Jews were not to hold public office, nor were they to testify against Christians in court, though we have cases in which they did. Jews were not to work openly on Sundays and Christian feast days. Jewish men were required to wear a badge, and Jewish women a headscarf. Both were to use the public baths only on Fridays. One restriction was particular to Marseille: no more than four Jews were allowed to travel at one time on Marseille ships. But these restrictions were observed in the breach, even in the late

120   J.L. MELL

fourteenth and fifteenth centuries. As Adolphe Crémieux, the historian of medieval Marseille Jewry, has emphasized, Marseille Jews were neither outcasts nor inferior; they were not humiliated, but in the main were treated as the equals of their Christian neighbors.[25]

Jewish Mercantile Activity in Marseille

Giraud d'Amalric's cartulary provides evidence on the nature and extent of Jewish commercial activity and the degree of professionalization among Jewish agents in mercantile sea trade. Jewish commercial activity appears to have been neither predominant nor insignificant. Jewish agents appear to have been professional merchants of a lower to middling stature. The depth and richness of the cartulary provides a cross section of Marseille trade at the height of the commercial revolution, but it can shed no light beyond the confines of 1248. To look beyond 1248, I shall turn at the end of this chapter to the other documents from late medieval Marseille and other Mediterranean ports. Though they are more fragmentary than Amalric's cartulary, these documents suggest that Jewish commercial activity in Marseille was not a unique or cursory phenomenon.

Almost half of the *notulae* in Amalric's cartulary are commenda contracts. They follow a typical formula, as in the following example: "I Modafar, Jew, son of a certain Bonasse, acknowledge and recognize to you Salomonetus, son of Salves, that I have received *in comanda* from you 105s. mixed money current in Marseille, invested in 15 pounds of cloves and 37 millares of gold, et cetera; which I will take, God willing, on the next sea-voyage to Bougie in the ship of Bertrandus Davini called the St. Franciscus. Witnesses: Peter de Villanova, Rainaudus de Cathedra, Gauterius de Templo. Done next to the moneychangers tables. By the mandate of the said Salomonetus, you acknowledge, et cetera."[26]

Of the 466 contracts in the cartulary, 11 percent have Jewish agents acting either as tractators or as commendators, that is, the traveling or investing partners, respectively (see Table 7.1). These percentages are strikingly similar to the 5–10 percent of the population often thought to be typical of Jewish population in European urban centers. Of the commendators named in the cartulary, 8.7 percent are Jewish, while 5 percent of the tractators are Jewish (see Table 7.2). The epithet "Jew" (*Judeus*) is used to establish identity. Its function is akin to an identification marker using place of origin, citizenship, or occupation, such as moneychanger,

COMMERCIALIZATION AMONG THE JEWISH MERCHANTS OF MARSEILLE 121

Table 7.1 Proportion of documents with Jewish agents in Amalric's register

	No. of documents*	No. documents with Jewish agents	% documents with Jewish agents
Commendae	466	51	11%
Other documents	565	13	2%
Total	1031	64	6%

*Count of all documents follows Pryor's count in his "Commenda," 299. Count of Jewish agents and Jewish documents is my own.

Table 7.2 Proportion of Jewish commendators and tractators in Amalric's register

	Totals*	No. of Jews	% of Jews
Commendators	297	26	9%
Tractators	244	12	5%

*Totals are derived from Pryor, "Commenda," 435, graph 4. Count of Jewish agents is my own. Jews who appear in both roles are counted twice.

spicer, drapier, and notary, commonly found in the Register.[27] As with all identification markers, the notary could exclude *Judeus* or include it at will. Giraud d'Amalric drops the marker *Judeus* for Bonusinfans, Bonus Dominus, and Bonafossus in *notulae* 694, 695, 696, 704, and 705 but includes it in 684, 693, and 697. He also drops the marker for Crestin f. Bonodominus de Monteil in 694, and for his father, Bonodominus de Monteil, in 963, but identifies the father as Jewish in 964. Amalric is similarly inconsistent with place of origin, citizenship, and occupation. This means that the numbers of Jews involved in commendae may be higher than we can verify. The historian is reliant on the notary's choice to include Jewishness as a means of identification. While marking Jewish identity was primarily functional, it may reflect a range of valences on the notary's part, including otherness and antipathy. However, the Register attests to legal discrimination only in one respect: Jews never appear as witnesses in the documents, seemingly because of the canonical pressure to exclude Jews as witnesses testifying against Christians in court.

The assumption that most Jews were moneylenders would lead one to presuppose that the Jewish agents in commenda contracts were mostly

122 J.L. MELL

passive investors (commendators) with ready cash, not merchants sailing the high seas. But to the contrary, the documents with Jewish tractators outnumber those with Jewish commendators. A total of 8.6 percent of all the commendae in Amalric's cartulary have Jewish tractators, and 6.2 percent have Jewish commendators. In fact, only one-fifth of the commendae with a Jewish agent have Christian tractators, while one-half have Christian commendators. This suggests that the group of Jewish agents which will be considered here are relatively highly involved in the merchant trade.

However, the roles of tractator and commendator are not clear identifications that an agent was a professional merchant or a passive landbound investor. Because tractators made sea voyages and traded goods for a profit, one generally assumes that they were professional merchants knowledgeable about foreign trade and foreign markets. However, travelers were known in the twelfth century to take goods in commenda to cover the expenses of their voyage. Thus, even tractators merit closer analysis to determine the extent of their professionalization. Conversely it might seem that commendators, being in the position of passive investors, often were occasional investors unskilled in long-distance trade, with a small nest egg they sought to put to good use. Yet commendators were often active merchants investing a part of their capital with another merchant to minimize risk. In fact, the most successful merchants often moved in the course of their careers from active tractator to the more settled position of commendator—these then would be anything but passive, novice investors.[28] A careful examination of the range and types of activity as well as the forms of investment within a condensed period of time, such as the four months of Amalric's register, should allow us to determine with some accuracy the degree of professionalization.

TRACTATORS

The Jewish tractators composed 5 percent of all the tractators in Amalric's register. But these Jewish tractators carried 8.6 percent of all commendae, and they carried twice the number of commendae that tractators on average carried.[29] Seventy-five percent of the Jewish tractators contracted three or more commendae in Amalric's register in the spring shipping season alone (see Table 7.3). The high number of commendae over the short period of four months indicates that these Jewish tractators were professional merchants.

Table 7.3 Number of commendae per Jewish agent

No. of commendae contracted per agent	1	2	3	4	5	6	7	8	9	10	11	12	13	14	15
No. of Jewish tractators	1				2	4	1	1					2	1	
No. of Jewish commendators	18	8													

The highest volume of trade was contracted by three Jewish tractators, primarily working in partnership: Bonafossus f. Vitalis de Turribus, Bonusinfans f. Jacob, and Bonus Dominus f. Astruc, citizens of Marseille.[30] On 8 May early in the day, Bonusinfans and Bonus Dominus made two commendae, one with Bono Isaac Ferrerio and one with Salvago f. Salomon.[31] Later in the day, they returned to Amalric's booth with Bonafossus to make an additional seven commendae.[32] On 12 May, the three men made two more commendae, and on 22 May one more commenda.[33] Seven of the commendators in these commendae were Christian, two of whom were moneychangers, possibly working next to Amalric's booth. Two of the contracts had commendators acting as partners, including one Jewish and Christian partnership. All the commendae taken in partnership were designated for the ship called the Leopardus of Bertrandus Belpel bound for Valencia (Spain), on which at least some of the three tractators were bound.

Prior to partnering with Bonusinfans and Bonus Dominus, Bonafossus f. Vitalis had made four commendae.[34] On 8 April, acting as commendator, he deposited 100s with a Christian tractator, Petrus Bartholomeus, bound on a ship to Pisa. On 28 April, he deposited six pounds of saffron with a tractator bound for Bougie. And on 29 April and 4 May, he took two commendae as tractator bound for Valencia on the ship of Basso. He clearly split his capital between three ports and three to four voyages.

On 8 May, after Amalric entered seven commendae held by Bonafossus, Bonusinfans, and Bonus Dominus in his register, he entered an additional *notula* stipulating the details of their partnership. Using the Latin contract of *societas*, the three partners specified that their partnership extended to all commendae made by them together or separately for the voyage of the Leopard, and they were each to receive profit shares equivalent to their investment on any additional sums they invested.[35] The partnership was ratified by an oath taken with their hands on "the Law of Moses" (either a Torah scroll or a Humash). This partnership could have been constructed in a form according with rabbinic law. The choice of a Latin contract undoubtedly was so that they could sue in Marseille's courts for breach of contract in regard to the division of profits or losses on the voyage. Though these types of partnerships were not unusual in Mediterranean trade, this is the only one to appear among Jewish or Christian merchants in Amalric's spring register.[36]

The contracts held by these Jewish partners often reveal intriguing details about the rich interrelationships between Jews and Christians active in commercial life. For instance, the three partners took in commenda sulfur worth £27.8.8 on 8 May from two commendators, one a Christian moneychanger, Dulcianus de Sancto Victore, and one a Jewish agent, Bonanatus Judeus f. Bonifilii.[37] Bonanatus Judeus f. Bonifilii took as tractator two commenda a month earlier (6 and 8 April) on a ship bound to Acco.[38] This same Dulcianus acted as witness to a commenda contract made directly after his and Bonanatus' with these same three partners.[39] The commendator of this contract, W. de Narbona, similarly acted as a witness for Dulcianus and Bonanatus.

We can appreciate the brisk business of these tractators, their professional status, and the upswing of commerce when we compare the records of Genoese merchants a hundred years earlier. In the records of 300 tractators taking Genoese investments overseas between 1155 and 1164, only 50 reappear as tractators in a 10-year period.[40] A majority of the Jewish tractators in Marseille, in contrast, appear multiple times within a four-month period.

While the Jewish tractators from Marseille were professional merchants, the commendae which they carried were of modest value. The deposits made with Jewish tractators ranged from £100 to 10s. The combined total reached £690 4s 11d, but the average value for a commenda taken by a Jewish tractator was £17 4s., as compared to the £62 for all commendae in mixed money in Amalric's cartulary.[41] We must conclude that Jewish tractators were active merchants, but of modest to middling means.

INVESTMENTS

From the types of investments, their values, and destinations, the tractators' professional character emerges even more clearly.[42] Investments documented in the Jewish commendae span the range of investment types found in Amalric.[43] In the commendae with Jewish agents, spices, herbs, and medicinals were the most important by far, with saffron the leading export and cloves a close second. Cloth was also important in the form of

COMMERCIALIZATION AMONG THE JEWISH MERCHANTS OF MARSEILLE 125

toile, silk, or finished capes, as were coins. Of secondary importance were foodstuffs, chemicals, and dyes. While about one-half of the Jewish commendae were invested in spices, herbs, and medicinals, one-fifth were left to the discretion of the tractator himself. These commendae were suited especially to the small investor; and indeed over half were modest investments between 10 and 100s, though one reached the large sum of £100 (see Table 7.4).

The ratio between investments in merchandise and in the common investments of the tractator was comparable in the Jewish commendae and in the commendae generally (see Table 7.5). But the ratio of commendae invested in coin was significantly lower for Jewish commendae than the average. When Jewish tractators alone are considered, the ratio of commendae in coin drops yet further. The lower rate of investment in coin speaks decisively against facile presumptions of Jewish predominance in the money trade. In Marseille, in fact, in the year 1248, not a single Jewish moneychanger appears among the 26 to 28 moneychangers who figure in Amalric's cartulary. Moreover, Jews appear more frequently as borrowers than as lenders.[44]

The higher ratio of commendae in merchandise suggests greater professionalization in long-distance trade. In the twelfth century, investments in coin predominated over merchandise. After a hundred years of commercialization, the economy strengthened and long-distance trade from western Europe increasingly exported merchandise rather than coin.[45] The shift from the bilateral commenda (*societas maris*) to the unilateral commenda (*accomendatio*) was closely linked. For the unilateral commenda was more flexible and suitable for investments in goods.[46] The investments made by Jewish commendators and investments carried by Jewish tractators were typical both in type and range of merchandise.

The ports to which Jewish tractators traveled and the number of ships on which they set sail also indicate a high level of mercantile trade. From Amalric's register, we know of 54 ships that left the port of Marseille in the spring of 1248. Jewish tractators made commendae assigned to sail on seven of these ships[47] (see Table 7.6). On Bertrand Davini's ship, the St. Francis, no less than six Jewish tractators sailed to Bougie (Maghreb) carrying two-thirds of the commendae, which we know were contracted for the ship. On Bertrandus Belpel's, the Leopardus, as mentioned before, three Jewish partners sailed to Valencia carrying a large number of commendae, while one of the partners, Bonafossus f. Vitalis, may have taken another two commendae on a second ship to Valencia. He was not the only one

126 J.L. MELL

Table 7.4 Types of investments made in Jewish commendae

Category	Type	No.	Total
Coin			**8**
	Besants of Acre	2	
	Besants of Millares	3	
	Marabotins	1	
	Sicilian Tarins	2	
Combined investments			**13**
Listed as "in the tractator's general investments"		13	
Merchandise			**46**
	Cloth		7
	Capes of Metz	1	
	Cotton	1	
	Silk	1	
	Skins	3	
	Toile	1	
	Foodstuffs		3
	Rhubarb	1	
	Licorice	1	
	Angelot Cheese	1	
	Spices, Herbs, and Medicinals		29
	Camphor	1	
	Cardamom	1	
	Cloves	5	
	Cumin	2	
	French (Spike) Lavender	1	
	Galangal	2	
	Gresse (Tartar?)	5	
	Musk	1	
	Nutmeg	2	
	Saffron	7	
	Scammony	2	
	Metals, Chemicals, and Dyes		5
	Amenlon (alum)?	1	
	Borax	1	
	Brazil-wood	1	
	Coral	1	
	Sulfur	1	
	Miscellaneous		2
	Chests	1	
	Boudron?	1	

COMMERCIALIZATION AMONG THE JEWISH MERCHANTS OF MARSEILLE 127

Table 7.5 Comparison of types of investments expressed as a ratio of common investments

	Common investment		Coin		Merchandise	
	Ratio	*No.*	*Ratio*	*No.*	*Ratio*	*No.*
Jewish commendators	1	10	0.4	4	1.6	16
Jewish tractators	1	12	0.16	2	2.34	28
Jewish commendae	1	16	0.38	6	1.94	31
All commendae*	1	113	0.76	86	2.04	231

*The figures for "all commendae" are from Pryor, "Commenda," 430 and note 43. The numbers for Jewish figures are my own.

to split his risk by sending commendae on two different ships sailing to the same location. Crescas Ferrusolus sent two commendae to Bougie on the St. Nicholas and then another commenda on the St. Gilles. Modafar f. Bonasse contracted a commenda on 24 April bound for Bougie on the St. Gilles, then three days later contracted for two commendae bound for Bougie on the St. Francis.[48]

Jewish tractators favored travel to Bougie (Maghreb) and Valencia (Spain) (see Table 7.7). This was in marked contrast to the Marseille commendae as a whole, in which the Levant was the favored market in 1248 and the Kingdom of Sicily took second place. Forty percent of the trade in 1248 recorded by Amalric was bound for Acre—a total of 173 commendae.[49] But only one Jewish tractator carried two commendae to Acre in the spring of 1248, although four Jewish commendators sent commendae with Christian tractators.[50] The high volume of trade with Acre may have been untypical. As Pryor notes:

> St. Louis' crusade was gathering in Southern France and in August Joinville boarded his ship at Marseille, bound for Cyprus. Intelligent businessmen might have hoped to make a good profit from the forces in the East or from the opportunities for expanded commerce which their conquests might create.[51]

The absence of Jewish tractators in the trade to the Levant may perhaps reflect anxiety about traveling in the direction of crusaders. In contrast, Jewish tractators made for the western Mediterranean and the Maghreb, to which they respectively transported 69 percent and 34 percent of the commendae bound for these destinations in the spring of 1248.

128   J.L. MELL

Table 7.6   Ships carrying Jewish tractators from Marseille in 1248

Ship name, type, master/owner, destination, no. of commendae on ship, name of Jewish tractator (commendae no. in Blancard)	Date ship was in port
St. Antonius, *bucius navis*, Bernardus de Narbona, Acre, 3 Bonanatus (also Benaciatus) f. Bonifilii (388, 411)	2–9 April
St. Nicholas, *navis*, Raimundus de Mossano, Bougie, 5 *Crescas Ferrusolus (466, 474)*	10–3 April
St. Gilles, *navis*, Raimundus de Mossono, Bougie, 21 Crescas Ferrusolus (613) *Modafar (Medafort) f. Bonasse (581)*	26 March–8 May
St. Franciscus, *bucius (navis)*, Bertrandus Davini, Bougie, 25 Astuguetus f. Samuelis (125, 341) Bonus Jusas f. Salomonis Ferrusoli (568, 572, 586) Juceph f. Mosse de Palerma (499, 500, 578, 598, 599) Leonetus Ferrusolus f. Salomonis Ferrusoli (603, 618, 621) Modafar (Medafort) f. Bonasse (594, 597) Mosse d'Accone (577)	23 March–8 May
—, *Navis*, de Basso, Valencia, 2 *Bonafossus f. Vital de Turribus (628, 647)*	**29 April–4 May**
Leopardus, *lignus*, Bertrandus Belpel, Valencia, 12 Bonafossus f. Vital de Turribus, Bonus Infans f. Jacob, and Bonus Dominus f. Astrugui (658, 659, 683, 684, 687, 693, 694, 695, 696, 704, 705, 759)	**8–22 May**
—, *Lignus*, Dominici de Fonte, Majorca-Barbary, 4 Bonisaac Ferrusol f. Bonjudas (807, 810, 814, 815)	**27–8 May**

This table follows the format of Pryor's Table 2 in "Commenda," 407–8, so that they can be compared. Ships in bold carry only Jewish tractators as recorded in Amalric. The names and document numbers which appear in italics indicate tractators and commendae who shortly afterwards contracted on a different ship bound for the same port. Therefore, they would have sailed on only one of these ships, though they may have sent goods on two different ships to split their risk

COMMENDATORS

The Marseille Jewish commendators can be classed in three groups: One-sixth were merchants acting both as tractators and commendators. One-quarter seem to have been actively involved in trade by virtue of investing in multiple commendae within a very short period of time, though perhaps not as merchants in long-distance sea trade. One-half invested in only one commenda, which was typical for commendators in Amalric's register. One-time investors can be presumed to have been small-time passive investors. But almost half of the Jewish commendators

COMMERCIALIZATION AMONG THE JEWISH MERCHANTS OF MARSEILLE 129

Table 7.7 Destination of commendae exported from Marseilles, spring 1248

Destination	All commendae	Jewish commendae	% of Jewish commendae
Southern France	8	0	
Northern France	10	0	
Northern Italy	43	1	2
Kingdom of Sicily	116	4	3
Western Mediterranean	29	20	69
Maghreb	72	24	34
Levant	184	6	3

Totals for "all commendae" are from Pryor, "Commenda," 403, Table 1. In calculating the totals for Jewish commendae, I followed Pryor's practice of counting each destination mentioned separately. Hence the number of destinations exceeds the number of commendae.

can be identified as active in trade in some degree beyond that of a small-time investor. This is a significant proportion, similar to the two-thirds of tractators who could be identified as active merchants.

The quickest and surest way of identifying mercantile commendators is through an individual's dual role as commendator and tractator. In such instances, agents were trading with the capital of others, investing their own capital with another tractator to reduce their risk of loss, and likely trading with their own capital, of which we have no monetary record. Their double activity as tractator and commendator indicates clearly that they were professionally involved in long-distance trade; they were Jewish merchants of the commercial revolution. For example, Mosse d'Accone, a Jewish citizen of Marseille, made reciprocal commenda contracts with a Christian, Petrus Cresteng, in two *notulae* on 23 April.[52] Petrus Cresteng took in commenda from Mosse d'Accone 40 Metz capes on a ship bound for Sicily. The capes were worth the high sum of £142 10d *monete miscue*, of which Mosse's son Salomon held £42 20d in the commenda. (The value of this commenda is twice that of the average in Amalric's cartulary.[53]) Then Mosse d'Accone took in commenda from Petrus Cresteng 150 besants of millares worth £45 *monete miscue* bound for Bougie. From other *notulae*, we find that Mosse d'Accone had not only a son Salomon, but a son Joseph who took four commendae ranging from £8 to £32 as tractator to Bougie on the same ship for which Mosse d'Accone was bound.[54] The profile of Mosse d'Accone's family, as minimal as it is, gives us a glimpse of a multi-generational Jewish merchant family who were citizens of Marseille.

Bonafossus f. Vitalis figures twice as commendator on 8 April and 28 April for ships headed to Pisa and Bougie. On one of these, he sent saffron. From 29 April to 22 May, he took in commenda as tractator no less than 14 commendae in spices: cumin, saffron, galangal, rhubarb, musk, camphor, cardamom, and licorice all bound for Valencia.[55] Bonafossus f. Vitalis and Mosse d'Accone were obviously professional merchants, as were the others who appear in both the roles of tractator and commendator in a single shipping season.

Over one-quarter of the Jewish commendators made multiple commendae within a period of several weeks, but did not act, at least in Amalric's register, as tractators. By dividing their investments, they split their risks between different ships, ports, and cargos. Cresquo f. Bonodominus de Montilio, for example, invested £8 on 23 April in a tractator's common investment to Bougie; on 8 May he invested another £8 4s in a tractator's common investment to Valencia.[56] Bonafossus Boc f. Astruc on 24 April sent in commenda coral worth £11 to Bougie and on 27 May sent in commenda 20 pounds of cloves and 20 pounds of nutmeg worth £10 to Majorca and the Barbary.[57] Again the sums invested were low, indicating that these Jewish individuals, whether investors or merchants, were of middling financial means.

Slightly over half of the Jewish commendators appear only once in Amalric's cartulary with no indication of profession or stature other than an occasional marker of citizenship in the commune of Marseille. They may perhaps have figured as tractators or commendators in other cartularies or other shipping seasons, but we have no way of knowing.

Overall the professionalization of the Jewish commendators is striking when compared with that of commendators generally in Genoa of the mid-twelfth century. Only 7 percent of the twelfth-century Genoese merchants acted as both commendator and tractator over the 10-year period running from 1155 to 1164.[58] This stands in marked contrast to the 16 percent of Jewish agents who acted as both commendator and tractator in four months. The numbers of course depend on the representative quality of the extant notarial registers. But scholars agree that a general shift between the twelfth and thirteenth centuries can be discerned, which was due to the progress of commercialization and the professionalization of long-distance trade. The Jewish merchants from Marseille appear to be part and parcel of this process of commercialization.

However, the relatively low value of the commendae made by Jewish investors suggests that these commendators were small-time investors and

COMMERCIALIZATION AMONG THE JEWISH MERCHANTS OF MARSEILLE 131

lesser merchants. The total value of investments made by Jewish commendators was about 3 percent of the total recorded in mixed money in Amalric's cartulary (£767 2s 11d of £23,921 2s 3d). The combined value of Jewish investments is therefore strikingly smaller than the percentage of commendae (6 percent) made by Jewish commendators. The highest Jewish investment, £142 10d, was a significant sum, twice the average value of commendae, but the lowest was a mere 10s.[59] The average Jewish investment (£26) was far below the average (£62) found in the cartulary (see Table 7.8).

As with Jewish tractators, the most popular destinations chosen by Jewish commendators were Bougie (the Maghreb) and Valencia (Spain), in marked contrast to the preferred destination of the Levant for Christian investors (see Table 7.9). Five Jewish commendators sent investments to northern Italy and Sicily, and these with Christian tractators.[60] Jewish commendators, more than the average, invested in merchandise over currency, particularly in spices.

To summarize, two-thirds of the tractators and one-third of the commendators can be identified as active merchants, while one-half of the commendators are more active in trade than would be true for small-time investors. Jewish commercial activity during the thirteenth-century

Table 7.8 Values of commendae recorded in mixed money

	No. commendae	High	Low	Average	Total
Jewish tractator	40	£100	10s	£17	£690.6.11
Jewish commendator	29	£142.0.10	10s	£26	£767.2.11
All commendae*	385			£62	£23,921.2.3

*Totals for "all commendae" are from Pryor, "Commenda" 412, Table 3, and include only commendae valued in mixed money, that is, 84 percent of the whole. The numbers for Jewish commendae are my own.

Table 7.9 Destination of Jewish commendae by agent

	Jewish tractator	Jewish commendator
Northern Italy	0	1
Kingdom of Sicily	0	4
Western Mediterranean	18	8
Maghreb	24	13
Levant	2	4

132   J.L. MELL

peak of the commercial revolution was solid and established, neither dominant nor nonexistent. The Marseille commendae do not represent the passive investments of moneylenders made prosperous by usury from consumption loans, but rather the active commercial activity of Jewish merchants of middling means. The Marseille records refute, at least for one Mediterranean community, the stereotype of the dominant early medieval Jewish merchant pushed out of trade at the beginning of the commercial revolution and the stereotype of the high medieval Jewish moneylender cut off from trade, crafts, and merchandising.

These documents likewise indicate that Jewish merchants were well integrated. Many were Marseille citizens, and many had close connections with Christian merchants. More importantly, if the commenda is considered the linchpin of the commercial revolution, then Jews' use of the Latin commenda must be considered evidence of their assimilation into the new forms of commercialization and active role in the commercial revolution. This "Jewish commercialization" is even more marked where both parties were Jewish. Significantly, over half of the Jewish commendae were contracted between Jewish commendators and Jewish tractators. This means that a Jewish commendator and a Jewish tractator sought out a Christian notary to have a Latin contract drawn up for use in a municipal (Christian) court, with Christian witnesses attesting the act lest the two Jewish partners have a disagreement. These Jewish individuals chose the Latin commenda over the rabbinic *iska*, the Christian municipal court over the rabbinic *bet din*. By contracting a commenda, Jews were participating in a much broader nexus of legal institutions, embedded within political and cultural bodies.[61] The commendae with Jewish tractators and commendators are thus a weighty testimony to Jewish acculturation in the economic, legal, and civic institutions of Marseille.

JEWISH MERCHANTS—LOOKING BEYOND 1248

The commendae from the spring of 1248 depict Jews already commercialized and active in the central movements of the commercial revolution. Yet the very qualities that make Amalric's cartulary invaluable are those that limit its usefulness. As the earliest extant cartulary for modern France, it stands alone. Around the brief but rich cross section of Marseille commercial life, darkness falls. Little can be discerned until well after the waning of Marseille's medieval commercial life. This gap leaves many questions unanswered: Was the Jewish presence in Marseille commercial life

COMMERCIALIZATION AMONG THE JEWISH MERCHANTS OF MARSEILLE 133

in the spring of 1248 characteristic for thirteenth-century Marseille? Was Marseille a unique and rare case in the thirteenth century or were there other Mediterranean Jewish communities active in long-distance trade?

Two other sets of documents from thirteenth-century Marseille can help determine the typical or atypical nature of the information in Amalric's register: the de Manduel charters spanning 1191–1263 and the notarial cartularies from 1278 to 1300. The charters of the de Manduel family, a prominent Marseille merchant family, record 73 commendae between the years 1191 and 1263 in which three men of the family, Stephen, Bernard, and John de Manduel, acted as commendator. In four commendae between 1226 and 1255, Jews were employed as tractators.[62] Six percent is a small but not insignificant number, for it accords with that of Amalric's register. A couple of other de Manduel charters, though written as a *mutuum* (loan) and an *emptio* (sale in which the buyer promises to pay in the future), appear to be commercial in character or to support a Jewish mercantile family.[63] For example, the first mutuum specifies the ship and destination to which the borrower, David f. Pesati, will carry the funds, just as for a commenda, and even adds the phrase *causa mercadarie* to make the commercial character of the mutuum absolutely clear.[64] The second mutuum appears to be a straight loan given, we are told, "gratis et pro amore," to the Daisona, wife of Salomon Ferrusol, and his son Ferrusol. But the Ferrusol family emerges 14 years later in Amalric's register as an active mercantile family, when two of Salomon's sons, Leon and Bonus Jusas, act as tractators for five commendae en route to Bougie on the St. Francis.[65] Was this a consumption loan to tide over the wife of Salomon while her husband was trading in another port, or was it perhaps used as capital by Leon and Bonus Jusas on one of their first voyages?

Although modern economic historians concerned with tracing commercialization and canon lawyers concerned with identifying usury may draw sharp distinctions between a loan (mutuum) and a commercial investment (commenda), the de Manduel merchants seem not to have regarded one type of borrowing as significantly different from another. For in a list of "money owed" (*pecunia debetur*) to the principal members of the family, namely, Stephen, Bernard, and John, the commendae and mutui, as well as other forms of contract, are all lumped together.[66] Similarly, the short notes made on the back of the charters, probably made to aid in quickly locating a charter, all use the bland language of a sum "owed" (*debet*) whether for a commenda or a mutuum.[67] The artificial division between merchant and moneylender, born out of the nineteenth-century German

134   J.L. MELL

Historical School's economic theories, has skewed much of the historical investigation of Jewish economic activity.

Among Marseille's late-thirteenth-century cartularies, only 68 commendae contracts are found, plus 14 indirect references to other commendae. This dearth of commercial information for late-thirteenth-century Marseille may be explained by the fact that the registers that survived belonged to notaries located outside the commercial center of the city, as well as by a general decline in the quantity of Marseille's commerce.[68] Jews appear a few times as agents in these commendae. Despite the small numbers, the documents demonstrate a continued mercantile presence for Marseille Jews.[69]

Jewish mercantile activity in Marseille continued into the fourteenth and fifteenth centuries as well. Salvet and Gassonet Durand made numerous voyages to Majorca between 1325 and 1340; Astrug Moise received commendae from the most important merchants of his time; together with Mosson Salomon, he sailed a route with multiple stops in the western Mediterranean in 1391; Marseille Jews had frequent commercial contact with Sardinia, concentrating particularly in the trade of coral.[70] Early in the fourteenth century, Bondavid, made famous by Joseph Shatzmiller's microhistory *Shylock Reconsidered*, made his fortune in maritime trade of spices and cloth.[71] At the end of the fourteenth century, a number of Jews were active in Mediterranean trade: Léon Passapayre, Abraham Bonehore, Abraham and Gardet de Bédarride, Cregut Profach, and above all Venguessete de Monteil.[72] Édouard Baratier, the historian who uncovered this evidence, emphasizes several important facts: Jewish merchants were of middling status, and they formed only a small group among the Jews of Marseille. Jews were more prominent as doctors, craftsmen especially in the working of coral, and middlemen in the internal trade in wool, tartar, and almonds, while Marseille Jews were rarely prominent in banking and moneychanging.[73]

The evidence, piecemeal though it is, suggests that Jewish commercial activity in Marseille extended over several hundred years, persisting through a half-century of economic upswing during the commercial revolution and a subsequent contraction in western Europe's economy. Marseille's Jewish merchants were neither the wealthiest nor the most prominent merchants, nor was international commerce the most common profession among Marseille Jews. The rather average, typical, and mediocre status of Marseille Jewry supports all the more the thesis of a Jewish commercialization consonant with that of Christian Europeans.

COMMERCIALIZATION AMONG THE JEWISH MERCHANTS OF MARSEILLE 135

But does the commercial activity of Marseille Jewry represent merely a carryover of early medieval Jewish mercantile activity, a late, rare bloom, which escaped the freeze that had already fallen on Jewish commerce throughout Europe? For it has long been an axiom that by the late middle ages Jews were excluded from long-distance international trade in the Mediterranean, principally by the Italian merchant republics. There is some truth in this. For the Genoese did not permit Jews to live in their town at all, and the Venetians excluded Jews from trade to the eastern Mediterranean by prohibiting them from traveling on Venetian galleys. Even Marseille Jews seem to have had little trade with the Levant.[74] But even this traditional picture has begun to be modified.

Salo Baron assembled diffuse references to Jewish trade, seaborne and land based, in his 1967 volume on Jewish economic history in the high and late middle ages.[75] Particularly prominent were Jewish merchants from Aragon, the Balearic Islands, and Portugal. But Baron studiously avoided challenging the conventional paradigm, though the facts he collected stretched the conventional narrative to the breaking point. That task was left to Eliyahu Ashtor.

From the notarial archives of Venice, Sicily, and the southern Italian mainland, Ashtor culled much data on Jews in fifteenth-century Mediterranean trade.[76] He has shown that Jews in areas not under the control of the Italian merchant cities of Venice and Genoa, such as the northern coastal towns of Tripoli and Tunisia, were actively trading with Sicily; the Jews of Sicily were trading with North African ports; and the Jews of Apulia were trading with Venice. Even the Jews in Venetian and Genoese dominions overseas, such as Crete and Corfu, Chios and Famagusta, respectively, were active in trade. Venetian subjects were even granted the privileged status of *fidelis* (faithful), a lesser form of citizenship which offered Jewish merchants the protection extended to Venetian merchants proper. Fifteenth-century Mediterranean Jewish merchants exported grain, cloth, cheese, and spices to Tunisia and Tripoli, Malta, and Sardinia; they invested in commendae and acted as tractators for other commendators; three Jews of Syracuse even founded a company for export to North Africa in 1486. Indeed "in the central basin of the Mediterranean [there was] no maritime line on which Jewish merchants were not active."[77] Fifteenth-century Jewish merchants traded both within the Venetian and Genoese commercial empires and with the Muslim countries of the Near East, moving back and forth between these two cultural spheres.

The sole branch of maritime trade from which Venice excluded Jews and foreigners was the Levantine trade, that is, trade between Venice proper or the Venetian dominions in the Adriatic and the Levant.[78] By the sixteenth century, even this prohibition was removed in the wake of Iberian Jews' mercantile activity in the Ottoman Empire, as the research of Benjamin Ravid on the "Jewish merchants of Venice" has shown.[79] Ravid's tongue-in-cheek title pokes fun at the stereotyped dichotomy between the Christian merchant and the Jewish moneylender epitomized in Shakespeare's *The Merchant of Venice*, to which the title of the concluding chapter in this book also alludes.

In light of the evidence for Jewish mercantile activity in thirteenth-century Aragon, in fifteenth-century Mediterranean ports including those under Venetian and Genoese dominion, and in sixteenth-century Venice itself, the Jewish merchants of Marseille cannot be considered a unique instance, or a vestige of an early medieval phenomenon. Ashtor has argued for fifteenth-century Italy, as I have for thirteenth-century Marseille, and Ravid for sixteenth-century Venice, that documentary evidence strongly contradicts the conventional image of the medieval Jew as the moneylender. Ashtor's conclusions for the late middle ages are all the more true for the thirteenth-century commercial revolution: the Jewish merchants of Marseille were economically assimilated into the expanding Mediterranean maritime trade of the commercial revolution. And this is as one would expect. For during the economic expansion of the commercial revolution, Jews should have had more openings for commerce than during the fifteenth century, a period of economic contraction when the great Italian maritime republics had consolidated their power. The data certainly suggests a long-term presence for European Jews in Mediterranean trade extending from the commercial revolution through the economic decline of the late medieval and early modern periods.

I have argued that the use of commenda contracts by Marseille Jews reflects Jews' assimilation in the new European commercial currents of the thirteenth century. The significance of this fact becomes clearer when the commendae are compared with the letters of the Geniza merchants from Fatimid Egypt. Jessica Goldberg's recent study *Trade and Institutions in the Medieval Mediterranean: The Geniza Merchants and Their Business World* corrects inflated notions of Jewish dominance in long-distance trade and presumptions of religious cohesion in cross-cultural trade.[80] Unlike the early modern European Jewish merchants of Livorno studied recently by Francesca Trivellato in *The Familiarity of Strangers*,[81] the Geniza merchants

COMMERCIALIZATION AMONG THE JEWISH MERCHANTS OF MARSEILLE 137

were not cross-cultural agents, but embedded in their local Islamic environment. Geniza merchants resembled their Islamic counterparts in status, reputation, and family structures, and often collaborated with them. Their Jewishness marked them, but it was only one among a range of factors that might have aided a merchant in creating a trade network. The most important factors were a merchant's reputation, knowledge, and connections. Relationships of reciprocal agency, known as *suhba*, stood at the heart of the Geniza merchants' trade networks. Two merchants would designate each other as unpaid agents for particular goods as often as they liked, with the understanding that the service would be repaid with a like service within a finite period of time.

Earlier scholars have contrasted the *suhba* with the European commenda, describing the former as informal and communal, and the latter as formal and individualistic. Goldberg rejects this characterization, noting that the *suhba* was "informal" only in that it was unwritten, and unremunerated only in that it did not receive monetary pay. Each transaction was legally binding on an agent, was upheld by both Jewish and Islamic courts, and necessitated reciprocal services. The network itself also "informally" reinforced the system of reciprocal services through the high value placed on reputation. Geniza merchants also used partnerships and junior associates to manage their business. But, Goldberg argues, Geniza merchants found reciprocal agency a more effective institution for managing labor and compensation, because they retained full property rights at all times and had legal protection against agents' misconduct.

Consequently, Goldberg concludes, European merchants did not have a monopoly on individualistic pursuit of profit or institutions that guaranteed trust. Individualism and institutionally based trust were present in the Islamic Mediterranean as well, but configured differently. The key difference determining the form of contract lay in the political structures of Islamic empires and European city-states, and the position of merchants within them. Italian merchant guilds were the political elites of their city-states and therefore controlled the means of violence; their ships were used equally to trade, make war, and prey upon other Mediterranean ships. Conversely they lacked a legal infrastructure beyond their own city-state. Islamic merchants were not part of the political elite and had no control over the state's monopoly on violence. But they could rely on a legal infrastructure that spanned the Islamic Mediterranean. These differences explain European preference for the commenda and Islamic preference for *suhba*. In the last analysis, the Mediterranean economy was not structured by its ecological unity or diversity.[82] Rather, local and long-distance exchanges were enmeshed in trade networks sustained by cultural, legal, and political institutions defined in macro-zones that aligned with Islamic or European spheres of influence.

The Geniza merchants did not forge ties with Jews in Latin Europe, because Geniza merchants relied upon Islamic institutions with which European Jews had no ties. Jewishness was but one factor among others that may have aided Geniza merchants in making business connections within the Islamic environment. But it neither predetermined nor ensured such ties, and it played no role beyond the Islamic zone. The Marseille Jewish merchants similarly were embedded within a European cultural and institutional framework. Their mercantile trade relied on the political and legal infrastructures of the Euro-Mediterranean city-state and its civic courts. Hence, the European merchants, whether Jewish or Christian, found the commenda the most useful form of partnership, just as the Fatimid merchants, whether Jewish or Muslim, found the *suḥba* the most useful form of partnership. There was no religious cohesion that trumped local institutions. The determining factor in the medieval Mediterranean was one's inclusion in a macro-zone defined by legal and political institutions. No simple dichotomy between gift exchange and profit exchange, or between Islamic *suḥba* and European commenda, can be maintained, as the next chapter will discuss.

NOTES

1. The term *lex mercatoria* suggests a coherency that cannot be assumed for what was a local and piecemeal customary law. On the development of European commercial law from the early middle ages, see: John Pryor, *Business Contracts of Medieval Provence: Selected Notulae from the Cartulary of Giraud Amalric of Marseilles, 1248* (Toronto, 1981), 1–19.

2. Richard Emery, *The Jews of Perpignan in the Thirteenth Century* (New York, 1959). Emery's study is an excellent one, but unfortunately, because of the strength of the stereotype on Jewish moneylending, it is open to being misread as applying throughout medieval Europe, though the sources are good only for a single town during 25 years. It is essential to remember the following: (1) Emery himself framed his study as a balance to the works of earlier French Jewish historians, such as Gustave Saige and Jean

Regné, who emphasized Jews as merchants, craftsmen, and land-owners. And (2) Perpignan, though part of modern-day France, was under Aragonese control at this time. It was certainly not representative of Capetian France, where Jewish moneylending had been outlawed. In fact, the immigration of Jewish moneylenders to Perpignan, revealed by Emery's study, may have been a result of the eradication of Jewish moneylending in France under Louis IX.

3. For a recent attempt to recapture the full range of Jewish occupations, see: Michael Toch, *The Economic History of European Jews: Late Antiquity and Early Middle Ages* (Leiden, 2013). On Jewish doctors, see: Joseph Shatzmiller, *Jews, Medicine, and Medieval Society* (Berkeley, 1994). On rabbis and the professionalization of the rabbinate, see: Yedidya Alter Dinari, *The Rabbis of Germany and Austria at the Close of the Middle Ages: Their Conceptions and Halachic Writings* [Hebrew] (Jerusalem, 1984); Avraham Grossman, *The Early Sages of Ashkenaz* [Hebrew] (Jerusalem, 1988); Simon Schwarzfuchs, *A Concise History of the Rabbinate* (Oxford, 1993); E.E. Urbach, *The Tosaphists: Their History, Writings and Methods* [Hebrew] (Jerusalem, 1954); Israel Jacob Yuval, *Scholars in Their Time: The Religious Leadership of German Jewry in the Late Middle Ages* [Hebrew] (Jerusalem, 1988). On Jews in crafts, see the references in Léon Poliakov, *Jewish Bankers and the Holy See from the Thirteenth to the Seventeenth Century* (London, 1977), 10. On Jewish agriculture and land ownership, see: Toni Oelsner, "The Economic and Social Condition of the Jews of Southwestern Germany in the 13th and 14th Centuries," Toni Oelsner Collection, AR 3970, Box 1, Folder 8, Leo Baeck Institute, New York; Gustave Saige, *Les Juifs de Languedoc antérieurement au XIVe siècle* (Paris, 1881); Jean Regné, "Étude sur la condition des Juifs de Narbonne du Ve au XIVe siècle," *Revue des études juives* 55 (1908): 1–36, 221–43; 58 (1909): 75–105, 200–25; 59 (1910): 59–89; and 61 (1911): 228–54. On Jewish vintners, see: Haym Soloveitchik, *Yayin bi-yeme ha-benayim* (Jerusalem, 2008). On Jewish merchants, see: Salo Baron, *A Social and Religious History of the Jews*, 2nd ed., vol. 12, *Economic Catalyst* (New York, 1967), 100–31; Eliyahu Ashtor, "The Jews in Mediterranean Trade in the Fifteenth Century," in his *The Jews and the Mediterranean Economy 10th–15th Centuries* (London, 1983), part VII; Eliyahu Ashtor, "New Data for the History of

Levantine Jewries in the Fifteenth Century," *Bulletin of the Institute of Jewish Studies* 3 (1975): 67–102; Benjamin Ravid, "The First Charter of the Jewish Merchants of Venice, 1589," *AJS Review* 2 (1977): 187–222; Benjamin Ravid, "An Introduction to the Charters of the Jewish Merchants of Venice," in *The Mediterranean and the Jews: Society, Culture and Economy in Early Modern Times,* ed. Elliott Horowitz and Moises Orfali (Ramat-Gan, 2002), 2:203–48.

4. Robert Lopez and Irving Raymond, *Medieval Trade in the Mediterranean World: Illustrative Documents* (New York, 1955), 174. Cf. John Pryor, "Commenda: The Operation of the Contract in Long Distance Commerce at Marseilles during the Thirteenth Century," *Journal of European Economic History* 13 no. 2 (1984): 397; John Pryor, "Mediterranean Commerce in the Middle Ages: A Voyage under Contract of Commenda," *Viator* 14 (1983): 133–94.

5. For the best brief summaries of the commenda, see: Lopez and Raymond, *Medieval Trade*, 174; N.J.G. Pounds, *An Economic History of Medieval Europe*, 2nd ed. (New York, 1994), 422–5; Pryor, "Mediterranean Commerce."

6. E.H. Byrne, "Commercial Contracts of the Genoese in the Syrian Trade of the Twelfth Century," *Quarterly Journal of Economics* 31 no. 1 (1916): 128–70. See also: his *Genoese Shipping in the Twelfth and Thirteenth Centuries* (Cambridge, MA, 1930) and his "Genoese Trade with Syria in the Twelfth Century," *American Historical Review* 25 (1920): 191–219.

7. John Pryor, "The Origins of the Commenda Contract," *Speculum* 52 no. 1 (1977): 5–37; Abraham Udovitch, "At the Origins of the Western Commenda: Islam, Israel, Byzantium?" *Speculum* 37 no. 2 (1962): 198–207.

8. I follow the opinion of Pryor and Lopez. The citation is from Lopez and Raymond, *Medieval Trade*, 174.

9. Hillel Gamoran, tracing the development of rabbinic law in these three areas, has suggested that rabbinic authorities responded to the "needs of the Commercial Revolution" (Hillel Gamoran, "Investing for Profit: A Study of *Iska* up to the Time of Rabbi Abraham Ben David of Posquieres," *Hebrew Union College Annual* 70–1 (1999–2000): 153–65, esp. 156. See also: Hillel Gamoran, "Lending—No, Investing—Yes: Development of the *Iska* Law

from the 12th to the 15th Centuries," *Jewish Law Association Studies. XII: The Zutphen Conference Volume*, ed. Hillel Gamoran (Binghamton, 2002), 79–93). Gamoran is the first to study the *iska* in its own right. Previously secondary literature has treated the *iska* only as a possible origin for the commenda, and therefore as a static and unchanging legal institution. See: Udovitch, "At the Origins of the Western Commenda"; Pryor, "The Origins of the Commenda Contract"; Irving Agus, *The Heroic Age of Franco-German Jewry* (New York, 1969), 127–30.

10. Rather than imagining the *iska* as a continuous practice transmitting a "pure" halachic form, it may be that we should see the medieval *iska* as more of a theoretical possibility latent for medieval European Jews through its presence in the Talmud, as were the concepts of Roman law for contemporary Christians. With the convergence of the cultural renaissance and commericialization of the twelfth and thirteenth centuries, the *iska* may have been developed in practice in relation to European commercialization just as Roman legal concepts did. In other words, local customary partnerships might have shaped the medieval development of the *iska*.

11. Pryor, *Business Contracts: The Cartulary of Giraud Amalric*, 20–2.

12. M.T. Clancy, *From Memory to Written Record: England 1066–1307* (Cambridge, 1979).

13. Archives Communales de la Ville de Marseille, Serie II, I, edited and published by Louis Blancard as *Les Notules Commerciales d'Almaric Notaire Marseillais du XIII siècle*, in *Documents inédits sur le commerce de Marseille au Moyen Age*, 2 vols. (Marseille, 1884–5), 1:261–417 and 2:7–367. (Cited hereafter as Blancard, ed., *Notules*. All citations reference the document number, not the volume and page numbers.) I have been able to consult the original manuscript owing to the generosity of the Archives of Marseille, which provided me with a microfilm of Amalric's register. John Pryor republished selected *notulae* in *Business Contracts: The Cartulary of Giraud Amalric*. The following discussion relies on Pryor, introduction to ibid., 31–51.

14. Pryor, "Commenda," 397–401. All three were edited in Blancard, *Documents inédits sur le commerce de Marseille*. Pryor also uncovered additional documents: *Business Contracts: The Cartulary of Giraud Amalric*, 41.

15. Robert Lopez, "The Unexplored Wealth of the Notarial Archives in Pisa and Lucca," in *Mélanges d'histoire du Moyen Age dédiés à la mèmoire de Louis Halphen* (Paris, 1951), 417–32.

16. Hilmar C. Krueger, "Genoese Merchants, Their Partnerships and Investments, 1155–1164," in *Studi in onore di Armando Sapori* (Milan, 1957), 255–71.

17. Isidore Loeb, "Les Négociants Juifs à Marseille au milieu du XIIIe siècle," *Revue des études juives* 16 (1888): 73–83.

18. Pryor, "Commenda," 431–3. The presence of Jews comes out particularly clearly in his analysis of commendators' and tractators' place of origin, when Pryor oddly lumps Jews together as a group, rather than incorporating them in the various places of origin. Pryor discusses the Jewish agents at more length in his introduction to a partial edition of Amalric's register: Pryor, *Business Contracts: The Cartulary of Giraud Amalric*, 86–8. Unfortunately he bends the facts to the grand narratives of Jews as outcasts, failing to recognize that the Marseille evidence contradicts these old tropes.

19. The most important study of the medieval Marseille Jewish community is that of Adolphe Crémieux, "Les Juifs de Marseille au Moyen Age," *Revue des études juives* 46 (1903): 1–47, 246–68. See also: Baron, *Social and Religious History of the Jews*, 12:104–5.

20. Emery, *Jews of Perpignan*, 6–9. Emery offers Giraud d'Amalric's register from Marseille as an example of this danger and downplays the significance of the Jewish commenda contracts found within it (ibid., 5–6, note 1). While Emery is correct in cautioning against using one sole register as a representative sample, he unjustly dismisses the positive evidence of Jewish commenda contracts contained in this register.

21. Many of the contracts in the registry are crossed out, signaling that they were completed. I have checked the Jewish commendae in the manuscript and found most marked as completed. On Amalric's method and its relationship to the later Marseille regulations, see: Pryor, *Business Contracts: The Cartulary of Giraud d'Amalric*, 43–5.

22. On the Jewish community of Marseille, see: Crémieux, "Les Juifs de Marseille"; Pryor, *Business Contracts: The Cartulary of Giraud Amalric*, 86–8; and Édouard Baratier and Félix Reynaud, *Histoire du commerce de Marseille* (Paris, 1951), 2:89–96. On the history of Marseille more generally, see: Édouard Baratier, *Histoire de Marseille* (Toulouse, 1973); Victor-L. Bourrilly, *Essai sur l'histoire*

politique de Marseille des origines à 1264 (Aix-en-Provence, 1925); Raoul Busquet, *Histoire de Marseille*, ed. Pierre Guiral (Paris, 1977). The legal culture and documents of Marseille have been explored in several recent works: Daniel Lord Smail, *The Consumption of Justice: Emotions, Publicity, and Legal Culture in Marseille, 1264–1423* (Ithaca, 2003) and *Imaginary Cartographies: Possession and Identity in Late Medieval Marseille* (Ithaca, 1999); as well as, Susan McDonough, *Witnesses, Neighbors, and Community in Late Medieval Marseille* (New York, 2013).

23. On the synagogues, see: Daniel Lord Smail, "The Two Synagogues of Medieval Marseillie: Documentary Evidence" *Revue des études juives* 154 (1995): 115–24. On the Jewish quarter in the cartographic imaginary, see: Smail, *Imaginary Cartographies*.

24. Loeb, "Les Négociants Juifs à Marseille," 80–1.

25. Crémieux, "Les Juifs de Marseille," 68, 86–8.

26. Blancard, ed., *Notules*, no. 597.

27. See, for instance: ibid., nos. 395, 518, 567, 891.

28. Krueger, "Genoese Merchants," 259–62. See also: his "Genoese Merchants, Their Associations and Investments, 1155–1230," in *Studi in onore di Amintore Fanfani* (Milan, 1962), 415–26.

29. The average for Jewish tractators can be calculated in two ways, because of the unusual partnership between three Jewish tractators. If the number of commendae is counted once for each agent, the average for Jewish tractators is 4.8 as opposed to 1.9 for tractators in general. If the commendae of the Jewish partners are counted only once, the average is 3.3, a number still far higher than the average.

30. Citizenship is noted by Amalric: Blancard, ed., *Notules*, no. 683.

31. Ibid., nos. 658, 659.

32. Ibid., nos. 683, 684, 687, 693, 694, 695, 696.

33. Ibid., nos. 704, 705, 759.

34. Ibid., nos. 415, 618, 628, 647.

35. Ibid., no. 697; and Pryor, *Business Contracts: The Cartulary of Giraud Amalric*, no. 84.

36. Pryor, *Business Contracts: The Cartulary of Giraud Amalric*, 87.

37. Blancard, ed., *Notules*, no. 683.

38. Ibid., nos. 388, 411; f. 55r, 58r. Both commendae are later crossed out as completed. It is unclear how to account for this discrepancy.

39. Ibid., no. 684.

40. Krueger, "Genoese Merchants," 263.

41. The average for all commendae in mixed money is taken from Pryor, "Commenda," 412, Table 3. These contracts represent a significant number of the whole, for 84 percent of the commendae in Amalric's cartulary were valued in mixed money.

42. The following information pertains to the commendators as well, though only half of these commendators are Jewish.

43. Compare my Table 7.4 to Pryor's Table 6 in "Commenda," 418–29.

44. Loeb, "Les négociants Juifs à Marseille," 80–1.

45. Pryor, "Commenda," 431.

46. Byrne, "Commercial Contracts of the Genoese in the Syrian Trade of the Twelfth Century," 158–9.

47. Several contracts were followed by others in which tractators took merchandise or coin bound to the same port, but on another ship. My hunch is that the tractators were reducing their risk by sending goods on two ships to the same port.

48. I have checked the manuscript carefully for marginal comments indicating that these commenda were cancelled prior to the voyage or moved to another ship. Because I found none, and on the contrary found evidence that at least some were still "open accounts," I have concluded that the merchants were splitting their risks by sending merchandise to a single port on two ships. See, for example: no. 647 on f. 89v. On Marseille rules for cancellation enacted in 1253 and Amalric's methods, see: Pryor, *Business Contracts: The Cartulary of Giraud Amalric*, 43–5.

49. Pryor, "Commenda," 403, Table 1.

50. Blancard, ed., *Notules*, nos. 388, 411 and 65, 127, 140, 277, respectively.

51. Pryor, "Commenda," 399–401.

52. Blancard, ed., *Notules*, nos. 576, 577.

53. Pryor, "Commenda," 412, Table 3. The average value is £62, calculated from 84 percent of Amalric's contracts which are valued in *monete miscue*.

54. Blancard, ed., *Notules*, nos. 499, 500, 578, 598.

55. Ibid., nos. 415, 618, 628, 647, 658, 659, 683, 684, 687, 693, 694, 695, 696, 697, 704, 705, 759.

56. Ibid., nos. 578, 694.

57. Ibid., nos. 591, 807. The commendator Jacob f. Astruc Maurel also made two commendae: ibid., nos. 572, 695.

COMMERCIALIZATION AMONG THE JEWISH MERCHANTS OF MARSEILLE 145

58. Krueger, "Genoese Merchants," 263–4.
59. Blancard, ed., *Notules*, nos. 576, 628.
60. Ibid., nos. 415, 576.
61. On the regulation of the commenda by civic law, see: Pryor, "Mediterranean Commerce." On the legal institutions and developments within which the commenda was embedded, see: Pryor, *Business Contracts: The Cartulary of Giraud Amalric*, 1–88.
62. Blancard, ed., *Les Chartes Commerciales des Manduel*, in *Documents inédits sur le commerce de Marseille*, nos. 17, 61, 81, 126. (References are to document numbers.)
63. Ibid., nos. 37, 55, 57, 60; see also no. 113, which renegotiates nos. 55 and 57. On *mutuum* and *emptio*, see: Pryor, *Business Contracts: The Cartulary of Giraud Amalric*, 204–6 and 174–5, respectively.
64. Blancard, ed., *Chartes commerciales*, no. 37. This mutuum, like many others in the collection, is made to husband and wife, but only the husband is mentioned as traveling to Ceuta on the ship Puelle Grandulphi Arfure.
65. Blancard, ed., *Notules*, nos. 572, 586, 603, 618, 621.
66. Blancard, ed., *Chartes commerciales*, nos. 137, 138, 139.
67. Cf.: ibid., nos. 17 and 113.
68. Pryor, "Commenda," 400–1.
69. Blancard, ed., *Pièces commerciales diverses*, in *Documents inédits sur le commerce de Marseille*, nos. 14, 15. (References are to document numbers.)
70. Baratier and Reynaud, *Histoire du commerce de Marseille*, 2:92–3.
71. Ibid., 2:95; Joseph Shatzmiller, *Shylock Reconsidered: Jews, Moneylending, and Medieval Society* (Berkeley, 1990), 28–35.
72. Baratier and Reynaud, *Histoire du commerce de Marseille*, 2:96.
73. Ibid., 2:89–96.
74. I follow closely here the comments of Eliyahu Ashtor in his "New Data for the History of Levantine Jewries in the Fifteenth Century," esp. 68–9.
75. Baron, *Social and Religious History of the Jews*, 12:100–31, esp. 12:104–7.
76. Ashtor, "Jews in Mediterranean Trade," vii, and "New Data for the History of Levantine Jewries in the Fifteenth Century."
77. Ashtor, "Jews in Mediterranean Trade," 444.
78. Ibid., 449.

79. Ravid, "The First Charter of the Jewish Merchants of Venice, 1589." See also his other articles on the Jewish merchants in Venice: "The Jewish Mercantile Settlement of Twelfth and Thirteenth Century Venice: Reality or Conjecture?" *AJS Review* 1 (1976): 201–25; and Ravid, "An Introduction to the Charters of the Jewish Merchants of Venice."

80. Jessica Goldberg, *Trade and Institutions in the Medieval Mediterranean: The Geniza Merchants and Their Business World* (Cambridge, 2012).

81. Francesca Trivellato, *The Familiarity of Strangers: The Sephardic Diaspora, Livorno, and Cross-Cultural Trade in the Early Modern Period* (New Haven, 2009).

82. Fernand Braudel, *The Mediterranean and the Mediterranean World in the Age of Philip II* (New York, 1972–3); contra Braudel, see: Peregrine Horden and Nicholas Purcell, *The Corrupting Sea: A Study of Mediterranean History* (Oxford, 2000).

CHAPTER 8

From Gift Exchange to Profit Economy Reconsidered: Toward a Cultural History of Money

Das Geld ist der eifrige Gott Israels, vor welchem kein andrer Gott bestehen darf. Das Geld erniedrigt alle Götter des Menschen, – und verwandelt sie in eine Waare. Das Geld ist der allgemeine, für sich selbst constituirte Werth aller Dinge. Es hat daher die ganze Welt, die Menschenwelt, wie die Natur, ihres eigenthümlichen Werthes beraubt. Das Geld ist das dem Menschen entfremdete Wesen seiner Arbeit und seines Daseins und dies fremde Wesen beherrscht ihn, und er betet es an.—Karl Marx, "Zur Judenfrage"[1]

Chapter 3 discussed three classics in medieval economic history that appeared in the 1970s: Robert Lopez's *The Commercial Revolution of the Middle Ages, 950–1350* (1971), Georges Duby's *Early Growth of the European Economy* (1973), and Lester Little's *Religious Poverty and the Profit Economy* (1978).[2] Lopez was presented as representative of the broad and path-breaking scholarship in medieval economic history in the mid-twentieth century, and his monograph *Commercial Revolution of the Middle Ages* as a synthesis of the scholarship on the high medieval expansion of trade, markets, and money by a generation of medieval economic and business historians on both sides of the Atlantic. Duby and Little were discussed as representatives of the trajectory flowing from Polanyi (and Mauss), which expanded the definition of economy beyond the categories of money, market, and trade. Duby in his *Early Growth of the European Economy* applied the sociological concept of "gift exchange" to early medieval economy, and in the conclusion contrasted this early

© The Author(s) 2018
J.L. Mell, *The Myth of the Medieval Jewish Moneylender*,
DOI 10.1007/978-3-319-34186-6_3

147

148   J.L. MELL

medieval "gift economy" with Lopez' commercial "takeoff" of the high middle ages. Little adopted Duby's juxtaposition of early medieval "gift economy" and high medieval "profit economy" as the starting point for a study of the social and cultural effects of the commercial revolution.[3] Little posited that the radical economic transition from a gift economy to a profit economy generated a disjuncture between the new socioeconomic realities and a traditional, unresponsive clergy and theology resulting in a "spiritual crisis of medieval urban culture."[4]

For Little, medieval antisemitism was a major piece of evidence for this crisis. Duby and Little both positioned money as a central, causal agent for the emergence of a new "profit economy," understood as synonymous with Lopez' commercial revolution. Money, in their accounts, both effected *and* symbolized the "profit motive," becoming a locus for anxiety among medieval Christians over a new money economy. (This concept of money as an abstract, impersonal element dissolving social bonds came directly from Max Weber and the Younger Historical School of Political Economy.) For Little, "the Jew came to be increasingly associated in Christian minds with the Commercial Revolution." He explained the association in this way: "the Jew was *so* identified with the money trade, and the money trade was such a source of uneasiness to Christians that the Christians just reversed the identification: they identified the entire money trade with the Jews."[5] Little retained Roscher's concept of an "economic function of the Jews," but transformed that function into one of a scapegoat for Christian guilt: Jews "were being blamed by Christians for doing what countless Christians were doing, but without being able to admit the fact."[6] It is ironic that the concept of gift exchange, originally formulated by Mauss to counter the Historical School's theory of economic stages, has been the means, when paired with "profit economy," for the reintroduction into medieval history of the Weberian/Sombartian version of the economic stages.[7]

The paradigm of early medieval gift economy against high medieval profit economy set forth by Duby and Little continues to stimulate scholarship and spur critical engagement among a wide range of medievalists, although not typically among economic historians.[8] Since 2000, four collections of articles have been published around these themes, with contributions from over 40 medievalists across Eurasia and North America representing disciplines as diverse as art history, English, Romance languages, history, music, and paleography.[9] The themes and chronologies evident in the titles of the two most recent volumes demonstrate

FROM GIFT EXCHANGE TO PROFIT ECONOMY RECONSIDERED... 149

the continuing force of the paradigm: *The Languages of Gift in the Early Middle Ages* and *Money, Morality, and Culture in Late Medieval and Early Modern Europe*.[10] The intellectual problem defined by the editors of *Money, Morality, and Culture* is set within Little's framework: "this volume explores the contradictions, fears, and anxieties that arose as capitalist values competed with traditional classical and Christian ethics."[11] The editors refer repeatedly to "the developing monetary economy." They see "money itself in the late Middle Ages" as the target of "theological condemnation" and regard Christian ethics as the site of contestation.[12]

Occasionally, individual contributors challenge the paradigm and raise new questions. Chris Wickham makes the most explicit attack in the conclusion to *The Languages of Gift in the Early Middle Ages*, where he argues:

> We see no significant difference between the economic structures of the early and central Middle Ages, even if the eleventh century was rather more economically active than before....There was commerce in both; negotiation in both; contract in both. It is not only unhelpful and misleading, but pointless, to exoticize the pre-1050 period, to turn it into the only period without the profit motive, or whichever other aspect of 'modernity' any given scholar wishes to privilege.[13]

Wickham builds on an earlier critique by Florin Curta that challenges the concept of an early medieval gift economy.[14] But this critique has not yet seeped fully into the scholarship on the early middle ages. Nor has it carried beyond early medieval scholarship to that on the high middle ages, despite the continued appearance of studies on money, markets, and trade in early medieval Europe.[15] Rather, historians of high medieval Europe are all too comfortable with the notion of the "merchant's function as a hero of a self-centered rationality."[16] Even less has the linkage of Jews with profit economy been challenged: the only substantive critique has come from Toni Oelsner and Giacomo Todeschini, as discussed in earlier chapters.

This chapter contributes to these critiques by applying recent cross-cultural anthropological studies of money and the morality of exchange to the concepts of gift economy/profit economy. I focus on "value," which cuts across the binaries gift/profit, human/divine, moral/amoral, Christian/Jew, which structure older scholarship. I argue that neither "money" nor the "money economy" *in and of themselves* generated anxiety among the medieval Christian authors. Rather, high medieval religious

150   J.L. MELL

authors had a sophisticated ideology of value that recognized economic value, but insisted upon moral value tied to that economic value. Their anxiety lay in the potential for a "disequilibrium" between these two values. They resolved the difficulty by constructing an elaborate divine economy in which money functioned as a Maussian gift that carried one's moral value with it even as it circulated among others.[17]

The evidence for this argument is taken from collections of *exempla* (short moral tales) produced in the high medieval period principally by the Franciscan and Dominican clergy important in Little's analysis of a moral crisis. The genre of exempla flowered in the second half of the twelfth and first half of the thirteenth centuries along with a new interest in preaching to the laity.[18] Exempla, though akin to folktales, are distinct in being shaped for a specific didactic end and in being treated as factual reports of events (from this derives their didactic force). From the mid-thirteenth century on, authors and collectors were often mendicants who had a particular interest in economic issues. These collections may have been used in the usury campaigns discussed in Chapter 6 to pepper sermons preaching moral reform. Two of the earliest texts, however, are not by mendicant preachers. They are the early-thirteenth-century texts *Sefer Ḥasidim* (The Book of the Pious) and *Dialogus Miraculorum* (The Dialogue on Miracles). *Sefer Ḥasidim* is a Hebrew collection composed in the vicinity of Regensburg principally by Judah the Pious (Yehudah he-Ḥasid), who has been compared with Francis of Assisi.[19] *Sefer Ḥasidim* is one of our few full-fledged collections of Hebrew exempla, though Hebrew exempla can be found scattered in *responsa*, texts on customs, ethics, and mysticism.[20] *Dialogus Miraculorum* is a Cistercian collection composed by Caesarius of Heisterbach, in the vicinity of Cologne, as a teaching aid for novices.[21] But many other Latin collections will be drawn on here, which come from across western Europe and over a century and a half or more. The diffuse geographical and chronological range means that the exempla speak with a multiplicity of voices (which the academic argument here tends to mute in its quest for larger patterns). Yet, alongside their diversity, the exempla have a cultural unity owing to the genre itself. They are tales told and retold, circulating far and wide, as they move from one collection to another. When recorded by literate clerics, the tales become part of literate culture preserved in a collection of exempla. A collection was meant to be pillaged by preachers, and thereby the tales were transported back into oral culture. An exempla collection thus represents a richer, more multivocal cultural artifact than the elite texts of high theology or philosophy.

FROM GIFT EXCHANGE TO PROFIT ECONOMY RECONSIDERED... 151

This makes exempla an ideal source for exploring cultural ideas about money and profit.

The first part of this chapter examines the cultural ideas about money in the moral texts of high medieval Christian authors, particularly in regard to moral value, the danger of "bad" moral value, and the place of penance in this moral economy. The second part demonstrates the parallels to these Christian ideas in the text of *Sefer Ḥasidim*. These texts, I argue, reveal complex concepts of value that cut across binary categories of gift and profit. Contrary to Little (and the editors of *Money, Morality, and Culture*), I suggest that money is not feared as an abstract holder of value, anonymous and impersonal, generating an anonymous and impersonal profit economy. Rather the medieval authors considered here recognize metallic currency as an abstract placeholder of economic value and argue against its potential to be anonymous and impersonal. Both the Christian monastics and the Jewish author(s) of *Sefer Ḥasidim* argue against the assumption that "a coin is a coin is a coin" by insisting on a moral value that inheres in coins. Moral value is determined by the mode of acquisition governed by the theological definitions of just and unjust price.[22] Money with "bad" moral value is dangerous, both to its owner and to those through whose hands it passes. In its capacity to acquire moral value, money acts like a classic Maussian gift, taking on the personal, moral characteristics of its owners. What these medieval religious texts feared was the potential for a disjuncture, a disequilibrium, between economic value and moral value. Money in this medieval thinking is then neither a causal agent nor a symbolic representation of profit economy. This refined reading of anxiety ultimately then challenges the very categories of gift economy and profit economy.

Recognizing the complexity of the concepts of value in these medieval texts has two implications for historical thinking. It deconstructs a clear binary of gift and profit precisely at the chronological pivotal point and precisely in the religious thinkers who in Little's account were most attuned to the anxieties of a "new money economy." Therefore, these concepts of value challenge us to reconsider the grand narrative of a radical shift from gift economy to profit economy. Second, the same ideology of "values" found in the moral literature of Latinate Christian authors and in the contemporary Jewish author(s) of *Sefer Ḥasidim* deconstructs the half-conscious linkages between Judaism and profit, on the one hand, and Christianity and gift, on the other, in popular and scholarly conceptions of premodern European culture. Whereas Chapter 6 explained from

Christian sources how the stereotyping of Jews as usurers emerged out of the confluence of the usury campaign, crusading and moral reform, and the contestation of legal jurisdiction, this chapter shows from Hebrew sources that Jews were not an economic "other," but shared a common economic culture with medieval western Christians. Though only a single Jewish text, *Sefer Ḥasidim* negates the assumption in Little's model that Christianity is the defining structure *and* the causal agent for the changes in economic attitudes. Because *Sefer Ḥasidim* precedes most of the Christian texts, it cannot be treated as derivative of Christian thought. Therefore medieval attitudes toward economic values, I argue, ought to be approached as *European*, rather than Christian, for this ideology was not limited by, or defined by, medieval Christianity. Medieval Jews were not "always already" commercialized and therefore were not fundamentally different in their economic activities and economic thought from medieval Christians. Jews were fellow travelers undergoing commercialization along with Christians.

MORAL VALUE

A humorous exemplum from the late-thirteenth-century English collection *Speculum Laicorum* provides a good example of the moral taint adhering to coins, or, in this example, literally, the *stench*.[23] The exemplum tells of a man who made his fortune through "unjust means of acquisition." Wishing to visit again Flanders, the land of his birth, he converted all his worldly wealthy into gold and set sail on a ship. The man brought along a tame ape he intended as a gift for his lord. When the ship was in the middle of the sea, the ape seized his bag of gold coins and scaled the mast. The ape opened the bag and held each coin in turn to his nose. He then threw most of the coins in the sea, but a few he threw onto the ship's deck. When the owner of the ape learned of it, he wished to throw himself in the sea. But a wise old man among the company stopped him, saying, "The ape is just, for that which was unjust he destroyed and that which was just he preserved. So collect those which were preserved and cease weeping for that which was less than justly acquired."[24]

The coins on the surface are anonymous and impersonal: they all look the same, and they all are mixed up in a single moneybag. But the ape sorting the coins by smelling them dramatizes the didactic point that not all coins are alike. Superficially their economic value is evident and equivalent, but their moral value depends upon the mode of acquisition.

FROM GIFT EXCHANGE TO PROFIT ECONOMY RECONSIDERED... 153

Those coins quite literally stink that were acquired in an unjust way. We are not told what the illicit economic activity was, and different versions cast the tale differently. The *Speculum Laicorum* categorizes the tale under "unjust acquisition." Another version describes the principal character as a Flemish merchant who made his fortune "contra sententiam Cardinalis" at the taking of Constantinople in 1204, suggesting that the sin was participating in the conquest of Constantinople against papal orders.[25] The oldest version, the French *Tabula Exemplorum*, probably compiled by a Franciscan, casts the principal character as a pilgrim but categorizes the tale under the rubric "usury."[26] The potential for using "bad" money for a sacred journey heightens the danger, just as the stench of the coins heightens the central didactic function of the exemplum—to underscore the differential between economic value and moral value. The nature of the illicit activity itself is less the issue, as the nebulous character of the mode of acquisition and the shifting contours of the characters and settings clarify. The exemplum rather plays off the audience's supposition that all coins are alike. The exemplum dislodges the anonymity and impersonal nature of the coins by insisting on the moral specificity that adheres to each coin.

The juxtaposition between the ape and the merchant is a careful, literary construction that underscores the tale's central concerns. The exemplum draws on rich symbolic motives connected with apes in medieval art: the ape as the figure of fallen man, sinful, sunk in animal appetites, lacking *ratio*; the figure of the tame, fettered ape whose antics amused the audiences of jongleurs and musicians and whose chains symbolized for moralists humankind's fetters to animal desires; the ape in the *monde reverse* of gothic marginalia whose aping of human actions amused and delighted its viewers, the ape as fool, folly, and *vanitas*.[27] The visual picture of the ape seizing its owner's moneybag, scaling the mast, melodramatically smelling the coins, and throwing the coins into the sea must have raised a chuckle from a medieval audience used to viewing the antics of apes as amusement. But in the sorting of the bad coins from the good, the roles of ape and human are reversed. The ape, sinful and desirous, lacking reason, sees beyond the face value of the coin to its inherent moral value. The man, blinded by his avarice, mistakes a coin for a coin for a coin. The ape, playing the holy fool, purges the purse of its ill-gotten gain, and thereby purges its master of bad money.

Here money is neither anonymous nor impersonal as modern social and economic theory would have it. Nor is money unequivocally evil for medievals as some historians have suggested. The exemplum starts from the assumption that money is an abstract holder of value. But both the humor of the exemplum and its deadly serious didactic lesson work to negate the presumption that a coin is a coin is a coin. Its lesson: that one ought not forget that moral value is created by the economic mode of acquisition; that those coins tainted with ill deeds ought to be cast aside and destroyed.

Destruction

The ape destroys the "bad" coins simply because they are tainted. But other exempla warn explicitly of the danger bad coins pose through contact and circulation. The early-thirteenth-century Cistercian collection *Dialogus Miraculorum* describes the danger posed to "good" money by contact with "bad" money.

> A usurer once entrusted a certain sum of money to a cellarer of our Order to keep for him. He sealed up this money and put it in the safe by the side of the monastery money. Later when the other reclaimed his deposit, the cellarer, unlocking the safe, found that both it and the monastery money had disappeared. Now when he found that the locks of the safe were untouched, and the seals of the bags unbroken, so that there could be no suspicion of theft, he understood that the money of the usurer had destroyed both the monastery money and itself.[28]

The money literally consumed itself after consuming the monastery's money. The exemplum illustrates the point that money acquired by usury not only diminishes, but is destructive. In the commentary following the exemplum, the narrator (depicted as a Cistercian monk training a novice) states: "It ['bad' money] quickly fails in itself and sometimes destroys that which is mixed or associated with it." Not only should one not give safe harbor to the money of usurers, but one should guard against contact with "bad" money. For "the property of a monastery is not only not increased, but actually diminished by the alms of usury."[29] Like the classic "gift" in Marcel Mauss' essay, the coin carries with it a part of its owner: "bad" moral value circulates under the cover of economic value.[30] "Bad" moral value is dangerous, because it spreads by contact. The exemplum forms part of a larger set of teachings that consider gray areas around usurious money: alms generated from usury, handling money acquired through usury in economic transactions, safe harbor given to a usurer's money. The

FROM GIFT EXCHANGE TO PROFIT ECONOMY RECONSIDERED... 155

point for our historical purpose is clear: while each coin looks like another, the mode of acquisition marks each coin with a different moral value. Ill-gotten gain is dangerous, but not money in and of itself.

The destructive quality of the coins spreads beyond material objects to human agents. Usurers and misers meet untimely and graphic deaths through the moneybags and money chests holding their money. In an early-fourteenth-century exempla collection, a usurer plays with his money, while his people go to church. "One day the lid of his money chest falls on him," and his people on returning find him dead within the chest."[31] An often repeated exemplum reports the death of a usurer in Dijon. As he was being betrothed before the church portal, the stone statue of a usurer threw his moneybag onto the head of the living usurer and killed him instantly.[32] The usurer was quite literally "knocked off" by moneybags.

Other Latin exempla equate the danger of "dirty" money to that of commodities with "bad" economic value. One tells of a man whose soul was claimed by devils, because he died wearing a coat that once belonged to a usurer.[33] The moral character of the possessor inheres in their posses-sions. Here the contagion spreads from person to person, and the locus of "bad" moral value is not a coin, but a coat. The equivalency of commodi-ties and currency is yet another indication of the sophistication of the eco-nomic thought of the medieval monastics. They recognize the principle of abstract economic value while insisting on the presence of moral value. All of the above exempla insist on the moral difference between coins and attempt to diminish the dangerous differential between moral value and economic value through moral exhortation.

These rather crude miracles can contain highly sophisticated theo-logical principles.[34] The exempla in which a usurer's coins consume the monastery's coins play upon the intellectual and theological definition of metallic currency as a nonproductive thing. Metallic currency does not generate or produce itself. It has no body, and therefore neither con-sumes nor produces. Nor can it be consumed or made to reproduce. The miracle of the exemplum is a reversal of nature. (This is, in fact, the definition of a miracle.) It is a supernatural occurrence for a nonbodied thing to consume a nonbodied thing. And the unnatural consumption reveals the truth of the unnatural act of usury. Usury produces money from money. Hence, in the miracle, the usurer's money devours money. To this the additional horror is added of a thing consuming itself. So the usurer's money becomes embodied in the full meaning—it produces, con-sumes, and is consumed. And each of these acts, we are to understand, is

156 J.L. MELL

unnatural. But the process of consumption rectifies the unnatural process of usury by reversing the production of profit.

REDEMPTION

In a more gruesome tale, the usurer himself is devoured by the fruits of his usury. Touched by divine mercy, the repentant usurer went to a priest, made confession, and promised to give all his goods to the poor to appease God. The priest instructed him to take alms from his loaves of bread and place them in a chest. The next morning when the chest was opened, the alms had turned to reptiles, the food of hell. The didactic aim of the exemplum is clear: money acquired by usury cannot be used for alms. Terrified by the divine rejection of his offering, the usurer begged the priest to tell him what he had to do to be saved. The priest instructed him to lie naked among the reptiles all night. The priest closed him in the box and left. In the morning, nothing was found but a skeleton. It was buried in the porch of the church of the martyr St. Gereon, "and it is said that the bones are of so great sanctity that up to this day no living reptile has been able to pass them."[35] The unnatural act of usury is underscored by the unnaturalness of the miracle: bread devours the body, rather than the body bread. The earthly suffering seems to substitute for eternal suffering. The usurer is redeemed, but his property is not.

But in another tale, alms were given from the possessions of a usurer and were not rejected. The narrator of *Dialogus Miraculorum*, who tells the tales for the instruction of a novice, explains: In this case, the usurer on his deathbed had begged an abbot to take over the care of his soul. The usurer, carried to the monastery with all his goods, promptly died. "The abbot, not unmindful of his promise, took pains to restore the products of usury as far as he possibly could and bestowed bountiful alms for the soul of the usurer; the rest he used for the good of the convent." But the novice's teacher emphasized that if "contrition had been lacking, his alms would have profited him but little."[36] The negative moral value of the usurer's property had been redeemed by his contrition and restitution, before positive moral value had been "purchased" with alms. Only because restitution of ill-gotten gains had first been made by agency of the abbot were his alms acceptable.

Giving of alms without contrition never diminishes the disequilibrium between moral and economic value. Contrition begins as sincere repentance, but typically ends through some kind of mortification (except when the sinner dies too quickly as in the example above). Another exemplum tells of a repentant usurer who was instructed first by a bishop to give all his money for the building of the Church of Notre Dame. The usurer, uncomfortable with this advice, asked a precentor what he should do. Now he was instructed to make restitution to all from whom he had taken more than was due. Only from what was left over might he give alms. Then he was instructed to do penance by walking naked through the streets shamed by a servant.[37] "Bad money" must be redeemed through restitution, and bad moral value through contrition.

These Latin exempla all recognize the following: (1) Money (metallic currency) is an abstract holder of economic value, and in this respect, anonymous and impersonal. (2) In addition to economic value, there is moral value generated by the mode of acquisition. "Bad" moral value makes coinage and commodities dangerous and destructive. (3) Money with "bad" moral value cannot be rectified by a good economic deed (alms). (4) The sinner must do penance for the bad moral value and redeem the money through restitution. Some exempla, particularly those from Caesarius of Heisterbach, show awareness of the high theological and intellectual definition of coins as a nonproductive holder of value, which neither produce (nor consume) nor are consumed. In summary then, money in the medieval worldview of regular clergy is neither simply impersonal, anonymous, and abstract, nor simply a dangerous evil, corroding society. Rather, the danger that lurks in coins arises from the potential for disjuncture between their economic face value and their inherent moral value.

Shared Culture: Moral Value

The general contours of this pattern of thought emerge in the Hebrew exempla as well. "Bad" moral value is created through unjust acquisition or ungenerous hoarding, and this immaterial value adheres to the material coins acquired unjustly and those held or used ungenerously. "Bad money" becomes dangerous, just as in the Latin exempla. *Sefer Ḥasidim*, speaking of misers and usurers, says: "One who is a miser, or who deposits his money with another without allowing them to make a profit from him or who will not lend anything of his own to another, or one who takes usury (*ribit*): those into whose hands come that man's money never will prosper; either they will die or they will become poor."[38] This exemplum recognizes the face value of the coin, that is, the economic value that is equivalent from coin to coin. But the exemplum insists on the negative moral value created through unjust acquisition or ungenerous use.

While economic value is anonymous and impersonal (a coin is a coin is a coin), moral value is highly personal and dangerous. All those through whose hands the money passes are endangered. The concluding lines of the passage from the Parma text of *Sefer Hasidim* refer to the money acquired through these acts as *menudeh*, which can be translated as "untouchable" or even "excommunicated." Money, here, itself becomes a repository for moral value. The negative "moral value" of the coins remains even when it circulates beyond the wrong-doers: "It is decreed that that money (in whoever's hand it comes) will be lost."[39] Money with negative moral value becomes dangerous, because this negative value circulates through the coins.

Another passage warns against coins with bad *mazal* (fortune or fate): "Don't take money from many people [for the purpose of] making a profit with it, lest the *mazal* of one of them will cause him to lose what he has in his hands, even the money of others which he has in his hands. For, there is a man, who in every instance that his money touches, in whoever's hands it is, his goods will decrease, or he will die. Therefore one should be careful."[40] *Mazal*, moral value, is transferred from person to person through the coins, just like material value. Like the *hau*, the spirit of the thing, in Marcel Mauss' classic study, the *mazal* of the owner circulates with the coin.[41]

SHARED CULTURE: DEATH AND DESTRUCTION

In *Sefer Hasidim*, the potential of money to circulate negative value is marked. The refrain "therefore one should be careful" is used to conclude a number of passages. For example, "Money of usurers and misers and shaved coins and that which comes from their money—whoever hands it touches, his possessions will decrease. Therefore one should be careful."[42] The most frequently mentioned danger is that "bad" money, like a bad apple, will rot the rest in the barrel. At times, *Sefer Hasidim* warns that not only will one suffer the destruction of one's worldly goods, but one will suffer death oneself, as in the passages quoted above.

The taint of rotten money, *Sefer Hasidim* often warns, passes beyond the wrong-doer to the wrong-doer's business associates, dependents, and supporters: "One who lends on usury (*ribit*): his money will be destroyed.

One who clips coins or who cheats in weighing, measuring, trade, or in any other way: in the end they will become impoverished, and *their children* will be separated from each other in a strange land, and they will be needy. *All those who are their associates and all who are their dependents*: they will lose their money *as will any who assist them*."[43] Here, *Sefer Ḥasidim* does not emphasize coins as the medium for circulating negative moral value, but rather networks of economic association. The sinner is not linked to children, associates, dependents, and benefactors by a single, limited market exchange, but by economic circles of consumption, association, or support. The distinction resembles the one made by Karl Polanyi between formal and substantive meanings of "economic" in which the "formal" refers to market exchange, and the "substantive" to cycles of reciprocity and redistribution.[44] In the economic conceptions of *Sefer Ḥasidim*, coins carry "bad" moral value across market exchanges. But "bad" moral value completely permeates substantive economic networks.

This subtle distinction may be particular to *Sefer Ḥasidim*. But the kernel of the exemplum contains the same principle asserted in the Latin exemplum where a dead man's soul was carried off by devils because he was wearing a usurer's coat: enjoyment of the "fruit" of an unjust gain brings down heavenly punishment appropriate to that gain, whether or not one committed the unjust act oneself. Both the Latin and Hebrew exempla mark out moral value, alongside economic value, and warn of the dangers.

Objects too tainted by negative moral value will suffer destruction in *Sefer Ḥasidim*, just as the usurer's money devoured itself in *Dialogus Miraculorum*. "If you see books being burnt, know that in sin they were acquired, or in sin they came to the hands of the owner's fathers, or they were not loaned to others desiring to study them, or they were not written for their own sake."[45] Books are burnt when acquired unjustly or composed unjustly. Unjust acquisition, unjust use, or a profit motive in their making becomes bound up with the materiality of the books: their loss and their owners' impoverishment are the result of the owners' or their ancestors' sins.[46]

The Hebrew exempla like the Latin exempla treat commodities no differently than metallic currency. Both contain economic value and moral value. Economic value is created through an economic act; and moral value is formed through either an act or a failure to act. Both commodities and currency circulate moral value together with the economic value. An exemplum, fascinating for its description of Jewish participation in urban

160 J.L. MELL

crafts, contrasts a bad Jewish employer (perhaps a master craftsman) with a good Christian employer:[47]

> One man did not allow his workers to leave their work until sundown, and these craftsmen were Jewish. Nearby was a non-Jew who let his workers go before sundown. On *erev Shabat*, the Jew would oppress his Jewish and Christian craftsmen making them work until it was time to go to the synagogue, even until it was time to say the *barechu*.[48] But the non-Jew let his hired laborers and workers go on *erev Shabat* a full hour before evening. The sage said, "I would be surprised if the buildings of the Jew remain standing or if they are inherited by his heirs." And furthermore, the non-Jew paid his workers in a spirit of goodwill (*be-ayin yafah*), while the Jew postponed payment. God did not restrain himself [from punishing] all this. And it happened according to the words of the sage: the building of the non-Jew was inherited by his heirs.[49]

Like Latin exempla that move effortlessly between coins, coats, and bread, this Hebrew exemplum moves between the economic value of labor and the economic value inherent in capital. Moreover, the sophistication in notions of economic value is matched by the sophistication in notions of moral value. For negative moral value is generated not just through hoarding, cheating, or usury, but rather through the more nebulous act of oppressing laborers by being stingy, either in paying wages reluctantly or in releasing laborers from work. The Hebrew exempla like the Latin exempla attempt to inculcate positive values in their audience by demonstrating the real danger that lurks in negative moral value.

Conversely, good moral value can generate economic gain. In the same cluster of exempla, *Sefer Ḥasidim* defines good moral value around generosity, but generosity is not set in opposition to commercial ventures or profit.

> One who is liberal with his money towards others so that they may profit from him, and he is happy and loans on half profit and is not miserly towards others who may benefit by him and welcomes guests warmly: all those into whose hands his money comes will prosper. Such was the case with the money of Job. "Whoever took a *prutah* from Job had luck with it" (Bava Batra 15b).[50]

The reference here to "lending on half profit" is to a standard commercial loan (*iska*) permitted in rabbinic law, which parallels the Christian

FROM GIFT EXCHANGE TO PROFIT ECONOMY RECONSIDERED... 161

commenda discussed in Chapter 7.[51] The commenda, historians often note, did not violate the canonical laws on usury, because the investor shared the risk. But this passage in *Sefer Ḥasidim* emphasizes sharing profit, rather than sharing risk. The investor by providing a source of livelihood to another becomes like a generous host welcoming guests into his home. The coins of the investor like the penny of Job has good *mazal.* Judah the Pious deploys Talmudic proof texts (here the *midrash* on Job from Bava Batra)[52] and again and again Talmudic principles, such as "midah ke-neggd midah." But by framing these in new textual contexts *and* by virtue of writing a new text in a new historio-cultural context, *Sefer Ḥasidim* makes them medieval and European. The economic issues with which Judah the Pious grappled were ones shared by Christian authors in western Europe. The answers that he devised were built out of rabbinic precepts and rooted in rabbinic texts, but moved, all the same, in a trajectory shared with Christian authors.

Shared Culture: Redemption

Sefer Ḥasidim shares in the religious culture of medieval Europe in one striking way in particular. It too developed an economic system that fused materiality and morality in a penitential logic. In many passages in *Sefer Ḥasidim* penitential practices are directed by a sage (*ḥasid*). External evidence for the practice of penance is attested by the penitential manuals of the *Ḥasidei Ashkenaz,* and at least one prominent scholar considers penance the only decisive influence that *Sefer Ḥasidim* had on Ashkenazic Judaism.[53] As in the Latin exempla, *Sefer Ḥasidim* insists on the insufficiency of alms alone as a means of rectification. Restitution of ill-gotten gains can be a part of the penance, but penance must encompass physical mortification. For rotten money cannot redeem a sin through its own exchange. The following exempla from *Sefer Ḥasidim* illustrate this principle.

A Jewish merchant had a cart loaded with garments for sale. When he reached the town where he wished to sell them, his cart broke down. As it was Friday, he "sanctified the Shabbat" at the inn there. But when marauders entered the town that evening, pillaging homes, the merchant acted to save his merchandise. Though it was the Shabbat, he fixed the cart and harnessed horses, even though by doing so he violated the strictures against work on Shabbat. In the meantime, messengers of the king came and ordered the marauders not to take anything from Jews.

162   J.L. MELL

> When the Jewish merchant returned home, he went to a sage who instructed him how to make full penance. The sage said to him, "Fill the cart with the same quantity of garments; place your hand on the earth, and have them pass the wheel over your hand; and give the money that you received for the garments to charity or hire [a scribe] to copy books...let orphans and the children of poor who cannot afford books read them....If there is any money left over, give it to [the poor] who are children of good men and ashamed to accept [charity] openly."[54]

Negative moral value must be redeemed through the penance of physical suffering and the dispersal of the equivalent economic value for which the merchant violated the Shabbat. The "bad" moral value of the garments is redeemed by using their economic value to produce books that are circulated among the poor. (Only the leftover money is distributed to the righteous poor.) But as in the Latin exempla where usurers must both make restitution and show true contrition, usually through bodily mortification, here too the act of giving away the value of the goods is not enough. The dispersal of economic value must be joined to a physical penance.[55]

In another exemplum, where a man violated the Shabbat by carrying money, we also find that both almsgiving to the worthy poor *and* physical penance must be done. The man who carried money on Shabbat "came before a sage to receive instruction on making penance. The sage said to him, 'The money or its equivalent value must be distributed among the children of good men who are ashamed to take charity.' The man did not want to give away the money. So the sage did not give him a penance to do."[56] Carrying in public space (but not private space) on Shabbat is a form of prohibited work.[57] The nature of the object carried is of little consequence. Money here is not "impure" in and of itself. Rather the violation pertains to the Shabbat laws that protect the Shabbat's essence as a day of rest by carefully prohibiting work. Sin is the Hasid's concern here, not money. The exemplum specifies money rather than another object, it seems, because it helps illustrate the central point about the necessity of material and immaterial penance for sin. The sage refuses to give a penance to the sinner, because the sinner refuses to complete the first step toward contrition. Sin must be compensated for with both a *material* and an *immaterial* penance. The didactic point of the exemplum is that the sinner must first show true contrition through a material act equivalent to a usurer's restitution and then complete that act with bodily mortification. This is the same point as was made in the Christian tales.

FROM GIFT EXCHANGE TO PROFIT ECONOMY RECONSIDERED... 163

The general contours of a medieval *mentalité* of value emerge out of *Sefer Ḥasidim* and Latin exempla—moral value over and above economic value, the danger of negative moral value, and the necessity of penance. Within this shared *mentalité*, strains of religious difference are evident. The economic concepts are grounded in a different set of religious texts and laws—rabbinic and Hebrew on the one hand, Latinate and canonical on the other. Sinful acts are tied at times to the religions' distinct legal traditions. Yet, overall, they exhibit similar concepts grounded in a common genre. The genre of exempla mediates a common religious goal (the aim of bringing one's audience through the miraculous but true tales to penance) and a common morality (the valuing of moral value over economic value).

Sefer Ḥasidim is only one text and a text from a religious current deemed by some to be marginal in contemporary medieval life, however influential the text and its author(s) became among early modern European Jews, however important it has become in the scholarship on medieval Judaism and Jewish history. The claim here is not that *Sefer Ḥasidim* influenced medieval Judaism and spread a new concept of moral value—that would presume far too much. All the more, the central claim is not that the Christian literature influenced the Jewish text of *Sefer Ḥasidim*; that is patently contradicted by the chronology of the texts. Rather, the intellectual project here is one of cultural history, which sketches a shared *mentalité*, not one of intellectual history, which traces intellectual influence. The attempt here has been to document parallels across medieval Judaism and Christianity in order to demonstrate the evidence for a medieval European culture of value that is *not rooted in a particular religious culture*. Though *Sefer Ḥasidim* is but one text, it demonstrates the fact that this shared *mentalité* is European, rather than specifically the result of Christianity. The supposition here, which cannot be fully proven, is that examples from multiple authors (whether Jewish or Christian) are fragmentary remains of a broader and more extensive European culture which transcends religious difference. The approach, in short, follows the established methodology of social historians of premodern cultures in which stray references are woven together to form a full picture. Both the author(s) of *Sefer Ḥasidim* and the authors of the Latin exempla, while they may have had limited influence in their day, have historical importance as creative thinkers responding to economic change. This shared *mentalité* has significance for European history as well as Jewish history.

Conclusions

First, money and the so-called new monetary economy (which in fact is not new at all) cannot be regarded as generating a spiritual crisis, as Little and those who follow him have maintained. Money per se was not a locus of anxiety; much less was it a causal agent for historical change. The religious authors considered here had a sophisticated and abstract notion of economic value that applied across currency and commodities. They did not treat money as something distinct and special. Rather, the authors were intent upon asserting that objects of economic value had multiple layers of value created in acts of exchange and transferred through networks of economic association or secondary market exchanges. These layers of value ranged from superficial economic value that they recognized and found unproblematic to all-important moral value. These authors were intent upon transmitting the ideology of multiple layers of value, and they were anxious about the potential for a disequilibrium between economic value and moral value.

What Little mistook for anxiety over "profit economy" was the didactic aim, the ideology, of the religious authors to impress upon their flocks the reality of moral value. The exempla tell their gruesome tales to educate listeners to value moral value over economic value. The genre of exempla works its didactic magic precisely from the "true event" that jars its audience into action with thrilling tales of money turned into flesh-eating serpents and stone moneybags knocking usurers stone dead. The exempla literature was generated, at least in part, out of the movement for preaching penance, and penance was, at least in part, its aim. The danger inherent in "bad" money was emphasized precisely to create new values in the audience: the valuing of "moral value."

According to this ideology, moral value adheres to a coin (or commodity) and circulates with it. Just as an individual possesses the economic value, she/he "possesses" the sin attached to that value, similar to the "spirit of the thing" (*hau*) in Marcel Mauss' discussion of gift exchange. Moral value remains bound to the economic value, so that as ill-gotten acquisitions are converted to another medium, the sin committed in the original economic act is transferred as well. Coins become a moral currency whose circulation circulates the original owner's vice or virtue through bringing poverty or wealth, death or life. Money functions as both an economic and a moral medium of value. If one were to hold to the old binary categories of gift/profit, one would have to say that money functions simultaneously as both gift and commodity in the worldview of medieval religious authorities. In the view of medieval religious authorities, money is neither a causal agent of economic change nor perhaps even a symbol of a new profit economy.

Second, the sophisticated ideology of a multilayered value inherent in commodities implodes the very categories of gift economy and profit economy, inasmuch as a concept of multilayered value fuses materiality and morality. This complex concept of value was developed precisely at the chronological juncture where Little held that gift economy radically shifted to profit economy. The shift, he claimed, caused a spiritual crisis through a disjuncture between material structure and cultural suprastructure. Because commercialization occurred, but cultural and religious change did not keep pace, he concluded that a radical reaction against the new economy in the repression of "usury" and persecution of Jews was followed by a gradual moderation of the crisis with the creation of new urban saints.

Certainly, there was greater economic expansion in western Europe until the economic crisis of the fourteenth century.[58] Certainly economic thought developed around these issues in canon law, scholastic theology, and moral literature. And this Christian literature developed real complexity and sophistication, as a generation of scholars has documented.[59] But as I discussed in Chapter 6, the new ideology on economy worked out the boundaries of permissible and impermissible economic activity, in ever-greater sophistication. To put it baldly, this theology of economic thought constructed "usury" as it simultaneously undid "usury."

Rather than describing European economic development as Little does, as a radical disjuncture between gift economy and profit economy eliciting a spiritual crisis, one might use this countermodel: As commercialization progressed, religious leaders constructed a more sophisticated, multivalent model of value that contained both moral value and economic value. The multivalent concept of value cuts against the binaries gift/profit, money/nonmoney, economy/religion. This model shucks a "profit economy," envisioned as the rude beginnings of capitalism, and a "gift economy," envisioned as a primitive system of obligations, for a model that approaches economic and religious exchange as embedded in complex webs of social meaning and action. This model is more in accord with Karl Polanyi's revolutionary notion of "economy as an instituted process" than that of gift economy to profit economy.

The fact that this *mentalité* can be found in Jewish author(s), as well as contemporary and later Christian authors, cuts against a binary opposition between medieval Christianity (linked to the spirit of the gift) and modernizing Judaism (linked to the spirit of capitalism). Although the economic models of the Historical School of Political Economy have not supplied the standard historical narratives on the economic development of Europe for half a century, they are still operative as assumptions of fundamental economic differences between medieval Jews and Christians, because commercialization is set in opposition to medieval Christianity. The Historical School's model of an "always already" commercialized Judaism over against a pre-commercial Christianity still undergirds much historical thinking, as in the classics by Little and Duby, and recent textbooks.[60] It is time to move beyond them. The complex thinking on value in *Sefer Ḥasidim* shows that medieval Jews were Europeans undergoing commercialization together with their Christian neighbors. Economic ideology and activities on both sides of the religious divide shared more than their religious differences suggest. If historical investigation were to begin from the assumption that Jewish economic activity and thought were part and parcel of European economic expansion and commercialization, historians would accept more readily the obvious parallels between rabbinic law and canon law on usury, between the commercial contract of the *iska* and the commenda, and between the deep moral grappling of Jewish and Christian thinkers noted by several generations of Jewish historians.

NOTES

1. Karl Marx, "Zur Judenfrage," *Deutsch-Französische Jahrbücher* 1–2 (1844): 182–214, citation on 211.
2. Robert Lopez, *The Commercial Revolution of the Middle Ages, 950–1350* (Cambridge, 1976); Georges Duby, *The Early Growth of the European Economy: Warriors and Peasants from the Seventh to the Twelfth Century*, trans. Howard Clarke (Ithaca, 1974); and Lester Little, *Religious Poverty and the Profit Economy in Medieval Europe* (Ithaca, 1978).
3. Little also draws heavily from Marc Bloch, Duby's predecessor in the Annales school (Little, *Religious Poverty*, ix–x).
4. Ibid., x.
5. Lester Little, "The Function of the Jews in the Commercial Revolution," in *Povertà e Ricchezza nella Spiritualità dei secoli XI e XII* (Todi, 1969), 271–87, citation on 285–6.

FROM GIFT EXCHANGE TO PROFIT ECONOMY RECONSIDERED... 167

6. Ibid.

7. For a full discussion of these ideas and the contradictions in the literature, see: Chap. 3.

8. See, for example: Barbara Rosenwein, *To Be the Neighbor of Saint Peter: The Social Meaning of Cluny's Property, 909–1049* (Ithaca, 1989); Stephen White, *Custom, Kinship, and Gifts to Saints: The Laudatio Parentum in Western France, 1050–1150* (Chapel Hill, 1988); Patrick Geary, *Living with the Dead in the Middle Ages* (Ithaca, 1994); and Florin Curta, "Merovingian and Carolingian Gift Giving," *Speculum* 81 (2006): 671–99. Also see the works cited in the following note. A recent example of the application of the concept of gift exchange to early modern European history is Natalie Zemon Davis, *The Gift in Sixteenth-Century France* (Madison, 2000). All these works concern gift exchange. For the use of Little's thesis of an anxiety over money, see: Joel Kaye, *Economy and Nature in the Fourteenth Century: Money, Market Exchange, and the Emergence of Scientific Thought* (Cambridge, 1998).

9. Esther Cohen and Mayke B. de Jong, eds., *Medieval Transformations: Texts, Power, and Gifts in Context* (Leiden, 2001); Gadi Algazi, Valentin Groebner, and Bernhard Jussen, eds., *Negotiating the Gift: Pre-modern Figurations of Exchange* (Göttingen, 2003); Wendy Davies and Paul Fouracre, eds., *The Languages of Gift in the Early Middle Ages* (Cambridge, 2010); Juliann Vitullo and Diane Wolfthal, eds., *Money, Morality, and Culture in Late Medieval and Early Modern Europe* (Farnham, 2010).

10. Not all scholarship fits into the Duby/Little paradigm. See, for example: Algazi, Groebner, and Jussen, *Negotiating the Gift*. They explicitly constructed the volume as "concerned with pre-modern societies which are neither 'archaic' nor 'modern' in accordance with any prevalent acceptation of those terms. In all of them, gift exchange was neither the sole nor necessarily the dominant transaction mode; they were all stratified societies, familiar with both political authority and market exchange" (14).

11. Vitullo and Wolfthal, introduction to *Money, Morality, and Culture*, 3.

12. Ibid., 1–4.

13. Chris Wickham, conclusion to *Languages of Gift*, 259–60. Although Wickham wrote on behalf of all the contributors, there is little evidence that all the contributors have moved as far in their perspective.

Some, like Wendy Davies, undoubtedly do, while Janet Nelson only edges in this direction in the introduction to *Languages of Gift*, 5–6. See also the articles in the volume by Wendy Davies and Chris Wickham which complicate any simple division of gift and sale: Wendy Davies, "When Gift Is Sale: Reciprocities and Commodities in Tenth-Century Christian Iberia," and Chris Wickham, "Compulsory Gift-Exchange in Lombard Italy, 650–1150," in *Languages of Gift*, 217–37, 193–216, respectively.

14. Curta, "Merovingian and Carolingian Gift Giving," esp. 673–4, where he refers to Duby and Little. One of the contributions to *Money, Morality, and Culture*—the essay by Giacomo Todeschini—might be read as unraveling Little's framework, though no author explicitly makes this argument (Giacomo Todeschini, "The Incivility of Judas: 'Manifest' Usury as a Metaphor for the 'Infamy of Fact' (*infamia facti*)," in *Money, Morality, and Culture*, 33–52).

15. See, for example: Rory Naismith, *Money and Power in Anglo-Saxon England: The Southern English Kingdoms, 757–865* (Cambridge, 2012); and Michael McCormick, *Origins of the European Economy: Communications and Commerce, AD 300–900* (Cambridge, 2001).

16. Recently, James Davis has taken up this issue, in his *Medieval Market Morality: Life, Law, and Ethics in the English Marketplace, 1200–1500* (Cambridge, 2012). Giacomo Todeschini comments: "Currently, the main problem lies in a historiography that asserts a forced and timeless separation between the lay and religious rationalities and assumes an everlasting conflict between economic and moral codes" (Giacomo Todeschini, "Theological Roots of the Medieval/Modern Merchant's Self-Representation," in *The Self-Perception of Early Modern Capitalists*, ed. Margaret Jacob and Catherine Secretan (New York, 2008), 17–48, citation on 18).

17. In this respect, I depart from Wickham, who says that he "cannot detect a specifically religious or spiritual element to the obligation to reciprocate...which Mauss was so keen on." His "readings of gift stress their alienability and their social and strategic nature" (Wickham, conclusion, *Languages of Gift*, 258). I stress the inalienability and the presence of moral value in monetary exchanges, whether in an unreciprocated gift or in sale and loan.

18. For an overview of the genre of exempla and their historical development, see: Claude Bremond, Jacques Le Goff, and Jean-Claude

Schmitt, *L'"Exemplum,"* Typologies des sources du Moyen Âge Occidental 40 (Turnhout, 1982); Jacques Berlioz and Marie Anne Polo de Beaulieu, eds., *Les Exempla médiévaux: nouvelles perspectives* (Paris, 1998).

19. Modern scholarship on *Sefer Hasidim* refers to two recensions, the Bologna printed edition and the Parma manuscript. The following notes refer to the Parma text as SHP from the edition by Judah Wistinetzki, *Sefer Hasidim* (Frankfurt am Main, 1924), and the Bologna text as SHB from the edition by Reuven Margoliot, *Sefer Hasidim* (Jerusalem, 1964). For information on the recensions and the 14 manuscripts and printed editions belonging to either SHP, SHB, or a mixture of the two, see: The Princeton University *Sefer Hasidim* Database (PUSHD), https://etc.princeton.edu/sefer_hasidim/index.php (I thank Edward Fram for making me aware of this resource); and Ivan Marcus, "The Recensions and Structure of *Sefer Hasidim*," *Proceedings of the American Academy for Jewish Research* 45 (1978): 131–53.

For a general introduction to *Sefer Hasidim*, see: Eli Yassif, *The Hebrew Folktale: History, Genre, Meaning*, trans. Jacqueline Teitelbaum (Bloomington, 1999), 283–97; and Israel Zinberg, *A History of Jewish Literature* (Cleveland, 1972), 2:35–56. There is a rich secondary literature on *Sefer Hasidim* and the *Hasidei Ashkenaz*. The most important secondary literature for this chapter was Ivan Marcus, *Piety and Society: The Jewish Pietists of Medieval Germany* (Leiden, 1981), and *Jewish Culture and Society in Medieval France and Germany* (Farnham, 2014); Yitzhak Baer, "Ha-Megamah ha-Datit ha-Hevratit shel *Sefer Hasidim*," *Zion* 3 (1937): 1–50; Haym Soloveitchik, "Three Themes in the *Sefer Hasidim*" *AJS Review* 1 (1976): 311–57; E. Yassif, "Ha-Sipur ha-eksemplari be-Sefer Hasidim" [The Exemplary Tale in *Sefer Hasidim*], *Tarbiz* 57 (1987–8): 217–55; Talya Fishman, "The Penitential System of Hasidei Ashkenaz and the Problem of Cultural Boundaries," *Journal of Jewish Thought and Philosophy* 8 (1999): 201–29; Haym Soloveitchik, "Piety, Pietism and German Pietism: *Sefer Hasidim I* and the Influence of *Hasidei Ashkenaz*," *Jewish Quarterly Review* 92 (2002): 455–93; and Tamar Alexander-Frizer, *The Pious Sinner: Ethics and Aesthetics in the Medieval Hasidic Narrative* (Tübingen, 1991). Many of the passages discussed in this chapter are also discussed in reference to social justice

170   J.L. MELL

in Abraham Cronbach, "Social Thinking in the *Sefer Hasidim*," *Hebrew Union College Annual* 22 (1949): 1–147.

20. Eli Yassif also notes that a fundamental difference exists between the Latin and Hebrew exempla in that Judah the Pious composed most of his own, and his did not circulate widely orally or textually.

21. Caesarius of Heisterbach, *Dialogus Miraculorum*, ed. Joseph Strange (Cologne, 1851).

22. On just price, see: John Baldwin, "The Medieval Theories of the Just Price: Romanists, Canonists, and Theologians in the Twelfth and Thirteenth Centuries," *Transactions of the American Philosophical Society* n.s. 49 (1959): 1–92. "Just price" in rabbinic law is defined in the Babylonian Talmud, Bava Metziah 40b.

23. Jean-Thiébaut Welter, ed., *Le Speculum Laicorum* (Paris, 1914) 6, no. 14. This exemplum is found in many collections with minor variations. The earliest that I know of comes from a late-thirteenth-century French collection drawn on heavily by *Speculum Laicorum*: Jean-Thiébaut Welter, ed., *Tabula Exemplorum secundum ordinem alphabeti* (Paris, 1926), 83, no. 306.

24. *Speculum Laicorum*, 6, no. 14.

25. J.A. Herbert, ed., *Catalogue of Romances in the Department of Manuscripts in the British Museum* (London, 1910), 3:497, describing ms. Royal D7i.

26. *Tabula Exemplorum*, 83, no. 306.

27. H.W. Janson, *Apes and Ape Lore in the Middle Ages and the Renaissance* (London, 1952), chs. 4–7.

28. Caesarius of Heisterbach, *Dialogus Miraculorum*, 1:108, no. 34. English text cited from Caesarius of Heisterbach, *The Dialogue on Miracles*, trans. H. von E. Scott and C.C. Swinton Bland (London, 1929), 1:121, no. 34.

29. Ibid.

30. See, for example: the discussion on "The Spirit of the Thing Given" in Marcel Mauss, *The Gift: Forms and Functions of Exchange in Archaic Societies* (New York, 1967), 10–13.

31. Herbert, *Catalogue of Romances*, 3:548, no. 106.

32. Stephanus de Borbone, *Anecdotes historiques, légendes et apologues, tirés du recueil inédit d'Étienne de Bourbon, Dominicain du XIIIe siècle* (Paris, 1877), 60, no. 53. This exemplum also appears in the thirteenth-century *Liber de dono timoris*, the early-fourteenth-century *Alphabetum narrationem*, and the fifteenth-century English

FROM GIFT EXCHANGE TO PROFIT ECONOMY RECONSIDERED... 171

translation of the *Alphabetum narrationem* (Frederic Tubach, *Index Exemplorum: A Handbook of Medieval Religious Tales* (Helsinki, 1969), 381, no. 5044).

33. Herbert, *Catalogue of Romances*, 3:476, no. 67.

34. On the theological principles underlying the exempla, see: Odd Langholm, *Economics in the Medieval Schools: Wealth, Exchange, Value, Money, and Usury according to the Paris Theological Tradition, 1200–1500* (Leiden, 1992), and *The Merchant in the Confessional: Trade and Price in the Pre-Reformation Penitential Handbooks* (Leiden, 2003); John Baldwin, *Masters, Princes, and Merchants: The Social Views of Peter Chanter and His Circle* (Princeton, 1970). See also the discussion in Chap. 6.

35. Caesarius of Heisterbach, *Dialogus Miraculorum*, 106–7; *Dialogue on Miracles*, 1:118–9.

36. Caesarius of Heisterbach, *Dialogus Miraculorum*, 103–5; *Dialogue on Miracles*, 1:116–8.

37. Caesarius of Heisterbach, *Dialogus Miraculorum*, 107–8.

38. SHP 1233; SHB 1075. In pairing usury and miserliness, the passage in *Sefer Ḥasidim* goes beyond the unjust acquisition of the merchant with the ape in the Latin exemplum with which it is likened here. This may reflect a subtle difference between the conceptual categories of sin in *Sefer Ḥasidim* and the Latin exempla discussed above. While the Latin texts would categorize both usury and miserliness under "avarice," the linkage may be more tightly constructed in Judaism. While the variations between medieval European Christianity and Judaism are not unimportant, the principal point here emphasized is their general similarity. Both *Sefer Ḥasidim* and the Christian exempla regard the immoral action of the coins' possessor as inhering in the physical coins.

39. SHP 1233.

40. SHB 1072.

41. Mauss, *Gift*, 11.

42. SHB 1073.

43. SHP 1233; SHB 1076. Italics are my own.

44. Karl Polanyi, "Economy as an Instituted Process," in *Trade and Market in the Early Empires: Economies in History and Theory*, ed. Karl Polanyi, Conrad Arensberg, and Harry Pearson (New York, 1957), 139–74.

45. SHP 677; SHB 871. See also: SHP 673; SHB 869.

46. On books in *Sefer Ḥasidim*, see: Talya Fishman, "The Rhineland Pietists' Sacralization of Oral Torah," *Jewish Quarterly Review* 96 no. 1 (2006): 9–16.
47. SHP 1499.
48. The *barechu* is the liturgical formula which marks the beginning of the evening prayer service. In the thirteenth century, the evening prayers on *erev Shabbat* would have begun with the *barechu*, as the *Kabbalat Shabbat* was only to be developed by the early modern Kabbalists. The scenario here seems to be one in which the Jewish employer kept his craftsmen at work until moments before Shabbat began. Had he kept them longer he would have been violating the Shabbat, but the general sense of the exemplum seems to tell against this. The sin is one of stinginess, not of Shabbat violation.
49. SHP 1499.
50. SHP 1233; SHB 1075.
51. On the *iska* and *commenda*, see the discussion and works cited in Chap. 7.
52. Babylonian Talmud, Bava Batra 15b.
53. On penance among the *Hasidei Ashkenaz*, see: Marcus, *Piety and Society*; and Fishman, "The Penitential System of Ḥasidei Ashkenaz." On Hebrew penitentials in manuscript, see: Ivan Marcus, "*Hasidei' Ashkenaz* Private Penitentials: An Introduction and Descriptive Catalogue of Their Manuscripts and Early Editions," in *Studies in Jewish Mysticism*, ed. Joseph Dan and Frank Talmage (Cambridge, MA, 1982), 57–83. For an evaluation of the influence of *Sefer Ḥasidim*'s penitential system (and lack of other types of influence), see: Soloveitchik, "Piety, Pietism and German Pietism."
54. SHP 630.
55. Both the Latin and Hebrew texts make a distinction between "restitution" and "alms." Restitution can and often must be made before penance, while alms cannot be given until after true contrition is effected by the penance plus restitution.
56. SHP 629; SHP 112; SHB 181.
57. The construction of an *eruv* transforms public space into private space, making it possible to carry objects. If an *eruv* is assumed to have been extant in the case discussed in the exemplum, then the Shabbat violation would be different. In that case, the exemplum would refer to a man violating the Shabbat by touching an

instrument used in prohibited forms of work. This class of objects, of which money is one, is designated *muktzeh*. Again, in this case, there is nothing intrinsic to money that is at the heart of the issue, but rather the Shabbat laws prohibiting work.

58. It is still an open question whether growth was qualitative or only quantitative. In addition to Lopez, *Commercial Revolution*, see: R.H. Britnell, *The Commercialisation of English Society 1000–1500* (Cambridge, 1993); and R.H. Britnell and Bruce Campbell, eds., *A Commercializing Economy: England 1086 to c. 1300* (Manchester, 1995). Even after the crisis of the fourteenth century, some historians, such as Raymond de Roover, have argued that even during the economic contraction, business methods grew in sophistication, and in his eyes these methods formed the basis for the later growth of capitalism: Raymond de Roover, *Business, Banking, and Economic Thought in Late Medieval and Early Modern Europe: Selected Studies of Raymond de Roover*, ed. Julius Kirschner (Chicago, 1974). See the discussion of commercial revolution and commercialization in Chap. 3.

59. T.P. McLaughlin, "The Teaching of the Canonists on Usury," *Mediaeval Studies* 1 no.1 (1939): 81–147; J.T. Noonan, *The Scholastic Analysis of Usury* (Cambridge, MA, 1957); J.T. Gilchrist, *The Church and Economic Activity in the Middle Ages* (London, 1969); Benjamin Nelson, *The Idea of Usury: From Tribal Brotherhood to Universal Otherhood* (Chicago, 1969); Baldwin, "The Medieval Theories of the Just Price"; Langholm, *Economics in the Medieval Schools*; Giacomo Todeschini, *Un trattato di economia politica francescana: il "De emptionibus et venditionibus, de usuris, de restitutionibus" di Pietro di Giovanni Olivi* (Rome, 1980); Diana Wood, *Medieval Economic Thought* (Cambridge, 2002); Giacomo Todeschini, *Credito e usura fra teologia, diritto e amministrazione: linguaggi a confronto, sec. XII–XVI* (Rome, 2005). See the discussion of this literature in Chap. 6.

60. Again, a recent example is Wood, *Medieval Economic Thought*, 167: "The original manifest usurers of Europe were the Jews, who were not subject to the jurisdiction of the Church. They were also not subject to qualms of conscience, for there seemed to be clear sanction for their activities in Deuteronomy 23.19–20." Note that the usury prohibition is numbered 23:20–21 in the Hebrew Bible.

CHAPTER 9

Which Is the Merchant Here? And Which the Jew?

Duke. You heare the learnd Bellario what he writes,
and heere I take it is the doctor come.
Give me your hand, come you from old Bellario?
Portia. I did, my Lord.
Duke. You are welcome, take your place:
are you acquainted with the difference
that holds this present question in the Court?
Por. I am enformed throughly of the cause,
which is the Merchant here? And which the Jew?
—William Shakespeare, *The Merchant of Venice*[1]

The title for this chapter has been taken from the deceptively simple question that Portia poses in *The Merchant of Venice* upon entering the courtroom in the guise of a young doctor of law. The various plots and subplots of Belmont's wooing and Venice's Rialto have come to a head. Antonio, the merchant of the play's title, has defaulted on a loan to Shylock the Jew. The penalty made half in jest is one pound of Antonio's flesh, and Shylock now intends to take it closest to Antonio's heart. Antonio made the loan gratuitously on behalf of his kinsman Bassanio, a Venetian youth seeking the heiress Portia in marriage. Bassanio's venture has succeeded, but Antonio's merchant ventures have been wrecked at sea. When Shylock discovers that his own daughter Jessica has run off with a Venetian youth, Lorenzo, a friend of Bassanio, the Jew's antipathy for Antonio deepens to a thirst for vengeance.

© The Author(s) 2018
J.L. Mell, *The Myth of the Medieval Jewish Moneylender*,
DOI 10.1007/978-3-319-34186-6_4

175

When Portia enters the court, the life of the merchant Antonio hangs in the balance, and Shylock "will have his bond"—even when offered thrice the sum. The happiness of the principal lovers too hangs in the balance.[2] Bassanio will be forever indebted to Antonio morally and financially if Antonio dies, and his and Portia's love will be forever marred by Antonio's sacrifice. Lorenzo's theft of Jessica and Jessica's theft of her father's jewels will remain thefts, unsanctioned by the paternal permission that would transform them into legal forms of marriage, dowry, and inheritance.

Shylock's knife would cut to the quick all the principal characters. But Portia's quick wit will right all: "Take then thy bond," she says. "Take thou thy pound of flesh;/But in the cutting it, if thou dost shed/ One drop of Christian blood, thy lands and goods/Are by the laws of Venice confiscate."[3] When Shylock would leave the court defeated and dejected, Portia detains him. The tables are turned. Portia accuses him of seeking Antonio's life. For, if it is proved against an alien that he sought the life of a citizen of Venice by direct or indirect means, one-half of his goods shall go to the party against whom he contrived and the other half to the state, and his life shall lie at the mercy of the Duke. Now Shylock is dependent upon Antonio's mercy, and Antonio gives it. Shylock should be left his life and half his goods, Antonio says, provided two conditions are met—that Shylock bequeath all he has at death to Lorenzo and Jessica, and the Jew be converted to Christianity. Shylock concedes and departs utterly destroyed. Shakespeare has effected the happy ending essential to all comedies through a quick series of inversions: A woman saves a man *with reason*, and a Christian defeats a Jew *with the law*. The prosecutor has become the prosecuted; Jewish revenge has been supplanted by Christian mercy; a Jew has become a Christian; a theft, an inheritance; and enemies have become members of an extended Christian family.

The words with which Portia assumes control of the legal case and sets in motion these inversions are simple and business-like: "Which is the merchant here? And which the Jew?"[4] But what an astonishing question it is.[5] The inversions with which the case will close mark the categories of "Jew" and "merchant" as fixed binary opposites. And yet, in the moment between Portia's question and its answer, the identities of Jew and merchant are suspended, unfixed, and ambiguous. It is this moment of ambiguity that I take for concluding this historical study. For the ambiguity of Jew and merchant reflects historical reality. For historically speaking, there

WHICH IS THE MERCHANT HERE? AND WHICH THE JEW? 177

never has been a merchant in Venice (or elsewhere) who "neither len[t] nor borrow[ed]/by taking nor by giving of excess!"[6]—except, that is, in *The Merchant of Venice.*

The juxtaposition of "merchant" and "Jew" is one that has shaped our sober historical accounts and our fantastical stereotypes from the turn of the thirteenth to today. (Shakespeare did not create it. That was the work of medieval Christian economic thought.) Portia's question suspends the rigid binaries—just for a moment. Then, the binaries come crashing down around Shylock, Antonio, and the audience. Associated with Judaism and the Jew is usury, the harsh justice of the law, revenge, enmity, the murder of (a) Christ(ian). Associated with Christianity and the Christian is fair trade, charity, mercy, forgiveness, friendship, and salvation. Shylock lends on usury; Antonio lends freely, charitably, and binds himself to Shylock only out of love for his friend Bassanio. Shylock demands the harsh justice of the law out of revenge: "I crave the law,/the penalty and forfeit of my bond." Antonio acts mercifully: "So please my lord the Duke and all the court/To quit the fine for one half his goods,/I am content; so he will let me have/The other half in use, to render it,/Upon his death, unto the gentleman/ That lately stole his daughter."[7] This gift mimics inheritance. Antonio becomes a kind of kinsman of Lorenzo and by extension of Shylock. Antonio substitutes ties of friendship and family for enmity and revenge. Shylock, when a Christian, will have legitimated Lorenzo's marriage to his daughter and become part of the kin networks that tie together the Venetian men. And this inscription of the Jew into the Christian network is an essential, if brutal, part of the "happy ending" of the Shakespearian comedy.

Underlying this resolution—and underlying the juxtapositions of usury/charity, law/mercy, enmity/friendship—is the great drama of Judaism and Christianity as presented in Christian theology. One cannot help noticing that the scene in the courtroom plays out the final judgment as envisioned in Pauline theology. Shylock, who demands "his bond," holds firm to "the law" and rejects any jot of mercy. But through this law, the Jew will be caught, and his life lie at the mercy of the Duke. Not by the law but by mercy alone will (the) man be saved. The words of Paul the Apostle resonate in the background:

> For all who rely on the works of the law are under a curse…it is evident that no one is justified before God by the law; for "The one who is righteous

will live by faith." But the law does not rest on faith....Christ redeemed us from the curse of the law by becoming a curse for us...in order that in Christ Jesus the blessing of Abraham might come to the Gentiles, so that we might receive the promise of the Spirit through faith.[8]

When Portia upholds Shylock's legal right to the bond, she is playing her fish out on a line:

> PORTIA: A pound of that same merchant's flesh is thine.
> The court awards it, and the law doth give it.
> SHYLOCK: Most rightful judge!
> PORTIA: And you must cut this flesh from off his breast.
> The law allows it, and the court awards it.
> SHYLOCK: Most learned judge!

Now Portia reels her fish in cruelly by making the law a curse.

> PORTIA: Therefore prepare thee to cut off the flesh.
> Shed thou no blood, nor cut thou less nor more
> But just a pound of flesh: if thou cut'st more
> Or less than a just pound, be it but so much
> As makes it light or heavy in the substance,
> Or the division of the twentieth part
> Of one poor scruple, nay, if the scale do turn
> But in the estimation of a hair,
> Thou diest and all thy goods are confiscate.[9]

The tide has turned and Gratiano takes up Shylock's previous cries of approbation for the young clerk: "O upright judge....O learned judge!" Life can be granted only through grace.

Antonio himself is both the figure of the Christian saved by Christ and a Christ-like figure whose willingness to die to pay his friend's debt echoes Christ's death on the cross to pay the wages of sin for all humankind. In turn, Antonio, like Christ, can plead for the sinner's life, and he does plead for Shylock so long as Shylock undergoes conversion. The conversion of the Jew prefigures the in-gathering of Israel at the end of days described by Paul in Romans 11. The salvation of Antonio, the condemnation of Shylock by the law, and Shylock's ultimate salvation through grace resonate deeply with the Pauline concepts linking Jew-law-death against Christian-grace-life.

WHICH IS THE MERCHANT HERE? AND WHICH THE JEW? 179

But the influence of Pauline theology stops short of economic matters. Paul makes no linkage to economic categories of unrighteous usurer and righteous merchant. These are inscribed into the Pauline binaries first in the high medieval period with the onset of what Giacomo Todeschini has recently called "Franciscan economics."[10] This Christian economics resonates in the juxtaposition of Jew and merchant in Portia's question, "Which is the merchant here, and which the Jew?" And the case will resolve the problematic binary opposition through conversion, in short, through the supersession of the Jew.[11]

Shakespeare's comedy does not end with the shaky exit of the crushed Shylock, but with the lovers back in idyllic Belmont. The moment is one suspended between night and day, between the marriage ceremony and the consummation of marriage in lovemaking. Like that silence between Portia's question and answer, it is a moment of ambiguity in which fixed identities and binaries are suspended, and a series of quick inversions resolves the charges of perjury and the threat of infidelity. Portia and her traveling company, the maid Nerissa, had given rings to their husbands on parting. Bassanio and Gratiano in taking the rings swore oaths that they should never part with them. But in the guise of the doctor of law and his clerk, the women had taken the rings back as payment for their legal service. Back in Belmont, their double identities still undisclosed, the women accuse their husbands of giving the rings to women (which they did), and the husbands, swearing they did not, perjure themselves yet again. When Portia declares she'll have that doctor for her "bedfellow" and Nerissa, his clerk, Antonio once again offers himself up in a mirroring of the courtroom scene. Antonio begs mercy for another and re-inscribes those at odds in peaceful ties of kinship. Here it is but playacting: Portia and Nerissa are playing an elaborate joke on their men. Bassanio receives back the ring he gave the doctor, and Gratiano, the clerk's. The women let their husbands think that they have broken their marriage vows, just as their husbands broke their oaths. The rather crude Gratiano, taken in by the joke, rails that "they are cuckolded before they ever deserve it."[12] But the return of the rings symbolizes quite the opposite. When Portia reveals the true identity of the doctor and his clerk, she again sets all to rights with a series of inversions. Men are made women; unfaithful wives, faithful; perjured husbands, true.

The fixed identities of Portia and doctor, Nerissa and clerk are blended as night blends with day in those two hours before dawn. Antonio is struck dumb, but Bassanio and Gratiano question their own obfuscation: "Were you the doctor and I knew you not? Were you the clerk that is to make me cuckold?"

> NERISSA: Ay, but the clerk that never means to do it,
> Unless he live until he be a man.
> BASSANIO: Sweet doctor, you shall be my bed-fellow:
> When I am absent, then lie with my wife.[13]

The resolution in Venice's court effected by the brutal conversion of Shylock from Jew to Christian is replaced in Venus' Belmont by the gentle conversion of maids to matrons. Portia promises to "answer all things faithfully." And the play concludes with the playful, ribald teasing of Gratiano—"That the first question my Nerissa shall be sworn on is"

> Whether till the next night she had rather stay,
> Or go to bed now, being two hours to day:
> But were the day come, I should wish it dark,
> That I were couching with the doctor's clerk.
> Well, while I live I'll fear no other thing
> So sore as keeping safe Nerissa's ring.[14]

The play ends not with the crushing defeat of Shylock, but with Gratiano's ringing play on the double entendre of Nerissa's ring.

The lovemaking and happily-ever-married ending (necessary to all proper comedies) do not disguise the dis-ease with which this play sits in the genre of comedy. Producers and audiences have struggled to square the brutal erasure of the Jew with the lighthearted and comic lovemaking. And I have lingered on the lovers at the end to bring out the dialectic that underlies the play as a whole. This discomfort can be seen in the closing scene of the recent film version directed by Michael Radford, which constructs Jessica as remaining faithful to her Jewish faith and family. The film closes with Jessica wistfully twisting a ring on her finger, the turquoise ring that her father received from her mother, a ring, Shakespeare has us know, that Shylock would never have given away as the Christian husbands did theirs.[15] In the film, the ring symbolizes Jewish faithfulness—faithfulness to Jewish family and Jewish identity. In the play, the ring symbolizes faithlessness, when Shylock hears that it was given away by Jessica for a monkey. Michael Radford's film ends with Jessica not in her husband's bedchamber like Nerissa and Portia, but alone, longingly gazing out to

WHICH IS THE MERCHANT HERE? AND WHICH THE JEW? 181

sea, her thoughts lingering on her lost Jewish faith and family symbolized by the turquoise ring she twists. Long before the horrors of the twentieth-century antisemitism, Heinrich Heine tells of seeing Shylock performed in Drury Lane: "There stood back of me in the box a pale British beauty who wept violently at the end of the fourth act and frequently cried out, 'The poor man is wronged!' Hers was a face of the noblest Grecian cut, and her eyes were large and black. I could never forget them, those great black eyes, that wept for Shylock."[16] The play, though written as comedy, can be, and continues to be, experienced as tragedy.

Behind the Janus-faced nature of the play as both comedy and trag-edy lie the double readings, both antisemitic and philosemitic, of the Jew Shylock as demon and pitiable, wronged wretch. Shakespeare draws on overt antisemitic stereotypes of ritual murder, Christian hater, and Christ-killer in his presentation of Shylock's enmity, lack of mercy, and blood-thirsty cruelty (Shylock sits on stage sharpening his knife for the kill). But at the same time, Shakespeare elicits our sympathy through Jessica's betrayal and makes Shylock's vengeance understandable. For Shylock was an affectionate husband and loving father. He has been wronged. And Shylock's self-defense mouthed through Shakespeare's glorious cadence rings as the lament of the Jewish people.

> Hath not a Jew eyes? Hath not a Jew hands, organs, dimensions, senses, affections, passions? – fed with the same food, hurt with the same weapons, subject to the same diseases, healed by the same means, warmed and cooled by the same winter and summer as a Christian is? If you prick us, do we not bleed? If you tickle us, do we not laugh? If you poison us, do we not die? And if you wrong us, shall we not revenge?[17]

Shakespeare's presentation of Shylock as wronged—despite the man's wrath—and audiences' response to the play as tragedy—despite its fram-ing as comedy—have made Shylock a resonant symbol for Jewish histori-cal studies, as in the works *Shylock Reconsidered*, *Shylock's Children*, and "Shylock's Daughters."[18] Yet Shylock holds together the opposing quali-ties of antisemitic stereotype and philosemitic history.

I have taken not Shylock but Portia's displacement of Shylock as the motto for concluding this book. For now that we "are informèd thor-oughly of the case," can we say "which is the merchant here, and which the Jew?" Portia's question suspends the fixed binaries "Jew" and "mer-chant." In the Introduction I invoked another doubling as a symbol for the myth of the Jewish moneylender and its two-sided nature as antisemitic distortion and philosemitic history. I likened the windmills, which Sancho saw, to the sober historical accounts of the beneficial economic role of the medieval Jewish moneylender; the many-armed ogres, which Don Quixote saw, to the antisemitic fantasies of the enemy-Jew. Janus-faced, the one will always be joined with and sustain the other. If we are to defeat the ogres of antisemitism, we must do away with the windmills, as with the giants. For both are rooted and given life in the medieval Christian category of "Jewish moneylender" opposed to "Christian merchant," dramatized so vibrantly by Shakespeare. Perhaps I have been no more successful than Don Quixote. But to those who say that "there aren't giants, only windmills," I reply with Don Quixote, "Obviously, you don't know much about adventures."

Conclusions

The object of this historical study has been the modern historical narrative on the medieval Jewish economic function. It has not, properly speaking, been a study of Jewish economic activity or Jewish economic thought, though it touches on both. It has analyzed how the narrative on the Jewish economic role as moneylenders came into being in nineteenth-century academic discourse, why it had such staying power in the twentieth century even when the growth of medieval economic history undercut its foundations, and why overturning the myth of the Jewish economic function is significant for Jewish *and* European history in the twenty-first century. The word "myth" is used not as a denial of the fact that Jews lent money in medieval Europe, nor of the fact that a small Jewish elite were professional moneylenders. The "myth of the medieval Jewish moneylender" is used as a shorthand for the grand narrative of the "Jewish economic function" with all of its assumptions and implications. In challenging this meta-narrative, I have critiqued a set of assumptions which do not have a factual, textual, or documentary basis. When taken as a given, these assumptions limit and distort interpretation of the past. These assumptions are as follows: Jews were the quintessential moneylenders of medieval Europe; in this role, they filled a function denied to Christians yet necessary for European economic development; Jews had to lend money, because they could not work the land, practice crafts, or trade; Jews were able to fill the credit niche, because they were always highly commercialized, unlike the Europeans among whom they lived, and were unrestricted

WHICH IS THE MERCHANT HERE? AND WHICH THE JEW? 183

by their religious law from profiting on credit. Underlying these assumptions is a slippage from "some Jews" to "most Jews" to "*the* Jews," and a presumption of Jewish difference and otherness. A presumption of Jewish difference reinforced by institutional divisions has led scholars to insulate Jewish history from European economic history. The result has been the persistence of a binary construction: the Christian merchant against the Jewish moneylender. This binary, forged in the high and late middle ages, still haunts modern economic thought today. Indeed, in the modern period, it has come to play a more prominent role in antisemitism than it did in the medieval period.

The heart of this book (Part 2) challenged the paradigm of the Jewish moneylender through an empirical study of the Jewish community most representative of the Jewish economic function—the Jews of medieval England. England was chosen as a case study not only because it offered the strongest support for the traditional narrative, which I aimed to challenge, but because it offered the best archival sources for a statistical analysis of Jewish wealth and Jewish moneylending. The two ironically are linked, as I shall shortly explain. Chapter 4 analyzed the distribution of wealth among Anglo-Jewry and showed that a projected 75 percent of the Jewish population eked out a living on the urban margins. Only a handful of men were high-end, professional moneylenders, and these were out-done by Christian lenders in the first half of the twelfth century and in the later half of the thirteenth century. Contrary to the methodology of social history, Jewish historians have for too long focused on the exceptional individual, the elite and wealthy Jewish moneylender, as a representative for all medieval Jews.

This striking economic information led to a reexamination in Chapter 5 of the assumption that Anglo-Jews were privileged and protected in order to be exploited by the Crown. The counterargument was made that medieval Jews were neither privileged nor extorted. Their legal status was akin to that of free, urban burgesses, but the community was treated differently by being marked out as Jews. The exchequer of the Jews was not a mechanism for aiding Jewish loans, but merely a branch of the great exchequer devoted to the auditing and collecting of royal revenue. Anglo-Jews' legal actions before the court of the exchequer and participation in the procedures of communal tallage were comparable to those of urban burgesses. I do not deny that Jews were more vulnerable to exploitation, as the tallages of a third in 1239 and 1275 indicate, and to the erosion of their right to residence, as the expulsion of 1290 shows. But there was no special protection for Jews as moneylenders. They were as close to being urban

184 J.L. MELL

burgesses as Jews could come while remaining Jewish. The sole difference was that they were segregated administratively more and more over the thirteenth century. The Jewish exchequer and Jewish loan chests did not protect Jewish moneylending for the rapacious Crown; rather these institutions aimed to protect Christians from Jewish maleficence. The administrative segregation of Jews in England, which has undergirded the assumption of a special Jewish role, ironically preserved the documentation allowing a reassessment of the Jewish economic function. As Chapter 6 argued, ultimately the deciding factor was the monarchies' assumption of the mantle of "most-Christian king," under which they pressed forward the Church's program of anti-Judaism. Jews became the symbolic referent for "usurer" not because they were the most important moneylenders, but because "infidel" became identified with economic sin, and Jews were the most prescient symbol of the infidel as the historic agents who were offered the Messiah, yet rejected and "killed" Christ.[19] The administrative record-keeping which allowed this reassessment was driven by a system prejudiced against Jews as anti-Christians.

Because the meta-narrative has had such staying power, I challenged it from two directions, one empirical and medieval, the other theoretical and modern. Part 1 showed how the narrative entered modern mainstream German academic discourse *before* economic history proper was practiced, how the narrative was fashioned as a philosemitic and liberal response to antisemitism in the 1870s and then refashioned in the mid-twentieth century in response to twentieth-century antisemitism. The narrative effectively countered antisemitism by first conceding that there was a special connection between Jews, Judaism, and money and then flipping the moral valence of these connections: Jews provided credit essential for European economic development, aiding Europe even when they suffered an antisemitic backlash. In the midst of the trauma of the Holocaust, Roscher's historical narrative was both celebrated and denounced by Jewish historians. Kisch celebrated it as a philosemitic response to contemporary antisemitism, while Oelsner denounced it as a source for contemporary antisemitism. I argued that both were correct: Roscher's argument in its historical context was philosemitic, but it had dangerous antisemitic potential, as Sombart's work showed. Oelsner's critique has been a guiding light for this study, and I see my own work as a completion of hers.

At the same time that Kisch and Oelsner were writing on Roscher, Sombart, and Weber, two other émigré scholars—Lopez and Postan—were synthesizing the broad economic histories of the twentieth century.

WHICH IS THE MERCHANT HERE? AND WHICH THE JEW? 185

They directly challenged Sombart's and the German Historical School's depiction of medieval European economy as static and traditional by recovering nascent capitalist strains. They crystallized the new economic research in the paradigms of the commercial revolution/economic expansion of the high middle ages. Following Marcel Mauss, anthropologists and sociologists critiqued the Historical School's economic stages, and historians associated with the Annales School applied the new theories of gift economy to early medieval Europe. But ironically, Kisch's reworking of Roscher became the basis for the standard postwar narrative of medieval Jewish economic history. The very experience of trauma and emigration surrounding WWII prompted émigré figures like Robert Lopez to sustain and celebrate Kisch's narrative of the medieval Jewish moneylender in *The Commercial Revolution of the High Middle Ages*. Only in the post-Holocaust period could historians, like Gavin Langmuir and Lester Little, neither Jews nor émigrés, but Americans galvanized by the Civil Rights movement, begin to think in new ways about medieval antisemitism and refashion the "Jewish economic function" to function as a scapegoat.

I argued that these trajectories in the subfields of Jewish history, economic history, and Annales School cultural history should be looked at as a unified whole. Although the historians who constructed the postwar models were aware of each other's work, we, the heirs of these historians, have failed to analyze the logical contradictions, lacunae, and limitations that have emerged between these models. Critical attention to the narrative of the Jewish economic function provides us with a tool for propelling forward each of these trajectories, precisely because the concept of Jewish commercialism was so closely bound up with the economic theories and models of the late nineteenth and early twentieth centuries against which the postwar models were constructed. Now, in the post-Holocaust period, with the formative scholarship on antisemitism having been published and absorbed, it is thinkable to cast the tropes of Jews and money as part of antisemitism without offering an apologia via Roscher's economic function.

Volume II explored how new insights can emerge in European and Jewish histories when the "Jewish economic function" is dissolved. The working assumption underlying this volume was that Jews were Europeans whose social, economic, and cultural practices roughly mirrored those of urban Christians: Among Jews, as among Christians, were found poor and rich—but mostly poor. Among Jews, as among Christians, those on the urban margin pieced together a living from various economic activities—

the range and diversity of which remain hidden from view. Among Jews, as among Christians, were found professional moneylenders, but these moneylenders were a small minority in both communities. Most medieval individuals, whether elite or common, urban or peasant, Jewish or Christian, had recourse to credit in the form of future sales on produce, mortgage of land, currency exchange, investments of extra cash, and consumption loans. Credit permeated the lives of thirteenth-century individuals and religious corporations. Commercialization was a process which Jews and Christians experienced at the same time, and its moral and legal dilemmas were explored in similar ways by Jewish and Christian religious leaders.

Chapters 6, 7, and 8 each engaged one of the postwar responses to the Roscher-Weber-Sombart paradigms in the subfields of Jewish history, economic history, and Annales School cultural history laid out in Chapter 3. By making these engagements, I attempted to realize one of my theoretical principles as a Jewish historian committed to writing Jewish history as European history. That principle briefly stated is that Jewish history has real relevance to European history: to understand deeply a piece of Jewish history must by necessity impact, even revolutionize, our understanding of European history.

Chapter 6 took up the trajectory set in motion by Stobbe with his question—why did the status of the Jews decline in the high middle ages? It reframed Roscher's answer to this question—the "Jewish economic function"—as a medieval discourse on Jewish usury. By doing so, Chapter 6 made three contributions to Jewish and European history. First, in regard to studies of usury, the chapter showed that the usury campaign was not directed first and foremost at Jewish usury, but at the reform of Christians. The campaign came, in time, to extend to Jews, as a problematic group that did not fall under Church jurisdiction and required the intervention of secular rulers. The specific and separate references to Jewish usury reflect this jurisdictional issue and the fraught religious attitude toward unbelievers within Europe during the crusades, not a special economic role fulfilled by Jews. Second, in regard to studies of medieval antisemitism, it showed that the discourse on Jewish usury was actually a component of a broader anti-Judaic movement, which manifested itself in legal disabilities, on the one hand, and in the classic medieval antisemitic charges of ritual murder, blood libel, and host desecration, on the other. The chapter suggested that the definition of medieval antisemitism as "irrational religious fantasy" over against "rational economic antagonism" must be reconfigured as part of the same "rational" religious animosity rooted in endemic crusading, as

WHICH IS THE MERCHANT HERE? AND WHICH THE JEW? 187

well as the jurisdictional competition of papal and secular monarchies of the late twelfth and thirteenth centuries. Third, the chapter contributed to a deeper understanding of the relationship between economic change and economic thought during medieval commercialization: the traditional understanding of the Christian usury campaign as coming from a regressive Church whose morals reflected the agrarian economy of the early middle ages and which only slowly and reluctantly ceded ground to the new commercial life was shown to be ill-founded on a theoretical assumption of a deep split between religion and economy. What had previously been seen as accommodation to commercialization was rather the development of sophisticated economic thought in concert with the usury campaign.

Chapter 7 took up the trajectory of the European commercial revolution and commercialization. It analyzed the commercial contracts and long-distance shipping patterns of Marseille's Jewish merchants as a counterpoint to Emery's study of Perpignan's Jewish moneylenders. The use of the *commenda* by Marseille's Jewish merchants during the thirteenth century, even when investing with coreligionists, showed Jewish participation in the commercial revolution and the parallel process of commercialization. Contra Sombart, Jews had no monopoly on individualistic pursuit of profit. Contra Roscher and Kisch, Jews were not pushed out of trade and into moneylending at the peak of the commercial revolution. The preference of the Jewish merchants of Marseille for the Latinate contract of the commenda and Marseille's legal courts as the institutions guaranteeing their trade confirms recent conclusions about the decisive role of political and legal structures on long-distance trade in the medieval Mediterranean. The Marseille Jewish merchants participated in the Latinate Christian mercantile system in contrast to their coreligionists from Islamic Cairo, who participated in the Islamic mercantile system. Individualism and institutionally based trust were present in the Islamic as well as the Italian trading spheres, but configured differently. The key difference between the two, as Jessica Goldberg has argued, was that of the political structures of empires and city-states, and the position of merchants within them.[20] Italian merchant guilds were the political elites of their city-states and therefore controlled the means of violence; their ships were used equally to trade, make war, and prey upon other Mediterranean ships. Conversely they lacked a legal infrastructure beyond their own city-state. Islamic merchants were not part of the political elite and had no control over the state's monopoly on violence. But they could rely on a legal infrastructure that spanned the Islamic Mediterranean. These differences explain Italian preference for partnership (commenda) and Islamic preference for reciprocal agency (*suḥba*). Jews in each of these cultural spheres adopted the mechanisms of the majority culture, within whose political and legal framework they lived. The dissolution of the old narrative on the Jewish economic function, therefore, allows us to use the presence of Jewish merchants within both Islamic and Christian Mediterranean zones as a test case which confirms more general conclusions about Mediterranean trade.

Chapter 8 reexamined Duby and Little's application of the concept of "gift economy" and "profit economy" to the medieval commercial revolution. The chapter suggested that recent deconstructions of gift and profit by anthropologists could be usefully applied to medieval history as the beginning point for a cultural history of money. Rather than aligning Jews with profit economy and Christians with gift economy, the chapter deconstructed both concepts within medieval Hebrew and Latin moral literature (*exempla*). The prevailing narrative posits the emergence of a "new money economy" in the high middle ages, in which money is positioned as a causal agent: money is said to effect and symbolize the "profit motive," becoming a locus for anxiety about the new money economy. But a close reading of moral literature, Jewish and Christian, suggests that money per se was not a locus of anxiety. Moralists had a sophisticated understanding of economic value and its relation to moral economy. Anxiety among Jewish and Christian religious authorities focused on the possible disjuncture between moral and economic values, not on economic value per se. Through close readings of medieval exempla, I suggested that moralists regarded the economic act of acquisition as creating a moral value. When "bad" moral value adhered to coins, they sought to devise means for redeeming bad moral value through penitential acts. This suggests that a European economic development narrated as a shift from gift exchange to profit exchange ought to be problematized. Binary oppositions between gift and profit, and between an altruistic Christianity (linked to gift economy) and a modernizing Judaism (linked to profit economy), ought to be broken down.

New Directions

The endpoint of this book is a new beginning. Its aim has been accomplished if it has cleared the ground for fresh historical exploration by deconstructing the narrative of the Jewish economic function founded on the binaries of "Jew" and "merchant." This new horizon was only

WHICH IS THE MERCHANT HERE? AND WHICH THE JEW? 189

made possible with a sea change that occurred in the aftermath of the Holocaust. Medieval antisemitism is recognized and studied for what it is, and the discourse on Jewish usury can be recognized as a component of it. No longer is the most effective response to antisemitic tropes on Jews and money an indirect assertion of a liberal economic function for the Jews. It is now thinkable to respond that medieval European Jews had no economic role, no economic function in Europe. Medieval Jews were on the whole paupers, thieves, bards, butchers, merchants, and merry wives. They lived on the urban margins, eking out a living like so many others. They were neither the heroes of progressive rationalization nor the minions of a Mr. Moneybags, spreading "their worldly religion—huckstering" and "their worldly God—money."[21] The same argument can and should be made in regard to sixteenth-century Italian Jewish moneylenders and seventeenth-century German court Jews.

This book has sought to displace both the many-armed ogres and the windmills, both the stereotype of the greedy Jew and the image of the Jewish modernizer, with a shared experience of European change symbolized in a moment of ambiguous identity evoked in Shakespeare's *The Merchant of Venice*. Portia's question points us toward a new beginning— the commensurability of Jewish and Christian culture and context, that is, to a joint European past within which difference may be discerned, but never constitutes incommensurability. But one of the main motives for clinging to the narrative of the Jewish economic function has been that it offered a mechanism for integrating Jewish history into European history. If the narrative is dissolved, one may ask: how can we integrate Jewish history into European history? And if one accepts the idea of a shared history, then how does one preserve Jewish history as something distinct?

The answer lies in how the category of "Jewish" is constructed against "European." In nineteenth- and early-twentieth-century historiography, "Jewish" was positioned as binary opposite to "European," and therefore alien and foreign. More recent work frames "Jewish" as a subset of "European," in which "European" is a bridge category including varieties of difference—ethnic, religious, legal, social, economic, gender, and so on. One can cite a number of recent studies on medieval Jewish thought and culture which emphasize a common European experience running beneath the religious divisions of Christianity and Judaism.[22] Elisheva Baumgarten in *Practicing Piety in Medieval Ashkenaz* suggests that in medieval Europe a "competitive piety developed that simultaneously emphasized mutually held ideas about religious expression and [yet] heightened divisions between Jews and Christians."[23] Medieval Jewish women who assumed positive time-bound commandments, such as tefillin and tzitzit, were part of a broader trend that encompassed Christian women's increased participation in religious and social rituals in the thirteenth century.[24] David Shyovitz has convincingly argued that the rapid spread of the Mourner's Kaddish in medieval Ashkenaz reflects a broad shift in Jewish conceptions of the afterlife that mirror the "birth of purgatory" among Christians.[25] Talya Fishman's *Becoming the People of the Talmud* takes the medieval European phenomenon of textualization as the starting point for understanding how the Talmud became a prescriptive guide to applied Jewish law in medieval Europe.[26] Ivan Marcus and Jeremy Cohen have shown how the shared dynamic of "renaissance and renewal" within the Hebrew chronicles of the First Crusade ironically solidified Jewish-Christian difference.[27] Ivan Marcus has subsequently conceptualized Jewish-Christian symbiosis as "inward acculturation," a term that captures this process of absorbing, yet transforming, Christian culture.[28] Malachi Hacohen's forthcoming *Jacob and Esau between Nation and Empire* goes one step further by "telling a European story out of traditional Jewish sources." Hacohen presents medieval Christian clerics and rabbinic authorities "as European figures, inhabiting a shared intellectual universe, often in dialogue with each other, addressing from different perspectives, European problems."[29] In all of these examples, Jewish religious and cultural changes are configured as medieval European experiences. Yet they retain their Jewish difference by virtue of the distinct Jewish language, texts, and culture within which broader changes are manifest. As Hacohen boldly puts it, "historians can now 'Europeanize' the rabbis and set an example for European integration that welcomes cultural pluralism."[30]

This model can and should be applied to Jewish economic thought and Jewish economic practice. Several paths were explored in Volume II, but much work remains to be done. The history of medieval economic thought has been carefully studied by scholars of both rabbinic Judaism and canon law: the classic studies of Joel Rosenthal and T.P. McLaughlin have been complemented by the probing explorations of Haym Soloveitchik and John Noonan, and have culminated in the surveys of Hillel Gamoran and Odd Langholm.[31] The parallels between the two traditions are striking, but remain virtually unexplored.[32] The state of the field is perhaps best exemplified by Soloveitchik's comment that the Jewish attitude to usury in the high and late middle ages is "radically different" from the

WHICH IS THE MERCHANT HERE? AND WHICH THE JEW? 191

Latin Christian one, which elicited "aversion," even "revulsion," in the theological tracts and preaching campaigns of the twelfth and thirteenth centuries.[33] On the one hand, I agree with Soloveitchik's assessment that we find nothing similar to the Christian usury campaign in Jewish sources. In Chapter 6, I attempted to explain the Christian usury campaign as the confluence of crusading, a movement for moral reform with roots in the Gregorian reform, and the growth of monarchies—including the papal monarchy. None of these apply to Jewish history with the exception, perhaps, of moral reform, if one regards *Hasidei Ashkenaz* as representing a major stream in Ashkenazi culture—a matter still open to debate. But on the other hand, the legal developments in medieval rabbinic law share general characteristics with legal developments in canon law. The *Schadennehmen* and "the pawned pawn," which Soloveitchik probes so deeply, are gray areas, just as are the 13 exceptions to taking "more than the principal" developed in thirteenth-century canon law.[34] Underlying both rabbinic and canon laws on usury is unquestioned adherence to the Deuteronomic prohibition, according to each religion's interpretive tradition, and basic economic concepts such as the incommensurability of money and material objects in economic exchanges.[35] The probing of gray areas sharpens conceptions of usury, deepens economic thought, and leads to the creation of legal forms, such as interest in canon law or the gentile intermediary in Jewish law. There will, of course, be many differences in the two legal systems, particularly in the details. Yet there will be many fundamental parallels, which derive in part through the roots of both legal systems in the Roman world and in part through their shared contemporary social context, as well as their shared sacred text, the Hebrew Bible. In short, the work of McLaughlin and Rosenthal, Soloveitchik and Noonan, Gamoran and Langholm provides a solid foundation on which to begin constructing the relationships between canon law and rabbinic law on usury as facets of a common European experience, an experience which generated new economic concepts out of striving to fulfill divine precepts.[36]

In regard to economic history, the range and diversity of Jewish economic occupations and strategies awaits fresh exploration unhindered by the blinders that obscured our historical vision with preconceptions about Jewish moneylenders. Documents are sparse to be sure, but the difficult terrain is nothing unusual for the medievalist, and several new forays are under way. Most notably, Michael Toch has undertaken a new survey and synthesis, *The Economic History of European Jews*, a task not undertaken since Caro's work a century ago.[37] The first volume has appeared on the early middle ages, and future volumes are promised on the high and late middle ages. But it remains to be seen how much Toch will dare to depart from the long-held tropes on Jews and money and moneymaking. In a recent article titled "Economic Activities of German Jews in the Middle Ages," he offers a preview of the lines of argument his later volume will likely contain.[38] He uncovers substantial evidence for the range of economic occupations, and the large portion of the Jewish population on the urban margins, and references Todeschini's work on antisemitism. Given all this, it is perplexing that he nonetheless concludes, "the traditional picture of the preponderance of trade, and later of money-lending, [is] largely valid."[39]

With the exponential growth of texts on the high and late middle ages, our knowledge can be extended greatly on Jewish economic occupations. In particular, renewed exploration of Jewish landownership and urban life promises to overturn presumptions about the absence of Jews in agriculture and guilds.[40] Equally important is the history of poverty, charity, and life on the urban margins, a topic that remains untouched in medieval European Jewish history, though explored for the Christian population by Annalist historians and in medieval Egypt for the Jewish population.[41] Perhaps the most intriguing intellectual path waiting to be explored is that of the commercialization of the Jewish population in regard to parallels and divergences with Christian populations. Recent demographic studies of Jewish settlement[42] have suggested that the Jewish population shared in the European demographic growth of the high middle ages, but with the contrary result. Rather than undergoing urbanization, the formerly urban Jewish population underwent ruralization, moving out into the countryside in smaller and smaller settlements. Ironically, this process was exacerbated with the expulsions of the late thirteenth and fourteenth centuries and the ghettoizations of the fifteenth and sixteenth centuries, as Debra Kaplan's *Beyond Expulsion* reveals.[43]

One of the subsidiary functions that the narrative on Jewish moneylenders has served is as a narrative mechanism for integrating the Jewish minority into mainstream European history. As the only religious minority whose visible presence was tolerated in medieval Europe, Jews have figured (particularly perhaps among North American medievalists shaped by the multicultural ethic of their immigrant nations) as the main mode for fashioning a more inclusive premodern European history. But abandoning the myth of "the Jewish economic function" can help deepen existing paths and spur the exploration of others. Research into medieval antisemitism widely acknowledged as important in the aftermath of the Holocaust has quietly assumed room in the standard textbooks of medieval history. The links between the emergence of medieval antisemitism and the persecution of heretics and other out-groups have been mapped out by R.I. Moore. His *Formation of a Persecuting Society* sparked rancorous debate, but much more effort has gone into contesting it than into developing his insight. Heresy and antisemitism are still largely treated separately, even when researchers acknowledge that both are the outgrowth of changes in Christian theologies and institutions. Above all, however, the impetus to integrate minority and majority history, Jewish and European, points to the necessity of rethinking the main narratives of medieval European history. Two themes of pressing importance today call for our historical attention: immigration/emigration in the formation of Europe and the history of expulsion and ethnic cleansing prior to the formation of the nation-state. Both are histories waiting to be written, and the latter in particular is one in which the Jewish case figured foremost in premodern Europe and shaped modern trajectories. This history would form an important part of the new transnational European histories beginning to be written for the modern period.

History is memory. The best history tells us how our world was made and illuminates how we came to be the people and communities and societies that we are. History is also an act of dreaming. It can linger over the still waters of a pond stirred but by a dragonfly's wings or it can rage in the tossed froth of a sea storm's waves. Whether born in quiet backwaters or sea storms, dreams of the past guide our future. What has gone before shapes structurally the paths toward the future, and determines the dreams and longings that carry us forward. Zionists forged the kibbutzim in response to the discourse on Jewish economic difference, in active negation of the Jewish past imagined as a nonproductive economic existence. The Hebrew colloquialism for the geographic location of the modern nation-state of Israel, "ha-Aretz" (the Land), encodes the opposition between productive and unproductive labor. Encoded within this term is also another set of oppositions between Diaspora and Homeland, and nonhistory and history. By returning diaspora Jews to history and denying the dichotomies of unproductive and productive, Jew and merchant, this book hopes to change in a small way the paths forward by changing our memories of the past.

194   J.L. MELL

NOTES

1. William Shakespeare, "The most excellent historie of the merchant of Venice: With the extreame crueltie of Shylocke the Jewe towards the sayd merchant" (1600), Early English Books Online, http://gateway.proquest.com.proxy.lib.duke.edu/openurl?ctx_ver=Z39.88-2003&res_id=xri:eebo&rft_id=xri:eebo:image:11589:26.
2. *The Merchant of Venice*, ed. David Bevington (Glenview, IL, 1980), IV, i. References are to act and scene.
3. Ibid.
4. Ibid.
5. I echo Tony Tanner here, who emphasizes how astonishing Portia's question is at the outset of his introduction to *The Merchant of Venice* (William Shakespeare, *Comedies: Volume 2,* Everyman's Library 226 (New York, 1996), xi–xxxix, citation on xi). Tanner closes the essay by suggesting that Shakespeare may have subtly undercut the radical opposition between "merchant" and "Jew" in the play by playing off the "*very* close" association of "buggery" and usury in the "contemporary mind as unnatural acts." He reads Antonio as "mooningly in love with Bassanio" and "conspicuously uninvolved with, and unattracted to, any woman," in short as displaying "a homosexual passion, which must now be frustrated since Bassanio is set on marriage" (ibid., xxxviii). My reading does not foreclose Tanner's, but turns the deconstructive element in a different direction. My thanks to David Halperin for drawing my attention to this line by suggesting it as an epigraph.

   The other two works that have influenced my thinking on the play are James Shapiro, *Shakespeare and the Jews* (New York, 1996); and Jonathan Elukin, "Is Shylock Really Jewish? The Devil, Theology and the Meaning of *The Merchant of Venice*" (paper presented at a joint session of the Jewish Studies & Medieval Studies Seminars of the Triangle, Durham, NC, 27 Feb. 2012). On the historical fate of Shylock, see: James Gross, *Shylock: A Legend and Its Legacy* (New York, 1992). My thanks to Karen Kletter, who continually drew my attention to the ahistorical nature of the "Jew" and the "merchant."
6. Shakespeare, *The Merchant of Venice*, I, iii.
7. Ibid., IV, i.
8. Gal. 3:10–4 (New Revised Standard).
9. Shakespeare, *The Merchant of Venice*, IV, i.

WHICH IS THE MERCHANT HERE? AND WHICH THE JEW? 195

10. Giacomo Todeschini, "Franciscan Economics and Jews in the Middle Ages: From a Theological to an Economic Lexicon," in *Friars and Jews in the Middle Ages and Renaissance*, ed. Steven McMichael and Susan Myers (Leiden, 2004), 111.
11. The Jew is not erased, but superseded. On the logic of Christian supersession, see: Kathleen Biddick, *The Typological Imaginary: Circumcision, Technology, History* (Philadelphia, 2003).
12. *The Merchant of Venice*, V, i.
13. Ibid.
14. Ibid.
15. Michael Radford, director, "William Shakespeare's The Merchant of Venice" (Movision & Arclight Films, 2005).
16. Heinrich Heine, *Heine on Shakespeare: A Translation of His Notes on Shakespeare Heroines*, trans. Ida Benecke (Westminster, 1895), 66.
17. Shakespeare, *The Merchant of Venice*, III, i.
18. Derek Penslar, *Shylock's Children: Economics and Jewish Identity in Modern Europe* (Berkeley, 2001); Joseph Shatzmiller, *Shylock Reconsidered: Jews, Moneylending, and Medieval Society* (Berkeley, 1990); Jonathan Hess, "Shylock's Daughters: Philosemitism, Popular Culture, and the Liberal Imagination" (paper presented at the Third Biennial German Jewish Workshop, Durham, NC, 10–12 Feb. 2013). See also: Robert Chazan, *Reassessing Jewish Life in Medieval Europe* (Cambridge, 2010), 107–32.
19. See the discussion of Todeschini's work in Chap. 6.
20. Jessica Goldberg, *Trade and Institutions in the Medieval Mediterranean: The Geniza Merchants and Their Business World* (Cambridge, 2012).
21. Karl Marx, "On the Jewish Question," in *The Marx-Engels Reader*, ed. Robert Tucker, 2nd. ed. (New York, 1978), 48.
22. I focus here on cultural history, but there is another stream emphasizing the coexistence of Jews and Christians from the perspective of social history. See, for example: Jonathan Elukin, *Living Together, Living Apart: Rethinking Jewish-Christian Relations in the Middle Ages* (Princeton, 2007).
23. Elisheva Baumgarten, *Practicing Piety in Medieval Ashkenaz: Men, Women and Everyday Religious Observance* (Philadelphia, 2014), citation on 8. See also: her *Mothers and Children: Jewish Family Life in Medieval Europe* (Princeton, 2004).
24. Baumgarten, *Practicing Piety*, 138–71.

25. David Shyovitz, "'You Have Saved Me from the Judgment of Gehenna': The Origins of the Mourner's Kaddish in Medieval Ashkenaz," *AJS Review* 39 (2015): 49–73.
26. Talya Fishman, *Becoming the People of the Talmud: Oral Torah as Written Tradition in Medieval Jewish Cultures* (Philadelphia, 2011).
27. Ivan Marcus, "The Dynamics of Jewish Renaissance and Renewal," in *Jews and Christians in Twelfth-Century Europe*, ed. Michael Signer and John Van Engen (Notre Dame, 2001), 27–45; Jeremy Cohen, *Sanctifying the Name of God: Jewish Martyrs and Jewish Memories of the First Crusade* (Philadelphia, 2004).
28. Ivan Marcus, "A Jewish-Christian Symbiosis: The Culture of Early Ashkenaz," in *Cultures of the Jews: A New History*, ed. David Biale (New York, 2002), 449–518.
29. Malachi Hacohen, *Jacob and Esau between Nation and Empire: A Jewish-European History* (Cambridge, forthcoming 2018), introduction and Chap. 4. Citations from introduction. For the modern period, Hacohen makes the radical claim that Jewish history provides the best foundation for European history, because it is already transnational and cosmopolitan by virtue of being Jewish.
30. Ibid.
31. For rabbinic law, see: Judah Rosenthal, "Ribit min-ha-Nokri," *Talpiyot* 5 (1952): 475–92 and 6 (1953): 130–52; Haym Soloveitchik, *Halakhah, Kalkalah ve-Dimui 'Atsmi: ha-Mashkona'ut bi-Yemei ha-Beinayim* (Jerusalem, 1985), originally published in a shorter English version as "Pawnbroking: A Study in Ribbit and of the Halakhah in Exile," *Proceedings of the American Academy of Jewish Research* 38–9 (1972): 203–68, and republished in a revised English version in his *Collected Essays* (Oxford, 2013), I:57–166; Hillel Gamoran, *Jewish Law in Transition: How Economic Forces Overcame the Prohibition against Lending on Interest* (Cincinnati, 2008).

    For canon law and theology, see: T.P. McLaughlin, "The Teaching of the Canonists on Usury," *Mediaeval Studies* 1 (1939): 81–147, and 2 (1940):1–22; John Noonan, *The Scholastic Analysis of Usury* (Cambridge, MA, 1957); John Baldwin, *Masters, Princes, and Merchants: The Social Views of Peter the Chanter and His Circle* (Princeton, 1970); Odd Langholm, *Economics in the Medieval Schools: Wealth, Exchange, Value, Money, and Usury according to the Paris Theological Tradition, 1200–1500* (Leiden, 1992), and *The Merchant in the Confessional: Trade and Price in the Pre-Reformation Penitential Handbooks* (Leiden, 2003).

WHICH IS THE MERCHANT HERE? AND WHICH THE JEW? 197

32. Two exceptions are Giacomo Todeschini, *La Ricchezza degli ebrei. Merci e denaro nella riflessione ebraica e definizione cristiana dell'usura alla fine del Medioevo* (Spoleto, 1989); and Aaron Kirschenbaum, "Jewish and Christian Theories of Usury in the Middle Ages," *Jewish Quarterly Review* 75 (1985): 270–89. For my reservations on Kirschenbaum and my acclamation of Todeschini, see: Chap. 6.

33. Haym Soloveitchik, "The Jewish Attitude to Usury in the High and Late Middle Ages (1000–1500)," in *Credito e usura fra teologia, diritto e amministrazione*, ed. Diego Quaglioni et al. (Rome, 2005), 115–27, esp. 123–6, republ. in Soloveitchik, *Collected Essays*, 1:44–56.

34. The *Schadennehmen* involves a case where a Jewish borrower takes a loan from a Christian lender on a pledge with interest and the Christian lender subsequently turns around and borrows from a second Jew on the same pawn ($J^1 > G > J^2$). The "pawned pawn" is a loan taken by a gentile on a pawn from a Jew. This Jewish creditor turns around and borrows from a second Jewish creditor on the basis of the pawn ($g > J^1 > J^2$). The same question arises for both: can the second Jew receive interest or would he or she be violating the Deuteronomic prohibition on intra-Jewish usury? Rashi rules that the second Jewish creditor can receive interest in both cases. Why? Because a gentile cannot be an agent for a Jew in rabbinic law, and therefore the *Schadennehmen* ($J^1 > g > J^2$) is two discrete transactions and not one. Thus interest is paid from Jew to gentile, but not from Jew to Jew. The "pawned pawn" ($g > J^1 > J^2$) is in fact one transaction, for the first Jewish creditor acts as an agent for the second Jewish creditor in the loan with the gentile. Therefore usury is paid from gentile to Jew, but not from Jew to Jew. These cases involve additionally subtle components, in particular the distinction between a material object and money encoded in the pawn.

   For the 13 exceptions, see: McLaughlin, "Teaching of the Canonists on Usury," 1:125–44.

35. See the discussion of the polemics in Chap. 6 for the difference in the interpretive traditions.

36. Unfortunately, the one book that attempts a comparative history of usury in Christianity, Judaism, and Islam is deeply flawed and obscures more than it illuminates: Susan Buckley, *Teachings on Usury in Judaism, Christianity and Islam* (Lewiston, NY, 2000).

37. Michael Toch, *The Economic History of European Jews: Late Antiquity and Early Middle Ages* (Leiden, 2013); Georg Caro,

198 J.L. MELL

Sozial- und Wirtscahftsgeschichte der Juden im Mittelalter und der Neuzeit, 2 vols. (Leipzig, 1908–20).

38. Michael Toch, "Economic Activities of German Jews in the Middle Ages," in *Wirtschaftsgeschichte der mittelalterlichen Juden: Fragen und Einschäzungen*, ed. Michael Toch (Munich, 2008), 181–210 (see his comment to this effect in *Economic History of European Jews*, 205, note 78). Toch has published extensively on Jewish economic history and his full oeuvre cannot be cited here, but see especially: Michael Toch, *Die Juden im Mittelalterlichen Reich* (Munich, 1998), and his collected essays *Peasants and Jews in Medieval Germany: Studies in Cultural, Social, and Economic History* (Aldershot, 2003).

39. Toch, "Economic Activities of German Jews," 210. His judgment seems to be based on a traditional methodology in social history which erringly, I argue, treats individual examples of Jewish moneylenders as typical of the whole Jewish population. Why should an elite male define the economic profile of "Jewry" more than an impoverished Jew/ess?

40. The unpublished, but path-breaking, research of Toni Oelsner on Jewish agriculture in the upper Rhineland has still not been followed up: "The Economic and Social Condition of the Jews of Southwestern Germany in the 13th and 14th Centuries," Toni Oelsner Collection, Archives of the Leo Baeck Institute, New York (126 pages). See also: Toch, "Economic Activities of German Jews," 205–8; and Haym Soloveitchik, *Yayin bi-yeme ha-benayim: yen nesekh: perek be-toldot ha-halakhah be-Ashkenaz* (Wine in Ashkenaz in the Middle Ages: Yeyn nesekh—a study in Halakhah) (Tel Aviv, 2003).

41. Mark Cohen, *Poverty and Charity in the Jewish Community of Medieval Egypt* (Princeton, 2005); Mark Cohen, *The Voice of the Poor in the Middle Ages: An Anthology of Documents from the Cairo Geniza* (Princeton, 2005); Michel Mollat, *The Poor in the Middle Ages: An Essay in Social History* (New Haven, 1986); Bronislaw Geremek, *Poverty: A History* (Oxford, 1994).

42. Alfred Haverkamp, ed., *Geschichte der Juden im Mittelalter von der Nordsee bis zu den Südalpen: Kommentiertes Kartenwek*, 3 vols. (Hannover, 2002); *Germania Judaica*, 4 vols. (Tübingen, 1963).

43. Debra Kaplan, *Beyond Expulsion: Jews, Christians and Reformation Strasbourg* (Stanford, 2011).

BIBLIOGRAPHY

ARCHIVES AND MANUSCRIPTS

Archives de la Ville de Marseille (Marseille)
Registre de Giraud Amalric (1248). 1, Serie II, 1.

Biblioteca Palatina (Parma)
Meir ha-Meili, *Milḥemet Mitzvah*. MS 2749 (De Rossi 155).

Leo Baeck Institute (New York)
Guido Kisch Collection, AR787, Leo Baeck Institute, New York. https://archive.org/details/guidokisch
Toni Oelsner Collection, AR 3970, Leo Baeck Institute, New York. https://archive.org/details/tonioelsnercolle01lsne

National Archives— United Kingdom (Kew)
E 101/249/1 King's Remembrancer: Accounts Various. Jews.
E 101/249/2 King's Remembrancer: Accounts Various. Jews.
E 101/249/3 King's Remembrancer: Accounts Various. Jews.

© The Author(s) 2018
J.L. Mell, *The Myth of the Medieval Jewish Moneylender*,
DOI 10.1007/978-3-319-34186-6

200 BIBLIOGRAPHY

E 101/249/4 King's Remembrancer: Accounts Various. Jews.
E 101/249/12 King's Remembrancer: Accounts Various. Jews.
E 101/249/16 King's Remembrancer: Accounts Various. Jews.
E 101/249/17 King's Remembrancer: Accounts Various. Jews.
E 101/249/19 King's Remembrancer: Accounts Various. Jews.
E 101/249/32 King's Remembrancer: Accounts Various. Jews.
E 401/1 Exchequer of Receipt. Receipt Rolls and Registers.
E 401/2 Exchequer of Receipt. Receipt Rolls and Registers.
E 401/3A Exchequer of Receipt. Receipt Rolls and Registers.
E 401/4 Exchequer of Receipt. Receipt Rolls and Registers.
E 401/8–9 Exchequer of Receipt. Receipt Rolls and Registers.
E 401/48 Exchequer of Receipt. Receipt Rolls and Registers.
E 401/1568 Exchequer of Receipt. Receipt Rolls and Registers.
E 401/1569 Exchequer of Receipt. Receipt Rolls and Registers.
E 401/1570 Exchequer of Receipt. Receipt Rolls and Registers.
E 401/1571 Exchequer of Receipt. Receipt Rolls and Registers.
E 401/1572 Exchequer of Receipt. Receipt Rolls and Registers.
E 401/1573 Exchequer of Receipt. Receipt Rolls and Registers.
ZBOX 1/39/1 Part 1. Note on calendaring receipt and issue rolls of the exchequer of receipt by S.C. Ratcliff. Manuscript.
ZBOX 1/39/2 Part 2. 10, 17 Hen III. Transcript of receipt rolls and registers: E 401/8–10. Manuscript.

Yale University Library Manuscripts & Archives (New Haven)

Robert Sabatino Lopez Papers, Yale University, New Haven, CN.

MEDIEVAL TEXTS — PRINTED AND ONLINE

Abrahams, Israel. "The Northampton 'Donum' of 1194." *Miscellanies of the Jewish Historical Society of England* 1 (1925): lix–lxxiv.

Abrahams, Israel and Henry Stokes, eds. *Starrs and Jewish Charters Preserved in the British Museum*. 3 vols. Cambridge: Cambridge University Press, 1930.

Agus, Irving. *The Heroic Age of Franco-German Jewry*. New York: Yeshiva University Press, 1969.

Alberigo, Giuseppe et al., eds. *Conciliorum Oecumenicorum Decreta*. Basil: Herder, 1962.

An Alphabet of Tales: An English 15th century translation of the Alphabetum narrationum of Étienne de Besançon. Translated by Mary Banks. London: K. Paul, Trench, Trübner & Co., 1904.

BIBLIOGRAPHY 201

Amalric, Giraud. *Les notules commerciales d'Almaric notaire Marseillais du XIIIme siècle*. In *Documents inédits sur le commerce de Marseille au Moyen Age*. Edited by Louis Blancard. Marseille: Barlatier-Feissat, 1884–5.

Baratier, Édouard and Félix Reynaud. *Histoire du commerce de Marseille*. 2 vols. Paris: Plon, 1951.

Berger, David. *The Jewish-Christian Debate in the High Middle Ages: A Critical Edition of the Nizzahon vetus with an introduction, translation, and commentary*. Philadelphia: Jewish Publication Society of America, 1979.

Bernard of Clairvaux. *The Letters of St. Bernard of Clairvaux*. Edited and translated by Bruno James. Kalamazoo: Cistercian Publications, 1998.

———. *Sämtliche Werke: lateinisch/deutsch*. 10 vols. Innsbruck: Tyrolia-Verlag, 1990–9.

Blancard, Louis. *Documents inédits sur le commerce de Marseille au Moyen Age*. 2 vols. Marseille: Barlatier-Feissat, 1884–5.

Bonusvillannus. *Notai liguri del sec.XII. III. Bonvillano (1198)*. Edited by J.E. Eierman, H.C. Krueger, and R.L. Reynolds. Turin: Editrice Libraria Italiana, 1939.

Bouquet, Martin et al., eds. *Recueil des Historiens des "Gaules et de la France*. 24 vols. Paris: Palmé, 1869–1904.

Bracton, Henry de. *Bracton on the Laws and Customs of England*. Translated by Samuel Thorne. 4 vols. Buffalo: W.S. Hein, 1997.

———. *De Legibus et Consuetudinibus Angliæ*. Yale Historical Publications. Manuscripts and Edited Texts 3. 4 vols. New Haven: Yale University Press, 1915–1942.

Caesarius of Heisterbach. *Dialogus Miraculorum*. Edited by Joseph Strange. Cologne: J.M. Heberle, 1851.

———. *The Dialogue on Miracles*. Translated by H. von E. Scott and C.C. Swinton Bland. 2 vols. London: George Routledge & Sons, 1929.

———. *Die Fragmente der Libri VIII Miraculorum des Caesarius von Heisterbach*. Rome: Herder, 1901.

Calendar of Documents Relating to Ireland, preserved in Her Majesty's Public Record Office, London, 1171–1307. 5 vols. London: Longman, 1875–86.

Calendar of the Charter Rolls Preserved in the Public Record Office. London: H.M. Stationery Office, 1903–27.

Calendar of the Close Rolls Preserved in the Public Record Office. London: H.M. Stationery Office, 1892 –.

Calendar of the Patent Rolls. London: H.M. Stationery Office, 1925 –.

Calendar of the Plea Rolls of the Exchequer of the Jews. 6 vols. London: Macmillan, 1905–2005.

Causton, Ann, ed. *Medieval Jewish Documents in Westminister Abbey*. London: Jewish Historical Society of England, 2007.

Chew, Helena. "A Jewish Aid to Marry, A.D. 1221." *Jewish Historical Society of England—Transactions* 11 (1924–27): 92–111.

202 BIBLIOGRAPHY

Curia Regis Rolls Preserved in the Public Record Office. London: H.M. Stationery office, 1922–2002.

Davis, M.D. *Hebrew Deeds of English Jews before 1290.* London: Jewish Chronicle, 1888.

Delaborde, Henri-François, ed. *Oeuvres de Rigord et de Guillaume le Breton, historiens de Philippe-Auguste.* 2 vols. Paris: Renouard, 1882–5.

———. *Recueil des actes de Philippe Auguste.* 3 vols. Paris: Impr. nationale, 1916–79.

Delisle, Léopold, ed. *Recueil de jugements de l'echiquier de Normandie au XIIIe siècle (1207–1270).* Paris: Impr. impériale, 1864.

———. *Recueil Historiens des Gaules et de la France.* Vol. 24, 2 parts. Paris: Impr. impériale, 1904.

Eidelberg, Shlomo, trans. and ed. *The Jews and the Crusaders: The Hebrew Chronicles of the First and Second Crusades.* Madison: University of Wisconsin Press, 1977.

Epstein, Isidore, ed. *The Hebrew-English edition of the Babylonian Talmud.* London: Soncino Press, 1989.

Étienne de Bourbon. *Anecdotes historiques légendes et apologues tirés du recueil inédit d'Etienne de Bourbon, Dominicain du XIIIe siècle.* Paris: Librairie Renouard, 1887.

Fitz Nigel, Richard. *Dialogus de Scaccario: The Dialogue of the Exchequer.* Emilie Amt, editor and translator. Clarendon Press, Oxford, 2007.

Friedberg, Emil, ed. *Corpus Iuris Canonici.* 2 vols. Leipzig: Bernhardi Tauchnitz, 1879. Reprinted Graz: Akademische Druck- u. Verlagsanstalt, 1959.

———. *Quinque Compilationes Antiquae.* Graz: Druck, 1882; reprt., 1956.

Giovanni di Guiberto. *Giovanni di Guiberto (1200–11).* Edited by Margaret Winslow Hall. 2 vols. Turin: Editrice Libraria Italiana, 1939.

Giovanni Scriba, *Il Cartolare di Giovanni Scriba.* Edited by Mario Chiaudano and Mattia Moresco. 2 vols. Turin: Lattes, 1935.

Glaber, Rodulfus. *Raoul Glaber. Les cinq livres de ses histoires (900–1044).* Edited by Maurice Prou. Paris: A. Picard, 1886.

Grayzel, Solomon. *The Church and the Jews in the XIIIth Century.* Vol. 1. New York: Hermon Press, 1966.

———. *The Church and the Jews in the XIIIth Century.* Edited by Kenneth Stow. Vol. 2. Detroit: Wayne State Press, 1989.

The Great Roll of the Pipe for the second– tenth year of the reign of King Richard the First, Michaelmas 1190–1198 (Pipe Roll 36–44). Publications of the Pipe Roll Society 39–41, 43–47. Edited by Doris Stenton. London: Pipe Roll Society, 1925–32.

Grosseteste, Robert. *The Letters of Robert Grosseteste, Bishop of Lincoln.* Translated and edited by F.A.C. Mantello and Joseph Goering. Toronto: University of Toronto Press, 2010.

BIBLIOGRAPHY 203

————. *Roberti Grosseteste episcopi quondam lincolniensis. Epistolae.* Edited by Henry Luard. London: Longman, 1861.

Guglielmo Cassinese. *Guglielmo Cassinese (1190–1192).* Edited by H.C. Krueger, Margaret W. Hall, and Robert Reynolds. 2 vols. Turin: Lattes, 1938.

Habermann, Avraham, ed. *Sefer Gezirot Ashkenaz ve-Sarfat.* Jerusalem: Tarshish, 1945.

"Henry III Fine Rolls Project: A window into English History, 1216–72." http://www.finerollshenry3.org.uk/index.html

Hoffman, Moses, ed. *Der Geldhandel der deutschen Juden während des Mittelalters bis zum Jahre 1350.* Leipzig: Duncker & Humblot, 1910.

Jacobs, Joseph. *The Jews of Angevin England: Documents and Records from the Latin and Hebrew Sources, Printed and Manuscript.* New York: Putnam's Sons, 1893.

Jenkinson, Hilary and Beryl Formoy, ed. *Select Cases in the Exchequer of Pleas.* London: B. Quaritch, 1932.

Jocelin de Brakelond. *Chronica Jocelini de Brakelond.* London: Camden Society, 1840.

————. *Chronicle of Jocelin of Brakelond.* London: T. Nelson, 1949.

Jordan, William. "Jewish-Christian Relations in mid-thirteenth century France: An unpublished *Enquête* from Picardy." *Revue des études juives* 138 (1979): 47–55.

Judah ha-Kohen. *Sefer Ha-Dinim.* Edited by Avraham Grossman. Jerusalem: Merkaz Zalman Shazar, 1977.

Kimḥi, Joseph. *The Book of the Covenant of Joseph Kimḥi.* Translated by Frank Talmage. Toronto: Pontifical Institute of Mediaeval Studies, 1972.

————. *Sefer ha-Brit.* Edited by Efraim Talmage. Jerusalem: Bialik Institute, 1974.

Lanfranco of Milan. *Lanfranco (1202–1226).* Edited by H.C. Krueger and R.L. Reynolds. Genoa: Società ligure di storia patria, 1951–3.

Layettes du Trésor des Chartes. Edited by Alexandre Teulet, J. de Laborde, E. Berger and H.-F. Delaborde. 5 vols. Paris: Henri Plon, 1863–1909.

Lespinasse, René de. *Le Nivernais et les comtes de Nevers.* 3 vols. Paris: H. Champion, 1909–14.

Lopez, Robert, and Irving Woodworth Raymond, trans. *Medieval Trade in the Mediterranean World: Illustrative Documents.* New York: Columbia University Press, 1955.

Maccoby, Hyam, ed. and trans. *Judaism on Trial: Jewish-Christian Disputations in the Middle Ages.* London: Associated University Presses, 1982.

Mansi, G.D., ed. *Sacrorum Conciliorum Nova et Amplissima Collectio.* 54 vols. Paris: H. Welter, 1901–27.

Marcus, Jacob, trans and ed. *The Jew in the Medieval World*, rev. ed. Cincinnati: Hebrew Union College Press, 1999.

204 BIBLIOGRAPHY

Meir ha-Meili. "Milḥemet Mitzvah shel R. Meir HaMeili." Edited by Zeev Herskowitz. In William Herskowitz, "Judaeo-Christian Dialogue in Provence as Reflected in *Milḥemet Mitzva* of R. Meir Hameili." Ph.D. diss., Yeshiva University, 1974.

The Memoranda Roll for the Michaelmas term of the first year of King John (1199–1200). Publications of the Pipe Roll Society 59, n.s. 21. Edited by John Ruddock. London: Pipe Roll Society, 1943.

Monumenta Germaniae Historica – eMGH. Turnhout: Brepols, last update 2014-12-30. Digitized version of *Monumenta Germaniae Historica*. Hannover: Impensis Bibliopolii Hahniani, 1826–1934.

Nahon, Gérard. "Les ordonnances de Saint Louis sur les juifs." *Les Nouveaux cahiers* 6 (1970): 18–35.

Neubauer, Adolf. "Documents inédits." *Revue des études juives* 9 (1884): 51–65.

Nicene and Post-Nicene Fathers of the Christian Church. Second Series. New York: The Christian Literature Company, 1890–1900.

Nichols, John. *History and Antiquities of the county of Leicester*. 4 vols. London: J. Nichols, 1795–1815.

Oberto Scriba de Mercato. *Oberto Scriba de mercato (1186)*. Edited by Mario Chiaudano. Turin: Editrice libraria italiana, 1940.

Oberto Scriba de Mercato. *Oberto Scriba de Mercato (1190)*. Edited by Mario Chiaudano and Raimondo Morozzo della Rocca. Turin: Editrice libraria italiana, 1938.

Olszowy-Schlanger, Judith, ed. *Hebrew and Hebrew-Latin Charters and Tallies from Medieval England*. Turnhout: Brepols, 2015.

Ordonnances des rois de France de la troisième race. Edited by Eusèbe de Laurière et al. 21 vols. Paris: Impr. royale, 1723–1849.

Patrologia Latina Database. ProQuest, 1996–2015. Digitized version of *Patrologiae cursus completus...Latina*. 1st ed. Edited by Jacques-Paul Migne. Paris: Migne, 1844–65.

Paul the Deacon. *Historia Langobardorum*. In *eMGH*. Turnhout: Brepols, 2014.

Peter the Venerable. *The Letters of Peter the Venerable*. Edited by Giles Constable. 2 vols. Cambridge, MA: Harvard University Press, 1967.

Powell, James, trans. *The Deeds of Pope Innocent III by an Anonymous Author*. Washington DC: Catholic University of America Press, 2004.

Pryor, John, ed. *Business Contracts of Medieval Provence: Selected Notulae from the Cartulary of Giraud Amalric of Marseilles, 1248*. Toronto: Pontifical Institute of Mediaeval Studies, 1981.

Quantin, Maximilien, ed. *Cartulaire général de l'Yonne, Recueil de documents authentiques pour servir à l'histoire des pays qui forment ce département*. Paris: Durand, 1854–60.

Rangeard, Pierre, ed. *Histoire de l'université d'Angers*. Angers: E. Barassé, 1877.

BIBLIOGRAPHY   205

Receipt and Issue Rolls for the Twenty-sixth Year of the Reign of King Henry III, 1241–2. Publications of the Pipe Roll Society 87, n.s. 49. Edited by Robert Stacey. London: Pipe Roll Society, 1992.

The Receipt Roll of the Exchequer for Michaelmas Term XXXI Henry II, A.D. 1185. Edited by Hubert Hall. London: London School of Economics, 1899.

Receipt Rolls for the fourth, fifth, and sixth years of the Reign of Henry III Easter 1220, 1221, and 1222. Publications of the Pipe Roll Society 90, n.s. 52. Edited by Nick Barratt. London: Pipe Roll Society, 2003.

Receipt Rolls for the seventh and eighth years of the Reign of Henry III, Easter 1223 and Michaelmas 1224. Publications of the Pipe Roll Society 93, n.s. 55. Edited by Nick Barratt. London: Pipe Roll Society, 2007.

Records of the Borough of Leicester, Being a series of Extracts from the Archives of the Corporation of Leicester, 1103–1327. Edited by Mary Bateson. London: C.J. Clay, 1899.

Rigg, J.M., ed. *Select Pleas, Starrs, and other records from the Rolls of the Exchequer of the Jews, A.D. 1220–1284.* London: B. Quaritch, 1902.

Robert de Courson. *Le traité "De Usura" de Robert de Courson.* Edited by George Lefevre. Travaux et mémoires de l'Université de Lille, 10/30. Lille: Au siège de l'Université, 1902.

Robinson, James Harvey, ed. *Readings in European History.* Boston: Ginn & Co., 1904–6.

Roger of Hoveden. *Annals of Roger of Hoveden.* Translated by Henry Riley. 2 vols. London: H.G. Bohn, 1853.

———. *Chronica Magistri Rogeri de Hovedene.* Edited by William Stubbs. 4 vols. London: Longman, 1868–71.

Rotuli Litterarum Clausarum in Turri londinensi asservati. Edited by Thomas Hardy. London: G. Eyre and A. Spottiswoode, 1833–44.

Simson, Bernard von, ed. *Ottonis et Rahewini Gesta Friderci I Imperatoris.* Scriptores Rerum Germanicarum in usum scholarum, 3rd ed. Hannover: Hahnsche Buchhandlung, 1978.

Statutes of the Realm (1225–1713). London: G. Eyre and A. Strahan, 1810–22.

Stephanus de Bourbon, *Anecdotes historiques, légendes et apologues, tirés du recueil inédit d'Etienne de Bourbon, dominicain du XIIIe siècle.* Paris: Renouard, 1887.

Stubbs, William, ed. *Gesta regis Henrici Secundi Benedicti abbatis. The Chronicle of the Reigns of Henry II and Richard I.* 2 vols. London: Longmans, 1867.

———. *Select Charters and other illustrations of English Constitutional History.* 9th ed. Oxford: Oxford University Press, 1913.

Tanner, Norman, ed. *Decrees of the Ecumenical Councils.* 2 vols. London: Sheed & Ward, 1990.

Thomas de Chobham. *Summa Confessorum.* Edited by F. Broomfield. Louvain: Éditions Nauwelaerts, 1968.

206 BIBLIOGRAPHY

Thomas of Monmouth. *The Life and Miracles of St. William of Norwich.* Cambridge: Cambridge University Press, 1896.

Thompson, James, ed. *History of Leicester from the time of the Romans to the end of the seventeenth century.* Leicester: J.S. Crossley, 1849.

Thorpe, Benjamin, ed. *Ancient Laws and Institutes of England.* Clarke, NJ: Lawbook Exchange, 2003.

Three Rolls of the King's Court in the Reign of King Richard I. A.D. 1194–95. Edited by Frederick Maitland. Publications of the Pipe Roll Society 14. London: Wyman & Sons, 1891.

Veterum scriptorum et monumentorum historicorum. Edited by Edmond Martène and Ursin Durand. 8 vols. Paris: Montalant, 1724–33.

Welter, Jean-Thiébaut, ed. *Speculum Laicorum.* Paris: A. Picard, 1914.

———. *Tabula Exemplorum secundum ordinem alphabeti.* Paris: E.H. Guitard, 1926.

Wilkins, David, ed. *Concilia Magnae Britanniae et Hiberniae.* 4 vols. London: C. Davis, 1737.

Yehudah he-Ḥasid. *Sefer Ḥasidim.* Edited by Judah Wistinetzki. Frankfurt am Main: Wahrmann, 1924.

———. *Sefer Ḥasidim.* Edited by Reuven Margoliot. Jerusalem: Mosad ha-Rav Kook, 1964.

———. *Sefer Ḥasidim Database* (PUSHD). Princeton University. https://etc. princeton.edu/sefer_hasidim/index.php

MODERN TEXTS — PRINTED AND ONLINE

Abel, Wilhelm. *Agricultural Fluctuations in Europe: From the Thirteenth to the Twentieth Centuries.* London: Methuen & Co., 1980.

Abraham, Gary. *Max Weber and the Jewish Question.* Urbana: University of Illinois Press, 1992.

Abrahams, Sir Lionel. "Condition of the Jews of England at the time of their Expulsion in 1290." *Jewish Historical Society of England—Transactions* 2 (1894–5): 76–105.

———. "The Economic and Financial Position of the Jews in Mediaeval England." *Jewish Historical Society of England—Transactions* 8 (1915–7): 171–88.

———. "The Expulsion of the Jews from England in 1290." *Jewish Quarterly Review* 7 (1894–5): 75–100, 236–58, 428–58.

———. *The Expulsion of the Jews from England in 1290.* Oxford: Blackwell, 1895.

Abu-Lughod, Janet. *Before European Hegemony: The World System AD 1250–1350.* Oxford: Oxford University Press, 1989.

Abulafia, Anna Sapir. *Christian-Jewish Relations, 1000–1300: Jews in the Service of Medieval Christendom.* Harlow: Pearson Education, 2011.

BIBLIOGRAPHY 207

————. *Christians and Jews in Dispute: Disputational Literature and the rise of Anti-Judaism in the West (c. 1000–1150).* Aldershot: Variorum, 1998.

————. *Christians and Jews in the Twelfth Century Renaissance.* London: Routledge, 1995.

————. "Theology and the Commercial Revolution: Guibert of Nogent, St. Anselm and the Jews of Northern France." In *Church and City, 1000–1500: Essays in Honour of Christopher Brooke.* Edited by David Abulafia, Michael Franklin and Miri Rubin. Cambridge: Cambridge University Press, 1998.

Abulafia, David. *The Two Italies: Economic Relations between the Norman Kingdom of Sicily and the Northern Communes.* Cambridge: Cambridge University Press, 1977.

Adams, George Burton. *History of England from Norman Conquest to the Death of King John, 1066–1216.* London: Longmans, 1905.

Adler, Michael. *Jews of Medieval England.* London: Jewish Historical Society, 1939.

————. "The Testimony of the London Jewry against the Ministers of Henry III." *Jewish Historical Society of England—Transactions* 14 (1935–9): 141–85.

Alexander-Frizer, Tamar. *The Pious Sinner: Ethics and Aesthetics in the Medieval Hasidic Narrative.* Tübingen: J.C.B. Mohr, 1991.

Algazi, Gadi, Valentin Groebner and Bernhard Jussen, eds. *Negotiating the Gift: Pre-modern Figurations of Exchange.* Göttingen: Vandenhoeck & Ruprecht, 2003.

Allgemeine Deutsche Biographie. Leipzig: Duncker & Humblot, 1893–1907.

Angelos, Mark. "Urban Women, Investment, and the Commercial Revolution of the Middle Ages." In *Women in Medieval Western European Culture.* Edited by Linda Mitchell. New York and London: Garland Publishing, 1999.

————. "Women in Genoese Commenda Contracts, 1155–1216." *Journal of Medieval History* 20 (1994): 299–312.

Anglo-Jewish Historical Exhibition, *Papers Read at the Anglo-Jewish Historical Exhibition, Royal Albert Hall, 1887.* London: Office of the Jewish Chronicle, 1888.

Anti-Defamation League. "Anti-Semitism and 'The Merchant of Venice:' A Discussion Guide for Educators," (2006). http://www.adl.org/assets/pdf/education-outreach/Merchant_Venice_Discussion_Guide.pdf. Accessed Feb. 3, 2013.

————. "Press Release: ADL Survey in Ten European Countries Finds Anti-Semitism at Disturbingly High Levels," (March 20, 2012). http://www.adl.org/press-center/press-releases/anti-semitism-international/adl-survey-in-ten-european-countries-find-anti-semitism.html-.USd30-hTuPc. Accessed Feb 22, 2013.

Ashkenazi, Ofer. "Home-Coming as a National Founding Myth: Jewish Identity and German Landscapes in Konrad Wolf's 'I was Nineteen.'" *Religions* 3 (2012): 130–50. doi:10.3390/rel3010130. Also published in *Central European*

208 BIBLIOGRAPHY

Jewish Émigrés and the Shaping of Postwar Culture: Studies in Memory of Lilian Furst (1931–2009). Edited by Julie Mell and Malachi Hacohen, 218–37. Basel: MDPI, 2014.

Ashley, W.J. "The Present Position of Political Economy." *The Economic Journal* 17 (1907): 467–89.

———. *Surveys Historic and Economic*. New York: Longmans,1900.

Ashtor, Eliyahu. "Gli ebrei nel commercio Mediterraneo nell-alto medioeve (sec. x–xi)." In *The Jews and the Mediterranean Economy 10th–15th Centuries*. London: Variorum Reprints, 1983.

———. "The Jews in Mediterranean Trade in the Fifteenth Century." In *The Jews and the Mediterranean Economy 10th–15th Centuries*. London: Variorum Reprints, 1983.

———. "New Data for the History of Levantine Jewries in the Fifteenth Century." *Bulletin of the Institute of Jewish Studies* 3 (1975):67–102.

Assis, Yom Tov. *Jewish Economy in the Medieval Crown of Aragon, 1213–1327*. Leiden: Brill, 1997.

Aston, T.H., and C.H.E. Philpin, eds. *The Brenner Debate: Agrarian Class Structure and Economic Development in Pre-Industrial Europe*. Cambridge: Cambridge University Press, 1985.

Astuti, Guido. *Origini e Svolgimento Storico della Commenda fino al secolo xiii*. Turin: S. Lattes & C. Editori, 1933.

Awerbuch, Marianne. "Petrus Venerabilis: Ein Wendepunkt im Anti-judaismus des Mittelalters?" In *Christlich-jüdische Begegnung im Zeitalter der frühscholastik*. Munich: Chr. Kaiser, 1980.

Backhaus, Jürgen. "Introduction: Wilhelm Roscher (1817–1894)—a Centenary Reappraisal." Special issue, *Journal of Economic Studies* 22/3 (1995): 4–15.

Baer, Yitzhak. "Ha-Megamah ha-Datit ha-Hevratit shel *Sefer Ḥasidim*" [The Religious-Social Orientation of *Sefer Ḥasidim*]. *Zion* 3 (1937): 1–50.

Bailey, Mark. "Historiographical Essay: The Commercialisation of the English Economy, 1086–1500." *Journal of Medieval History* 24/3 (1998): 297–311.

Baldwin, John. *The Government of Philip Augustus*. Berkeley: University of California Press, 1986.

———. *Masters, Princes, and Merchants: The Social Views of Peter the Chanter and His Circle*. 2 vols. Princeton: Princeton University Press, 1970.

———. "The Medieval Theories of the Just Price: Romanists, Canonists, and Theologians in the Twelfth and Thirteenth Centuries." In *Pre-Capitalist Economic Thought: Three Modern Interpretations*. New York: Arno, 1972. Originally published in *Transactions of the American Philosophical Society* n.s. 49 (1959): 1–92.

Baldwin, John et al., ed., *Les Registres de Philippe Auguste*. Paris: Impr. nationale, 1992.

Baratier, Édouard. *Histoire de Marseille*. Toulouse: Privat, 1973.

BIBLIOGRAPHY   209

———. "L'influence de la politique Angevine sur le declin de Marseille au xiiie et xive siècles." In *VI Congreso de historia de la corona de Aragon*. Madrid: Dirección General de Relaciones Culturales del Ministerio de Asuntos Exteriores, imp., 1961.

Barkai, Avraham. "The German Jews at the Start of Industrialisation: Structural Change and Mobility 1835–1860." In *Revolution and Evolution: 1848 in German-Jewish History*. Edited by Werner Mosse et al., 123–49. Tübingen: J.C.B. Mohr, 1981.

———. "Zur Wirtschaftsgeschichte Der Juden in Deutschland: Historiographische Quellen und Tendenzen vor und nach 1945." *Tel Aviver Jahrbuch für Deutsche Geschichte* 20 (1991): 195–214.

———. "Yahadut, ha-Yehudim, ve-ha-Hitpatchut shel Kapitalism" [Judaism, the Jews, and the Development of Capitalism]. In *Dat ve-Kalkalah* [Religion and Economy]. Edited by Menahem Ben-Sasson, 53–63. Jerusalem: Zalman Shazar, 1995.

Baron, Salo. "Ghetto and Emancipation: Shall We Revise the Traditional View?" *The Menorah Journal* 14 (1928): 515–26.

———. *A Social and Religious History of the Jews*. 3 vols. 1st ed. New York: Columbia University Press, 1937.

———. *A Social and Religious History of the Jews*. 18 vols. 2nd ed. New York: Columbia University Press, 1952–93.

———. "Medieval Nationalism and Jewish Serfdom." *Studies and Essays in Honor of Abraham A. Neuman*. Philadelphia: Dropsie College, 1962.

Barton, J.L. "The Mystery of Bracton." *Journal of Legal History* 14 (1993): 1–142.

Baum, Gregory. *Karl Polanyi on Ethics and Economics*. Montreal: McGill-Queen's University Press, 1996.

Baumgarten, Elisheva. *Mothers and Children: Jewish Family Life in Medieval Europe*. Princeton: Princeton University Press, 2004.

———. *Practicing Piety in Medieval Ashkenaz: Men, Women and Everyday Religious Observance*. Philadelphia: University of Pennsylvania Press, 2014.

Bautier, Robert-Henri. *The Economic Development of Medieval Europe*. Translated by Heather Karolyi. New York: Harcourt Brace Jovanovich, 1971.

Becker, Marvin. *Medieval Italy: Constraints and Creativity*. Bloomington: Indiana University Press, 1981.

Bedos, Brigitte. "Les sceaux." In *Art et archeology des Juifs en France médiévale*. Edited by Bernard Blumenkranz, 207–28. Toulouse: Privat, 1980.

Ben-Sasson, Hillel H., ed. *A History of the Jewish People*. Cambridge: Harvard University Press, 1976.

Bendix, Reinhard. *Max Weber: An Intellectual Portrait*. Berkeley: University of California Press, 1977.

Bennett, Judith. *Medieval Europe: A Short History*. 10th ed. Boston: McGraw-Hill, 2006.

210 BIBLIOGRAPHY

Berg, Maxine. *A Woman in History: Eileen Power 1889–1940*. Cambridge: Cambridge University Press, 1996.

Berger, David. "The Attitude of St. Bernard of Clairvaux toward the Jews." *Proceedings of the American Academy for Jewish Research* 40 (1972): 89–108.

———. *From Crusades to Blood Libels to Expulsions*. New York: Touro College, 1997.

———. *Persecution, Polemic, and Dialogue: Essays in Jewish-Christian Relations*. Boston: Academic Studies Press, 2010.

Berlioz, Jacques and Marie Anne Polo de Beaulieu, eds. *Les Exempla médiévaux: nouvelles perspective*. Paris: H. Champion, 1998.

Bessner, Daniel. "Rather More than One-Third had no Jewish Blood: American Progressivism and German-Jewish Cosmopolitanism at the New School for Social Research 1933–39." *Religions* 3 (2012): 99–129. doi:10.3390/rel3010099 Also published in *Central European Jewish Émigrés and the Shaping of Postwar Culture: Studies in Memory of Lilian Furst (1931–2009)*. Edited by Julie Mell and Malachi Hacohen, 1–32. Basel: MDPI, 2014.

Biddick, Kathleen. *The Typological Imaginary: Circumcision, Technology, History*. Philadelphia: University of Pennsylvania Press, 2003.

Bird, Jessalynn. "Reform or Crusade? Anti-Usury and Crusade Preaching during the Pontificate of Innocent III." In *Pope Innocent III and his World*. Edited by John Moore, 165–85. Brookfield: Ashgate, 1999.

Bird, Jessalynn, Edward Peters, and James Powell, eds. *Crusade and Christendom: Annotated Documents in Translation from Innocent III to the fall of Acre, 1187–1191*. Philadelphia: University of Pennsylvania Press, 2013.

Blaug, Mark. *Economic Theory in Retrospect*. 5th ed. Cambridge: Cambridge University Press, 1997.

Bloch, Marc. *Esquisse d'une histoire monétaire de l'Europe*. Paris: A. Colin, 1954.

———. "Économie-nature or économie-argent." In *Mélanges Historiques*, 2:868–877. Paris: S.E.V.P.E.N., 1966.

———. "Natural Economy or Money Economy: A Pseudo-Dilemma." In *Land and Work in Mediaeval Europe*, 230–43. Berkeley: University of California Press, 1967.

Bloomfield, Morton. *The Seven Deadly Sins: An Introduction to the History of a Religious Concept*. East Lansing: Michigan State College Press, 1952.

Blumenkranz, Bernhard. *Les auteurs chrétiens latins du Moyen Âge sur les juifs et le judaïsme*. Paris: Mouton, 1963.

Bohannan, Paul, and George Dalton. *Markets in Africa*. Chicago: Northwestern University Press, 1962.

Bolton, Brenda. *The Medieval Reformation*. New York: Holmes & Meier, 1983.

Bormuth, Matthias. "Meaning and Progress in History – A Comparison between Karl Löwith and Erich Auerbach." *Religions* 3 (2012): 151–62. doi:10.3390/rel3020151 Also published in *Central European Jewish Émigrés and the Shaping*

BIBLIOGRAPHY 211

of Postwar Culture: Studies in Memory of Lilian Furst (1931–2009). Edited by Julie Mell and Malachi Hacohen, 33–44. Basel: MDPI, 2014.

Botticini, Maristella and Zvi Eckstein. *The Chosen Few: How Education Shaped Jewish History, 70–1492.* Princeton: Princeton University Press, 2012.

Bouchard, Constance. *Strong of Body, Brave and Noble: Chivalry and Society in Medieval France.* Ithaca: Cornell University Press, 1998.

Bourdieu, Pierre. "The Forms of Capital." In *The Sociology of Economic Life.* Edited by Mark Granovetter and Richard Swedberg, 96–111: Westview Press, 2001.

Bourrilly, Victor-L. *Essai sur l'histoire politique de Marseille des origines à 1264.* Aix-en-Provence: A. Dragon, 1925.

Bowers, Richard. "From Rolls to Riches: King's Clerks and Moneylending in Thirteenth-Century England." *Speculum* 58/1 (1983): 60–71.

Brand, Paul. "Introduction: The Exchequer of the Jews, 1265–1290." *Plea Rolls of the Exchequer of the Jews,* 6:1–73. London: Macmillan, 2005.

Braudel, Fernand. *The Mediterranean and the Mediterranean World in the age of Philip II.* New York: Harper & Row, 1972–3.

Bremond, Claude, Jacques Le Goff, and Jean-Claude Schmitt. *L' "Exemplum."* Typologies des sources du Moyen Âge Occidental 40. Turnhout: Brepols, 1982.

Brenner, Robert. "The Origins of Capitalist Development: A Critique of Neo-Smithian Marxism." *New Left Review* 104 (1977): 25–92.

———. "Agrarian Class Structure and Economic Development in Pre-Industrial Europe." In *The Brenner Debate: Agrarian Class Structure and Economic Development in Pre-Industrial Europe.* Edited by T.H. Aston and C.H.E. Philpin, 10–63. Cambridge: Cambridge University Press, 1985.

———. "Postan, Michael Moissey (1899–1981)." In *New Palgrave Dictionary of Economics.* 2nd ed. New York: Palgrave, 2008.

Bretherton, Luke. *Resurrecting Democracy: Faith, Citizenship, and the Politics of a Common Life.* New York: Cambridge University Press, 2015.

Bridbury, A.R. *Economic Growth in the Later Middle Ages.* London: G. Allen & Unwin, 1962.

Britnell, R.H. *The Commercialisation of English Society 1000–1500.* Cambridge: Cambridge University Press, 1993.

Britnell, R.H., and Bruce Campbell, eds. *A Commercializing Economy: England 1086 to c.1300.* Manchester: Manchester University Press, 1995.

Brooke, Christopher. *Europe in the Central Middle Ages, 962–1154.* Edited by Denys Hay. A General History of Europe. 3rd ed. London: Longman, 2000.

Brown, Elizabeth. "The Tyranny of a Construct: Feudalism and Historians of Medieval Europe." In *Debating the Middle Ages.* Edited by Lester Little and Barbara Rosenwein, 148–69. Malden, MA: Blackwell, 1998.

212 BIBLIOGRAPHY

Brown, Reva and Sean McCartney. "The business activities of Jewish women entrepreneurs in medieval England." *Management Decisions* 39 (2001): 699–709.

Brundage, James. *Medieval Canon Law*. London: Longman, 1995.

———. *Medieval Canon Law and the Crusader*. Madison: University of Wisconsin Press, 1969.

Buckatzsch, E.J. "Geographical distribution of wealth in England, 1086–1843." *Economic History Review* n.s, 3 (1950): 180–202.

Buckley, Susan. *Teachings on Usury in Judaism, Christianity and Islam*. Lewiston: Edwin Mellen Press, 2000.

Bücher, Carl. *Industrial Evolution*. Translated by S. Morley Wickett. London: George Bell and Sons, 1901.

Burrow, John. "Historicism and Social Evolution." In *British and German Historiography, 1750–1950: Traditions, Perceptions, and Transfers*. Edited by Benedikt Stuchtey and Peter Wende, 251–64. Oxford: Oxford University Press, 2000.

Busquet, Raoul. *Histoire de Marseille*. Paris: R. Laffont, 1945.

Byrne, E.H. "Commercial Contracts of the Genoese in the Syrian Trade of the Twelfth Century." *The Quarterly Journal of Economics* 31/1 (1916): 128–70.

———. "Easterns in Genoa." *Journal of the American Oriental Society* 38 (1918): 176–87.

———. *Genoese Shipping in the Twelfth and Thirteenth Centuries*. Cambridge: Medieval Academy of America, 1930.

———. "Genoese Trade with Syria in the Twelfth Century." *American Historical Review* 25 (1920): 191–219.

Caenegem, R. C van. *The Birth of Common Law*. Cambridge: Cambridge University Press, 1973.

Cam, Helen. *Liberties and Communities in medieval England: Collected Studies in Local Administration and Topography*. Cambridge: Cambridge University Press, 1944.

Caro, Georg. *Sozial- und Wirtschaftsgeshichte der Juden im Mittelalter und der Neuzeit*. 2 vols. Leipzig: G. Fock, 1908–20.

Carpenter, D.A. *The Reign of Henry III*. London: Hambledon Press, 1996.

Carrier, James. *Gift and Commodities: Exchange and Western Capitalism since 1700*. London: Routledge, 1995.

Cazel, Fred. "The Fifteenth of 1225." *Bulletin of the Institute of Historical Research* 34 (1961): 67–81.

Chaloupek, Günther. "Wiens Großhandel in Der Kommerziellen Revolution." *Wiener Geschichtsblatter* 39 (1984): 105–25.

Cervantes Saavedra, Miguel de. *Don Quijote*. Translated by Burton Raffel. New York: Norton, 1999.

BIBLIOGRAPHY 213

———. *The ingenious gentleman Don Quixote of La Mancha*, London: G. Bell and Sons, 1913. http://hdl.handle.net/2027/uc1.31158005388797?urlappend=%3Bseq=126

Chazan, Robert. *European Jewry and the First Crusade*. Berkeley: University of California Press, 1987.

———. "From the First Crusade to the Second: Evolving Perceptions of the Christian-Jewish Conflict." In *Jews and Christians in Twelfth-Century Europe*. Edited by Michael Signer and John Van Engen, 46–62. Notre Dame: University of Notre Dame Press, 2001.

———. *Jews of Medieval Western Christendom, 1000–1500*. Cambridge: Cambridge University Press, 2006.

———. "Medieval Anti-Semitism." In *History and Hate: The Dimensions of Anti-Semitism. Edited by* David Berger, 49–66. Philadelphia: Jewish Publication Society, 1986.

———. *Medieval Jewry in Northern France: A Political and Social History*. Baltimore: John Hopkins University Press, 1973.

———. *Medieval Stereotypes and Modern Antisemitism*. Berkeley: University of California Press, 1997.

———. *Reassessing Jewish Life in Medieval Europe*. Cambridge: Cambridge University Press, 2010.

———. "Twelfth-Century Perceptions of the Jews: A Case Study of Bernard of Clairvaux and Peter the Venerable." In *From Witness to Witchcraft: Jews and Judaism in Medieval Christian Thought*. Edited by Jeremy Cohen, 187–201. Wiesbaden: Harrassowitz, 1996.

Chazan, Robert, ed. *Church, State, and Jew in the Middle Ages*. West Orange, NJ: Behrman House, 1980.

Chiaudano, Mario. *Contratti Commerciali Genovesi del secolo XII*. Turin: Fratelli Bocca, 1925.

Cipolla, Carlo. *Before the Industrial Revolution: European Society and Economy 1000–1700*. Translated by Christopher Woodall. 3rd ed. 1993 ed. London: Routledge, 1976.

———. *Money, Prices, and Civilization in the Mediterranean World*. Princeton: Princeton University Press, 1956.

———, ed. *The Fontana Economic History of Europe: The Middle Ages*. Edited by Carlo Cipolla, The Fontana Economic History of Europe: Fontana Books, 1972.

Çizakça, Murat. *A Comparative Evolution of Business Partnerships: The Islamic World and Europe, with Specific Reference to the Ottoman Archives*. Leiden: E.J. Brill, 1996.

Clancy, M.T. *England and Its Rulers, 1066–1307*. Oxford: Blackwell, 2006.

———. *From Memory to Written Record: England 1066–1307*. Cambridge: Harvard University Press, 1979.

214 BIBLIOGRAPHY

Clapham, J.H. and Eileen Power, eds. *The Agrarian Life of the Middle Ages*. Vol. 1 of *The Cambridge Economic History of Europe*. 1st ed. Cambridge: Cambridge University Press, 1941.

Cleary, Patrick. *The Church and Usury*. Dublin: M.H. Gill, 1914.

Cohen, Arnold. *An Introduction to Jewish Civil Law*. Jerusalem: Philip Feldheim, 1991.

Cohen, Esther and Mayke B. de Jong, eds. *Medieval Transformations: Texts, Power, and Gifts in Context*. Leiden: Brill, 2001.

Cohen, Jeffrey Jerome. *Hybridity, Identity, and Monstrosity in medieval Britain: on difficult middles*. New York: Palgrave, 2006.

Cohen, Jeremy. *The Friars and the Jews: the Evolution of Medieval Anti-Judaism*. Ithaca: Cornell University Press, 1982.

———. "The Jews as the killers of Christ in the Latin Tradition, from Augustine to the Friars." *Traditio* 39 (1983): 1–27.

———. *Living Letters of the Law: Ideas of the Jew in Medieval Christianity*. Berkeley: University of California Press, 1999.

———. "Recent Historiography on the Medieval Church and the Decline of European Jewry." In *Popes, Teachers, and Canon Law in the Middle Ages*. Edited by James Sweeney and Stanley Chodorow, 251–62. Ithaca: Cornell University Press, 1989.

———. *Sanctifying the Name of God: Jewish Martyrs and Jewish Memories of the First Crusade*. Philadelphia: University of Pennsylvania Press, 2004.

Cohen, Jeremy, ed. *From Witness to Witchcraft: Jews and Judaism in Medieval Christian Thought*. Wiesbaden: Harrassowitz, 1996.

Collins, Roger. *Early Medieval Europe, 300–1000*. History of Europe. New York: St. Martin's Press, 1999.

Constable, Giles. *Crusaders and Crusading in the Twelfth Century*. Farnham: Ashgate, 2008.

———. "The Financing of the Crusades in the Twelfth Century." In *Outremer: Studies in the history of the Crusading Kingdom of Jerusalem*. Edited by B.Z. Kedar et al., 64–88. Jerusalem: Yad Izhak Ben-Zvi Institute, 1982.

Cramer, Alice. "The Jewish Exchequer: An Inquiry into Its Fiscal Functions." *American Historical Review* 45 (1940): 327–37.

———. "The Origins and Functions of the Jewish Exchequer." *Speculum* 16 (1941): 226–29.

Crémieux, Adolphe. "Les Juifs de Marseille au Moyen Age." *Revue des études juives* 46 (1903): 1–47, 246–68.

Cronbach, Abraham. "Social Thinking in the *Sefer Ḥasidim*." *Hebrew Union College Annual* 22 (1949): 1–147.

Cromarty, D., and R. Cromarty, eds. *The Wealth of Shrewsbury in the early Fourteenth Century: Six Local Subsidy Rolls 1297 to 1322: Text and Commentary*. Shrewsbury: Shropshire Archaeological and Historical Society, 1993.

BIBLIOGRAPHY   215

Crouzet, François. *A History of the European Economy, 1000–2000*. Charlottesville: University Press of Virginia, 2001.

Cunningham, William. *The Growth of English Industry and Commerce*. Cambridge: Cambridge University Press, 1882.

Curta, Florin. "Merovingian and Carolingian Gift Giving." *Speculum* 81 (2006): 671–99.

Dahan, Gilbert. "Bernard de Clairvaux et les Juifs." *Archives juives* 23 (1987): 59–64.

———. *The Christian Polemic against the Jews in the Middle Ages*. Translated by Jody Gladding. Notre Dame: University of Notre Dame Press, 1998.

———. *Les intellectuels chrétiens et les juifs au Moyen Âge*. Paris: Cerf, 1990.

Dahan, Gilbert, ed. *Le Brûlement du Talmud à Paris, 1242–4*. Paris: Cerf, 1999.

Dalton, George. *Economic Anthropology and Development*. New York: Basic Books, 1971.

———. "Introduction." In *Primitive, Archaic, and Modern Economies: Essays of Karl Polanyi*. Edited by George Dalton, ix–liv. Garden City: Anchor Books, 1968.

———. "Writings That Clarify Theoretical Disputes over Karl Polanyi's Work." In *The Life and Work of Karl Polanyi*. Edited by Kari Polanyi-Levitt, 161–70. Montreal: Black Rose Books, 1990.

Darby, H.C., J. Sheail, and G.R. Verset. "The changing geographical distribution of wealth in England, 1066–1334–1525." *Journal of Historical Geography* 5 (1979): 247–52.

Davies, Wendy and Paul Fouracre, eds. *The Languages of Gift in the Early Middle Ages* Cambridge: Cambridge University Press, 2010.

Davis, James. *Medieval Market Morality*. Cambridge: Cambridge University Press, 2012.

Davis, Natalie Zemon. *The Gift in Sixteenth-Century France*. Madison: University of Wisconsin Press, 2000.

Davis, Ralph. *A Commercial Revolution: English Overseas Trade in the Seventeenth and Eighteenth Centuries*. London: Historical Association, 1967.

Davis, R.H.C. *A History of Medieval Europe: From Constantine to Saint Louis*. London: Longmans, 1957.

de Roover, Florence Edler. "The Business Records of an Early Genoese Notary, 1190–1192." *Bulletin of the Business Historical Society* 14 (1940): 41–46.

———. "Partnership Accounts in Twelfth Century Genoa." *Business History Review* 15 (1941): 87–92.

de Roover, Raymond. *Business, Banking, and Economic Thought in Late Medieval and Early Modern Europe: Selected Studies of Raymond de Roover*. Edited by Julius Kirschner. Chicago: University of Chicago Press, 1974.

———. "The Cambium Maritimum Contract according to the Genoese Notarial Records of the Twelfth and Thirteenth Centuries." *Explorations in Economic History* 7 (1969–70): 15–33.

216 BIBLIOGRAPHY

———. "The Commercial Revolution of the Thirteenth Century." In *Enterprise and Secular Change: Readings in Economic History*. Edited by Frederic Lane and Jelle Riemersma. Homewood: Richard Irwin, 1953.

———. *Money, Banking and Credit in Mediaeval Bruges: Italian Merchant-Bankers Lombards and Money-Changers, a Study in the Origins of Banking*. Cambridge: Mediaeval Academy of America, 1948.

Dickson, Ch. "Vie de Robert de Courson." *Archives d'histoire Doctrinale et Littéraire du Moyen Âge* 9 (1934): 53–142.

Dinari, Yedidya. *Hakhme Ashkenaz be-shilhe Yeme-ha-benayim: darkhehem ye-khitvehem ba-halakhah* [The Rabbis of Germany and Austria at the Close of the Middle Ages: Their Conceptions and Halachaic Writings]. Jerusalem: Bialik Institute, 1984.

Dobb, Maurice. *Studies in the Development of Capitalism*. London: Routledge & Kegan Paul Ltd., 1946.

Dobson, Barrie. "The Decline and Expulsion of the Medieval Jews of York." *Jewish Historical Society of England—Transactions* 26 (1979): 34–52.

———. *The Jews of Medieval York and the Massacre of March 1190*. York: St. Anthony's Press, 1974.

Dopsch, Alfons. *The Economic and Social Foundations of European Civilization*. New York: Harcourt, Brace and Company, 1937.

———. *Naturalwirtschaft und Geldwirtschaft in der Weltgeschichte*. Vienna: Seidel & Sohn, 1930.

Dowell, Stephen. *History of Taxation and Taxes in England*. London: Longmans, 1888.

Dubnow, Arie. *Isaiah Berlin: the Journey of a Jewish Liberal*. New York: Palgrave, 2012.

Duby, Georges. *The Early Growth of the European Economy: Warriors and Peasants from the Seventh to the Twelfth Century*. Translated by Howard Clarke. Ithaca: Cornell University Press, 1974.

———. *History Continues*. Chicago: University of Chicago Press, 1994.

———. *Rural Economy and Country Life in the Medieval West*. Columbia: University of South Carolina Press, 1968.

Duggan, Catherine. "Money from Strangers: Indirect Regulation in Developing Financial Markets." Ph.D. diss., Stanford, 2008.

Dyer, Alan. "Appendix: Ranking Lists of English medieval towns." In *Cambridge Urban History of Britain*, 1:747–770. Cambridge: Cambridge University Press, 2000.

Dyer, Christopher. *Lords and Peasants in a Changing Society: The Estates of the Bishopric of Worcester, 680–1540*. Cambridge: Cambridge University Press, 1980.

———. *Standards of Living in the Later Middle Ages: Social Change in England c. 1200–1520*. Cambridge: Cambridge University Press, 1989.

BIBLIOGRAPHY   217

————. "Taxation and communities in late medieval England." In *Progress and Problems in Medieval England: Essays in Honour of Edward Miller*. Edited by Richard Britnell and John Hatcher, 168–90. Cambridge: Cambridge University Press, 1996.

Edler, Florence. *Glossary of Medieval Terms of Business: Italian Series 1200–1600*. Cambridge: The Medieval Academy of America, 1934.

Elman, Peter. "The Economic Causes of the Expulsion of the Jews in 1290." *Economic History Review* 7 (1937): 145–154.

————. "Jewish Trade in Thirteenth Century England." *Historia Judaica* 1 (1938–9): 91–104.

Elukin, Jonathan. "Is Shylock Really Jewish? The Devil, Theology and the Meaning of 'The Merchant of Venice.'" Paper presented at a joint session of the Jewish Studies & Medieval Studies Seminars of the Triangle, Durham, NC, 27 February, 2012.

————. *Living Together, Living Apart: Rethinking Jewish-Christian Relations in the Middle Ages*. Princeton: Princeton University Press, 2007.

Emery, Richard. *The Jews of Perpignan in the Thirteenth Century*. New York: Columbia University Press, 1959.

Epstein, Catherine. *A Past Renewed: A Catalog of German-Speaking Refugee Historians in the United States after 1933*. New York: Cambridge University Press, 1993.

Epstein, Steven. *An Economic and Social History of Later Medieval Europe, 1000–1500*. Cambridge: Cambridge University Press, 2009.

Farmer, David. "Prices and Wages." In *The Agrarian History of England and Wales*. Edited by H.E. Hallam, 2:716–817. Cambridge: Cambridge University Press, 1988.

Favier, Jean. *Gold and Spices: The Rise of Commerce in the Middle Ages*. New York: Holmes & Meier, 1998.

Feiler, Arthur. Review of *Refugees: a Preliminary Report of a Survey, Social Research* by Sir John Hope Simpson. *Social Research* 6/1 (1939): 114–7.

Ferguson, W.K. "Recent Trends in the Economic Historiography of the Renaissance." *Studies in the Renaissance* 7 (1960): 7–26.

Festschrift Guido Kisch: Rechtshistorische Forschungen anlässlich des 60. Geburtstags dargebracht von Freunden, Kollegen und Schülern. Stuttgart: W. Kohlhammer, 1955.

Fields, Lee. "An Anonymous Dialog with a Jew: An Introduction and Annotated Translation." Ph.D. diss., Hebrew Union College, 2001.

Fink, Carole. *Marc Bloch: A Life in History*. Cambridge: Cambridge University Press, 1989.

Finley, Moses. *The World of Odysseus*. New York: Viking Press, 1954.

Fishman, Talya. *Becoming the People of the Talmud: Oral Torah as Written Tradition in Medieval Jewish Cultures*. Philadelphia: University of Pennsylvania Press, 2011.

218 BIBLIOGRAPHY

————. "The Penitential System of Hasidei Ashkenaz and the Problem of Cultural Boundaries." *Journal of Jewish Thought and Philosophy* 8 (1999): 201–229.

————. "The Rhineland Pietists' Sacralization of Oral Torah." *The Jewish Quarterly Review* 96 (2006): 9–16.

Flower, C.T. *Introduction to the Curia Regis Rolls.* Publications of the Selden Society 62. London: B. Quaritch, 1944.

Fourquin, Guy. *Histoire économique de l'occident médiéval.* 3rd ed. Paris: Armand Colin, 1979.

Foxman, Abraham. *Jews and Money: The Story of a Stereotype.* New York: Palgrave, 2010.

Frankel, Jonathan. "Assimilation and the Jews in Nineteenth-Century Europe: Towards a New Historiography?" In *Assimilation and Community: The Jews in Nineteenth-Century Europe.* Edited by Jonathan Frankel and Steven Zipperstein, 1–37. Cambridge: Cambridge University Press, 1992.

Frankforter, Daniel. *The Medieval Millennium: An Introduction.* Upper Saddle River, NJ: Prentice-Hall, 1999.

Freedman, Paul. "Robert S. Lopez (1910–1985)." In *Rewriting the Middle Ages in the Twentieth Century.* Edited by Jaume Aurell and Francisco Crosas, 279–93. Turnhout: Brepols, 2005.

Friedmann, Yvonne. "Anatomy of Anti-Semitism: Peter the Venerable's Letter to Louis VII, King of France (1146)." In *Bar-Ilan Studies in History,* 87–102. Ramat-Gan: Bar-Ilan University Press, 1978.

Funkenstein, Amos. "Changes in Christian Anti-Jewish Polemics in the Twelfth Century." In *Perceptions of Jewish History,* 172–201. Berkeley: University of California Press, 1993. Originally published as "Changes in Patterns of Christian Anti-Jewish Polemic in the Twelfth Century" [Hebrew]. *Zion* 33 (1968): 125–44.

Gamoran, Hillel. "Investing for Profit: A Study of *Iska* up to the Time of Rabbi Abraham Ben David of Posquieres." *Hebrew Union College Annual* 70–1 (1999–2000): 153–65.

————. *Jewish Law in Transition: How Economic Forces Overcame the Prohibition against Lending on Interest.* Cincinnati: Hebrew Union College, 2008.

————. "Lending — No, Investing — Yes: Development of the *Iska* Law from the 12th to the 15th Centuries." In *Jewish Law Association Studies XII.* Edited by Hillel Gamoran, 79–93. Binghamton: Global Publications, 2002.

————. "The Tosefta in Light of the Law against Usury." In *Jewish Law Association Studies IX.* Edited by E.A. Goldman. Atlanta: Scholars Press, 1997.

Garlan, Yvon. "La Place de l'économie dans les sociétés anciennes." *La Pensée* 171 (1973): 118–27.

Geary, Patrick. "Exchange and Interaction between the Living and the Dead in Early Medieval Society." In *Living with the Dead in the Middle Ages,* 77–92. Ithaca: Cornell University Press, 1994.

BIBLIOGRAPHY 219

————. "Sacred Commodities: The Circulation of Medieval Relics." In *Living with the Dead in the Middle Ages*, 194–218. Ithaca: Cornell University Press, 1994.

Geary, Patrick, ed. *Readings in Medieval History*. 3rd ed. Peterborough, ON: Broadview Press, 2003.

Geremek, Bronislaw. *The Margins of Society in Late Medieval Paris*. Cambridge: Cambridge University Press, 1987.

————. *Poverty: A History*. Oxford: Oxford University Press, 1994.

Germania Judaica. Tübingen: J.C.B. Mohr, 1963–.

Gilchrist, John. "The Canonistic Treatment of Jews in the Latin West in the Eleventh and Early Twelfth Centuries." *Zeitschrift der Savigny-Stiftung für Rechtsgeschichte Kanonistische Abteilung* 75 (1989): 70–103.

————. *The Church and Economic Activity in the Middle Ages*. London: Macmillan, 1969.

Gimpel, Jean. *The Medieval Machine: The Industrial Revolution of the Middle Ages*. New York: Penguin, 1976.

Godden, M.R. "Money, Power and Morality in Late Anglo-Saxon England." *Anglo-Saxon England* 19 (1990): 41–65.

Godelier, Maurice. *The Enigma of the Gift*. Chicago: University of Chicago, 1999.

Goitein, S.D. *A Mediterranean Society: The Jewish Communities of the Arab World as Portrayed in the Documents of the Cairo Geniza*. 6 vols. Berkeley: University of California Press, 1967–93.

Goldberg, Jessica. *Trade and Institutions in the Medieval Mediterranean: The Geniza Merchants and their Business World*. Cambridge: Cambridge University Press, 2012.

Goldschmidt, Levin. *Universalgeschichte des Handelrechts*. Stuttgart: F. Enke, 1891.

Goldthwaite, Richard. "Raymond de Roover on Late Medieval and Early Modern Economic History." In *Business, Banking, and Economic Thought in Late Medieval and Early Modern Europe: Selected Studies of Raymond De Roover*. Edited by Julius Kirshner, 3–14. Chicago and London: University of Chicago Press, 1974.

Gordon, Adi. "The Need for the 'West': Hans Kohn and the North Atlantic Community," *Journal of Contemporary History* 46, 2011: 33–57.

Gould, Stephen Jay. *Full House: The Spread of Excellence from Plato to Darwin*. Cambridge, MA: Belknap Press, 2011.

Gow, Andrew. *The Red Jews: Antisemitism in an Apocalyptic Age, 1200–1600*. Leiden: Brill, 1995.

Grabois, Aryeh. "Du crédit juif a Paris au temps de Saint Louis." *Revue des études juives* 129 (1970): 5–22.

Graeber, David. *Toward an Anthropological Theory of Value: The False Coin of Our Own Dreams*. New York: Palgrave, 2001.

220 BIBLIOGRAPHY

Gras, N.S.B. *Business and Capitalism.* New York: F.S. Crofts & co., 1939.

———. "Capitalism — Concepts and History." *Bulletin of the Business and Historical Society* 16 (1942): 21–34.

———. "Stages in Economic History." *Journal of Economic and Business History* 2/3 (1930): 395–418.

Grayzel, Solomon. "An Adventure in Scholarship." *Historia Judaica* 23 (1961): 15–22.

Greenberg, Joanne. *The King's Persons.* New York: Holt, Rinehart and Winston, 1963.

Gregory, C.A. *Gifts and Commodities.* London: Academic Press, 1982.

———. "Gifts to Men and Gifts to God: Gift Exchange and Capital Accumulation in Contemporary Papua." *Man* n.s. 15/4 (1980): 626–52.

Greffath, Mathias, and Günther Anders, ed. "Bloch hielt einen Vortrag über Träume vom besseren Leben.' Gespräch mit Toni Oelsner." In *Die Zerstörung einer Zukunft: Gespräche mit emigrierten Sozialwissenschaftlern,* 223–47. Reinbek bei Hamburg: Rowohlt, 1979.

Grief, Avner. *Institutions and the Path to the Modern Economy: Lessons from Medieval Trade.* Cambridge: Cambridge University Press, 2006.

———. "On the Political Foundations of the Late Medieval Commercial Revolution: Genoa during the Twelfth and Thirteenth Centuries." *Journal of Economic History* 54/2 (1994): 271–87.

Grierson, Philip. "Commerce in the Dark Ages: A Critique of the Evidence." In *Studies in Economic Anthropology.* Edited by George Dalton, 74–83. Washington, D.C.: American Anthropological Association, 1971.

———. *The Origins of Money.* London: Athlone Press, 1977.

Gross, Charles. "The Exchequer of the Jews of England in the Middle Ages." In *Papers Read at the Anglo-Jewish Historical Exhibition, Royal Albert Hall, London 1887.* London: Office of the Jewish Chronicle, 1888.

Gross, James. *Shylock: A Legend and Its Legacy.* New York: Simon & Schuster, 1992.

Grossman, Avraham. *Hakhme Ashkenaz ha-rishonim* [The Early Sages of Ashkenaz]. Jerusalem: Magnes Press, 1988.

Güde, Wilhelm. "Leben und Werk des Rechtshistorikers Guido Kisch (1889–1985)." *Basler juristische Mitteilungen: Organ für Gesetzgebung und Rechtspflege der Kantone Basel-Stadt und Basel-Landschaft* 1 (2010): 1–24.

———. *Der Rechtshistoriker Guido Kisch (1889–1985).* Karlsruhe: Gesellschaft für Kulturhistorische Dokumentation, 2010.

Gurevich, Aaron. *Historical Anthropology of the Middle Ages.* Cambridge: Polity Press, 1991.

Gutsch, Milton. "A Twelfth Century Preacher — Fulk of Neuilly." In *The Crusades and other historical essays presented to Dana Munro.* Edited by Louis Paetow, 183–206. New York: F.S. Crofts, 1928.

BIBLIOGRAPHY 221

Guttman, Julius. "Die wirtschaftliche und soziale Bedeutung der Juden im Mittelalter." *Monatsschrift Geschichte und Wissenschaft des Judentums* 51,, n.s. 15 (1907): 257–90.

Gutwein, Daniel. "Kapitalism, Pariah-Kapitalism ve-Me'ut" [Capitalism, Pariah-Capitalism, and Minority]. In *Dat ve-Kalkalah* [Religion and Economy]. Edited by Menahem Ben-Sasson, 65–76. Jerusalem: Zalman Shazar, 1995.

Guyotjeannin, Oliver. "Innocent III." In *The Papacy: An Encyclopedia,* 2:785–90. New York: Routledge, 2002.

Habakkuk, H.J. "The Economic History of Modern Britain." *Journal of Economic History* 18/4 (1958): 486–501.

Hacohen, Malachi. *Jacob and Esau, Between Nation and Empire: A Jewish-European History.* Cambridge: Cambridge University Press, forthcoming.

———. "Typology and the Holocaust: Erich Auerbach and Judeo-Christian Europe." *Religions* 3 (2012): 600–45. doi:10.3390/rel3030600 Also published in *Central European Jewish Émigrés and the Shaping of Postwar Culture: Studies in Memory of Lilian Furst (1931–2009).* Edited by Julie Mell and Malachi Hacohen, 45–91. Basel: MDPI, 2014.

Hadwin, J.F. "Evidence on the Possession of 'Treasure' from the Lay Subsidy Rolls." In *Edwardian Monetary Affairs (1279–1344): a symposium held in Oxford, August 1976.* Edited by N.J. Mayhew, 148–165. Oxford: British Archaeological Reports, 1977.

———. "The Medieval Lay Subsidies and Economic History," *The Economic History Review,* n.s. 36 (1983): 200–217.

Hahn, Bruno. *Die Wirtschaftliche Tätigkeit der Juden im Fränkischen und Deutschen Reich bis zum 2. Kreuzzug.* Freibug: Hammerschlag, 1911.

Hall, Margaret Winslow. "Early Bankers in the Genoese Notarial Records." *Economic History Review* 6 (1935/36): 73–9.

Hall-Cole, Margaret. "The Investment of Wealth in Thirteenth Century Genoa." *Economic History Review* 8 (1937/8): 185–7.

Halperin, Rhoda. "Polanyi, Marx, and the Institutional Paradigm in Economic Anthropology." *Research in Economic Anthropology* 6 (1984): 245–72.

Hao, Yen-p'ing. *The Commercial Revolution in Nineteenth-Century China: The Rise of Sino-Western Mercantile Capitalism.* Berkeley: University of California Press, 1986.

Harriss, G.L. *King, Parliament, and Public Finance in Medieval England to 1369.* Oxford: Clarendon, 1975.

Harvey, Barbara F. "The Population Trend in England between 1300 and 1348." *Transactions of the Royal Historical Society,* 5th ser. 16 (1966): 23–42.

Hatcher, John, and Mark Bailey. *Modelling the Middle Ages: The History and Theory of England's Economic Development.* Oxford: Oxford University Press, 2001.

Haussherr, Hans. *Wirtschaftsgeschichte der Neuzeit vom Ende des 14. bis zur Höhe des 19. Jahrhunderts.* 3rd ed. Cologne: Böhlan, 1969.

222 BIBLIOGRAPHY

Haverkamp, Alfred. *Aufbruch und Gestaltung. Deutschland, 1056–1273.* Munich: C.H. Beck, 1984.

———, ed. *Geschichte der Juden im Mittelalter von der Nordsee bis zu den Südalpen: Kommentiertes Kartenwerk.* 3 vols. Hannover: Hahnsche Buchhandlung, 2002.

Heejebu, Santhi, and Deirdre McCloskey. "The Reproving of Karl Polanyi." *Critical Review* 13 (1999): 285–314.

Hefele, Karl Joseph von. *Conciliengeschichte: nach den Quellen bearbeitet.* 9 vols. Freiburg: Herder, 1869–90.

———. *A History of the Christian Councils.* Translated by William Clark. 5 vols. Edinburgh: T. & T. Clark, 1894–6.

Heine, Heinrich. *Heine on Shakespeare: A Translation of His Notes on Shakespeare Heroines.* Translated by Ida Benecke. Westminster: A. Constable and Co., 1895.

Helmolz, R.H. "Usury and the Medieval English Church Courts." *Speculum* 61/2 (1986): 364–80.

Hennis, Wilhelm. "A Science of Man: Max Weber and the Political Economy of the German Historical School." In *Max Weber and His Contemporaries.* Edited by Wolfgang Mommsen and Jürgen Osterhammel. London: Allen & Unwin, 1987.

Herbert, J.A., and H.L.D. Ward. *Catalogue of Romances in the Department of Manuscripts of the British Museum.* 3 vols. London: Longmans, 1910.

Herlihy, David. "The Economy of Traditional Europe." *Journal of Economic History* 31 (1971): 153–64.

Herskowitz, William. "Judaeo-Christian Dialogue in Provence as Reflected in *Milḥemet Mitzva* of R. Meir Hameili." Ph.D. Diss., Yeshiva University, 1974.

Herzog, Isaac. *The Main Institutions of Jewish Law.* 2 vols. London: Soncino Press, 1965.

Heschel, Susannah. *Abraham Geiger and the Jewish Jesus.* Chicago: University of Chicago Press, 1998.

Hess, Jonathan. "Shylock's Daughters: Philosemitism, Popular Culture, and the Liberal Imagination." Paper presented at the Third Biennial German Jewish Workshop, Durham, NC, 10–12 Feb. 2013.

Heynen, R. *Zur Entstehung des Kapitalismus in Venedig.* Stuttgart: J.G. Cotta'sche Buchhandlung Nachfolger, 1905.

Hildebrand, Bruno. "Natural-, Geld- und Kreditwirtschaft." *Jahrbuch Nationalökonomie* 2 (1864): 1–24.

Hilton, Rodney. *English and French Towns in Feudal Society: A Comparative Study.* Cambridge: Cambridge University Press, 1992.

———. "Introduction." In *The Brenner Debate: Agrarian Class Structure and Economic Development in Pre-Industrial Europe.* Edited by T.H. Aston and C.H.E. Philpin. Cambridge: Cambridge University Press, 1985: 1–9.

Hilton, Rodney, ed. *The Transition from Feudalism to Capitalism.* London: Verso, 1978.

BIBLIOGRAPHY 223

Hodges, Richard. *Dark Age Economics: The Origins of Towns and Trade AD 600–1000*. New York: St. Martin's Press, 1982.

Hodges, Richard, and David Whitehouse. *Mohammed, Charlemagne and the Origins of Europe: Archaeology and the Pirenne Thesis*. Ithaca, NY: Cornell University Press, 1983.

Hodgett, Gerald. *A Social and Economic History of Medieval Europe*. London: Methuen, 1972.

Holborn, Hajo. *A History of Modern Germany, 1840–1945*. Princeton: Princeton University Press, 1969.

Hollister, Warren. *Medieval Europe: A Short History*. 5th ed. New York: Wiley, 1982.

Hollister, Warren, and Judith Bennett. *Medieval Europe: A Short History*. 9th ed. ed. Boston: McGraw-Hill, 2001.

Holton, R.J. *The Transition from Feudalism to Capitalism*. New York: St. Martin's Press, 1985.

Hoover, Calvin Bryce. "The Sea Loan in Genoa in the Twelfth Century." *Quarterly Journal of Economics* 40 (1926): 495–529.

Horden, Peregrine and Nicholas Purcell. *The Corrupting Sea: A Study of Mediterranean History*. Oxford: Blackwell, 2000.

Hoselitz, Bert. "Theories of Stages of Economic Growth." In *Theories of Economic Growth*. Edited by Bert Hoselitz, et al., 193–238. Glencoe: Free Press, 1960.

Hoyt, Robert. *The Royal Demesne in English Constitutional History: 1066–1272*. Ithaca: Cornell University Press, 1950.

Hsia, Po-Chia. *The Myth of Ritual Murder: Jews and Magic in Reformation Germany*. New Haven: Yale University Press, 1988.

———. *Trent 1475: Stories of a Ritual Murder Trial*. New Haven: Yale University Press, 1992.

———. "The Usurious Jew: Economic Structure and Religious Representations in an Anti-Semitic Discourse." In *In and Out of the Ghetto: Jewish-Gentile Relations in Late Medieval and Early Modern Germany*. Edited by R. Po-Chia Hsia and Hartmut Lehmann, 161–212. Cambridge: Cambridge University Press, 1995.

Hübinger, Gangolf. "Historicism and the 'Noble Science of Politics' in Nineteenth-Century Germany." In *British and German Historiography, 1750–1950: Traditions, Perceptions, and Transfers*. Edited by Benedikt Stuchtey and Peter Wende, 191–209. Oxford: Oxford University Press, 2000.

Hughes, Diane Owen. "Domestic Ideals and Social Behavior: Evidence from Medieval Genoa." In *The Family in History*. Edited by Charles Rosenberg, 115–43. Philadelphia: University of Pennsylvania Press, 1975.

———. "From Brideprice to Dowry in Mediterranean Europe." In *The Marriage Bargain: Women and Dowries in European History*. Edited by Marion Kaplan, 13–58. New York: Haworth Press, 1985.

224 BIBLIOGRAPHY

―――. "Kinsmen and Neighbors in Medieval Genoa." In *The Medieval City*. Edited by H.A. Miskimin, D. Herlihy, and A.L. Udovitch, 95–111. New Haven: Yale University Press, 1977.

―――. "Urban Growth and Family Structure in Medieval Genoa." *Past & Present* 66 (1975): 3–28. doi:10.1093/past/66.1.3

Hughes, H. Stuart. *Between Commitment and Disillusion: The Obstructed Path and the Sea Change, 1930–1965*. Middletown: Wesleyan University Press, 1987.

Huizinga, Johan. *The Autumn of the Middle Ages*. Chicago: University of Chicago Press, 1996.

Humpreys, S.C. "History, Economics, and Anthropology: The Work of Karl Polanyi." *History and Theory* 8 (1969): 165–212.

Huscroft, Richard. *Expulsion: England's Jewish Solution*. Stroud: Tempus, 2006.

Hyams, Paul. "The Jewish minority in medieval England 1066–1290." *Journal of Jewish Studies* 25 (1974): 270–93.

―――. *King, Lords and Peasants in Medieval England: The Law of Villainage in the Twelfth and Thirteenth Centuries*. Oxford: Clarendon, 1980.

Iggers, Georg. *The German Conception of History: The National Tradition of Historical Thought from Herder to the Present*. Hanover: Wesleyan University Press, 1968.

Iggers, Georg and Harold Parker, eds. *International Handbook of Historical Studies*. Westport: Greenwood Press, 1979.

International Biographical Dictionary of Central European Émigrés, 1933–1945. 3 vols. Munich: K.G. Saur, 1980.

International Encyclopedia of the Social Sciences. Detroit: Macmillan Reference, 2008

Isaac, Barry. "Retrospective on the Formalist-Substantivist Debate." *Research in Economic Anthropology* 14 (1993): 213–33.

Jacob, Margaret and Catherine Secretan, ed. *The Self-Perception of Early Modern Capitalists*. New York: Palgrave, 2008.

Jackson, Richard. "From Profit-Sailing to Wage-Sailing: Mediterranean Owner-Captains and Their Crews during the Medieval Commercial Revolution." *Journal of European Economic History* 18/1 (1989): 605–28.

Janson, H.W. *Apes and Ape Lore in the Middle Ages and the Renaissance*. London: The Warburg Institute, 1952.

Jenkinson, Hilary. Introduction to *Calendar of the Plea Rolls of the Exchequer of the Jews*. Vol. 3, xi–lii. London: Macmillan, 1929.

―――. "Jewish entries in the *Curia Regis Rolls* and elsewhere." *Jewish Historical Society of England: Miscellanies* 5 (1948): 128–34.

―――. "Medieval Sources for Anglo-Jewish History: The Problem of Publication." *Jewish Historical Society of England—Transactions* 18 (1955): 285–294.

―――. "The Records of Exchequer Receipts from the English Jewry." *Jewish Historical Society of England—Transactions* 8 (1915–7): 19–54.

BIBLIOGRAPHY 225

———. "William Cade, a Financier of the Twelfth Century." *English Historical Review* 28/110 (1913): 209–227.

Jenks, S. "The lay subsidies and the state of the English economy, 1275–1334." *Vierteljahrschrift für Sozial- und Wirtschaftsgeschichte* 85 (1998): 1–39.

Jewish Year Book. London: Jewish Chronicle Publications, 1896/7 –.

Jordan, William. "An Aspect of Credit in Picardy in the 1240s: The Deterioration of Jewish-Christian Financial Relations." *Revue des études juives* 142 (1983): 141–52.

———. *The French Monarchy and the Jews: From Philip Augustus to the Last Capetians*. Philadelphia: University of Pennsylvania Press, 1989.

———. "Jews on Top: Women and the Availability of Consumption Loans in Northern France in the Mid-Thirteenth Century." *Journal of Jewish Studies* 29 (1978): 39–56.

———. *Louis IX and the Challenge of the Crusade*. Princeton: Princeton University Press, 1979.

———. "Shatzmiller's 'Shylock Reconsidered'." Review of *Shylock Reconsidered: Jews, Moneylending, and Medieval Society* by Joseph Shatzmiller. *Jewish Quarterly Review* 82 (1991): 221–3.

Jost, Isaak M. *Geschichte der Israeliten seit der zeit der Maccabaer bis auf unsre Tage*. Berlin: Schlesingerschen Buch- und Musikhandlung, 1820–9.

Jüdisches Museum Frankfurt am Main. "From Moneylending to Trading." http://juedischesmuseum.de/91.html?&L=1. Accessed Feb 3, 2013.

Jurkowski, M., C.L. Smith, and D. Crook. *Lay Taxes in England and Wales 1188–1688*. Kew: Public Record Office Publications, 1998.

Kaplan, Debra. *Beyond Expulsion: Jews, Christians and Reformation Strasbourg*. Stanford: Stanford University Press, 2011.

Kaplan, Marion. "Women's Strategies in the Jewish Community in Germany." *New German Critique* 14 (1978): 109–18.

Karabel, Jerome. *The Chosen: The Hidden History of Admission and Exclusion at Harvard, Yale, and Princeton*. Boston: Houghton Mifflin, 2005.

Karp, Jonathan. *The Politics of Jewish Commerce: Economic Thought and Emancipation in Europe, 1638–1848*. Cambridge: Cambridge University Press, 2008.

———. "The Politics of Jewish Commerce: European Economic Thought and Jewish Emancipation, 1638–1848." Ph.D. diss., Columbia University, 2000.

Katznellenbogen, Adolf. *Allegories of the Virtues and Vices in Medieval Art*. London: W.W. Norton, 1939.

Kaye, Joel. *Economy and Nature in the Fourteenth Century: Money, Market Exchange, and the Emergence of Scientific Thought*. Cambridge: Cambridge University Press, 1998.

Keen, Maurice. *A History of Medieval Europe*. London: Routledge & Kegan Paul, 1968.

226 BIBLIOGRAPHY

Keene, Derek and Alexander Rumble. *Survey of Medieval Winchester.* Oxford: Clarendon, 1985.

Kelly, A. *The Descent of Darwin: The Popularization of Darwin in Germany, 1860–1914.* Chapel Hill: University of North Carolina Press, 1981.

Kirschenbaum, Aaron. "Jewish and Christian theories of Usury in the Middle Ages." *Jewish Quarterly Review* 75 (1985): 270–89.

Kirschner, Julius. "Raymond De Roover on Scholastic Economic Thought." In *Business, Banking, and Economic Thought in Late Medieval and Early Modern Europe: Selected Studies of Raymond De Roover.* Edited by Julius Kirschner, 15–36. Chicago: University of Chicago Press, 1974.

Kisch, Guido. *Forschungen zur Rechts-, Wirtschafts- und Sozialgeschichte der Juden.* Ausgewählte Schriften, vol. 2. Sigmaringen: J. Thorbecke, 1979.

———. *Forschungen zur Rechts- und Sozialgeschichte der Juden in Deutschland während des Mittelalters.* Zurich: Europa Verlag, 1955. Republished: Ausgewählte Schriften, vol. 1. Sigmaringen: J. Thorbecke, 1978.

———. *Forschungen zur Rechts- und Sozialgeschichte des Mittelalters.* Ausgewählte Schriften, vol. 3. Sigmaringen: J. Thorbecke, 1980.

———. "Historia Judaica, 1938–1961: An Historical Account and Reminiscences of the Retiring Editor." *Historia Judaica* 23 (1961): 3–14.

———. *Jewry-law in Medieval Germany: Laws and Court Decisions concerning Jews.* New York: American Academy for Jewish Research, 1949.

———. "The Jews' Function in the Mediaeval Evolution of Economic Life in Commemoration of the Anniversary of a Celebrated Scholar and His Theory." *Historia Judaica* 6 (1944): 1–12.

———. *The Jews in Medieval Germany: A Study of the Legal and Social Status.* Chicago: University of Chicago Press, 1949.

———. *Der Lebensweg eines Rechtshistorikers: Erinnerungen.* Sigmaringen: Thorbecke, 1975.

———. *Die Prager Universität und die Juden, 1348–1848.* Mährisch-Ostrau: Kittl, 1935.

———. Review of *The Jews and Modern Capitalism* by Werner Sombart and translated by M. Epstein. *Historia Judaica* 13 (1951): 157–9.

———. Worte des Dankes in *Anlässlich der Vollendung meines achtzigsten Lebensjahres 1969.* Basel: [s.n.], 1969.

Kniewasser, Manfred. "Die antijüdische Polemik des Petrus Alfonsi und des Abtes Petrus Venerabilis von Cluny." *Kairos: Zeitschrift für Religionswissenschaft und Theologie* 22 (1980): 34–76.

Knight, Frank. "Historical and Theoretical Issues in the Problem of Modern Capitalism." *Journal of Economic and Business History* 1 (1928–9): 119–36.

Krabbe, J.J. *Historicism and Organicism in Economics: The Evolution of Thought.* Dordrecht: Kluwer Academic Publishers, 1996.

Krause, J. "The Medieval Household: Large or Small?" *Economic History Review* 9 (1957): 420–32.

BIBLIOGRAPHY 227

Krause, Werner, and Günther Rudolph. *Grundlinien des ökonomischen Denkens in Deutschland: 1848 bis 1945.* Berlin: Akademie-Verlag, 1980.

Kriegel, Maurice. "Mobilisation politique et modernisation organique: Les Expulsions de Juifs au Bas Moyen Âge." *Archives de sciences sociales des religions* 46 (1978): 5–20.

Krueger, Hilmar C. "Genoese Merchants, Their Associations and Investments, 1155–1230." In *Studi in onore di Amintore Fanfani*, 415–26. Milan: Dott. A. Giuffrè, 1962.

———. "Genoese Merchants, Their Partnerships and Investments, 1155–1164." In *Studi in onore di Armando Sapori*, 255–71. Milan: Instituto editoriale cisalpino, 1957.

———. "The Wares of Exchange in the Genoese-African Traffic of the Twelfth Century." *Speculum* 12 (1937): 57–71.

Krummel, Miriamne. *Crafting Jewishness in Medieval England: Legally Absent, Virtually Present.* New York: Palgrave, 2011.

La Touche, Robert. *The Birth of the Western Economy: Economic Aspects of the Dark Ages.* New York: Barnes & Noble, 1961.

Landes, David. "The Jewish Merchant: Typology and Stereotypology in Germany." *Leo Baeck Institute Year Book* 19 (1974): 11–24.

Lane, Frederic. "Investment and Usury." In *Venice and History: The Collected Papers of Frederic C. Lane.* Baltimore: Johns Hopkins Press, 1966.

———. "Venetian Shipping during the Commercial Revolution." *The American Historical Review* 38/2 (1933): 219–39.

Lane, Frederic and Jelle Riemersma, ed. *Enterprise and Secular Change.* Homewood: Richard Irwin, 1953.

Langholm, Odd. *Economics in the Medieval Schools: Wealth, Exchange, Value, Money, and Usury according to the Paris Theological Tradition, 1200–1500.* Leiden: Brill, 1992.

———. *The Merchant in the Confessional: Trade and Price in the Pre-Reformation Penitential Handbooks.* Leiden: Brill, 2003.

Langmuir, Gavin. *History, Religion, and Antisemitism.* Berkeley: University of California Press, 1990.

———. *Toward a Definition of Antisemitism.* Berkeley: University of California Press, 1990.

Lastig, G. *Die Accomendatio, die Grundform der heutigen Kommanditgesellschaft in ihrer Gestaltung vom XIII. bis zum XIX. Jahrhundert.* Halle: Buchhandlung des Waisenhauses, 1907.

Le Blevec, Daniel. *Le part du pauvre: l'assistance dans le pays du Bas-Rhone du XIIe siècle au milieu du XVe siècle.* Rome: Ecole française de Rome, 2000.

Le Goff, Jacques. *Money and the Middle Ages: An Essay in Historical Anthrpology.* Translated by Jean Birrell. Cambridge: Cambridge University Press, 2012.

———. *Saint Louis.* Paris: Gallimard, 2013.

228 BIBLIOGRAPHY

————. *Your Money or Your Life: Economy and Religion in the Middle Ages.* Translated by Patricia Ranum. New York: Zone Books, 1998.

Le Roy Ladurie, Emmanuel. *Les paysans de Languedoc.* 2 vols. Paris: S.E.V.P.E.N., 1966.

————. *The Peasants of Languedoc.* Translated by John Day. Urbana: University of Illinois Press, 1974.

————. "A Reply to Robert Brenner." In *The Brenner Debate: Agrarian Class Structure and Economic Development in Pre-industrial Europe.* Edited by T. H. Aston and C. H. E. Philpin, 101–6. Cambridge: Cambridge University Press, 1985.

Leclerq, Jean. "L'Encyclique de Saint Bernard en faveur de la croisade." *Revue bénédictine* 81 (1971): 295–330.

Levin, Yuval. "With Interest," review of *Capitalism and the Jews* by Jerry Z. Muller. *Jewish Review of Books,* 2 (2010): 17–18.

Leonard, G.H. "The Expulsion of the Jews by Edward 1st— an essay in explanation of the Exodus A.D. 1290." *Transactions of the Royal Historical Society* 5 (1891): 103–46.

Leslie, Cliffe. *Essays in Political Economy.* 2nd ed. Dublin: Hodges, Figgis, & Co., 1888.

Lévi-Strauss, Claude. *Structural Anthropology.* New York: Basic Books, 1963.

Lewis, Archibald. "Mediterranean Maritime Commerce, AD 300–1100, Shipping and Trade." In *The Sea and Medieval Civilizations.* Edited by Archibald Lewis, 1–21. London: Variorum Reprints, 1978.

Lewis, Archibald, Jaroslav Pelikan, and David Herlihy. "Robert Sabatino Lopez." *Speculum* 63 (1988): 763–5.

Lewittes, Mendell. *Jewish Law: An Introduction.* Northvale: Jason Aronson, 1987.

Lexikon deutsch-jüdischer Autoren. Munich: De Gruyter, 2006.

Lieberman, Sharon. "English Royal Policy towards the Jews' Debtors, 1227–1290." Ph.D. diss., University of London, 1982.

Lifshitz, Berachyahu, and Eliaz Shochetman. *Mafteach ha-She'elot ve ha-Teshuvot shel Hakhme Ashkenaz, Tsarefat ve-Italyah.* Jerusalem: ha-Makhon le-heker ha-mishpat ha-'Ivrri, 1997–.

Lifshitz, Felice. "Lopez, Robert," in *Encyclopedia of Historians and Historical Writing,* 1: 732–3. London: Fitzroy Dearborn, 1999.

Lindenfeld, David. "The Myth of the Older Historical School of Economics." *Central European History* 26/4 (1993): 405–16.

————. *The Practical Imagination: The German Sciences of State in the Nineteenth Century.* Chicago: University of Chicago Press, 1997.

Lipman, Vivian D. "The Anatomy of Medieval Anglo-Jewry," *Jewish Historical Society of England—Transactions* 21 (1968): 65–77.

————. *The Jews of Medieval Norwich.* London: Jewish Historical Society of England, 1967.

BIBLIOGRAPHY   229

Lipson, E. *The Economic History of England*. London: Adam and Charles Black, 1937.

Lipton, Sara. *Images of Intolerance: The Representation of Jews and Judaism in the Bible Moralisée*. Berkeley: University of California Press, 1999.

———. "The Root of All Evil: Jews, Money and Metaphor in the *Bible Moralisée*." *Medieval Encounters* 1/3 (1995): 301–22.

Little, Lester. *Benedictine Maledictions*. Ithaca: Cornell University Press, 1993.

———. "The Function of the Jews in the Commercial Revolution." In *Povertà e Ricchezza nella Spiritualità dei secoli XI e XII*, 271–87. Todi: Presso l'Accademia Tudertina, 1969.

———. "Pride Goes before Avarice: Social Change and the Vices in Latin Christendom." *American Historical Review* 76/1–2 (1971): 16–49.

———. *Religious Poverty and the Profit Economy in Medieval Europe*. Ithaca: Cornell University Press, 1978.

Loeb, Isidore. "Les négociants Juifs à Marseille au milieu du XIIIe siècle." *Revue des études juives* 16 (1888): 73–83.

———. "Réflexions sur les Juifs," *Revue des études juives* 28 (1894): 1–31.

Logan, F.D. "Thirteen London Jews and conversion to Christianity: problems of apostasy in the 1280s." *Bulletin of the Institute of Historical Research* 45 (1972): 214–49.

Lopez, Robert. "An Aristocracy of Money in the Early Middle Ages." *Speculum* 28 (1953): 1–43.

———. "Back to Gold, 1252." *Economic History Review* 9 (1956): 219–40.

———. *The Commercial Revolution of the Middle Ages, 950–1350*. Cambridge: Cambridge University Press, 1976.

———. "Concerning Surnames and Places of Origin." *Medievalia et Humanistica* 8 (1954): 6–16.

———. "Market Expansion: The Case of Genoa." *Journal of Economic History* 25 (1964): 445–64.

———. "Mohammed and Charlemagne: A Revision." *Speculum* 18 (1943): 14–38.

———. *La Naissance de l'Europe*. Paris: A. Colin, 1962.

———. *La Prima crisi della banca in Genova, secolo XIII*. Milan: Università L. Bocconi, 1956.

———. *The Tenth Century: How Dark the Dark Ages?* New York: Rinehart, 1959.

———. "The Trade of Medieval Europe: the South." In *The Cambridge Economic History of Europe: Trade and Industry in the Middle Ages*. Vol. 2, 1st ed. Edited by Michael Postan and E.E. Rich. 1st ed. Cambridge: Cambridge University Press, 1952.

———. "The Unexplored Wealth of the Notarial Archives in Pisa and Lucca." In *Mélanges d'histoire du Moyen Âge dédicées à la mémoire de Louis Halphen*, 417–32. Paris: Presses Universitaires de France, 1951.

230   BIBLIOGRAPHY

Love, John. "Max Weber's *Ancient Judaism.*" In *The Cambridge Companion to Weber.* Edited by Stephen Turner. Cambridge: Cambridge University Press, 2000.

Lück, Heiner. "Der Rechtshistoriker Guido Kisch (1889–1985) und sein Beitrag zur Sachsenspiegelforschung." In *Hallesche Rechtsgelehrte Judischer Herkunft.* Edited by Walter Pauly and Hans Lilie, 53–66. Cologne: C. Heymann, 1996.

Luzzatto, Gino. *An Economic History of Italy from the Fall of the Roman Empire to the Beginning of the Sixteenth Century.* Translated by Philip Jones. New York: Barnes & Noble, 1961.

———. "Small and Great Merchants in the Italian Cities of the Renaissance." In *Enterprise and Secular Change.* Edited by Frederic Lane and Jelle Riemersma, 41–52. Homewood: Richard Irwin, 1953.

———. "The Study of Medieval Economic History in Italy: Recent Literature and Tendencies." *Journal of Economic and Business History* 4 (1931–2): 708–27.

Lyon, Bryce. *Henri Pirenne: A Biographical and Intellectual Study.* Ghent: E. Story-Scientia, 1974.

Lyotard, Jean-François. *Post-modern Condition: A Report on Knowledge.* Minneapolis: University of Minnesota Press, 1984.

Maddicott, J.R. *Simon de Montfort.* Cambridge: Cambridge University Press, 1994.

Marcus, Ivan. "The Dynamics of Jewish Renaissance and Renewal." In *Jews and Christians in Twelfth-Century Europe.* Edited by Michael Signer and John Van Engen, 27–45. Notre Dame: University of Notre Dame Press, 2001.

———. "*Hasidei' Ashkenaz* Private Penitentials: An Introduction and Descriptive Catalogue of their Manuscripts and Early Editions." In *Studies in Jewish Mysticism.* Edited by Joseph Dan and Frank Talmage, 57–83. Cambridge, MA: Association for Jewish Studies, 1982.

———. "A Jewish-Christian Symbiosis: The Culture of Early Ashkenaz," in *Cultures of the Jews: A New History.* Edited by David Biale, 449–518. New York: Schocken Books, 2002.

———. *Jewish Culture and Society in Medieval France and Germany.* Farnham: Ashgate, 2014.

———. *Piety and Society: The Jewish Pietists of Medieval Germany.* Leiden: Brill, 1981.

———. "The Recensions and Structure of *Sefer Hasidim.*" *Proceedings of the American Academy for Jewish Research* 45 (1978): 131–53.

Margolis, Ethan. "Evidence That the Majority of Medieval English Jews Were Not Moneylenders, with an Emphasis on Document E. 101/249/4." Master's thesis, North Carolina State University, 2015.

Marx, Karl. *Capital: A Critique of Political Economy.* Translated by Ben Fowkes. London: Penguin, 1976–8.

———. *The Marx-Engels Reader.* Edited by Robert Tucker. 2nd ed. New York: Norton, 1978.

BIBLIOGRAPHY   231

————. "Zur Judenfrage." *Deutsch-Französische Jahrbücher* 1–2 (1844): 182–214.
Mattes, Barbara. *Jüdisches Alltagsleben in einer Mittelalterlichen Stadt: Responsa des Rabbi Meir von Rothenburg.* Berlin: De Gruyter, 2003.
Mauss, Marcel. *The Gift: Forms and Functions of Exchange in Archaic Societies.* New York: Norton, 1967.
Mayer, H.E. *Marseilles Levantehandel und ein akkonenisches Fälscheratelier des XIII Jhdts.* Tübingen: M. Niemeyer, 1972.
McCormick, Michael. *Origins of the European Economy: Communications and Commerce, AD 300–900.* Cambridge: Cambridge University Press, 2001.
McGovern, John F. "The Documentary Language of Medieval Business, Ad 1150–1250." *Classical Journal* 66 (1970/1): 227–39.
McKitterick, Rosamond. *The Early Middle Ages, Europe 400–1000.* Edited by T.C.W. Blanning. The Short Oxford History of Europe. Oxford: Oxford University Press, 2001.
McLaughlin, T.P. "The Teaching of the Canonists on Usury." *Mediaeval Studies* 1 (1939): 81–147 and 2 (1940): 1–22.
McNamara, Jo Ann and Suzanne Wemple. "The Power of Women through the Family in Medieval Europe: 500–1100." In *Clio's Consciousness Raised: New Perspectives on the History of Women.* Edited by Mary and Lois Banner Hartman, 103–18. New York: Harper, 1974.
McRee, Benjamin and Trisha Dent. "Working Women in the Medieval City." In *Women in Medieval Western European Culture.* Edited by Linda Mitchell. New York and London: Garland Publishing, 1999.
Meekings, C.A.F. "Justices of the Jews, 1218–1268: A Provisional List." *Bulletin of the Institute of Historical Research* 28 (1955): 173–88.
Mell, Julie. "Hybridity in a Medieval Key: The Paradox of Jewish Participation in Self-Representative Political Processes." *Jewish Historical Studies: Transactions of the Jewish Historical Society of England* 44 (2012): 127–38.
Mell, Julie and Malachi Hacohen, ed. *Central European Jewish Émigrés and the Shaping of Postwar Culture: Studies in Memory of Lilian Furst (1931–2009).* Basel: MDPI, 2014.
Menache, Sophia. "Faith, Myth and Politics — the stereotype of the Jews and their expulsion from England and France." *Jewish Quarterly Review* 75 no. 4 (1985): 351–74.
————. "The King, the Church and the Jews: some considerations on the expulsions from England and France." *Journal of Medieval History* 13 (1987): 223–36.
Mendell, Marguerite, and Daniel Salée, eds. *The Legacy of Karl Polanyi: Market, State and Society at the End of the Twentieth Century.* New York: St. Martin's Press, 1991.
Mendes-Flohr, Paul. "Werner Sombart's *The Jews and Modern Capitalism*: An Analysis of Its Ideological Premises," *Leo Baeck Institute Year Book* 21 (1976): 87–107.

232 BIBLIOGRAPHY

Mentgen, Gerd. "Die Ritualmordaffäre um den 'Guten Werner' von Oberwesel und ihre Folgen." *Jahrbuch für Westdeutsche Landesgeschichte* 21 (1995): 159–98.

———. "Die Vertreibungen der Juden aus England und Frankreich im Mittelalter." *Aschkenas* 7 (1997): 11–53.

Mieder, Wolfgang. *"Tilting at Windmills": History and Meaning of a Proverbial Allusion to Cervantes'* Don Quixote. Burlington: University of Vermont, 2006.

Milford, Karl. "Roscher's Epistemological and Methodological Position: Its Importance for the *Methodenstreit*." *Journal of Economic Studies* 22/3–5 (1995): 26–52.

Miller, Edward. "Michael Moissey Postan: 1899–1981." *Proceedings of the British Academy* 69 (1983): 543–5.

Miller, Edward and John Hatcher. *Medieval England: Rural Society and Economic Change, 1086–1348*. A Social and Economic History of England. London and New York: Longman, 1978.

———. *Medieval England: Towns, Commerce and Crafts, 1086–1348*. A Social and Economic History of England. London and New York: Longman, 1995.

Mills, Mabel. "Experiments in Exchequer Procedure (1220–1232)." *Transactions of the Royal Historical Society* 8 (1925): 151–70.

Miskimin, Harry, David Herlihy, and A.L. Udovitch, eds. *The Medieval City*. New Haven: Yale University Press, 1977.

Mitchell, Sydney. *Studies in Taxation under John and Henry III*. New Haven: Yale University Press, 1914.

———. *Taxation in Medieval England*. New Haven: Yale University Press, 1951.

Mitzman, Arthur. *The Iron Cage: An Historical Interpretation of Max Weber*. New York: Knopf, 1970.

———. *Sociology and Estrangement: Three Sociologists of Imperial Germany*. New York: Knopf, 1973.

Mollat, Michel. *The Poor in the Middle Ages: An Essay in Social History*. New Haven: Yale University Press, 1986.

Momigliano, Arnaldo. "A Note on Max Weber's Definition of Judaism as a Pariah-Religion." *History & Theory* 19 (1980): 313–8.

Montesquieu, Baron de. *The Spirit of the Laws*. Translated by Thomas Nugent. New York: Hafner Publishing, 1949.

Moore, John. *Pope Innocent III (1160/1–1216): To Root Up and to Plant*. Leiden: Brill, 2003.

———. "Pope Innocent III and Usury." In *Pope, Church, and City: Essays in Honour of Brenda M. Bolton*. Edited by Frances Andrews, et. al., 59–75. Leiden: Brill, 2004.

Moore, R.I. "Anti-semitism and the Birth of Europe," in Diana Wood, ed., *Christianity and Judaism*, Studies in Church History 29, 33–58. Cambridge: Ecclesiastical History Society, 1992.

BIBLIOGRAPHY 233

_____. *The Formation of a Persecuting Society: Authority and Deviance in Western Europe, 950–1250*. 2nd ed. Malden, MA: Blackwell, 2007.

Morimoto, Yoshiki. "Aspects of the Early Medieval Peasant Economy as Revealed in the Polyptych of Prüm." In *The Medieval World*. Edited by Peter Linehan and Janet Nelson, 605–20. London: Routledge, 2001.

Morris, Marc. *A Great and Terrible King: Edward I and the Forging of Britain*. London: Hutchinson, 2008.

Mosse, Werner. "Judaism, Jews and Capitalism: Weber, Sombart, and Beyond." *Leo Baeck Institute Year Book* 24 (1979): 3–15.

Muller, Jerry. *Capitalism and the Jews*. Princeton: Princeton University Press, 2010.

_____. *The Mind and the Market: Capitalism in Modern European Thought*. New York: Anchor Books, 2002.

Mundill, Robin. "The 'Archa' System and Its Legacy after 1194." In *Christians and Jews in Angevin England: The York Massacre of 1190, Narratives and Contexts*. Edited by Sarah Jones and Sethina Watson, 148–62. Woodbridge: York Medieval Press, 2013.

_____. "Christian and Jewish Lending Patterns and Financial Dealings during the Twelfth and Thirteenth Centuries." In *Credit and Debt in Medieval England, c. 1180–1350*. Edited by Schofield, P.R. and N.J. Mayhew, 48–67. Oxford: Oxbow, 2002.

_____. *England's Jewish Solution: Experiment and Expulsion, 1262–90*. Cambridge: Cambridge University Press, 1998.

_____. *The King's Jews: Money, Massacre and Exodus in Medieval England*. London: Continuum, 2010.

Mundy, John. *Europe in the High Middle Ages, 1150–1309*. A General History of Europe. London: Longman, 1973.

Murray, Alexander. *Reason and Society in the Middle Ages*. Oxford: Clarendon, 1978.

Myers, David. *Re-inventing the Jewish Past: European Jewish Intellectuals and the Zionist Return to History*. New York: Oxford University Press, 1995.

Nahon, Gérard. "Le credit et les Juifs dans la France du XIIIe siècle." *Annales, Histoire, Sciences Sociales* 24 (1969): 1121–48.

_____. "From the Rue aux Juifs to the Chemin du Roy: the classical age of French Jewry, 1108–1223." In *Jews and Christians in Twelfth-Century Europe*. Edited by Michael Signer and John Van Engen, 311–39. Notre Dame: University of Notre Dame Press, 2001.

Naismith, Rory. *Money and power in Anglo-Saxon England: the southern English Kingdoms, 757–865*. Cambridge: Cambridge University Press, 2012.

Nelson, Benjamin. *The Idea of Usury: From Tribal Brotherhood to Universal Otherhood*. 2nd ed. Chicago: University of Chicago Press, 1969. First published 1949.

234 BIBLIOGRAPHY

Nightingale, Pamela. *Trade, Money, and Power in Medieval England*. Aldershot: Ashgate, 2007.

Nirenberg, David. *Anti-Judaism: The Western Tradition*. New York: Norton, 2013.

Noonan, John. *The Scholastic Analysis of Usury*. Cambridge, MA: Harvard University Press, 1957.

North, Douglass and Robert Thomas. *The Rise of the Western World: A New Economic History*. Cambridge: Cambridge University Press, 1973.

Nussbaum, Frederick. *A History of the Economic Institutions of Modern Europe*. New York: Crofts, 1933.

"Obituary: Professor Sir Michael Moissey Postan, 1899–1981." *Economic History Review* n.s. 35 (1982): iv–vi.

O'Brien, Bruce. *God's Peace and King's Peace: The Laws of Edward the Confessor*. Philadelphia: University of Pennsylvania Press, 1999.

Oelsner, Toni. "'Bloch hielt einen Vortrag über Träume vom besseren Leben': Gespräch mit Toni Oelsner." In *Die Zerstörung einer Zukunft: Gespräche mit Emigrierten Sozialwissenschaftlern*. Edited by Mathias Greffrath, 223–47. Reinbek bei Hamburg: Rowohlt, 1979.

———. "Dreams of a Better Life: Interview with Toni Oelsner." In *Germans and Jews since the Holocaust: The Changing Situation in West Germany*. Edited by Anson Rabinbach and Jack Zipes, 98–119. New York: Holmes & Meier, 1986.

———. "The Economic and Social Condition of the Jews of Southwestern Germany in the 13th and 14th Centuries." In Toni Oelsner Collection; Archives of the Leo Baeck Institute, 126 pages. New York.

———. "The Economic and Social Condition of the Jews of Southwestern Germany in the thirteenth and fourteenth centuries." *The American Philosophical Society Year Book* (1963): 577–81.

———. "The Jewish Ghetto of the Past." *YIVO Annual of Jewish Social Science* 1 (1946): 24–43. Originally published in Yiddish in the *YIVO Bleter* 20 (1942): 232–242.

———. "The Place of the Jews in Economic History as Viewed by German Scholars: A Critical-Comparative Analysis." *Leo Baeck Institute Yearbook* 7 (1962): 183–212.

———. "Three Jewish Families in Modern Germany: Studies of the Process of Emancipation." *Jewish Social Studies* 4 (1942): 241–68, 349–98.

———. "Wilhelm Roscher's Theory of the Economic and Social Position of the Jews in the Middle Ages: A Critical Examination." *YIVO Annual of Jewish Social Science* 12 (1958-9): 176–95.

Oren, Dan. *Joining the Club: A History of Jews and Yale*. New Haven: Yale University Press, 2000.

Ormrod, W.M. "The crown and the English economy, 1290–1348." In *Before the Black Death: Studies in the 'crisis' of the early fourteenth century*. Edited by Bruce Campbell, 149–83. Manchester: Manchester University Press, 1991.

BIBLIOGRAPHY 235

Osterhammel, Jürgen. "'Peoples without History' in British and German Historical Thought." In *British and German Historiography, 1750–1950: Traditions, Perceptions, and Transfers.* Edited by Benedikt Stuchtey and Peter Wende, 265–87. Oxford: Oxford University Press, 2000.

Packard, Laurence. *The Commercial Revolution, 1400–1776.* New York: H. Holt, 1927.

Pakter, Walter. *Medieval Canon Law and the Jews.* Ebelsbach: Gremer, 1988.

Parkes, James. *The Jew in the Medieval Community: A Study of His Political and Economic Situation.* New York: Hermon Press, 1976.

Parry, Jonathon. "The Gift, the Indian Gift and the 'Indian Gift'." *Man,* n.s. 21/3 (1986): 453–73.

———. "On the Moral Perils of Exchange." In *Money and the Morality of Exchange.* Edited by J. Parry and M. Bloch. Cambridge: Cambridge University Press, 1989.

Parry, J., and M. Bloch. *Money and the Morality of Exchange.* Cambridge: Cambridge University Press, 1989.

Pascal, Roy. *The German Sturm und Drang.* London: Butler and Tanner, 1953.

Patschovsky, Alexander. "Das Rechtsverhältnis der Juden zum deutschen König (9–14 Jahrhundert)." *Zeitschrift der Savigny-Stiftung für Reschtsgeschichte* 123 (1993): 331–71.

———. "The Relationship between the Jews of Germany and the King (11th–14th Centuries): A European Comparison." In *England and Germany in the High Middle Ages.* Edited by Alfred Haverkamp and Hanna Vollrath, 193–218. New York: Oxford University Press, 1996.

Patterson, David. "The Renaissance of Jewish Learning in Post-World War II Europe." In *Jewish Centers and Peripheries: Europe between America and Israel Fifty Years after World War II.* Edited by S. Ilan Troen. New Brunswick: Transaction Publishers, 1999.

Pekic, Borislav. *How to Quiet a Vampire: A Sotie.* Chicago: Northwestern University Press, 2005.

Penslar, Derek. *Shylock's Children: Economics and Jewish Identity in Modern Europe.* Berkeley: University of California Press, 2001.

Pernoud, Régine. *Essai sur l'histoire du port de Marseille des origines à la fin du XIIIe siècle.* Marseilles: Institut historique de Provence, 1935.

Philipp, Alfred. *Die Juden und das Wirtschaftsleben. Eine antikritisch-bibliographische Studie zu Werner Sombart: Die Juden und das Wirtschaftsleben.* Strassburg: Heitz & Cie., 1929.

Pirenne, Henri. *Economic and Social History of Medieval Europe.* New York: Harcourt, Brace & World, 1937.

———. *Medieval Cities: Their Origins and the Revival of Trade.* Garden City: Doubleday Anchor Books, 1956.

———. *Mohammed and Charlemagne.* New York: Meridian, 1957.

236 BIBLIOGRAPHY

———. *Les périodes de l'histoire sociale du capitalism*. Brussels: Librairie du "Peuple," 1914.

———. "The Stages in the Social History of Capitalism." *American Historical Review* 19/3 (1914): 494–515.

Polanyi, Karl. *The Great Transformation: The Political and Economic Origins of Our Time*. Boston: Beacon Press, 2001. First published, 1944.

———. "Review: Studies in the Development of Capitalism." *Journal of Economic History* 8/2 (1948): 206–7.

Polanyi, Karl, Conrad Arensberg, and Harry Pearson, eds. *Trade and Market in the Early Empires: Economies in History and Theory*. New York: Free Press, 1957.

Polanyi-Levitt, Kari, ed. *The Life and Work of Karl Polanyi: A Celebration*. Montreal: Black Rose Books, 1990.

Polanyi-Levitt, Kari, and Marguerite Mendell. "Karl Polanyi: His Life and Times." *Studies in Political Economy* 22 (1987): 7–39.

Poliakov, Léon. *Jewish Bankers and the Holy See from the Thirteenth to the Seventeenth Century*. London: Routledge & Kegan Paul, 1977.

Pollak, Oliver. "Antisemitism, the Harvard Plan, and the Roots of Reverse Discrimination." *Jewish Social Studies* 45 (1983): 113–22.

Pollock, Sir Frederick, and Frederic Maitland. *The History of the English Law before the Time of Edward I*. 2 vols. 2nd ed. Cambridge: Cambridge University Press, 1898. Reprint, Indianapolis: Liberty Fund, 2010.

Poole, Austin Lane. *From Domesday Book to Magna Carta, 1087–1216*. 2nd ed. Oxford: Clarendon Press, 1955.

Poole, Reginald L. *The Exchequer in the twelfth century: The Ford lectures delivered in the University of Oxford in Michaelmas Term, 1911*. Oxford: Clarendon Press, 1912.

Postan, Michael M. *British War Production*. History of the Second World War. London: H.M. Stationary Office, 1952.

———. "Credit in Medieval Trade." *Economic History Review* 1, 1928: 234–61.

———. *Essays on Medieval Agriculture and General Problems of the Medieval Economy*. Cambridge: Cambridge University Press, 1973.

———. *Medieval Trade and Finance*. Cambridge: Cambridge University Press, 1973.

———. "Mediaeval Capitalism." *Economic History Review* 4 no. 2 (1933): 212–77.

———. *The Medieval Economy and Society: An Economic History of Britain 1100–1500*. Berkeley and Los Angeles: University of California Press, 1972.

———. "Partnership in English Medieval Commerce." In *Studi in Onore di Armando Sapori*, 519–50. Milan: Instituto Ediotriale Cisalpino, 1957.

———. "Private Financial Instruments." *Vierteljahrschrift für Sozial- und Wirtschaftsgeschichte* 23, 1930: 26–75.

BIBLIOGRAPHY   237

———. "Rapport de M.M. Postan." *IXe Congrès International des Sciences Historiques*, vol. 1, *Rapports*, 225–241. Paris: Colin, 1950.

———. "The Rise of a Money Economy." *Economic History Review* 14 no. 2 (1944): 28–40.

Postan, Michael, ed. *The Agrarian Life of the Middle Ages.* Vol. 1 of *The Cambridge Economic History of Europe.* 2nd ed. Cambridge: Cambridge University Press, 1966.

Postan, Michael and Denys Hay and J.D. Scott. *Design and Development of Weapons: Studies in Government and Industrial Organization.* History of the Second World War. London, H.M. Stationary Office, 1964.

Postan, Michael and Edward Miller, eds. *Trade and Industry in the Middle Ages.* Vol. 2 of *The Cambridge Economic History of Europe.* 2nd ed. Cambridge: Cambridge University Press, 1987.

Postan, Michael and E.E. Rich, eds. *Trade and Industry in the Middle Ages.* Vol. 2 of *The Cambridge Economic History of Europe.* 1st ed. Cambridge: Cambridge University Press, 1952.

Postan, Michael, E.E. Rich and Edward Miller, eds. *Economic Organization and Policies in the Middle Ages.* Vol. 3 of *The Cambridge Economic History of Europe.* 1st ed. New York: Cambridge University Press, 1963.

Postan, Michael and John Hatcher. "Population and Class Relations in Feudal Society." In *The Brenner Debate: Agrarian Class Structure and Economic Development in Pre-Industrial Europe.* Edited by T.H. Aston and C.H.E. Philpin, 64–78. Cambridge: Cambridge University Press, 1985.

Pounds, N.J.G. *An Economic History of Medieval Europe.* 2nd ed. New York: Longman Publishing, 1994.

"Pour une histoire anthropologique: la notion de réciprocité." Symposium in *Annales: Économies, Sociétés, Civilisations* 29/6 (1974): 1309–80.

Powell, Edgar. "The Taxation of Ipswich for the Welsh War in 1282." *Proceedings of the Suffolk Institute of Archaeology and Natural History* 12 (1906): 137–57.

Power, Eileen and M.M. Postan, eds. *Studies in English Trade in the Fifteenth Century.* London: G. Routledge & Sons, 1933.

Powicke, F.M. *King Henry III and the Lord Edward.* 2 vols. Oxford: Oxford University Press, 1947.

———. *Loss of Normandy (1189–1204): Studies in the history of the Angevin empire.* Manchester: Manchester University Press, 1960.

Prestwich, Michael. *Edward I.* Berkeley: University of California Press, 1988.

———. *Plantagenet England, 1225–1360.* Oxford: Clarendon Press, 2005.

Prynne, William. *Second Part of a Short Demurrer to the Jewes long discontinued remitter into England.* London: Edward Thomas, 1656.

———. *Short Demurrer to the Jewes long discontinued barred remitter into England.* London: Edward Thomas, 1656.

238 BIBLIOGRAPHY

Pryor, John. "Commenda: The Operation of the Contract in Long Distance Commerce at Marseilles during the Thirteenth Century." *Journal of European Economic History* 13/2 (1984): 397–440.

———. "Mediterranean Commerce in the Middle Ages: A Voyage under Contract of Commenda." *Viator* 14 (1983): 133–94.

———. "The Origins of the Commenda Contract." *Speculum* 52/1 (1977): 5–37.

Pugh, Ralph. "Some Mediaeval Moneylenders." *Speculum* 43 no. 2 (1968): 274–89.

Quaglioni, Diego, Giacomo Todeschini, and Gian Maria Varanini, eds. *Credito e usura fra teologia, diritto e amministrazione: linguaggi a confronto, sec. XII–XVI*. Rome: Ecole française de Rome, 2005.

Ramsay, Sir James. *A History of the Revenues of the Kings of England, 1066–1399*. 2 vols. Oxford: Oxford University Press, 1925.

Rapp, Richard. "The Unmaking of the Mediterranean Trade Hegemony: International Trade Rivalry and the Commercial Revolution." *Journal of Economic History* 35/3 (1975): 499–525.

Ravid, Benjamin. "The First Charter of the Jewish Merchants of Venice, 1589." *AJS Review* 2 (1977): 187–222.

———. "An Introduction to the Charters of the Jewish Merchants of Venice." In *The Mediterranean and the Jews: Society, Culture and Economy in Early Modern Times*. Edited by Elliott Horowitz and Moises Orfali. Ramat-Gan: Bar-Ilan University Press, 2002.

———. "The Jewish Mercantile Settlement of Twelfth and Thirteenth Century Venice: Reality or Conjecture?" *AJS Review* 1 (1976): 201–25.

Razi, Zvi. *Life, Marriage, and Death in a Medieval Parish*. Cambridge: Cambridge University Press, 1980.

Regné, Jean. "Étude sur la condition des Juifs de Narbonne du Ve au XIVe siècle." *Revue des études juives* 55 (1908): 1–36, 221–43; 58 (1909): 75–105, 200–25; 59 (1910): 59–89; and 61 (1911): 228–54.

Reynolds, Robert L. "In Search of a Business Class in Thirteenth Century Genoa." *Journal of Economic History* 5, suppl. (1945): 1–19.

Reynolds, Susan. *Fiefs and Vassals: The Medieval Evidence Reinterpreted*. Oxford: Clarendon, 2001.

Ricardo, David. *On the Principles of Political Economy and Taxation*. 2nd ed. London: John Murray, 1819.

Richard, Jean. *The Crusades, c. 1071–c. 1291*. Translated by Jean Birrell. Cambridge: Cambridge University Press, 1999.

Richardson, H.G. "Azo, Drogheda, and Bracton." *English Historical Review* 59 (1944): 22–47.

———. *The English Jewry under Angevin Kings*. London: Methuen, 1960.

———. "Studies in Bracton." *Traditio* 6 (1948): 61–104.

BIBLIOGRAPHY   239

Richardson, H.G. and G.O. Sayles. *Law and Legislation from Aethelberht to Magna Carta*. Edinburgh: Edinburgh University Publications, 1966.

Riemer, Eleanor S. "Women, Dowries, and Capital Investment in Thirteenth-Century Siena." In *The Marriage Bargain: Women and Dowries in European History*. Edited by Marion Kaplan, 59–80. New York: Institute for Research in History, 1985.

Rigby, Stephen. "Urban Society in early fourteenth-century England: the evidence of the lay subsidies." *Bulletin of the John Rylands University Library of Manchester* 72 (1990): 169–84.

Riley-Smith, Louise and Jonathan, eds. *The Crusades: Idea and Reality, 1095–1274*. London: Edward Arnold, 1981.

Rist, Rebecca. "The Power of the Purse: Usury, Jews, and Crusaders, 1198–1245." In *Aspects of Power and Authority in the Middle Ages*. Edited by Brenda Bolton and Christine Meek, 197–213. Turnhout: Brepols, 2007.

Rokéah, Zefira. "Crime and Jews in Late Thirteenth-Century England: Some Cases and Comments." *Hebrew Union College Annual* 55 (1984): 95–157.

———. "A Hospitaller and the Jews: Brother Joseph de Chauncy and the English Jewry in the 1270s." *Jewish Historical Studies: Transactions of the Jewish Historical Society of England* 34 (1994–6): 189–207.

———. "The Jewish Church-Robbers and Host Desecrators of Norwich (ca. 1285)." *Revue des études juives* 141 (1982): 331–62.

———. *Medieval English Jews and Royal Officials: Entries of Jewish Interest in the English Memoranda Rolls, 1266–1293*. Jerusalem, 2000.

———. "The State, the Church, and the Jews in Medieval England." In *Antisemitism Through the Ages*. Edited by Shmuel Almog. Oxford: Pergamon Press, 1988.

Roscher, Wilhelm. "Die Juden im Mittelalter, betrachtet vom Standpunkte der Allgemeinen Handelspolitik." In *Ansichten der Volkswirthschaft aus dem Geschichtlichen Standpunkte*, 321–54. Leipzig: Winter, 1878.

———. *Principles of Political Economy*. Translated by John Lalor. 2 vols. Chicago: Callaghan, 1878.

———. "The Status of the Jews in the Middle Ages Considered from the Standpoint of Commercial Policy." Translated by Solomon Grayzel. *Historia Judaica* 6/1 (1944): 13–26.

Rosenthal, Judah. "Ribit min-ha-Nokri." *Talpiyot* 5 (1952): 475–92 and *Talpiyot* 6 (1953): 130–52.

Rosenwein, Barbara. *To Be the Neighbor of Saint Peter: the Social Meaning of Cluny's Property, 909–1049*. Ithaca: Cornell University Press, 1989.

Roth, Cecil. *A History of the Jews in England*. Oxford: Oxford University Press, 1941; 1964.

———. *The History of the Jews of Italy*. Philadelphia: The Jewish Publication Society of America, 1946.

240 BIBLIOGRAPHY

————. "The Ordinary Jew in the Middle Ages: A Contribution to His History." In M. Ben-Horin et al, eds., *Studies and Essays in honor of Abraham A. Neuman*, 424–37. Leiden: Brill, 1962.

Roth, Guenther. "Duration and Rationalization: Fernand Braudel and Max Weber." In Guenther Roth and Wolfgang Schluchter, *Max Weber's Vision of History: Ethics and Methods*. Berkeley: University of California Press, 1979.

Rubin, Miri. *Charity and Community in Medieval Cambridge*. Cambridge: Cambridge University Press, 1987.

————. *Gentile Tales: the Narrative Assault on late medieval Jews*. New Haven: Yale University Press, 1999.

Russell, Josiah C. *Medieval British Population*. Albuquerque: University of New Mexico, 1948.

Rutledge, Elizabeth. "Immigration and Population Growth in early Fourteenth century Norwich." *Urban History Yearbook* (1988): 15–30.

Sahlins, Marshall. *Social Stratification in Polynesia*. Seattle: University of Washington Press, 1958.

————. *Stone Age Economics*. Chicago: Aldine–Atherton, 1972.

Saige, Gustave. *Les Juifs de Languedoc antérieurement au XIVe siècle*. Paris: A. Picard, 1881.

Sapori, Armando. "The Culture of the Medieval Italian Merchant." In *Enterprise and Secular Change*. Edited by Frederic Lane and Jelle Riemersma, 53–65. Homewood: Richard Irwin, 1953.

Sárkány, Mihály. "Karl Polanyi's Contribution to Economic Anthropology." In *The Life and Work of Karl Polanyi*. Edited by Kari Polanyi-Levitt, 183–7. Montreal: Black Rose Books, 1990.

Sayers, Jane. *Innocent III: Leader of Europe, 1198–1216*. London: Longman, 1994.

Sayles, G.O. "Henry Gerald Richardson, 1884–1974." *Proceedings of the British Academy* 61 (1975): 497–521.

Sayous, André. "Le Commerce de Marseille au Syrie" *Revue des études historique* 95 (1929): 391–408.

Schaube, Adolf. *Handelsgeschichte der Romanischen Völker des Mittelmeergebiets bis zum ende der Kreuzzüge*. Munich: R. Oldenbourg, 1906.

Schechter, Frank. "The Rightlessness of Medieval English Jewry." *Jewish Quarterly Review*, n.s. 4 (1913–4): 121–51.

Schefold, Bertram, ed. *Vadecum zu einem Klassiker der Historischen Schule*. Kommentarbeiband zur Faksimile-Ausgabe von Wilhelm Roschers *Ansichten der Volkswirthschaft aus dem Geschichtlichen Standpunkte*. Düsseldorf: Verl. Wirtschaft und Finanzen, 1994.

Schofield, P.R. and N.J. Mayhew, ed. *Credit and Debt in Medieval England, c. 1180–1350*. Oxford: Oxbow, 2002.

Schofield, R.S. "The Geographical distribution of wealth in England, 1334–1649." *Economic History Review* 2nd ser., 18 (1965): 483–510.

BIBLIOGRAPHY 241

Schorsch, Ismar. "The Lachrymose Conception of Jewish History." In *From Text to Context: The Turn to History in Modern Judaism*, 376–88. Hanover: Published for Brandeis University Press by University Press of New England, 1994.

Schwarzfuchs, Simon. *A Concise History of the Rabbinate*. Oxford: Basil Blackwell, 1993.

Scialoja, Antonio. "La Commenda nel diritto Commune del Mediterraneo dei secoli XI–XIII." In *Saggi di Storia del Diritto Marittimo*. Rome: Soc. ed. del "Foro italiano," 1946.

Shakespeare, William. *Merchant of Venice*. Edited by David Bevington. *The Complete Works of Shakespeare*, 3rd ed. Glenview, IL: Scott, Foresman and Co., 1980.

———. "The most excellent historie of the merchant of Venice: With the extreame crueltie of Shylocke the Jewe towards the sayd merchant." 1600. Early English Books Online. http://gateway.proquest.com.proxy.lib.duke.edu/openurl?ctx_ver=Z39.88-2003&res_id=xri:eebo&rft_id=xri:eebo:image:11589

Shapiro, James. *Shakespeare and the Jews*. New York: Columbia University Press, 1996.

Shatzmiller, Joseph. *Cultural Exchange: Jews, Christians and Art in the Medieval Marketplace*. Princeton: Princeton University Press, 2013.

———. *Jews, Medicine, and Medieval Society*. Berkeley: University of California Press, 1994.

———. *Shylock Reconsidered: Jews, Moneylending, and medieval society*. Berkeley: University of California Press, 1990.

Sheehan, James. *The Career of Lujo Brentano*. Chicago and London: University of Chicago Press, 1966.

Shmueli, Ephraim. "The 'Pariah-People' and Its 'Charismatic Leadership:' A Revaluation of Max Weber's 'Ancient Judaism'." *American Academy for Jewish Research: Proceedings* 36 (1968): 167–247.

Shyovitz, David. "'You have saved me from the Judgment of Gehenna': The Origins of the Mourner's Kaddish in Medieval Ashkenaz." *AJS Review* 39 (2015): 49–73.

Sieveking, G. *Genueser Finanzwesen vom 12. bis 14. Jhdt.* Freiburg-im-Breisgau: J.C.B. Mohr, 1898.

Signer, Michael and John van Engen, ed. *Jews and Christians in Twelfth-century Europe*. Notre Dame: University of Notre Dame Press, 2001.

Skinner, Patricia, ed. *The Jews in Medieval Britain: Historical, Literary, and Archaeological Perspectives*. Woodbridge: Boydell Press, 2003.

Smail, Daniel Lord. *The Consumption of Justice: Emotions, Publicity, and Legal Culture in Marseille, 1264–1423*. Ithaca: Cornell, 2003.

———. *Imaginary Cartographies: Possession and Identity in Late Medieval Marseille*. Ithaca: Cornell, 1999.

242 BIBLIOGRAPHY

———. "Notaries, Courts, and the Legal Culture of Late Medieval Marseille" in *Urban and Rural Communities in Medieval France: Provence and Languedoc, 1000–1500*, ed. Kathryn Reyerson and John Drendel (Leiden, 1998), 23–50.

———. "The Two Synagogues of Medieval Marseille: Documentary Evidence" *Revue des études juives* 154 (1995): 115–24.

Small, Albion. *Origins of Sociology*. Chicago: University of Chicago Press, 1924.

Soloveitchik, Haym. *Collected Essays*. 2 vols. Oxford: Littman Library of Jewish Civilization, 2013–4.

———. *Halakhah, Kalkalah ve-Dimui-ʿAtsmi: ha-Mashkona'ut bi-Yemei ha-Benayim*. Jerusalem: Magnes, 1985.

———. "The Jewish Attitude to Usury in the High and Late Middle Ages (1000–1500)." In *Credito e usura fra teologia, diritto e amministrazione*, eds. Diego Quaglioni et al., 115–27. Rome: Ecole française de Rome, 2005. Republished in his *Collected Essays*, 1:44–56.

———. "Pawn and Surety: Two Studies in *Ribit* and of the Halakah in Exile" [Hebrew]. Ph.D. diss., The Hebrew University, 1972.

———. "Pawnbroking: A Study in Ribbit and of the Halakhah in Exile." *Proceedings of the American Academy of Jewish Research* 38–9 (1972): 203–68. Republished in a revised and expanded version in his *Collected Essays*, 1:57–166.

———. "Piety, Pietism and German Pietism: *Sefer Ḥasidim I* and the influence of Ḥasidei Ashkenaz." *Jewish Quarterly Review* 92 (2002): 455–93.

———. "Three Themes in the *Sefer Ḥasidim*." *AJS Review* 1 (1976): 311–57.

———. *Yayin bi-yeme ha-benayim: yen nesekh: perek be-toldot ha-halakhah be-Ashkenaz* [Wine in Ashkenaz in the Middle Ages: yeyn nesekh—a Study in Halakhah]. Tel Aviv: Zalman Shazar, 2003.

Sombart, Werner. *Economic Life in the Modern Age*. New Brunswick: Transaction Publishers, 2001.

———. *The Jews and Modern Capitalism*. London: T.F. Unwin, 1913.

———. *Der moderne Kapitalismus*. 1st ed. 3 vols. Leipzig: Duncker and Humblot, 1902.

———. *The Quintessence of Capitalism: A Study of the History and Psychology of the Modern Business Man*. Translated by Mordecai Epstein. London: T. Fisher Unwin, 1915.

Spufford, Peter et al. *Handbook of Medieval Exchange*. London: Offices of the Royal Historical Society, 1986.

———. *Money and Its Use in Medieval Europe*. Cambridge: Cambridge University Press, 1988.

———. *Power and Profit: The Merchant in Medieval Europe*. London: Thames & Hudson, 2003.

Stacey, Robert. "1240–60: A Watershed in Anglo-Jewish relations?" *Historical Research* 61/145 (1988): 135–50.

BIBLIOGRAPHY 243

———. "The conversion of Jews to Christianity in thirteenth-century England." *Speculum* 67 (1992): 263–83.

———. "From Ritual Crucifixion to Host Desecration: Jews and the Body of Christ." *Jewish History* 12 (1998): 11–28.

———. "Jewish Lending and the Medieval English Economy." In *A Commercialising Economy: England 1086 to c. 1300*. Edited by Richard H. Britnell and Bruce Campbell. Manchester: Manchester University Press, 1995.

———. "The Massacres of 1189–90 and the Origins of the Jewish Exchequer, 1186–1226." In *Christians and Jews in Angevin England: The York Massacre of 1190, Narratives and Contexts*. Edited by Sarah Jones and Sethina Watson, 106–24. Woodbridge: York Medieval Press, 2013.

———. "Parliamentary Negotiation and the Expulsion of the Jews from England." *Thirteenth Century England: Proceedings of the New Castle Upon Tyne Conference* 6 (1995): 77–101.

———. *Politics, Policy, and Finance under Henry III: 1216–1245*. Oxford: Oxford University Press, 1987.

———. "Royal Taxation and the Social Structure of Medieval Anglo-Jewry: The Tallages of 1239–1242." *Hebrew Union College Annual* 56 (1985): 175–249.

Stanfield, J.R. *The Economic Thought of Karl Polanyi: Lives and Livelihood*. New York: St. Martin's Press, 1986.

Stanley, M.J. "Medieval Tax Returns as source material." In *Field and Forest: an historical geography of Warwickshire and Worcestershire*. Edited by T.R. Slater and P.J. Jarvis, 231–56. Norwich: Geo Books, 1982.

Stehr, Nico and Reiner Grundmann. Introduction to *Economic Life in the Modern Age*, by Werner Sombart. New Brunswick: Transaction Publishers, 2001.

Stein, Siegfried. "The Development of Jewish Law on Interest from the Biblical Period to the Expulsion of the Jews from England." *Historia Judaica* 1 (1955): 3–40.

———. "A Disputation on Moneylending between Jews and Gentiles in Me'ir b. Simeon's *Milḥemeth Miswah* (Narbonne, 13th Cent.)." *Journal of Jewish Studies* 10 (1959): 45–61.

———. *Jewish-Christian Disputations in Thirteenth Century Narbonne: An inaugural lecture delivered at University College London 22 October 1964*. London: H.K. Lewis, 1969.

Stenton, Doris. *English Society in the Early Middle Ages, 1066–1307*. Pelican History of England. 4th ed. Harmondsworth: Penguin, 1965.

Stephenson, Carl. *Borough and Town: A Study of Urban Origins in England*. Cambridge, MA: Medieval Academy of America, 1933.

———. *Medieval Institutions: Selected Essays*. Ithaca: Cornell University Press, 1954.

244 BIBLIOGRAPHY

Stern, Selma. *The Court Jews: A Contribution to the history of the period of Absolutism in Central Europe*. Philadelphia: Jewish Publication Society of America, 1950.

———. *The Spirit Returneth...A Novel*. Translated by Ludwig Lewisohn. Philadelphia: Jewish Publication Society of America, 1946.

Stobbe, Otto. *Die Juden in Deutschland während des Mittelalters*. Braunschweig: C.A. Schwetschke und Sohn, 1866. Republished: Amsterdam: B.R. Grüner, 1968.

Stokes, H.P. *A Short History of the Jews in England*. New York: Macmillan, 1921.

———. *Studies in Anglo-Jewish History*. Edinburgh: Jewish Historical Society of England, 1913.

Stow, Kenneth. *Alienated Minority: The Jews of Medieval Latin Europe*. Cambridge, MA: Harvard University Press, 1992.

———. *Jewish Dogs: An Image and Its Interpreters: Continuity in the Catholic-Jewish Encounter*. Palo Alto: Stanford University Press, 2006.

———. "The Jewish Family in the Rhineland in the High Middle Ages: Form and Function." *American Historical Review* 92 (1987): 1085–110.

———. "Papal and Royal Attitudes Toward Jewish Lending in the Thirteenth Century." *AJS Review* 6 (1981): 161–84.

———. *Theater of Acculturation: The Roman Ghetto in the Sixteenth Century*. Seattle and London: University of Washington Press, 2001.

Strathern, Marilyn. *The Gender of the Gift*. Berkeley: University of California Press, 1988.

Strauss, Raphel. *Die Juden im königreich Sizilien unter Normannen und Staufern*. Heidelberg: C. Winter, 1910.

Strayer, Joseph. *On the Medieval Origins of the Modern State*. Princeton: Princeton University Press, 1970.

Streider, Jacob. "Origin and Evolution of Early European Capitalism." *Journal of Economic and Business History* 2/1 (1929): 1–19.

Stubbs, William. *Constitutional History of England in Its Origins and Development*. 3 vols. 5th ed. Oxford: Clarendon Press, 1891.

"Symposium: Economic Anthropology and History: The Work of Karl Polanyi." Special issue, *Research in Economic Anthropology* 4 (1981): ix–285.

Tal, Uriel. "German-Jewish Social Thought in the Mid-Nineteenth Century." In *Revolution and Evolution: 1848 in German-Jewish History*. Edited by Werner Mosse et al., 299–328. Tübingen: J.C.B. Mohr, 1981.

Tamari, Meir. *"With All Your Possessions": Jewish Ethics and Economic Life*. London: Collier Macmillan, 1987.

Tanner, Tony. Introduction to *The Merchant of Venice*, by William Shakespeare, xi–xxxix. In *Comedies: Volume 2*. Everyman's Library 226. New York: Alfred Knopf, 1996.

Täubler, Eugene. "Zur Handelsbedeutung der Juden in Deutschland vor Beginn des Städtewesens." In *Beiträge zur Geschichte der Deutschen Juden*. Leipzig, 1916.

BIBLIOGRAPHY 245

Tawney, R.H. *Religion and the Rise of Capitalism*. Gloucester: P. Smith, 1962.
Thieme, Hans. "Nachrufe: Guideo Kisch." *Österreichische Akademie der Wissenschaften Almanach für das Jahr 1986* 136: 413–20.
Thomas, Nicholas. *Entangled Objects*. Cambridge, MA: Harvard University Press, 1991.
Thompson, James W. *Economic and Social History of the Later Middle Ages (1300–1350)*. New York: D. Appleton-Century Co., 1931.
Toaff, Ariel, and Simon Schwarzfuchs, eds. *The Mediterranean and the Jews: Banking, Finance and International Trade (XVI–XVIII Centuries)*. Ramat-Gan: Bar-Ilan University Press, 1989.
Toch, Michael. *The Economic History of European Jews: Late Antiquity and Early Middle Ages*. Leiden: Brill, 2013.
———. "Geldleiher und sonst nichts? Zur wirtschaftlichen Tätigkeit der Juden im deutschen Sprachraum des Spätmittelalters." *Tel Aviver Jahrbuch für deutsche Geschichte* 22 (1993): 117–26.
———. *Die Juden im Mittelalterlichen Reich*. Enzyklopädie Deutscher Geschichte, vol. 44. Munich: Oldenbourg, 1998.
———. *Peasants and Jews in Medieval Germany: Studies in Cultural, Social, and Economic History*. Aldershot: Ashgate, 2003.
———. "Die Wirtschaftsgeschichte der Juden im Mittelalter: Stand, Aufgaben und Möglichkeiten der Forschung." *Wiener Jahrbuch für Jüdische Geschichte Kultur & Museumswesen* 4 (1999–2000): 9–24.
Toch, Michael, ed. *Wirtschaftsgeschichte der mittelalterlichen Juden: Fragen und Einschäzungen*. Schriften des Historischen Kollegs Kolloquien 71. Munich: Oldenbourg, 2008.
Todeschini, Giacomo. "Christian Perceptions of Jewish Economic Activity in the Middle Ages." In *Wirtschaftsgeschichte der mittelalterlichen Juden Fragen und Einschäzungen*. Edited by Michael Toch, 1–16. Munich: Oldenbourg, 2008.
———. *Come Guida: la gente commune e i giochi dell'economia all'inizio dell'epoca moderna*. Bologna: Il Mulino, 2011.
———. "Franciscan Economics and Jews in the Middle Ages: from a theological to an economic lexicon." In *Friars and Jews in the Middle Ages and Renaissance*. Edited by Steven McMichael and Susan Myers, 99–117. Leiden: Brill, 2004.
———. *Franciscan Wealth: From Voluntary Poverty to Market Society*. Translated by Donatella Melucci. Saint Bonaventure, NY: The Franciscan Institute, 2009.
———. "Les historiens juifs en Allemagne et le débat sur l'origine du capitalisme avant 1914." In *Écriture de l'histoire et identité juive. L'Europe ashkénaze XIX–XX siècle*. Edited by D. Bechtel et. al., 209–28. Paris, 2003.
———. "The Incivility of Judas: 'Manifest' Usury as a Metaphor for the 'Infamy of Fact' (*infamia facti*)." In *Money, Morality, and Culture in Late Medieval and Early Modern Europe*. Edited by Vitullo, Juliann and Diane Wolfthal, 33–52. Farnham: Brill, 2010.

246 BIBLIOGRAPHY

———. "*Judas mercator pessimus*': Ebrei e simoniaci dall'XI al XIII secolo." *Zakhor* 1 (1997): 11–23.

———. *La ricchezza degli ebrei. Merci e denaro nella riflessione ebraica e nella definizione cristiana dell'usura alla fine del Medioevo*. Spoleto: Centro italiano di studi sull'alto Medioevo, 1989.

———. "Theological Roots of the Medieval/Modern Merchant's Self-Representation." In *The Self-Perception of Early Modern Capitalists*. Edited by Margaret Jacob and Catherine Secretan, 17–48. New York: Palgrave, 2008.

———. *Un trattato di economia politica francescano: il "De emptionibus et venditionibus, De usuris, De restitutionibus" di Pietro di Giovanni Olivi*. Rome: Istituto storico italiano per il Medioevo, 1980.

———. "Usura Ebraica e identità economica cristiana: la discussion medievale." In *Ebrei in Italia*, 291–318. Edited by C. Vivanti et al. Turin: G. Einaudi, 1996.

Torrell, Jean-Pierre. "Les Juifs dans l'oeuvre de Pierre le Vénérable." *Cahiers de civilization médiévale* 30 (1987): 331–46.

Tovey, D'Blossiers. *Anglia Judaica: or the History and Antiquities of the Jews in England*. Oxford, 1738. Republished: New York: B. Franklin, 1967.

Trachtenberg, Joshua. *The Devil and the Jews: The Medieval Conception of the Jew and Its Relation to Modern Antisemitism*. Philadelphia: Jewish Publication Society of America, 1983.

Tribe, Keith. "The Historicization of Political Economy?" In *British and German Historiography, 1750–1950: Traditions, Perceptions, and Transfers*. Edited by Benedikt Stuchtey and Peter Wende, 211–28. Oxford: Oxford University Press, 2000.

———. *Strategies of Economic Order: German Economic Discourse, 1750–1950*. Cambridge: Cambridge University Press, 1995.

Trivellato, Francesca. *The Familiarity of Strangers: the Sephardic diaspora, Livorno, and cross-cultural trade in the early modern period*. New Haven: Yale University Press, 2009.

Tubach, Frederic. *Index Exemplorum: A Handbook of Medieval Religious Tales*. Helsinki: Suomalainen Tiedeakatemia, 1969.

Tucker, Gilbert Norman. *The Canadian Commercial Revolution, 1845–1851*. Toronto: McClelland and Stewart, 1964.

Udovitch, Abraham. "At the Origins of the Western Commenda: Islam, Israel, Byzantium?" *Speculum* 37/2 (1962): 198–207.

———. *Partnership and Profit in Medieval Islam*. Princeton: Princeton University Press, 1970.

Urbach, E.E. *The Tosaphists: Their History, Writings, and Methods* [Hebrew]. Jerusalem: Bialik Institute, 1954.

Usher, Abbott Payson. *The Early History of Deposit Banking in Mediterranean Europe*. Cambridge, MA: Harvard University Press, 1943.

BIBLIOGRAPHY 247

Utterback, Kristine and Merrall Price, ed. *Jews in Medieval Christendom: "Slay them not".* Leiden: Brill, 2013.

Vaccari, Pietro. "'Accomandatio e Societas' negli atti dei Notai Ligure del xiii secolo." *Rivista di storia del diritto italiano* 26–7 (1953–4): 85–97.

Varsori, Antonio, ed. *Roberto Lopez: l'impegno politico e civile (1938–1945).* Florence: Università degli studi di Firenze, 1990.

Vermeersch, Arthur. "Usury." In *The Catholic Encyclopedia.* New York: Encyclopedia Press, 1913–4.

Vinogradoff, Paul. *Villainage in England: Essays in English Mediaeval History.* London: Oxford University Press, 1927.

Vitullo, Juliann and Diane Wolfthal, eds. *Money, Morality, and Culture in Late Medieval and Early Modern Europe.* Farnham: Brill, 2010.

Wallerstein, Immanuel. *The Modern World-System: Capitalist Agriculture and the Origins of the European World-Economy in the Sixteenth Century.* New York: Academic Press, 1974.

Watt, J.A. "The Jews, the Law, and the Church: the Concept of Jewish Serfdom in Thirteenth-Century England." In Diana Wood, ed., *The Church and Sovereignty, c. 590–1918: Essays in Honour of Michael Wilks,* 153–72. Cambridge, MA: Basil Blackwell, 1991.

Weber, Max. *Ancient Judaism.* Translated by Hans Gerth and Don Martindale. Glencoe: Free Press, 1952.

———. *Economy and Society.* Berkeley: University of California Press, 1978.

———. *The History of Commercial Partnerships in the Middle Ages.* Lanham: Rowman & Littlefield, 2003.

———. *The Protestant Ethic and the Spirit of Capitalism.* Translated by Talcott Parsons. New York: Charles Scribner's Sons, 1958.

———. "Roscher's 'Historical Method'." In *Roscher and Knies: The Logical Problems of Historical Economics,* 53–92. Translated by Guy Oakes. New York: Free Press, 1975.

———. *The Sociology of Religion.* Boston: Beacon Press, 1963.

Wechsler, Harold S. "The Rationale for Restriction: Ethnicity and College Admission in America, 1910–1980." *American Quarterly* 36/5 (1984): 643–67.

Weiner, Annette. *Inalienable Possessions: The Paradox of Keeping-While-Giving.* Berkeley: University of California Press, 1992.

———. *Women of Value, Men of Renown.* Austin: University of Texas Press, 1976.

Weinryb, Bernard. "Prolegomena to an Economic History of the Jews in Germany in Modern Times." *Leo Baeck Institute Yearbook* 1 (1956): 279–306.

White, Lynn. *Medieval Technology and Social Change.* Oxford: Clarendon Press, 1962.

White, Stephen. *Custom, Kinship, and Gifts to Saints: The* Lauditio Parentum *in Western France, 1050–1150.* Chapel Hill: University of North Carolina Press, 1988.

248 BIBLIOGRAPHY

Wilhelm, Joseph. "General Councils." In *The Catholic Encyclopedia*. New York: Encyclopedia Press, 1908.

Willard, James F. *Parliamentary Taxes on Personal Property, 1290 to 1334: a study in Mediaeval English Financial Administration*. Monographs of the Mediaeval Academy of America, vol. 9. Cambridge, MA: Medieval Academy of America, 1934.

———. "Taxes upon Movables of the Reign of Edward I." *English Historical Review* 28 (1913): 517–21.

Wolowski, M. "Preliminary Essay on the Application of the Historical Method to the Study of Political Economy." In Wilhelm Roscher, *Principles of Political Economy*. Translated by John Lalor, 1–48. Chicago: Callaghan, 1878.

Wood, Diana. *Medieval Economic Thought*. Cambridge: Cambridge University Press, 2002.

Yassif, Eli. *The Hebrew Folktale: History, Genre, Meaning*. Translated by Jacqueline Teitelbaum. Bloomington: Indiana University Press, 1999.

———. "Ha-Sipur ha-eksemplari be-Sefer Ḥasidim" [The Exemplary Tale in *Sefer Ḥasidim*]. *Tarbiz* 57 (1987–8): 217–255.

Yunck, John. *The Lineage of Lady Meed*. Notre Dame, 1963.

Yuval, Israel Jacob. *Scholars in Their Time: The Religious Leadership of German Jewry in the Late Middle Ages* [Hebrew]. Jerusalem: Magnes Press, 1988.

Yver, Georges. *Le commerce et les marchands dans l'Italie méridionale au XIIIe et au XIVe siècle*. Paris: A. Fontemoing, 1903.

Zinberg, Israel. *A History of Jewish Literature*. Cleveland: Case Western Reserve University Press, 1972.

Zunz, Leopold. "Etwas über die rabbinische Literatur." In *Gessammelte Schrfiten*. 3 vols. 1:1–31. Berlin: Louis Gerschel, 1875–6.

INDEX[1]

A

Abraham and Gardet de Bédarride, 134
Abraham Bonehore, 134
Abulafia, Anna, 82n15
Acre, 127, 128
"Ad liberandam" (1215), 54–5, 101n221
agrarian economy, viii–x, 4, 113, 185
Albi, church council of 1254, 19–20, 73
Albigensian Crusade, 21, 56, 65, 68, 80
Alexander III, 18, 23
Algazi, Gadi, 167n9
alms, 11, 75, 154, 156–7, 161–2, 172n55
'Amalric, Giraud d', notarial register of, 114, 117–33, 142n18, 144n41
Ambrose, 30, 91n120
Amoraim, 29
Angevin (Anglo-Norman) monarchs, 42, 64, 79–80
Anjou, expulsion from, 74–6

Annales School, viii, 148, 166n3, 185, 186
anti-Judaism, ix, x, 4, 6, 30–41, 74, 78–80, 113, 119, 184. *See also* antisemitism; medieval antisemitism
  in canonical legislation, 42
  and expulsion, 42, 73–5
  in French royal legislation, 42, 71–2
  Jews as enemy of Christendom, 46–52, 65, 80
  in Marseille, 119
antisemitism. *See also* medieval antisemitism
  development of, viii, 71–81
  and narrative of Jewish economic function, vii, viii, 113, 184–5, 193
  scholarship on, vii, viii, 193
  and Shylock stereotype, 181
apes, in medieval art, 152–4
Aragon, 135, 136

---

[1] Note: Page numbers followed by "n" refers to notes.

© The Author(s) 2018
J.L. Mell, *The Myth of the Medieval Jewish Moneylender*,
DOI 10.1007/978-3-319-34186-6

249

250 INDEX

archae (loan chests), 60, 77
ha-Aretz (the Land), 193
Arles, church councils of 1234 and
    1236, 21, 25, 88n85
Ashkenazic Judaism, 161, 191
Ashtor, Eliyahu, 135, 136, 145n74
Astrug Moise, 134
Auxerre, 102n235
auxilium, 50
avarice, 171n38
Avignon, church council of 1209,
    14–18, 21, 24–5, 73, 88n83,
    89n101

B
bailiffs, 15, 58, 60, 61, 62–4,
    103n244, 105n254, 106n257
Baldwin, John, 103n245, 105n254
Baratier, Édouard, 134
Barcelona, church council of 1263,
    31–2, 73
Baron, Salo, 135
Baumgarten, Elisheva, *Practicing Piety
    in Medieval Ashkenaz*, 189
Benedict XVI, 100n207
Bernard of Clairvaux, 3, 46–9, 51
    scholarship on, 97n188
Bernard of Pavia, 61, 91n120
bet din, 132
Béziers
    church councils, 19, 20, 21, 25, 34,
        73, 90n110
Bible moralisée, 7
biblical passages on usury, 28–9,
    30–41. *See also* Deuteronomy;
    Exodus; Psalms
biblical-moral school, 66
binary categories, xi, 93, 165, 193
    gift and profit, xi, xii, 149, 151,
        165, 188
    Jew and merchant, xi, 133–4,
        176–82, 183, 188

Blancard, Louis, 118
blasphemy, 20, 27, 47, 50, 56, 73, 77,
    79, 80
Bloch, Marc, 166n3
blood libel, 6, 186
Bolton, Brenda, 107n273
Bonafossus Boc f. Astruc, 130
Bonafossus f. Vitalis de Turribus, 121,
    123–4, 125, 128, 130
Bonanatus (Benaciatus) f. Bonifilii,
    124, 128
Bondavid, 134
Bono Isaac Ferrerio, 123
Bonodominus de Monteil, 121
Bonus Dominus f. Astruc, 121, 123–4,
    128
Bonusinfans f. Jacob, 121, 123–4
Bougie (Maghreb), 120, 123, 125,
    127–31, 133
Bretherton, Luke, 90n113
brother, biblical language of, 28–30,
    33–4, 36–40
Buckley, Susan, *Teachings on usury in
    Judaism, Christianity and Islam*,
    197n36
Byrne, Eugene, 115–6

C
Caesarius of Heisterbach, 150, 157
Cairo, Jewish merchants of, xi, 114,
    136–8, 187–8
canon law, 4–5, 8–10, 166. *See also*
    conciliar legislation; ecclesiastical
    jurisdiction
    anti-Judaism in, 24–8. *See also*
        anti-Judaism
    defining usury, 5, 14
    scholarship on, 6, 190–1
Canterbury, Archbishop of, 66, 78
Capetian kings of France, 9, 42–5, 80.
    See also Louis VIII; Louis IX;
    Philip Augustus

INDEX 251

capitalism. *See also* commercial
revolution; commercialization;
profit economy
growth of, viii, 113, 173n58
spirit of, xii, 166
captio, 9, 108n281, 108n282,
108n284
cartularies. *See* notarial registers
Celestine III, 23, 53
Central Europe, x, 99n195, 112n325
Chapitles Tuchaunz la Gyuerie (Articles
Touching the Jewry), 77
Charles II, King of Naples, 74–6,
79
Charles VI, 74, 111n303, 119
Charles VIII, 119
Châtelet du Petit Pont, Paris, 62
Chazan, Robert, 47, 94n159, 97n188,
98n190, 98n192, 100n208,
102n232, 103n240, 107n277
Medieval Jewry in Northern France,
42
Christendom, 55–8
moral reform of, 65–8, 71–4, 80
radicalization of, 55, 65, 68, 80
Christian burial, 10, 11, 13, 15
Christian economic thought, 5,
177
Franciscan, 7–8, 179
Christianity, xii, 23, 26, 30, 66, 75,
77, 100n208, 151, 152, 163,
166, 171n38, 176, 177–9, 188,
189, 197n36
Christians. *See also* Jewish-Christian
polemics
compared with Jews, 71, 114,
185–6
distribution of wealth, ix, 183
evil deeds of, 32–3
merchants, x, 7, 44, 124, 132, 136,
182, 183
prohibition on economic exchange
with Jews, 14, 86n64

church councils. *See* conciliar
legislation; councils, church
church lands, 58–9, 106n258
Church property, 57
Church vessels and ornaments, 50–1,
58, 59, 62, 77, 102n238
Cistercians, 46, 47, 54, 150, 154
clergy
taking loans from Jews, 62–3,
89n98, 102n238
usury, 10–11, 15, 21, 34
Cluny, 99n203
Cohen, Jeremy, 97n188, 190
commandments (*mitzvot*), 3, 32,
35–41, 190
allegorical interpretation of, 3, 35,
36
commenda (Latin contract), xi, 29,
114–20, 132, 161, 166
in Amalric's cartulary, 118, 120–33
compared to *suḥba* (reciprocal
agency), 114, 137–8, 188
and Jewish commercialization,
114–15, 132, 134, 187, 188
sharing of risk, 161
commendators, 115, 128–32
Christian, 122, 123
Jews as, 120–3, 125, 127–32
professionalization, 122, 130
commercialization, 113–46, 151–2,
165–6, 185–8, 192. *See also*
money
commercial revolution, vii, ix, xi,
113–6, 120, 129–38, 185, 187–8
scholarship on, ix, 147–8
commodities, 33
with 'bad' economic value, 155,
157, 159
value inherent in, 159, 160, 164,
165
Compilatio II, 53
Compilatio III (1210), 17, 23, 87n73
compound interest, 58, 59, 61, 64–5

252 INDEX

conciliar legislation
  on Christian usury, 6, 10–4, 21–2, 42
  on Jewish usury, 6, 14–22
  on Jews, 22–8, 56
  and secular legislation, 63, 72
consilio et auxilio, 50–1
Constantinople, 13, 101n228, 153
consumption, xi–xii, 65, 132–3, 155–6, 159, 186
contracts, xi, 114. *See also* commenda (Latin contract); iska (Hebrew contract)
  oral, 114, 118
contrition, 156–7, 162, 172n55
conversion of Jews, 23, 26, 35, 49, 52, 77–8, 80, 112n313, 178–9
Corpus Juris Civilis, 59
councils, church, 21, 25, 26. *See also* conciliar legislation
  Albi (1254), 19–20, 73
  Arles (1234 and 1236), 88n85
  Avignon (1209), 14–9, 73, 88n83, 89n101
  Barcelona (1263), 31–2, 73
  Béziers (1246), 19, 20, 34, 90n110
  Béziers (1255), 20, 34, 73, 88n88
  Elvira (305 or 306), 84–5n36
  jurisdiction of, 4, 12, 13, 72, 186. *See also* ecclesiastical jurisdiction
  Lateran II (1139), 10–4, 46, 48, 55, 84n34
  Lateran III (1179), 11–5, 17–9, 24, 48, 55–7, 72
  Lateran IV (1215), 3, 12, 14–9, 22, 24, 27, 34, 41, 55, 62, 67, 73, 87n73, 88n85, 89n104, 90n110
  local councils, 9, 12, 21, 86n64
  Lyon I (1245), 12, 16, 106n260
  Lyon II (1274), 12–14, 24, 76, 77
  Melun (1216), 21, 25, 63, 106n260

Melun (1230), 71, 73, 94n161
mixed councils, 20, 21, 34, 54, 68, 71, 73, 88n88, 101n219
Montpellier (1214), 67
Montpellier (1258), 20–1, 89n100
Narbonne (1227), 19, 24, 31, 34, 88n83, 90n110
Paris (1212), 12
Paris (1213), 67
Paris (1248), 63
provincial councils, 12, 14, 18, 19, 21, 34, 62, 63, 67, 73
Rouen (1214), 67
Rouen (1231), 21, 25, 63, 106n260
Vienna (1267), 12, 19
Vienne (1311-12), 12–14, 21, 24
courts, 23, 39, 71, 107n279, 114, 117, 123, 132, 137, 138, 187
credit, vii, 5, 14, 29, 115, 182–4, 186. *See also* loans; usury
credit economy, viii, 48
  legitimate and illegitimate forms of, x, 5, 14
creditors, 9, 16, 18, 23, 28, 37, 39, 53–4, 61, 63, 64, 69, 87n69, 91n121, 108n279, 197n34
Cregut Profach, 134
Crémieux, Adolphe, 120, 142n19
Crescas Ferrusolus, 127, 128
Cresquo f. Bonodominus de Montilio, 130
Crestin f. Bonodominus de Monteil, 121
crusader privilege, 46, 52–6, 62, 64, 69
  applied to all Christians, 62–5, 69
crusades, x, 16, 80, 127
  Albigensian, 21, 56, 65, 68, 80
  First, 43, 47–55, 98n190, 190
  Second, 3, 46–8, 52, 55, 64
  Third, 46, 52, 55, 65, 80
  Fourth, 16, 54, 56, 65, 67, 68, 80
  Fifth, 54, 55, 60, 65, 68, 80
  People's, 47

INDEX   253

and Post miserabile, 16, 54
  preaching on, 65–8
cultural history, 147–66, 185, 188
Curta, Florin, 149

D

David f. Pesati, 133
David, King, 36
Davies, Wendy, 168n13
Davis, James, 168n16
de Roover, Raymond, 173n58
death, 154–6, 158–61
debtors, 13, 15–20, 53, 58, 63–4, 69,
  71, 77, 105n251, 106n257, 119
despoiling, 50, 52, 75
destruction, 154–6, 158–61
Deuteronomy 23:20-22, 7, 28–30,
  33–4, 36–41, 91n121, 173n60,
  191, 197n34
dialogs, 31–3
Dialogus Miraculorum (The Dialogue
  on Miracles), 150, 154–7, 159
discrimination, legal, 121
disputations, 31–4, 38, 40, 73, 80,
  93n132. *See also* Jewish-Christian
  polemics
  Paris (1240), 31–32
divorce, 38–9, 58
Dominicans, 67, 72, 73, 77, 78
  exempla, 150
Dominic of Osma, 66
Don Quixote, 181–2
Duby, Georges, *Early Growth of the
  European Economy*, 99n203,
  147–8, 166, 167n10, 188
Dulcianus de Sancto Victore, 124

E

ecclesiastical jurisdiction, 14, 20, 22–8,
  30, 39, 41, 42, 46, 65, 68, 71–2,
  80. *See also* rabbinical jurisdiction

ecclesiastical law. *See* canon law;
  rabbinic law
economic activity, permissible and
  impermissible forms, x, 5–8, 14,
  29, 30–41, 165. *See also* usury
economic history, 114, 182–8, 191–2.
  See also medieval economic history
  "general", 114
  Jewish, xi, 114–15, 118, 135, 185
economic value
  of commodities, 155, 157, 159, 164
  disequilibrium between moral value
    and, 149–51, 156–7, 164, 188
  of labor, 160
  of money, xi–xii, 149–56, 158, 159,
    164–6, 188
ecumenical councils, 12–4, 16–8, 26,
  77. *See also* councils, church;
  Lateran II (1139); Lateran III
  (1179); Lateran IV (1215)
Edomites, 33, 37–8
"Edwardian experiment," 77
Edward I of England
  crusading by, 74
  expulsion of Jews, 4, 74–9
  letter to exchequer, 74, 76
  Statute of Jewry (1275), 74, 76–7
Edward II of England, 13
Elvira, church council of 305 or 306,
  84–5n36
Emery, Richard, *The Jews of Perpignan*,
  9, 114–15, 118, 138n2, 142n20,
  187
émigrés, viii, ix, 185
emptio, 133
England, Anglo-Norman
  administrative segregation of Jews,
    ix, 184
  Anglo-Jewry, ix, 183–4
  expulsion of Jews, 4, 74–80
  Jewish tallages, 61, 69, 183
  legal status, ix, 183
Ephraim of Bonn, 52, 64

254 INDEX

Esau, 33–4, 38
ethnic cleansing, 193
Eugenius III, 46–8, 52, 96n185
Europe
  central, x, 99n195, 112n325
  civic institutions, 114, 132
  immigration/emigration, 193
  medieval agrarian economy, vii–x, 4,
    113, 185, 187
European history
  role of Jewish history in, x, 113–15,
    151–2, 163, 182, 185–6,
    189–90, 192–3
  shared experiences of change, 163,
    189–90
Eustace of Flay, 66
exchequer, 74, 76, 183–4
excommunication, 12–16, 18, 19, 23,
    72
  "indirect," 16, 23
  "material," 14, 18, 23, 54
exempla (moral literature), xi, 150–63,
    188
  didactic aim of, 150, 164
  Hebrew, 150–2, 157–62, 170n20
  Latin, 150–7, 171n38, 188
Exodus 22:24-25, 28, 33, 35, 37, 39, 41
expulsion, 183, 192, 193
  of Jewish and Christian usurers, 73
  Jewish usury as justification for, x,
    3–4, 42, 74, 76–7
  of Jews, 42, 68, 73–81, 109n294,
    110n298, 119
  scholarship on, 193
  withdrawn and renewed, 79, 111n303

F
Fatimid Egypt, 136–8
Ferrusol family, Bonisaac, Bon Judas,
    Crescas, Leon, and Salomon, 127,
    128, 133

Fifth Crusade, 54, 55, 60, 65, 68, 80
First Crusade, 43, 47, 98n190, 190
Fishman, Tayla, *Becoming the People of
    the Talmud*, 190
Fourth Crusade, 16, 54, 56, 65, 67,
    68, 80
France. *See also* councils, church;
    French royal legislation;
    Marseille
  expulsion of Jews, 74, 79
  royal jurisdiction over Jews, 22,
    39, 41, 43, 44, 58, 67, 68,
    80
Franciscans, 67, 72, 78
  economic thought, 7–8, 179
  exempla, 150, 153
Francis of Assisi, 66, 150
fraud, 36–7, 49–50, 57, 59–61, 63,
    75, 85n47
French royal legislation on Jewish
    usury, 4, 22, 41–74
  and conciliar legislation, 22–9, 59,
    67
  crusading origins of, 46–58
  ordinance of 1206, 43, 56, 59,
    60–4, 88n78, 103n244,
    105n251, 106n258
  ordinance of 1219, 43, 56, 62–5,
    69, 103n244–5, 105n256
  ordinance of 1223, 43–5, 68–71
  ordinance of 1230, 44–5, 68, 70–1,
    94n161
  ordinance of 1235, 43, 71–3
  'Philip Augustus' decrees, 58–65
  rates of interest, 43, 58–65
  registration of debts, 61–2,
    104n245, 105–6n257
  seals on Jewish loans, 21, 43,
    58–65, 69, 106n257
friend, biblical language of, 36–40
fugitives, 58, 59, 102n236
Fulk of Neuilly, 66–7

INDEX 255

G

Gamoran, Hillel, 90n111, 140n9, 190–1
garments, bloody or stained, 58–9, 62
Gascony, expulsion of Jews (1287), 74, 78
generosity, 160–1
Geniza merchants, 136–8
Genoa, 115, 118, 130, 135–6
  merchants, 115–16, 118, 124, 130, 135
  notarial registers, 118
German Historical School of Political Economy, viii–ix, x, 113, 134. 148, 166, 184–5. *See also* Younger Historical School of Political Economy
  theory of economic stages, vii, 148, 185
gift economy, viii, xi–xii, 113–14, 138, 147–52, 164–6, 188
gift exchange, viii, xi, 138, 147–66, 188
Goldberg, Jessica
  Trade and Institutions in the Medieval Mediterranean, 136–8, 187
Gratian
  Decretum, 4, 10–11, 14
"Graves orientalis terrae" (1199), 54
Gregory VII, 65
Gregory VIII, 52–3
Gregory IX, 72
  Decretals, 17, 53
Gregory X, 13
guilds, vii, 13, 137, 187, 192
Guillaume I de la Brue, 94n160
Guy of Dampierre, 58

H

Hacohen, Malachi, *Jacob and Esau*, 190
halachah, 40, 95n166

Halperin, David, 194n5
Ḥasidei Ashkenaz, 161, 191
Hebrew literature *(exempla)*, 150–2, 157–62, 170n20
Heine, Heinrich, 181
Henry II of England, 54
Henry of Lausanne, 66
heretics, 12, 14, 27, 33, 56–7, 79, 93n133, 193
  Jews perceived as, 56, 93n133
  persecution of, 193
Historical School. *See* German Historical School of Political Economy; Younger Historical School of Political Economy
homosexuality, 194n5
Honorius III, 66
Honorius IV, 78
host desecration, 6, 78, 186
Hsia, R. Po-Chia, 7
Huguccio of Pisa, 23, 61

I

Iberian peninsula, 112n325, 136
immigration/emigration, 193
infidels, 7–8, 27, 55, 91n120, 184
Ingeborg of Denmark, 58
Innocent III, 14–18, 21, 23, 54–9, 65–7
  "Ad liberandam" (1215), 54–5
  "Graves orientalis terrae" (1199), 54
  letters to Philip Augustus on Jewish usury, 57–9
  moral reform and the crusades, 65–6
  "Post miserabile" (1198), 16–18, 23, 54
instrumentum (formal charter), 117
interesse (interest), 5, 14, 61
investments and investors, xi, 29, 114–9, 124–32

256 INDEX

iska (Hebrew contract), 29, 114, 116–18, 132, 140n9, 141n10, 160, 166
Islamic mercantile system, xi, 114, 136–8, 187–8. *See also* suḥba
Israel, 28–9, 37–8, 50, 51, 80, 178, 193
Italian merchant republics, 118, 131, 135–6, 187
    political elites, 137–8, 187

J

Jacob ben Reuben, 30
Jacob f. Astruc Maurel, 144n57
Jacques de Vitry, 65–6
James II of Aragon, 13
Jesus Christ, 31, 35, 178
    Jewish culpability for crucifixion, 47, 49
Jewish badge, 24, 73, 77, 80, 88n85, 109n296, 119
Jewish-Christian polemics, x, 6–7, 30–41, 91n121, 99n203
Jewish difference, 80, 114, 183, 190
Jewish economic function, historical narrative on, vii–x, 6, 42–5, 113, 148, 182–6, 188, 189, 193, 198n38
    deconstructing, 188–9
    meta-narrative, vii, 182, 184–5
    in post-Holocaust scholarship, vii, 185
Jewish economic history, xi, 114–15, 118, 135, 185, 191–2, 198n38. *See also* economic history
Jewish economic practice, 46, 190–2
Jewish economic thought, 182, 190–1
Jewish historians, viii, 6, 18, 68, 83n19, 103n245, 138n2, 166, 184, 186, 188–93
Jewish history, viii, x, 30, 68, 70, 113–15, 163, 183–93

role in European history, ix, x, 113–15, 151–2, 163, 182, 186, 189
Jewish identity, ix, 121, 180
Jewish merchants
    in Mediterranean trade, xi, 114, 135–8, 187–8
    in Marseille, xi, 114–15, 120–38, 187–8
Jewish moneylending, vii, ix, xi, 7, 9, 114, 138n2, 139n2, 183, 184. *See also* loans; Merchant of Venice; usury, Jewish
    conciliar legislation on, 14–22
    discourse on, vii, ix, 3–9, 182–93
    evidence, lack of, 22, 48
    evidence related to, 9
    French royal legislation on, 42–5, 58–65, 68–74
    as not representative of all medieval Jews, 183
    professional, ix, 182, 183, 186
Jewish religious practices, repression of, 25–7, 68
Jewish serfdom, 67–8, 74, 80, 107n276
Jews
    as "always already" commercialized, 152, 166, 182
    attitudes toward, 44–5, 78, 96n179. *See also* anti-Judaism
    banned from public office, 26–7, 56, 65
    compared with Christians, 30–2, 41, 124, 166, 185–6, 190
    conciliar legislation on, 22–8. *See also* Jewish moneylending, conciliar legislation on
    distribution of wealth, ix
    economic activities, xi, 7, 152, 114–15, 185, 192
    equal to Christians, 119–20, 183–4

excluded from international trade, 135

good deeds of, 32

imagined enmity and hostility toward Christians, 46–52, 56–7, 61, 74–81

legal status, 76–7, 183–4

loans to clergy, 59, 62–3, 89n98, 102n238

poverty, ix, 80, 192

as scapegoat, 148, 185

social separation, 24–7, 71, 80

subordinate status, 24–8, 76–7

as witnesses, 57, 121, 132

Job, 160–1

John II of France, 111n303

Jordan, William, 9, 42, 103n243, 103n244, 103–4n245, 105n252–5, 108n281

The French Monarchy and the Jews, 42

Joseph b. Nathan ha-Mekanne, 32, 94n157

Josias, Archbishop, 53

Judah the Pious (Yehudah he-Ḥasid), 150, 161, 170n20

Judaism. *See also* anti-Judaism; Ḥasidei Ashkenaz, Jews

Ashkenazic, 161, 191

in Christian theology, 31, 177–9

judaizare (Judaize), 3, 47, 49, 98n195

"Judgment of the Jews," 23, 54. *See also* excommunication

just price, 151, 170n22

K

Kabbalat Shabbat, 172n48

Kaplan, Debra, *Beyond Expulsion*, 192

Kilwardby, Robert, 78

Kimḥi, Joseph, *Sefer ha-Brit* (Book of the Covenant), 30, 32–4

Kirschenbaum, Aaron, 91n120, 91n121

Kisch, Guido, viii, 184–5, 187

Kletter, Karen, 194n5

L

laborers, 62, 64, 65

Langholm, Odd, 190–1

Langmuir, Gavin, 42–5, 99n203, 185

"'Judei Nostri' and the Beginning of Capetian Legislation," 42

Toward a Definition of Antisemitism, 82n15

The Languages of Gift in the Early Middle Ages, 148–9

Lateran II (1139), 10–14, 46, 48, 55, 84n34

Lateran III (1179), 11–5, 17–9, 24, 55–7, 72

Lateran IV (1215), 3, 12, 14–19, 22, 24, 27, 34, 41, 55, 62, 67, 73, 87n73, 88n85, 89n104, 90n110

Canon 67 ("On the Usury of the Jews"), 14, 17–19, 22, 24, 34, 41, 62, 67

on Jewish badge, 73

legal status of Jewry

administrative segregation, ix, 65, 184

as free urban burgesses, ix, 183, 184

Léon Passapayre, 134

Leopardus (ship), 123, 125, 128

Levant, 127, 129, 131, 135–6

Leviticus 25:35-38, 28, 37, 40–1

lex mercatoria, 114, 138n1

Lipman, Vivian, 112n311

Lipton, Sara, 7

Little, Lester, 147–52, 164–6, 168n14, 185, 188

Religious Poverty and the Profit Economy, 147–9

258 INDEX

loan chests *(archae)*, 60, 61, 184
loans. *See also* Jewish moneylending
  defaults on repayment, 60,
      104n250, 106n262, 175
  between Jews, 19–20
  mutuum, 133–4
  necessity of, 40, 186
  penalties for late payment, 60–5
  structure of, 104n247
  usury-free, 63
Loeb, Isidore, 118
Lopez, Robert, 114, 184–5
  *The Commercial Revolution of the
      Middle Ages*, 147–8
Louis I, 79
Louis VIII, 43–5, 52, 64, 94n161,
      67–70, 94n161, 105n257
  1223 ordinance, 43–4, 68–70
Louis IX, 9, 20, 41, 43, 45, 67–8,
      70–4, 88n88, 94n161
  crusading by, 72–3
  as "most Christian king," 41, 184
  1230 ordinance, 43, 44, 68, 70–1
  1235 ordinance, 43, 71–2
Louis X of France, 111n303
loving kindness, commandment of, 35,
      36, 40
lucrum, 5, 59, 61
Lyon I, church council of 1245, 12,
      16, 21, 106n260
Lyon II, church council of 1274,
      12–14, 21, 24, 76, 77

M
magic, 20, 26, 73
Maine, expulsion from, 74–6
Mainz, Archbishop of, 47
Manduel family charters, 117, 133–4
manifest usurers, 7, 11, 13, 18, 19,
      173n60
Marcus, Ivan, 190

market economy, viii, x
Marseille
  commendators, 128–32
  courts, 123, 132, 187
  investments, 124–8
  Jewish community in, 119–20
  Jewish merchants in, xi, 114–15,
      120–38, 187–8
  tractators, 122–33
Marx, Karl, 147
Matthew, book of, 35
Mauss, Marcel, viii, 147, 148, 150–1,
      154, 158, 164, 168n17, 185
mazal (fortune or fate), 158, 161
McLaughlin, T. P., 90n115, 190–1
medieval antisemitism, 82n15, 148,
      185, 186, 189, 193. *See also*
      anti-Judaism; antisemitism
  irrational fantasies, 6, 186. *See also*
      ritual murder
  as rational economic backlash, 6,
      186
  and spiritual crisis over money
      economy, 148, 164–6
medieval economic history, vii–ix, 113,
      147–50, 182–8. *See also* economic
      history
  20th century scholarship, 147–9, 184
medieval Reformation, 66, 107n273
Mediterranean trade, xi, 114–38,
      187–8. *See also* Jewish merchants;
      Marseille
  destinations, 125–31, 133–5
  ships, 123–8
Meir b. Simeon of Narbonne (Meili),
      Milḥemet Mitzvah, 31, 32, 34–40,
      80, 94n161
Melun
  church council of 1216, 21, 63,
      106n260
  church council of 1230, 71, 73,
      94n161

INDEX 259

mendicants, 67, 72–3, 78, 150
menudeh, 158
Merchant of Venice (Shakespeare), 136,
175–82, 189, 194n5
metallic currency (coin), 125–7,
144–7
moral value in, 151–5, 157–8, 164
as non-productive thing, 155–7
meta-narrative, vii, 182, 184–5
'milch-cow' (royal milk cow), ix, 44
miracles, 48, 150, 155–6
misers, 155, 157–8
Mishnah, 29, 116
mitzvot (commandments), 3, 32,
35–7, 38–41, 190
allegorical interpretation of, 3, 35,
36
money, xi–xii, 7–8, 147–66. *See also*
metallic currency
as anonymous and impersonal, 148,
151–3, 157, 158
anxieties of 'new money economy,'
xi, 27, 63, 65, 148–51, ,
164–5, 188
as causal agent, 148, 151–2, 164,
188
death and destruction, 154–6,
158–61
in Hebrew *exempla*, 150–2, 157–63
in Latinate Christian *exempla*, 151–7
moral value, 150–9, 162, 164, 188
and profit economy, 147–66
redemption of sin involving, 156–7,
161–3
stereotypes about Jews and, ix. *See
also* Jewish economic
function
moneychangers, xi, 117, 119, 120,
123–5
Jewish, absence of, 119, 125
moneylenders. *See also* Jewish
moneylending

as distinct from merchants, 133, 189
*Money, Morality and Culture in Late
Medieval and Early Modern
Europe*, 149, 151
Montpellier (1214), council of, 67
Montpellier (1258), council of, 20–1,
89n100
Moore, John, 18
Moore, R. I., *Formation of a
Persecuting Society*, 193
moral literature. *See* exempla
moral reform, 65–8, 71–4, 80, 150,
152, 191
moral value
disequilibrium between economic
value and, 149–51, 156–7,
164, 188
and economic act of acquisition,
152–9, 164, 171n38, 188
of money, xi–xii, 149–58, 164–6,
168n17, 188
negative ('bad'), 151–63, 188
positive ('good'), 156, 160–1
Moses of Paris, 94n157
Mosse d'Accone family, 128–30
Mosson Salomon, 134
Mundill, Robin, *England's Jewish
Solution*, 76, 78, 105n252
Muslims, 24, 67, 80, 98n191,
100n207, 116, 135, 138
mutuum (loan), 133–4

N

Nahmanides, 73
Nahon, Gérard, 9
Narbonne, Archbishop of, 16, 19,
38–40
Narbonne, church council of 1227,
19, 24, 31, 34, 88n83, 90n110
Nelson, Benjamin, *The Idea of Usury*, 6
Nelson, Janet, 168n13

260 INDEX

networks of economic association, 114, 137–8, 159, 164
Nevers, Count of, 17, 18, 57–8, 74, 79, 88n80, 101n228, 102n235
expulsion of Jews, 74
New Testament, parable of the talents, 14
Noonan, John, *Scholastic Analysis of Usury*, 190–1
Norwich Daybook, 104n247
notarial registers, 9, 114, 117–9, 130, 133, 135. *See also* Amalric, Giraud d', notarial register of
Jewish identification markers in, 120–1

O
oaths, 16, 19–20, 38–40, 46, 48, 59, 78, 87n69, 107n279, 123, 179
Odo of Sully, Bishop of Paris, 59, 66, 86n64
Oelsner, Toni, viii, 29, 149, 184, 198n40
organic folk (*Volk*) model, vii, viii

P
Pakter, Walter, 24
Paris
church council of 1212, 12
church council of 1213, 67
church council of 1248, 63
Paris disputation (1240), 31
Paris, Matthew, 109n294
Paris School, 65–7
Paul Christiani, 73
Paul the Apostle, 177–9
'pawned pawn,' 191, 197n34
Peckham, John, 78
penalties. *See also* excommunication

and Christian usury, 5, 10–16, 106n260
and Jewish usury, 5, 14–9, 23, 60–5
penance, 11, 67, 151, 156–7, 161–4, 172n53
People's Crusade (1096), 47
Perpignan, xi, 9, 114–15, 118, 138n2, 187
Peter Cantor. *See* Peter the Chanter
Peter of Benevento, 17
Peter of Castelnau, 56
Peter the Chanter, 5, 34, 55, 65–8
Peter the Venerable, 31, 46–51, 75, 98n191, 99n203, 99n204, 100n207
scholarship on, 96–7n188
Peter Waldo, 66
Petrus Bartholomeus, 123
Petrus Cresteng, 129
Philip Augustus of France, 17, 18, 42–3, 45, 53, 55, 103n243
decrees on Jewish lending, 42, 58–65, 67
statute of 1188, 53–5, 63–4, 69
Philip II, 55
Philip IV of France, 13
expulsion of Jews, 74, 79
Philip VI of France, 111n303
philosemitism
and narrative of Jewish economic function, vii, viii, x, 184–5, 192–3
and Shylock stereotype, 181
Polanyi, Karl, viii, 147, 159, 165
polemics. *See* Jewish-Christian polemics
poor, prohibition on usury in rabbinic law, 28, 37–40
popes, 12, 23. *See also* ecclesiastical jurisdiction; *individual popes*
relations with French crown, 41, 58
Postan, Michael, 184

INDEX 261

"Post miserabile" (1198), 16–18, 23, 54–5
poverty
  among Jews, ix, 80, 185, 192
  voluntary, x, 7–8, 36
prejudice, 184. *See also* anti-Judaism; antisemitism
profit. *See also* binary categories, gift and profit; just price; money and profit economy
  rates of, 58–65
  sharing, 160–1. *See also* commenda; iska
profit economy, viii, xi–xii, 113–14, 138, 147–66, 188. *See also* commercialization; commercial revolution
prostitution, 66, 68
Proverbs, 34, 90n112
Pryor, John, 118, 121, 127–9, 131
Psalms, 32, 33, 36, 40, 47

R
Rabanus Maurus, 91n120
Rabbenu Tam, 32, 52
rabbinical jurisdiction, 23, 27, 30, 34, 39–41, 80
rabbinic law, 4, 28–31, 37–41, 80, 89n104, 90n111, 116, 123, 140n9, 160, 166, 170n22, 191, 196n31, 197n34
  bet din, 132
  legislation against Jewish usury, 28–30
  polemics on permissible lending, 30–41
  scholarship on, 30, 32, 190–1
Radford, Michael, 180
radicalization of Christian society, 17, 21, 46, 55, 65, 68, 80
Rashi, 197n34

rates of interest, 43, 58. *See also* interesse; profit; usury
rational economic attitude, 6, 149, 168n16, 186
Ravid, Benjamin, 136
Raymund of Penafort, 61
redemption, 156–7, 161–3
registration of debts, 61–2, 104n245, 106n257
Regné, Jean, 138–9n2
remarriage, 38
remittance, 16
repentance, 13, 67, 156–7. *See also* penance
restitution, 11–8, 23–4, 172n55
  in Latin *exempla*, 156–7
  in *Sefer Ḥasidim*, 161–2
Richard I, 53, 60
righteousness, 35, 39
Rigord, 101n219
Rishonim, 29
ritual murder, 6–7, 47, 52, 77–8, 98n192, 181, 186–7
robbery, 85n47
Robert of Courson, 3, 5, 59–60, 65–7, 102n237, 107n275
  Summa, 3, 59, 66
Roman law, 18, 91n120, 141n10
Roscher, Wilhelm, vii–viii, 6, 114, 148, 184–7
Rosenthal, Joel, 190–1
Rouen
  church council of 1214, 67
  church council of 1231, 21, 25, 63, 106n260
Rudolph (Cistercian monk), 47, 78
ruralization, 192

S
Saige, Gustave, 138n2, 139n3
Saladin Tithe, 54, 68

262 INDEX

Salvago f. Salomon, 123
Salvet and Gassonet Durand, 134
Sardinia, 134–5
Schadennehmen, 191, 197n34
Scriba, Giovanni, 118
seals on Jewish loans, 21, 43, 58–65, 69, 106n257
Second Crusade, 3, 46–8, 52, 55, 64
secular judges, 19, 73, 79
secular rulers. *See also* French royal legislation; *individual rulers* participation in councils, 12
Sefer Ḥasidim (Book of the Pious), 150–2, 157–62, 163, 166, 169n19, 171n38
　on death and destruction, 158–61
　on moral value, 151, 157–8, 160
　on redemption, 161–2
　and shared medieval *mentalité*, 152, 163
Sefer Nizzahon Yashan, 32–4
Sefer Yosef HaMekanne, 33
segregation of Jews from Christians, ix, 65, 73, 80, 184
Shabbat observance, 33, 99n204, 161–2, 172n48, 173n57
Shakespeare, William, *The Merchant of Venice*, 136, 175–82, 189, 194n5
Shatzmiller, Joseph, *Shylock Reconsidered*, 81n7, 134, 181
Shylock (character), 175–81
Shylock Reconsidered (Shatzmiller), 81n7, 134, 181
Shylock's Children (Penslar), 181
"Shylocks's Daughters" (Hess), 181
Shyovitz, David, 190
Sicily, 16, 127, 129, 131, 135
sinners, 10, 157, 159, 162, 178. *See also* exempla moral literature
social history and Jewish history, 183, 195n22, 198n39

societas (Latin contract), 116, 123
Soloveitchik, Haym, 190–1
Sombart, Werner, vii–viii, 148, 184–7
Speculum Laicorum, 152–4, 170n23
"spirit of capitalism," xii, 166
spiritual crisis, xi–xii, viii–ix, 148, 150, 164–5
Stacey, Robert, 60
stages of civilization, vii–viii, 8
statistical analysis, 118–19, 183
Statute of the Jewry (1275), 74, 76–7
Stein, Siegfried, 91n119, 92n122, 94n161
Stephen Langton, 66–7, 107n275
St. Francis (ship), 120, 125–8, 133
St. Gilles (ship), 127, 128
St. Nicholas (ship), 127, 128
Stobbe, Otto, 6, 186
stolen goods, 50, 56, 59
Stow, Kenneth, 18, 87n73, 96n187
stranger, biblical language of, 28–9, 34, 36–41, 56, 91n121
suḥba (reciprocal agency), 114, 137–8, 188
substantive economic, 159
Syracuse, 135

T
Tabula Exemplorum, 153
tallages, Jewish, 9, 50, 61, 69, 183
Talmud
　definition of *iska*, 29, 116, 141n10
　'just price' in, 170n22
　midrash on Job, 161
　suppression of, 6, 20, 23, 32, 72, 78–80
Tannaim, 29
Tanner, Tony, 194n5
taxation. *See also* tallages, Jewish

INDEX 263

general, first instance of, 54
of Jews, ix
theft, 32, 35–6, 50–1, 85n47, 116,
   154, 176
theological interpretations, 27–41, 44,
   49, 51–2, 66, 68, 80
theological tracts, 3, 4, 9, 10, 59, 60,
   66, 107n275
theory of economic stages, vii–viii,
   148, 185
Third Crusade, 46, 52, 55, 65, 80
Thomas Aquinas, 5
Thomas of Chobham, 3, 66
tithes, 17, 23–4, 26, 36, 54, 56, 57,
   88n85
Toch, Michael
  Economic Activities of German Jews
    in the Middle Ages, 191–2,
    198n38
  *The Economic History of European
    Jews*, 139n3, 191–2
Todeschini, Giacomo, 7–8, 29,
   149, 168n14, 168n16, 179,
   192
Toledot Yeshu, 30
Torah passages on usury, 28–41
Trachtenberg, Joshua, 6–7, 82n16,
   99n195
tractators (travelling investment
   partner), 115, 120–33, 135,
   144n47
  Christian, 122, 123, 127, 131
  Jews as, 122–5, 127, 128, 131, 132,
   142n18, 143n29
  professionalization, 122, 125
trade. *See also* commenda; Jewish
   merchants
  expansion of, viii, 115, 136, 147
Tripoli, 135
Trivellato, Francesca, 136, 146n81
Troyes, Countess of, 58
Tunisia, 135

U
unjust means of acquisition, 152–4,
   157–9, 171n38
unjust price, 151
urban burgesses, ix, 183–4
Urban II, 46, 65
urbanization, 192
usufruct, 37, 63
usura, 5, 18, 59, 61, 63
usurers, 5, 7, 10–6, 18, 42, 46, 61,
   80, 113, 154–7, 179, 184. *See
   also* clergy; manifest usurers
usurious intent and practices, 13, 17,
   19, 20, 27–30, 43, 49, 55, 61,
   63, 70, 116, 154
usury
  biblical passages on, 28–41
  campaign, x, 3–22, 41–74, 80, 150,
   152, 186–7, 191
  centesimas usuras (1 out of 100
   pennies), 59, 102n237
  in Christian economic thought, 5, 8,
   177
  in Jewish-Christian polemics, 6,
   30–41, 142n18
  legislation before Lateran II, 10–2,
   14, 47, 84n34
  as target for moral reformers,
   65–8
  as unnatural act, 155–6
usury, Christian
  by clergy, 10–2, 28, 84n34,
   89n98
  commenda and avoidance of, 116
  conciliar legislation on, 10–4, 73
  penalties on, 5, 10–16
usury, Jewish, 3–112, 186–7, 189
  conciliar legislation on, 6, 14–22,
   63, 67, 72
  current historical model, 4–6
  discourse on, 3–4, 6–9, 46–52, 81,
   186, 189

264 INDEX

usury, Jewish (*cont.*)
"heavy and immoderate usury," 3, 17–9
iska and avoidance of, 116
in Jewish-Christian polemics, 30–41
as justification for expulsion, x, 3–4, 20, 42, 74–9
legislation secular, 3, 6, 9, 18, 41–74. *See also* French royal legislation; rabbinic law penalties on. *See* excommunication restraining, 14–6, 18, 20
rhetoric on, x, 42

V
Valencia (Spain), 25, 102n238, 117, 123, 125–8, 130, 131
value, xi–xii. *See also* economic value; moral value
disequilibrium between economic value and moral value, 149–51, 156–7, 164, 188
shared medieval *mentalité* of, 163
Venguessete de Monteil, 134
Venice, 117, 118, 135–6, 175–7, 180, 189
notarial registers, 118
Vermeersch, Arthur, 85n36
vices, 11
Vienna, church council of 1267, 12, 19
Vienne, church council of 1311-12, 12–14, 21, 24
Vikkuah le-ha-Radak, 31

violence against Jews, 5, 39, 46–7, 98n190
theological debate over, 49–51
voluntary poverty, x, 7–8, 36

W
W. de Narbona, 124, 128
wealth, distribution of, ix, 183
Weber, Max, vii–viii, 29, 148, 184, 186
Wickham, Chris, 149, 167n13, 168n13, 168n17
William of Norwich, 98n192
wills, 12, 13, 15
Wissenschaft des Judentums (WDJ), vii
Wladislaus, Duke, 97n189
Wood, Diana, *Medieval Economic Thought*, 173n60
Wurzburg, ritual murder accusation, 85n50, 87n65, 98n192

Y
Yassif, Eli, 169n19, 170n20
Yehiel mi-Paris, 31
Yosef ha-Mekanne, 31. *See also* Sefer Yosef HaMekanne
Younger Historical School of Political Economy, 148. *See also* German Historical School of Political Economy

Z
Zionists, 193
Zoën, 73